Proceedings of the 5th International Conference on Innovation and Entrepreneurship ICIE 2017

Hosted By

The Multimedia University
Kuala Lumpur, Malaysia

26 - 27 April 2017

Edited by

Dr Kamarulzaman Ab. Aziz

Review Process
Papers submitted to this conference have been double-blind peer reviewed before final acceptance to the conference. Initially, abstracts were reviewed for relevance and accessibility and successful authors were invited to submit full papers. Many thanks to the reviewers who helped ensure the quality of all the submissions.

Ethics and Publication Malpractice Policy
ACPIL adheres to a strict ethics and publication malpractice policy for all publications – details of which can be found here:
http://www.academic-conferences.org/policies/ethics-policy-for-publishing-in-the-conference-proceedings-of-academic-conferences-and-publishing-international-limited/

Conference Proceedings
The Conference Proceedings is a book published with an ISBN and ISSN. The proceedings have been submitted to a number of accreditation, citation and indexing bodies including Thomson ISI Web of Science and Elsevier Scopus.

Author affiliation details in these proceedings have been reproduced as supplied by the authors themselves.

The Electronic version of the Conference Proceedings is available to download from DROPBOX http://tinyurl.com/ICIE17-Proc Select Download and then Direct Download to access the Pdf file. Free download is available for conference participants for a period of 2 weeks after the conference.
The Conference Proceedings for this year and previous years can be purchased from http://academic-bookshop.com

E-Book ISBN: 978-1-911218-32-6
E-Book ISSN: 2049-6842
Book version ISBN: 978-1-911218-33-3
Book Version ISSN: 2049-6834

Published by Academic Conferences and Publishing International Limited
Reading
UK
44-118-972-4148
www.academic-publishing.org

Contents

Preface

These proceedings represent the work of researchers participating in the 5th International Conference on Innovation and Entrepreneurship (ICIE 2017) which is being hosted this year by the Multimedia University on 26 - 27 April 2017.

ICIE is a recognised event on the international research conferences calendar and provides a valuable platform for individuals to present their research findings, display their work in progress and discuss conceptual and empirical advances in the areas of Innovation and Entrepreneurship. It provides an important opportunity for researchers and practitioners to come together to share their experiences of researching in this varied and expanding field.

The conference this year will be opened with a keynote presentation by Prof Dr Murali Raman from the Multimedia University, speaking on *"Fearlessness of Failing: Injecting Creativity in Developing an Entrepreneurial Mindset in a Digital World"* and in the afternoon the international consultant Mr Philip Merry, who will discuss, *"Entrepreneurship, Synchronicity & Leading with Heart: Intuiting the Future in a Quantum World"*.

The second day of the conference will be opened by Prof George Teodorescu; the Chairman of the Danubius Academic Consortium Ecosystem for Integral Innovation, who will be talking about *"Integral Innovation, a Brain to Business strategy for Leadership"*. And an afternoon keynote presentation by Adjunct Prof Dato' Dr Ghazali bin Dato' Mohd. Yusoff who is an Honorary Doctor of Law at the University of Nottingham will address the topic *"Islam and Business: Innovation and Entrepreneurship Incorporating Values and Belief in God"*.

With an initial submission of 176 abstracts, after the double blind, peer-review process there are 26 academic Research papers, 2 PhD Research papers, and 1 Work in Progress paper published in these Conference Proceedings. These papers represent truly global research in the field, with contributions from Australia, Canada, China, Finland, France, Germany, India, Indonesia, Iran, Italy, Japan, Malaysia, Nigeria, Philippines, Poland, Romania, Russia, Saudi Arabia, Taiwan, UK and USA.

We wish you a most interesting conference.

Dr. Kamarulzaman Ab. Aziz
ICIE Conference Chair
Multimedia University
Cyberjaya
Malaysia

ICIE Committee

Executive committee

The ICIE 2017 executive committee are all from the Multimedia University, Cyberjaya, Malaysia.

Dr Kamarulzaman Ab. Aziz; Dr. Chong Lee Lee; Prof Dr. Nahariah; Dr Chan Kok Thim; Dr Mariati Binti Norhashim; Associate Prof Dr. Tan Siow Hooi; Prof Norzila Binti Mat Zain; Dr. Shaista; Dr. Choon Shay Wei; Dr. Yvonne Lee Lean Ee; Dr. Ong Hway Boon; Dr. Tan Siow Kian; Dr. Koong Seow Shin; Dr. Nik Mohamad Zaki Nik Salleh; Dr. Abdullah Sallehhuddin; Ms. Zarehan Selamat; Ms. Noor Shahaliza Othman; Ms. Nor Azliana Aridi; Ms. Hamsatulazura Hamzah; Ms. Kwan Jing Hui; Ms. Chong Choy Yoke; Mr. Muhamad Iruwan Ghuslan; Ms. Yee Chin Nee; Ms Nurul Nadia Binti Nordin; Ms Ruzanna Binti AB Razak; Ms Diyana Binti Abdul Mahad; Abdul Hamid; Mr Mohd Fairuz Bin ABD Rahim.

Conference Committee

Diyana Binti Abdul Mahad Abdul Hamid, Faculty of Management, Multimedia University, Malayisia; Ass. Prof.Dr. Nahariah Jaafar, Faculty of Management, Multimedia University, Malayisia; Dr. Kamarulzaman Ab. Aziz, Multimedia University, Malaysia; Prof Saber Abd-Allah, Beni Suef University, Egypt; Dr. Ghassan E. Abuyaghi, The Hashemite University, Amman, Jordan; Assc. Prof. Dr. Zafer Acar, Piri Reis University, Tuzla, Istanbul, Turkey; Dr. Bulent Acma, Anadolu University, Turkey; Dr. Mo'taz Amin Al Sa'eed, Al - Balqa' Applied University, Amman, Jordan; Saleh Al-Jufout, Tafila Technical University, Jordan; Dr. Maher Al-Mahrouq, The Jordanian Chamber of Industry (JCI), Jordan; Dr. Hanadi Al-Mubaaraki, Kuwait University, Kuwait; Dr. Hussein Al-Yaseen, Al-Ahliyya Amman University, Jordan; Mohammad Aladwan, Hashemite University, Jordan; Dr. Husam Aldeen Al-Khadash, The Hashemite University, Amman,, Jordan; Dr Mariam Aldhaheri, Higher Colleges of Technology, UAE; Dr. Mohammad Sadegh Allahyari, Islamic Azad University, Rasht Branch, Iran; Dr. Talah Arabiat, The German Jordanian University, Jordan; Omid Askarzadeh, Polad Saab Shargh, Tehran, Iran; Nor Azliana Aridi, Faculty of Management, Multimedia University, Malayisia; Dr. Daniel Badulescu, University of Oradea, Romania; Prof. Alina Badulescu, University of Oradea, Romania; Dr. Afsaneh Bagheri, University of Tehran, Iran; Ruzanna Binti AB Razak, Faculty of Management, Multimedia University, Malayisia; Nurul Nadia Binti Nordin, Faculty of Management, Multimedia University, Malayisia; Ass. Prof.Dr. Ong Hway Boon, Faculty of Management, Multimedia University, Malayisia; Eduardo Castro, National University de la Plata, Argentina; Prof. Jurate Cerneviciute, Vilnius Gediminas Technical University, Lithuania; Dr. Toly Chen, Feng Chia University, Taichung, Taiwan; Shi-Jay Chen, National United University, Taiwan; Dr Steve Childers, Radford University, United States; Yee Chin Nee, Faculty of Management, Multimedia University, Malayisia; Dr. Prof. Musabbir Chowdhury, Niagara College, Canada; Chong Choy Yoke, Faculty of Management, Multimedia University, Malayisia; Ms Tan Christine Nya-Ling, Multimedia University, Malaysia; Dr. Leonardo Costa, School of Economics and Management, Catholic University of Portugal, Portugal; Prof. Costas N. Costa, Cyprus University of Technology, Lemesos, Cyprus; Prof. Armando Carlos De Pina Filho, Federal University of Rio de Janeiro , Brazil; Dr. Mihaela Diaconu, The "Gheorghe Asachi" Technical University, Romania; Dr. Mercy Escalante Ludena, USP, Brazil; Prof. Iancu Eugenia, Stefan cel Mare University, Romania; Prof Iancu Eugenia, Stefan cel Mare University Suceava, Romania; Prof. Paula Odete Fernandes, Polytechnic Institute of Braganca, Portugal; Prof. Dr. Ramaswamy Ganesan, National Foundation for Entrepreneurship Development, India; Prof. Dr. Adriana Giurgiu, University of Oradea, Faculty of Economic Sciences, Dept. of International Business, Romania; Dr. Sayed Mahdi Golestan Hashemi, Iranian Research Center for Creatology, TRIZ & Innovation Management, Iran; Prof. Ken Grant, Ryerson University, Toronto, Canada; Dr. Ebru Gunlu, Dokuz Eylul University Faculty of Business, Turkey; Kaled Hameide, Montclair State University in New Jersey, USA; Hamsatulazura Hamzah, Faculty of Management, Multimedia University, Malayisia; Dr. Mahmoud Hassanin, Pharos University, Alexandria, Eygpt; Ass. Prof.Dr. Tan Siow Hooi, Faculty of Management, Multimedia University, Malayisia; Dr. Lilin Huang, American University of Madaba, Jordan; Dr Katarzyna Hys, Opole University of Technology, Poland; Dr. Andreea-Oana Iacobuta, Alexandru Ioan Cuza University of Iasi, Romania; Mohamad Iruwan Ghuslan, Faculty of Management, Multimedia University, Malayisia; Dr. Ayman Ismail, American University in Cairo, Egypt; Dr. Perwaiz Ismaili, Metropolitan State University, USA; Prof. Zhang Jianhong, North CHina university of Technology, China; Kwan Jing Hui, Faculty of Management, Multimedia University, Malayisia; Lawrence Jones-Esan, London Academy Business School, UK; Dr Nowshade Kabir, Trouvus, Canada; Prof. Konstantinos Kalemis, National Centre of Local Goverment and Administration, Greece; Yusniza Kamarulzaman, University of Malaya, Kuala Lumpur, Malaysia; Prof. Rajkumar Kannan, Bishop Heber College Autonomous, India; Dr Muhammad Rahatullah Khan`, Effat University, Saudi Arabia; Dr. Radwan Kharabsheh, Applied Science University, East Al-Ekir, Kingdom of Bahrain; Chang-Hee Kim, Republic Polytechnic, Singapore; Prof. Jesuk Ko, Gwangju University, Korea; Dr. Renata Korsakiene, Vilnius Gediminas Technical University, Lithuania; Dr. Yvonne Lagrosen, University West Trollhättan, Sweden; Brent Lane, Kenan-Flager Business School, University of North Carolina, USA; Dr. Yvonne Lee Lean Ee, Faculty of Management, Multimedia University, Malayisia; Dr. Chong Lee Lee, Faculty of Management, Multimedia University, Malayisia; Dr. Andriew Lim, Hotelschool The Hague, Netherlands; Angeline Low, University of Technology Sydney, Mosman, Australia; Dr. Ihab K. Magableh, The German Jordanian University, Jordan; Dr Mohammed Sanusi Magaji, Maryam Abacha American University, Maradi, Republic of Niger, Niger Republic; Randa Mahasneh, The Hashemite University, Jordan; Prof.

Biographies

Conference and Programme Chairs

Dr Kamarulzaman Ab. Aziz is currently an associate professor and Director of the Entrepreneur Development Centre at Multimedia University, member of the Centre of Excellence for Business Performance (CeBP) and the Centre for Knowledge & Innovation Management (CEKIM), and previously he was the Deputy Dean (R&D) of the Faculty of Management, Multimedia University. He is also the founding president of the AKEPT Young Researchers Circle (AYRC). His research interests includes Cluster Development, Technology and Innovation Management, Entrepreneurship and Commercialization.

Dr Chong Lee is currently a senior lecturer and Chairperson of Centre of Business Performance (CeBP) at Faculty of Management, Multimedia University. Previously, she was the Deputy Dean of the Faculty of Management. Her research interest covers Investment, Behavior Finance and International Finance. She also has vast teaching experience in both undergraduate and post-graduate levels.

Keynote Speakers

Adjunct. Prof. Dato Ghazali (PhD) graduated from Universiti Malaya and is an Honorary Doctor of Law from the University of Nottingham, UK. He is a Founding life member of Malaysian Institute of Directors. Dato is an advisor for University–Industry Collaboration for Universiti Utara Malaysia, UiTM and Universiti Malaysia Pahang. He is currently Executive Chairman, Nusantara Technologies Sdn. Bhd.

Philip Merry 36 Years Consulting Experience in 58 Countries (26 Years living in Asia). CEO/Founder of Singapore's Philip Merry Consulting Group helps leaders access the power of the heart and self-leadership for personal and business transformation. He has conducted leadership and team projects with global organizations for 37 years in 58 countries, boosting mindsets that grow inter-cultural co-operation and optimise personal excellence. Senior facilitator with United Nations and Duke Corporate Education, Regional Representative Belbin Team Roles, Marshall Goldsmith Coach, Appreciative Inquiry Certified, HeartMath certified, Philip is author of The Search for Singapore's Happiest People, and one-time London taxi driver.

Professor Dr. Murali Raman obtained his Doctorate in Management Information Systems from Claremont Graduate University, California in 2005. He is currently a Professor and Dean of the Management Faculty at Multimedia University, Cyberjaya, Malaysia. Murali also holds an MSC in Human Resource Management (London School of Economics, UK) and an MBA (Imperial College, London, UK). He has worked in the corporate sector with Maybank Bhd (1994-1996) and Accenture Consulting (1997-2001), before joining MMU. With Accenture, he managed and led more than 9 different IT projects in Malaysia and Singapore, mainly in the area of IT and Systems integration.

Prof. George Teodorescu is Chairman of the Danubius Academic Consortium Ecosystem for Integral Innovation, comprising 12 Universities from 10 European countries, several industry Associations and public Institutions. The mission of the DAC Ecosystem is to promote Creativity as a driving force for a prosperous economy and for a harmonious society. From 1992 to 2012 George led the Masters Program for Integral Innovation at the State Academy Stuttgart, Germany, where he designed the curriculum and developed a methodology for educating original problem solvers and creative entrepreneurs with a basic education in engineering, natural sciences, architecture or design. He was on the Executive Board of the World Design Organisation between 2001 and 2005. He is Visiting Professor to several Asian Universities and adviser to institutions in China and

South Korea. Since 2013 he has been cooperating with the Beijing Institute of Technology and several European Universities. He is author of a book entitled the 'Theory of Integral Innovation'. Born in Bucharest, George now lives in Cologne in Germany.

Workshop Facilitators and Mini Track Chair

Andriew Lim is Professor of Technopreneurship and Innovation in Hospitality at Hotelschool The Hague (hospitality business school), the Netherlands. He leads the research group focusing on entrepreneurship and innovation for hospitality industry. Next to his research activities, he also teaches Strategic Management and Business Model Innovation courses to the final year students. Andriew holds a PhD in Technology Policy and Innovation Management from Eindhoven University of Technology, the Netherlands. His main research interest is the interplay between technologies and business strategies in innovation management.

Dr. Siti Sarah Omar is a lecturer at the Faculty of Technology Management and Business, Universiti Tun Hussein Onn Malaysia (UTHM) Johor Malaysia. She is also a Certified Professional Entrepreneurial Educator awarded by the Ministry of Higher Education in Malaysia. She obtained her PhD Degree (Management-Entrepreneurship) in 2015 from University of Southampton, UK. Prior to joining UTHM she had two years teaching experience at the private higher institution in Kuala Lumpur. Her expertise is in the field of Entrepreneurial Networking, Human and Social Capital, Human Resource Management and Development as well as Talent Management. She is currently active in delivering talks and seminars to university students on the entrepreneurial mind and to public on self-development and improvement.

Biographies of Contributing Authors

Hossein Ada . Born September 1965. PhD in Industrial Management, Tehran, Iran. Fifteen years academic work at Industrial Management Department, Azad University (2001 to present). 26 years experience in Industrial Management Institute (IML) in position of Senior Consultant.

Wassim J. Aloulou is an assistant professor at the Department of Business Administration of the CEAS in IMSIU (Saudi Arabia). He received his Ph.D. degree in Management Sciences from the University of Grenoble 2 (UPMF), in France (2008). His research interests include (social) entrepreneurship and (social) entrepreneurial intentions and orientations of individuals and organizations.

Faouzi Ayadi is an Assistant Professor of Business Management at College of Economics & Administrative Sciences in Al Imam Mohammad Ibn Saud Islamic University (Saudi Arabia). He received his M.Sc. degree from Bordeaux 4 University (France) and his Ph.D. degree in Business Management (specialty: Management Information Systems) from Toulouse 1 University (France). In addition to his experience as an Assistant Professor in Tunisia and Saudi Arabia.

Anne Marie Bagadion is Currently taking up PhD Business in De La Salle University, Manila, is a full time faculty of the Department of Allied Business Courses, College of Business and Accountancy in Ateneo de Naga University. Prior to her academe life , Anne worked as a Product Manager of a major Telecommunications Company in Manila.

Mamoni Banerjee is doctorate in Agricultural Science. She served different organizations; State Bank of India, Indian council of Agricultural Science, Indo-French Centre for promotion of Advanced Research. Now, She work as Asst. Professor at Rajendra Mishra School of Engineering Science, IIT Kharagpur. Her research interests are in Phytochemicals, Bio pesticides, Pesticide bio-efficacy study, Rural Technology Development for entrepreneurship etc.

Jack Chang, is currently attaining his MBA degree from NSYSU and is a doctoral researcher at Warwick Business School, he has served as Director of Strategic Planning of iStaging. Before joining iStaging Corp., Jack served as an industry analyst at IEK of ITRI, and researcher of the China Productivity Center and Commerce Development Research Institute.

Tan Booi Chen is a senior lecturer in the Faculty of Management, Multimedia University, Malaysia. She received her PhD from Multimedia University in 2014. She has been an academician for over ten years and was involved actively in teaching, research and supervision. Her research interests include consumer behaviour, sustainable consumption behaviour, green

Jamel Choukir is a Professor in Management and Entrepreneurship at College of Economics and Administrative Sciences and atAl-Imam Mohammad Ibn Saud Islamic University and Sfax University He holds a Ph. D. from University of Montreal in Management and has Published many articles and books in Human Resource Management and Entrepreneurship

David Crick is the Paul Desmarais Professor of International Entrepreneurship and Marketing at the University of Ottawa, Canada. His current research interests involve work at the Marketing/International Entrepreneurship interface and particularly work that addresses a more effective public/private sector interaction. He is on the editorial boards of several journals and his work has been presented at various international conferences and published in journals including: the Journal of Business Venturing, Journal of Small Business and Enterprise Development, Journal of Small Business Management, and Small Business Economics.

Arif Hartono is a lecturer at Management Department, Faculty of Economics, Universitas Islam Indonesia, Yogyakarta, Indonesia. Currently he is undertaking PhD at Warwick Business School, University of Warwick, UK. Prior to join in academia job, Mr. Hartono had roles as a professional in logistics, marketing and business development fields in multinational, state-owned and private enterprises. His research interest includes open innovation and innovation value chain.

Rara (Hye-Seong) Jeon is a Assertive Consultant for Strategic Management & Business Development. Advisor for Educational Management and Instructor. She has 13 years of experiences as an owner, director, and manager in different organizations. She takes great joy in help organizations such as business development, creating strategies for marketing, HR, and management aspect. Recently, she is focus on start-ups in high-tech industry: finding a problem and building strategies such as business model, developing organizations' structure, creating marketing and management strategies.

Lee Jia En is a candidate under the Master of Philosophy (Management) program in Multimedia University, Cyberjaya, Malaysia. She is a member of the university's Centre of Excellence for Knowledge and Innovation Management.

Rosalina Loquias is a a graduate of Doctor of Philosophy, major in Educational Management, and Master in Business Administration. At present, an Associate Professor V of Ateneo de Naga University mentoring the business management courses students and other related courses. Previously, a payroll master and bookkeeper in other educational institution.

Lester Lloyd-Reason is Director of the Centre for Enterprise Development and Research (CEDAR) at ARU in Cambridge, UK. A collaborative venture between Cambridge entrepreneurs and expert academics, CEDAR embeds entrepreneurs to co-create and co-deliver innovative entrepreneurial programmes and advise governments around the world on developing and supporting entrepreneurial activity. With over 190 publications, at the last UK REF, his research work was judged to have 'world leading' impact.

Federica Marangio is a PhD researcher at the Department of Engineering for Innovation of University of Salento, Lecce, Italy. For her research, she spent one semester in China at the University of Guangzhou, as exchange PhD. Her topics of interest are the triple helix and the innovative entrepreneurship culture.

Jamal Nassar is a practicing trainer on Cross-Cultural Communication, Leading Global/Virtual Teams, Change Management and Islamic Finance. Jamal has over 14 years experience as a marketing manager, managing director and a training consultant. Jamal coaches technology startups in Malaysia. Jamal has a regional experience across SEA training C-level executives on Cultural Communication & Global Businesses. Jamal is a certified HRDF trainer and currently a Phd Candidate at INCEIF."

Florabel Nieva (PhD) is an Assistant Professor in the Department of Entrepreneurship of the College of Business Administration at Effat University in Jeddah, Kingdom of Saudi Arabia. A former Member of the Regional Quality Assessment Team (RQAT) for Business and Management Education in the Commission on Higher Education (CHED) in Bicol Region, Philippines.

Rojan Nori is a candidate under the Master of Philosophy (Management) program in Multimedia University, Cyberjaya, Malaysia.

Cletus Famous Nwankwo was a 2015/2016 Member of the National Youth Service Corps and served at Novena University, Nigeria. He is currently a Graduate Assistant at the Department of Geography,

University of Nigeria and he is pursuing a Master's Degree in Political Geography with a focus on public policy.

Kehinde Olanipekun obtained her B.Sc from Obafemi Awolowo University Metallurgical and Materials Engineering. She obtained her M.Sc and Ph.D from the same university in Technology Management from the Department of African Institute for Science Policy and Innovations (AISPI). Her focus is on Sustainable Entrepreneurship and Innovations.

Lim Ooi Wei was born in Kuala Lumpur, Malaysia, in 1969. She obtained her Master of Management degree from Universiti of Malaya and Bachelor of Arts (Business Administration) from Ottawa University, USA. She is currently pursuing a PhD in Health Economics in Faculty of Economics and Administration, University of Malaya. Having more than 15 years of experience in education, she has been involved in teaching UK Bachelor Degree programs and South Australian Matriculation program. Her expertise and passion in teaching will be continuously lead her to expose and instill independent learning among students. Her current research interests include women entrepreneurship, health economics, innovation management, entrepreneurship, and development studies.

Aneta Ptak-Chmielewska is senior lecturer in Warsaw School of Economics (Poland). Her research specialization is survival of enterprises. She applies advanced statistical and data mining methods in her research. She is publishing in high quality national and international journals.

Kalsom Salleh is currently attached at College University Poly-Tech MARA Kuala Lumpur as a senior lecturer. She was formerly an Associate Professor Dr and a senior lecturer at Faculty of Accountancy, Universiti Teknologi MARA, Shah Alam, Malaysia. Her research areas of interest include Knowledge Management, Intellectual Capital, Auditing and Public Sector Management and Accounting. She has published many of her research papers in international refereed journals, conference proceedings and book chapters as well as sitting on the editorial board and reviewing committee members of several journals.

Surendev Singh, is a degree graduate in Creative Multimedia and a Master graduate in MBA. Currently I am pursuing my studies in PHD with prior working experience both in the industry and academic. This will be my first time publishing and writing a paper for conference with the help of my co-authors.

Blair Stevenson (PhD) is an educator, researcher and manager with a broad range of experience in education, culture and technology. He is currently manager at the Oulu EduLAB program (www.oamk.fi/labs), and acting as coordinator of the LAB international partnerships at the Oulu University of Applied Sciences in Finland. Personal website: https://blairoulu.wordpress.com/

Hongyi Sun (PhD) is from City University of Hong Kong. Dr Sun has twice been the winner of the Teaching Excellence Award at his university and has won several other awards for his cross-disciplinary PIPE® model for integrating and teaching creativity, innovation and entrepreneurship. He is a regular speaker and trainer about PIPE®.

Sarath Tomy is currently a second year PhD student in the Department of Computer Science and Information Technology at La Trobe University, Australia. His research is focused on the application of data analytics for entrepreneurial process in IT Startups. His research interests include methods for decision-making under uncertainty in entrepreneurship, machine learning and predictive analytics.

Khimji Vaghjiani has 28 years of technology commercialisation experience across banking, telco, defence and government, and was awarded both Australian Innovator of the year 2010 for the solar off-grid product and the Australian International Design Award 2010 for internationalising the solar product. He also won the Tech23 in 2010: most innovative company (Global Sustainability) in Australia. He is currently the Engagement and Commercialisation manager at the NSW Government Data Analytics Centre, Australia. Previously, he managed a NSW Government fund supporting innovative start-ups across industry verticals.

Maxim Vlasov is a serious science worker of Institute of Economics, the Ural Branch of the Russian Academy of Sciences. He investigates the problems of institutional and knowledge economics modeling.

Asliza Yusoff received her B.B.A. in Finance from University of Wisconsin- Milwaukee, USA and M.B.A. from Universiti Teknologi MARA, Malaysia in 1998 and 2010 respectively. She is currently a full-time PhD candidate at Universiti Sains Malaysia and also a senior lecturer at Malaysian Polytechnic. Her research interests include small business and entrepreneurial intentions and behaviours.

Inclusive Innovation Adoption among Malaysian SMEs

Kamarulzaman Ab. Aziz
Multimedia University, Cyberjaya, Malaysia
kamarulzaman.aziz@mmu.edu.my

Abstract: This study proposes to explore the level of inclusive innovation adoption among Malaysian SMEs as well as their attitudes towards the idea, using Ajzen's theory of planned behavior (TPB). The inclusive innovation index (III) is used, derived from the definition by the Global Research Alliance (2012). The paper shares the findings of the pilot study conducted. Discussions on the robustness of the tool developed, descriptive statistics, preliminary findings and recommendations for the policymakers are given as well as implications for next stages of the work. In general, the findings indicated that the Malaysian SMEs moderately agreed on the inclusiveness of the goods currently available in the markets. However, the findings also indicated more can be done to enhance the level of inclusiveness. Furthermore, there appear to be certain differences in attitude towards inclusive innovation according to gender, generation and several other categories within the sample.

Keywords: inclusive innovation, inclusive innovation index, theory of planned behaviour, 1-InnoCERT

1. Introduction

Aids and charity had been the common and easy solutions used by many when addressing poverty and the variety of issues related to it. However, there had been increasing awareness that there should be better strategies for addressing these problems (Prahalad and Hammond, 2002; Prahalad, 2009; UNDP, 2008). No longer should the reponsibility falls only on government and NGOs (Prahalad and Hammond, 2002; Prahalad, 2009; UNDP, 2008; Hart, 2005; Kandachar and Halme, 2008; Srinivasa and Sutz, 2008; Prahalad and Hart, 2002). It had been reported of the tremendous market potential of the collective at the base of the economic pyramid (BOP) (Prahalad and Hart, 2002; World Resources Institute, 2007).

According to George, McGahan and Prabhu (2012) (p.663), inclusive innovation is "the development and implementation of new ideas which aspire to create opportunities that enhance social and economic wellbeing for disenfranchised members of society." The commonly disenfranchised or marginalized are often due to disability, poverty, gender, race and knowledge (Burton and Kagan, 2005). A major champion for inclusive innovation, Dr. R. A. Malshelkar of the Global Research Alliance defined inclusive innovation as "any innovation that leads to affordable access of quality goods and services creating livelihood opportunities for the excluded population, primarily at the base of the pyramid, and on a long term sustainable basis with a significant outreach"[1]. Given the importance placed nowadays towards achieveing inclusiveness in economic growth and societal development, there is a bigger need to ensure profileration of inclusive innovations as it can not only address the needs of the disenfrahcished but also help eradicate problems such as digital divide.

There had been numerous studies investigating inclusive innovation adoption among large corporations (Nestle Research, 2011; Halme, Lindeman and Linna; 2012; George, McGahan and Prabhu, 2012). The studies also highlighted initiatives implemented from around the globe (George, McGahan and Prabhu, 2012; Khayesi and George, 2011; Smith, Fressoli and Thomas, 2013; Rezaie, McGahan, Frew, Daar and Singer, 2011; Sonne, 2012; Ramani and Mukherjee, 2014; Hegger, Spaargaren, van Vilet and Frijns, 2011) but there is a dirth of Malaysian studies. Thus, there seems to be a research gap in the context of inclusive innovation among SMEs in Malaysia. This paper believes that it is important to investigate the level of inclusive innovation adoption among Malaysian SMEs as well as their attitudes towards the idea. The paper shares the findings of the pilot study conducted. The following sections explain the measure developed to determine the level of inclusive innovation adoption, descriptive statistics and preliminary findings from the pilot study as well as some recommendations.

2. Inclusiveness and Policies in Malaysia

Wu[2] highlight the importance for inclusive growth towards ensuring ASEAN countries economic development, and the Malaysian government specifically recognized the importance of inclusive growth with both

---

[1] http://theglobalresearchalliance.org/en/What-we-do/Inclusive-Innovation.aspx

[2] http://thediplomat.com/2013/05/rethinkingthe-development-gap-aseans-inclusive-growth-imperative/?allpages=yes&print=yes

innovation and inclusive development identified among the "10 Big Ideas" listed in the 10th Malaysia Plan. In the 10th Malaysia Plan, the government spelled out the move towards inclusive socio-economic development by elevating the livelihoods of the bottom 40% households, strengthening bumiputera entrepreneurs, improving infrastructure, etc. This theme is carried through in the current 11th Malaysia Plan which covers 2016 till 2020. Specifically, inclusiveness featured as the first strategic thrust for the 11th Malaysia Plan; "Enhancing inclusiveness towards an equitable society. This commitment to enable all citizens to participate in and benefit from the country's prosperity is anchored on a belief that inclusive growth is not only key to individual and societal well-being, but also critical for sustaining longer periods of solid economic growth."[3] These were all anchored to the New Economic Model (NEM)[4] which was unveiled in 2009 with the aim to make Malaysia a high income economy that is both inclusive and sustainable.

Along with the 5 year Malaysia plans (10th and 11th), based on the NEM, the Economic Transformation Plan (ETP)[5] was announced in 2010 outlining 12 National Key Economic Areas (NKEAs) and 6 Strategic Reform Initiatives (SRIs) designed to drive the transformation of the country towards developed nation status by the year 2020. Among the SRIs is narrowing disparity which aims to improve the economic status of the bumiputra where a large percentage of are still within the lower income brackets. According to the World Bank's country overview report on Malaysia[6], "pockets of poverty exist and income inequality remains high relative to the developed countries Malaysia aspires to emulate". Furthermore, the Malaysian government allocated MYR 5.9 billion[7] in 2016 from MYR 4.6 billion[8] in the 2014 budget for the financial assistance scheme (BR1M) targeting the low income groups. It was announced in October 2016 that a total of MYR 6.8 billion[9] will be allocated to the scheme in 2017. Perhaps the scheme would be more effective if there are inclusive innovation goods and services available in the markets for the recipients to purchase.

The policy framework targeting the Malaysian SMEs specifically is the SME Masterplan 2012-2020[10]. The plan consists of 32 initiatives designed to accelerate the growth of SMEs in the country to ensure more impactful contribution of the sector to the nation's economy. The 32 initiatives are grouped into 2 main categories; high impact programmes, and measures. There are 6 high impact programmes outlined in the plan and the measures are grouped into 6; 4 thematic measures, a set of measures specifically for East Malaysia (Sabah and Sarawak), and 7 additional supporting measures. Inclusiveness features prominently in the masterplan in the form of the 6th high impact programme (HIP6); foster inclusive innovation. Specifically the programme aims to motivate, identify, screen, adopt, upgrade, develop, and sustainably deliver inclusive innovations. Based on information gathered from the interview with the Deputy CEO of SME Corporation Malaysia (SME Corp. Malaysia), the lead agency for SME development in the country, the HIP6 defines inclusive innovation along similar lines of the definition by Global Research Alliance. It is then categorised further into 2; innovations targeted at the masses, and innovations from the grassroots, both should have the element of empowering the bottom 40% of the income pyramid. The implementation of HIP6 is entrusted to the Malaysian Foundation for Innovation[11]. From the interview conducted with the HIP6 Programme Director, it was learned that the focused for the programme had been more on the 2nd category i.e. grassroots innovation. This focused had led to the emphasis of HIP6 skewed towards innovators from the rural areas and the innovations featured more of in the nature of frugal or jugaad innovations (Radjou, Prabhu, and Ahuja, 2012; Radjou and Prabhu, 2015).

3. Inclusive Innovation Index

This study surveyed a total of 33 businesses from a list provided by the SME Corp. Malaysia. SME Corp. Malaysia is the agency under the Ministry of International Trade and Industry Malaysia that formulates overall policies and strategies for SMEs and coordinates the implementation of the various development programmes across the country. This study explores the level of inclusive innovation adoption among the SMEs as well as their attitudes towards the idea, using Ajzen's theory of planned behavior (TPB). Specifically, this study

[3] http://english.astroawani.com/malaysia-news/11th-malaysia-plan-six-strategic-thrusts-moving-towards-vision-2020-60389
[4] http://www.epu.gov.my/sites/default/files/nem.pdf
[5] http://etp.pemandu.gov.my/About_ETP-@-Overview_of_ETP.aspx
[6] http://www.worldbank.org/en/country/malaysia/overview.print
[7] http://www.thesundaily.my/news/1591875
[8] http://mybajet.my/budget-2014-full-text-of-prime-ministers-speech
[9] http://www.theborneopost.com/2016/10/21/budget-2017-increase-in-br1m-aid-across-the-board/
[10] http://www.smecorp.gov.my/index.php/en/resources/2015-12-21-11-07-06/sme-masterplan/book/11-sme-masterplan-english/3-sme-masterplan
[11] http://yim.my/yim_v3/index.html

proposes to explore the level of inclusive innovation adoption in Malaysian SMEs as well as their attitudes towards the idea using Ajzen's theory of planned behavior (TPB). TPB was developed by Ajzen in 1988 and later refined in subsequent works (Ajzen, 1988; 1991; 2006).

The theory of planned behavior is a theory which predicts deliberate behavior, because behavior can be deliberative and planned. The theory proposes a model which can measure how human actions are guided. It predicts the occurrence of a particular behavior, provided that behavior is intentional. The model outlines three variables which the theory suggests will predict the intention to perform behavior. The variables are attitudes (Att) - the respondents' attitudes towards inclusive innovation, subjective norms (SN) - the respondents own estimate of the social pressure to adopting inclusive innovation, specifically; beliefs about how other people, who may be in some way important to them, would like them to behave, and perceived behavioral controls (PBC) - is the extent to which the respondents feel able to enact the adopting inclusive innovation behavior. The intentions (Int) are the precursors of behavior, in other words, it is the cognitive representation of a respondents' readiness to adopting inclusive innovation, and it is considered to be the immediate antecedent of behavior.

Via the survey, the representatives for each SME were introduced to the concept of inclusive innovation. Next, they were asked to consider their portfolio of products/services and evaluate their inclusiveness. The measure for this is the inclusive innovation index (III), developed from operationalizing the definition of inclusive innovation by the Global Research Alliance where inclusive innovations are defined along the lines of five dimensions:

- Affordable Access (AA) – "Such inclusive innovation will have to be aimed at `extreme reduction' in both the costs of production as well as the distribution." Key elements for this dimensions are; I) significant reduction of production costs to enable affordable price, and II) significant reduction of distribution costs to enable affordable price.
- Sustainable Business (SB) – "This means that in the long term, the 'affordable access' must not depend on the government subsidies or generous government procurement support systems but should work by retaining the market principles with which the private sector works comfortably." Thus the key elements are; I) not dependent on government subsidies, II) not dependent on significant government procurement, III) not dependent on charity and CSR, and IV) a sustainable business model.
- High Quality (HQ) – "It is because we have to recognize the basic rights of the people at the base of the pyramid, who should be enjoying the more or less the same level of quality of basic services as people at the top of the pyramid." The elements are; I) meeting quality standards, II) do not sacrifice quality to bring down the costs, and III) comparable quality level with those of similar products available in the market
- Excluded Population (EP) – "The excluded population or the disenfranchised or commonly marginalized groups which could include the poor, the disabled, the migrants, the women, the elderly, certain ethnic group, and so on." The elements; I) designed for the poor, the disabled, the migrants, the women, the elderly, certain ethnic group, and so on, II) priced with the poor in mind, and III) distribution designed to ensure accessibility for the poor, the disabled, the migrants, the women, the elderly, certain ethnic group, and so on.
- Massive Outreach (MO) – "If the `true inclusion' has to happen then the benefits of inclusive innovation should reach a large scale, i.e. a significant portion of population, and not just a small section of the population (in many cases, the total target population may only be a few hundreds of thousands or a few million- and not necessarily hundreds of million)." The key elements; I) large market size, II) large market share, and III) reached sizeable percentage of the target market.

Based on the definitions and the key elements identified from the definitions of the five dimensions, survey items were developed for the III. Following table provide the list of items. Their intention towards inclusive innovation is then gauged via a survey develop based on Ajzen's TPB. The findings are presented in the following sections.

4. Findings

A total of 33 executives representing 33 SMEs took part in the study. Among them, 17 (51.5%) were males while the remaining 16 (48.5%) were females. The age ranged from 20-24 to 45-49 years old. Out of the 33, 2

(6.1%) have Master degrees, and 25 (75.8%) have Bachelor degrees. The participants had a mean of nearly 4 years work experience with their current organization, ranging from first year to the 10th year.

Among the 33 SMEs, majority have 75 employees or less and had been in operation up to 20 years. 69.7% of the SMEs develop their own products and 51.5% of them target up to the Asian markets. The mean annual sale is around MYR 7.8 million with the mean annual sale for the last 3 years is around MYR 6 million. The mean R&D budget is 18% of the annual sale. Furthermore, 8 (24.2%) of them are 1-InnoCERT SMEs. The 1-InnoCERT programme is a certification programme by SME Corp. Malaysia to promote and develop innovative companies in Malaysia[12].

Reliability analysis was conducted to determine the internal reliability of the items used to measure the constructs tested in this study. According to Sekaran (2000), Cronbach's Alpha is a reliability coefficient that indicates the extent to which the items are positively correlated to one another. Theoretically, the higher the coefficient values are, the more reliable the instrument. In this context, the coefficients for all constructs were within the range of 0.850 to 1.000. This indicates the survey instruments have high reliability and internal consistency (Leech, Barrett and Morgan, 2011). All of the constructs were considered as reliable and good as the Cronbach's Alpha were above 0.70 (see Table 2). A total of 66 items were used to measure the main constructs of the study, namely III (22 items), Att (16 items), SN (12 items), PBC (12 items) and Int (4 items). The items were measured by itemized rating scale with seven scale categories. Mean analysis was conducted to determine the average mean of the constructs.

Generally, the respondents agreed with all the items measuring the constructs with overall Int achieved the highest level of agreement with an average of 5.5530 and median of 5.5000; while overall SN scored the lowest with an average of 5.2778 and median of 5.3333. Meanwhile, overall Att achieved a mean of 5.3428 and median at 5.4375. Overall PBC achieved the second highest mean of 5.4091 and median at 5.2500. The respondents rated a moderate level of agreement on inclusiveness of goods currently being offered by their businesses to the markets with overall III of 5.2135 and median at 5.1818, suggesting that there is still the need to produce more inclusive goods. The overall Int mean being the highest gives a good indication of the managers in Malaysian SMEs intending to adopt inclusive innovation when developing goods and services for their customers in the future.

Table 1: Items for Inclusive Innovation Index

Dimension	Item
AA	• Our production costs are significantly low compared to industrial standard • Our production costs are significantly low compared to our competitors • Our distribution costs are significantly low compared to industrial standard • Our distribution costs are significantly low compared to our competitors • Our product is priced affordably low compared to industrial standard • Our product is priced affordably low compared to our competitors
SB	• We are not dependent on government subsidies • We are not dependent on significant government procurement • We are not dependent on a single major client • We are not dependent on social funding (charity or corporate donations) • There is a long term demand for our product • Even though our product is designed for the commonly marginalized groups it is appealing to the mass market as well
HQ	• Our product meet all relevant quality standards • We don't sacrifice quality to bring down the costs • We ensure any cost reduction does not compromise quality of our product • Our product quality is comparable with those of similar but higher priced products available in the market
EP	• Our product is designed for the commonly marginalized groups such as the poor / bottom 40% / disabled / migrants / women / elderly / minority groups / etc • Our product is priced affordably; with the poor / bottom 40% in mind • Our distribution channel is designed/selected to ensure our product is accessible by the commonly marginalized groups such as the poor / bottom 40% / disabled / migrants / women / elderly / minority groups / etc

[12] http://www.smecorp.gov.my/index.php/en/programmes/2015-12-21-09-57-03/1-innocert

Dimension	Item
MO	• There is a large market potential for our product • We have a large share of our target market • We have reached more than 50% of our product target market

Table 2: Reliability Analysis

Constructs	N	Items Mean	Std. Dev.	Cronbach's Alpha	No. of Items
Att	33	5.343	13.89721	0.931	16
SN	33	5.278	10.35817	0.914	12
PBC	33	5.409	9.19022	0.898	12
Int	33	5.553	4.06015	0.961	4
III	33	5.213	17.32499	0.914	22

Correlation analysis (see Table 3) indicated that Overall III, Overall Int, Overall PBC, Overall Att and Overall SN to have significant correlation with each other except for between Overall III and Overall SN. There is a probability for a mediating effect except for the relationships among Overall III, Overall Int and Overall SN. This could be due to the relatively small sample size. Comparing the means between the male and female respondents show marked difference in their overall attitude towards inclusive innovation with the male participant showing higher means than female (see Table 4), suggesting female executives have less than favourable attitude towards inclusive innovation in the context of their business.

Comparing the means between SMEs with 1-InnoCERT and those without the certification also show a significant difference in their attitude towards inclusive innovation with those with the certification showing higher means (see Table 4). However, when assessing the inclusiveness of their goods, their Overall III score is lower than those without the certification. The pattern is further reflected when comparing the means between those that develop their own product with those that don't.

Table 3: Correlations Analysis

		Overall III	Overall Int	Overall PBC	Overall Att	Overall SN
Overall III	Pearson Correlation	1	.399*	.512**	.553**	.293
	N	33	33	33	33	33
Overall Int	Pearson Correlation	.399*	1	.744**	.677**	.733**
	N	33	33	33	33	33
Overall PBC	Pearson Correlation	.512**	.744**	1	.499**	.509**
	N	33	33	33	33	33
Overall Att	Pearson Correlation	.553**	.677**	.499**	1	.603**
	N	33	33	33	33	33
Overall SN	Pearson Correlation	.293	.733**	.509**	.603**	1
	N	33	33	33	33	33

*. Correlation is significant at the 0.05 level (2-tailed).
**. Correlation is significant at the 0.01 level (2-tailed).

The SMEs were further categorized into those with High III and High Int (the median scores for each scale were used as the threshold) - High III (18, 54.5%), Low III (15, 45.5%), High Int (19, 57.6%) and low Int (14, 42.4%). It is found that 62.5% of the SMEs with 1-InnoCERT recorded High III, and 87.5% recorded High Int. 13 of those High III SMEs are those that do their own R&D and develop their product. Similarly, 13 of the High Int SMEs are the ones that develop their own products. Similar comparative analyses of the means were done for the High III and High Int and again clear differences between the groups with the high groups recording higher means across the board. Similar pattern seen when comparing means according to 1-InnoCERT is seen when looking at firms according to years in business, with those 10 years or less showing lower means in Overall Att, Overall SN, Overall PBC and Overall Int, but their Overall III is higher than those operating for more than 10 years.

5. Discussions

The findings indicated that the Malaysian SMEs have good attitude towards inclusive innovation in general with good level of intention for adoption. The current level of implementation of inclusive innovation among the SMEs is still at a moderate level with rooms for more implementation. This suggests that more educational exposure and promotions should be implemented by the relevant parties such as SME Corp Malaysia. If the level of awareness and understanding of inclusive innovations among SMEs can be enhanced, the adoption may also increase. Thus, SME Corp Malaysia needs to reposition their High Impact Programme (HIP) 6 on inclusive innovation under the Malaysian SME Masterplan (2012 - 2020), to be beyond grassroot innovation. In order to ensure HIP 6 become a vehicle that can empower the bottom 40% of the income group by leveraging on innovation, the SMEs need to be pushed towards inclusive innovation. Development of inclusive goods and services should be incentivized, with success stories being shared and celebrated. The Inclusive Innovation Index (III) developed for this study serves as a useful tool that can be used to help get this movement under way.

Table 4: Comparing Means

Gender	Overall III	Overall Att	Overall SN	Overall PBC	Overall Int
Male	5.3663	5.4522	5.3775	5.4657	5.7500
Female	5.0511	5.2266	5.1719	5.3490	5.3438
1-InnoCERT (No)	5.2182	5.2625	5.1533	5.3267	5.3500
1-InnoCERT (Yes)	5.1989	5.5937	5.6667	5.6667	6.1875
Develop Own Product (Yes)	5.2174	5.3451	5.3514	5.6159	5.6630
Develop Own Product (No)	4.5606	4.3542	4.7222	4.5833	4.3333
High III (No)	4.5788	4.8500	5.1000	5.1500	5.2333
High III (Yes)	5.7424	5.7535	5.4259	5.6250	5.8194
High Int (No)	4.8766	4.8438	4.8393	4.8512	4.5893
High Int (Yes)	5.4617	5.7105	5.6009	5.8202	6.2632

There are marked differences observed in the responses between the genders with male respondents rated higher across all measures compared to their female counterpart. This could be due to female respondents often are more reserve and careful in their rating decisions. When comparing the SMEs between those certified 1-InnoCERT SME against others, the certified SMEs show a significantly stronger attitude towards inclusive innovation. However, their III rating was lower. This could be due to the certified SMEs are more familiar with the innovation processes and thus have a better appreciation of the importance of inclusive innovation. Their better appreciation also may be the reason for them to rate more realistically of the inclusiveness of their goods leading to the lower III. In other words, those SMEs with the certification would have a more sophisticated understanding of innovation in general than those without the certification. Thus, their assessment may be more stringent and less generous i.e. more realistic. The difference is also seen when comparing between the SMEs that develop their own product against those that don't. However, it is not possible to deduce conclusively on the differences based on the findings of this study due to the small sample size. Thus, this study should be implemented with a larger sample size in order to gain better insights to the true state.

6. Conclusions

Some may still argue that ensuring inclusion is not the responsibility of the private sector. However, earlier studies have argued it otherwise. In Malaysia based the various policies and initiatives, it appear that there is political will towards achieving inclusiveness in the country via innovation and entrepreneurship. Thus, it is important to get the businesses to respond to call from the government. Thus, there is a need to understand the inclusive innovation landscape in Malaysia, specifically among the SMEs. Armed with insights provided from studies such as this, the inclusive agenda would have better probability of success. Further work in the area need to be carried out to gauge more accurately the level of adoption among the SMEs of inclusive innovations and this can be done with a refined research framework that include various dimensions of the individual decision-making process impacting SMEs' tendencies to engage in inclusive Behavior, specifically in adopting inclusive innovations as their offering to the consumers.

References

A. Smith, M. Fressoli, and H. Thomas, "Grassroots innovation movements: challenges and contributions." *Journal of Cleaner Production*. pp. 1-11, 2013.

C. K. Prahalad, and A. Hammond, "Serving the world's poor profitably," *Harvard Business Review*, vol. 80, pp. 48-57, 2002.

C. K. Prahalad, and S. Hart, "The fortune at the bottom of the pyramid." *Strategy+Business*. Vol. 26, pp. 1-13, 2002.

C. K. Prahalad, *The Fortune at the Bottom of the Pyramid, Revised and Updated 5th Anniversary Edition: Eradicating Poverty Through Profits*. 1st ed., Pearson FT Press, 2009.

D. L. T. Hegger, G. Spaargaren, B. J. M. van Vliet, and J. Frijns, "Consumer – inclusive innovation strategies for the Dutch water supply sector: Opportunities for more sustainable products and services." *NJAS-Wageningen Journal of Life Sciences*, vol. 58. pp.49-56, 2011.

G. George, A. M. McGahan, and J. Prabhu, "Innovation for inclusive growth: Towards a theoretical framework and a research agenda." *Journal of Management Studies*. 49 (4), pp. 661 – 683, 2012.

I. Ajzen, "Theory of Planned Behavior." *Organizational Behavior and Human Decision Processes*, vol. 50, pp. 179 – 211, 1991.

I. Ajzen, *Attitudes, Personality, and Behavior*. Chicago, IL.: Dorsey Press, 1988.

I. Ajzen, Constructing a TpB Questionnaire: Conceptual and Methodological Considerations. 2006. Available: http://www.people.umass.edu./aizen/pdf/tpb.measurement.pdf, March. 2010.

J. Khayesi, and G. George, "When does the socio-cultural context matter? Communal orientation and entrepreneurs' resource accumulation efforts in Africa." *Journal of Occupational and Organizational Psychology*, vol. 84. pp. 471-492, 2011.

L. Sonne, "Innovative initiatives supporting inclusive innovation in India: Social business incubation and micro venture capital." *Technological Forecasting & Social Change*, vol. 79. pp. 638-647, 2012.

M. Burton and C. Kagan, "Marginalization." in G. Nelson and I. Prilleltensky, (Eds). *Community psychology: in pursuit of wellness and liberation*. London, Palgrave Macmillan, 2005.

M. Halme, S. Lindeman, and P. Linna, "Innovation for Inclusive Business: Intrapreneurial Bricolage in Multinational Corporations." *Journal of Management Studies*, vol. 49, pp.743–784, 2012.

N. Radjou, J. Prabhu, and S. Ahuja, "Jugaad Innovation." India, Random House Publishers India Pvt. Ltd., 2012.

N. Radjou, and J. Prabhu, "Frugal Innovation: How to do better with less." London, Profile Books Ltd., 2015.

Nestle Research, *Popularity positioned products: Affordable and Nutritious*. Renens: Nestec SA, 2011.

P. Kandachar, and M. Halme, "Farewell to pyramids: how can business and technology help to eradicate poverty." in [5] P. Kandachar, and M. Halme (Eds) *Sustainability challenges and solutions at the base of the pyramid: Business, technology and the poor*. London: Greenleaf. pp. 1-28, 2008.

R. Rezaie, A. M. McGahan, S. Frew, A. Daar, and P. Singer, "Biopharmaceutical innovation in China, India, Brazil and South Africa: Implications for the United States." Working paper. University of Toronto, 2011.

S. Hart, *Capitalism at the crossroads: The unlimited business opportunities in serving the world's most difficult problems*. Upper Saddle River, NJ: Wharton School Publishing, 2005.

S. Ramani, and V. Mukherjee, "Can breakthrough innovations serve the poor (bop) and create reputational (CSR) value? Indian case studies." *Technovation*, vol. 34. pp. 295-305, 2014.

S. Srinivasa, and J. Sutz, "Developing countries and innovation: searching for a new analytical approach." *Technology in Society*, vol. 30. pp. 129-140, 2008.

UNDP, *Creating value for all: strategies for doing business with the poor. Report of the growing inclusive markets initiative*. New York, 2008.

World Resources Institute, *The Next 4 Billion: Market Size and Business Strategy at the Base of the Pyramid*. Washington, 2007.

Is There an Immediate Impact of an Entrepreneurship Course on TPB Antecedents, Intentions and Actual Behaviors of Final Year Saudi Business Students?

Wassim J. Aloulou
CEAS, Al Imam Muhammad Bin Saud Islamic University (IMSIU), Riyadh, KSA
wassim.aloulou@gmail.com

Abstract: This study has two main objectives. First, it aims to determine factors that affect intentions of final year Saudi Business students to become entrepreneurs before and after the completion of an Entrepreneurship Course at university. Second, it reports results of a longitudinal quasi-experimental study that focused on the impact of such course on intentions and behaviors of students to start a new business by applying the Theory of Planned Behavior (TPB) as a validated theoretical framework. Data were collected in two waves before and after the completion of an Entrepreneurship Course within a period of four months later. A sample composed of 151 Business college students (109 males and 42 females) at Al Imam Mohammad Ibn Saud Islamic University (IMSIU) at Riyadh was considered in this study from a population of 330 students. Analyses included hierarchical and multivariate regressions to identify the most significant factors that affect intentions and behaviors in the two waves. Analyses also included tests of significance of changes in TPB antecedents (attitudes toward behavior; subjective norms; and perceived behavioral control), intentions and actual behaviors of students immediately after the completion of the course. The results show small but non-significant changes in attitudes, subjective norms and intentions, but a slightly significant change for perceived behavioral control and strongly significant change for actual behaviors of students. Findings suggest that the TPB could be considered as a useful framework to predict intentions and behaviors of students and measure how an entrepreneurship course might influence students' entrepreneurial intentions and behaviors. We draw some implications for researchers about the role of entrepreneurship education in developing entrepreneurial intentions and behaviors.

Keywords: Entrepreneurial Intention; Actual Behavior; Theory of Planned Behaviour, Final Year Saudi Business Students, Linear and hierarchical regressions.

1. Introduction

Entrepreneurship has long been considered as a key driver of economic development, competitiveness, innovation, job creation and personal fulfillment throughout the world (European Commission, 2013). Viewed as a potential solution to the young people' unemployment, entrepreneurship is fostered by public policy in creating entrepreneurial culture and reigniting entrepreneurial spirits and activities among youth. Efforts are being pursued by university policy makers to introduce entrepreneurship education programs in different educational levels. Such programs aim to develop entrepreneurial skills amongst students and help them consider entrepreneurship as a career alternative (European Commission, 2013). There is a wide range of entrepreneurship education efforts that have been initiated in USA, Europe and other countries around the world and the state of the art has been assessed in higher education institutions (Kuratko, 2005; Jonathan, 2008). For developing countries, entrepreneurship education is an emerging trend with a dramatic rise in number and status of dedicated programs at universities. But, limited empirical research is available to evaluate its impact and intriguing results were provided (von Graevenitz et al, 2010). It has been noted that intentions are the best predictors of entrepreneurial activity and behavior (Bird, 1988; Krueger and Carsrud, 1993; Krueger et al, 2000). As a result, the study of entrepreneurial intention (EI) is vital to understand how to encourage entrepreneurial activity and behavior to emerge (Krueger et al, 2000). Therefore, it has been noted that entrepreneurship education has a positive impact on entrepreneurial mindset and skills of young people, their intentions towards entrepreneurship, their employability and finally their role in society and the economy (European Commission, 2013). But, its impact has remained unexplored (von Graevenitz et al, 2010).
Over the last few years, entrepreneurship is considered as an emerging field of interest for Saudi Arabia and its stimulation has become central to the economic policy agenda of the country (Porter, 2012) in order to face main challenges: diversification of its economic base away from the dependence on oil; and reduction of unemployment' rates estimated at more than 11% among youth ages. A national reform plan called the "*Saudi Arabia Vision to 2030*" aims to enable the country to meet these challenges (Saudi Council of Economic and

Development Affairs, 2016). Recent official statistics and forecasts showed that the country has to embrace significant change to its economic growth model in order to create six million jobs by 2030 and to employ the sizable cohort of young Saudi citizens that will enter the labor force over the next 15 years (Schwab and Sala-I-Martin, 2015; McKinsey and Company 2015). Therefore, entrepreneurship has been part of the curricula in Saudi higher education institutions since few years ago. It has been considered as a mean to develop entrepreneurial attitudes and intentions among young Saudis at different educational levels. However, Saudi Arabia still had a relative lack of EI (1% of respondents) compared to higher perceptions of entrepreneurship as potential career choice (86.6%) has been recognized during the last years as a challenging issue (Kelley et al, 2011), for Saudi public policy in general and university policy in particular, that has to be resolved to meet aforementioned challenges. Therefore, measuring the impact of entrepreneurship education programs on students' intentions and behaviors at university becomes a matter needing further investigation and interest.

The purpose of our study has twofold objective. First, It aims to apply the Theory of Planned Behavior (TPB) model to predict the formation of EIs of final year Saudi university business students before and after the completion of an Entrepreneurship Course (EC) and examine their main antecedents when considering entrepreneurship as a career option to face unemployment. Second, our study aims to assess the immediate impact of entrepreneurship education on students' attitudes, intentions and actual behaviors.

Limited empirical research in Saudi Arabia about intentions of final year students to start a new business is one of the reasons for conducting this study (e.g., Alexandre-Leclair et al, 2013; Aloulou, 2015a; 2015b; 2016). No empirical research found in Saudi Arabia until now for measuring the impact of entrepreneurship education on attitudes, intentions and behaviors and it is another reason for that choice. In addition, the decision taken to focus on this target audience is linked to the fact that such students, as future graduates, are reflecting on their future professional career and choosing between being employed by others or being self-employed. Thus, the enrollment in EC before graduation can help them in making adequate career decisions.

The reminder of the paper contains five sections. Next, we describe the theoretical framework and the research model of EIs and behaviors based on TPB. In section three, we introduce the longitudinal quasi-experimental design of the empirical study based on survey data collected from a sample of 151 final year Saudi university business students. This design includes the data analysis strategy. Section 4 presents empirical results while the last section discusses findings, limitations and implications for further research.

2. Literature review

2.1 Entrepreneurship as intentional planned behavior

As an important phenomenon, EI has attracted important cognitive research associated with a framework that underlies entrepreneurship as intentional behavior (Bird 1988; Krueger and Brazeal 1994; Krueger et al, 2000). Intention toward a behavior is referred to as the best predictor of planned behavior and the immediate antecedent of it (Ajzen 1991; Krueger and Carsrud 1993). Social-psychological studies also assume that intention is the best predictor of actual behavior (Bagozzi et al, 1989) and supported its predictive validity on actual behaviors (Sheeran, 2002). Consequently, a research stream grounded in social psychology theories has started to accumulate from a well-known theoretical model, the TPB (Ajzen 1991). This model has attracted particular attention from entrepreneurship researchers (Fayolle and Liñán 2014). According to Ajzen (1991), it captures the degree to which people show their motivation and willingness to implement the desired behavior. Since entrepreneurial behavior is intentional, particularly when it is rare, hard to observe, or involves unpredictable time lags (Ajzen, 1991; Bird 1988; Krueger and Brazeal 1994), many researchers agreed that it can be predicted by EI and that new business formation is a deliberately designed behavior (Autio et al, 2001; Krueger and Carsrud 1993; Krueger et al, 2000). Since, intention is crucial in the entrepreneurial process and forms the first in a series of actions to found an organization (Bird 1988), then, it can be strong indicator of that targeted behavior and powerful predictor of subsequent behavior (Krueger et al, 2000). Several researchers have emphasized students' increasing interest in entrepreneurship as a career choice (Kolvereid, 1996). In our study, EI is defined as a university student's cognitive inclination to pursue an entrepreneurial career after graduation (one's desire to start a business, Krueger and Brazeal 1994; Krueger et al, 2000).

2.2 Entrepreneurship education and evaluation of its impacts

Entrepreneurship is a discipline and can be learned (Kuratko, 2005; Matlay, 2008). There is an increased interest in entrepreneurship education and a variety of dedicated programs and pedagogies across the world.

These programs are based on the assumption that EIs and skills can be taught and learned. In fact, education for entrepreneurship can help to promote its spirit in schools and universities and make a difference as young people who go through entrepreneurial programs and activities start more companies (European Commission, 2013). Here, entrepreneurship education is meant as any pedagogical (program) or process of education for developing entrepreneurial attitudes, skills and knowledge among students preparing them for choosing entrepreneurial careers (Bae et al, 2014; European Commission, 2013; Fayolle et al, 2006; Linan, 2008). Most university-level programs are intended to influence students' entrepreneurial awareness, to prepare them as aspiring entrepreneurs and provide them with skills needed to start and successfully run their own businesses (Pittaway and Cope 2007; Weber, 2012).

A range of entrepreneurship education programs for different target audience and with different types are identified and discussed for example by Liñán (2004). Despite the lack of evidence on evaluating the effects of such education, the key role of entrepreneurship education must not be disregarded. In several studies, the benefits from entrepreneurship education programs are showed (e.g., Fayolle et al, 2006; Souitaris et al, 2007) and the importance for assessing their impacts on entrepreneurial careers is challenged (Matlay, 2008). In some recent years, several researchers were focused on investigating the entrepreneurship education's impacts, challenges and approaches (Duval-Couetil, 2013; Fretschner and Weber, 2013; Mwasalwiba, 2010; Oosterbeek et al, 2010; von Graevenitz et al, 2010). Academic research has shown that entrepreneurship education increases EI and results generally support its positive effect on it (Fayolle and Gailly, 2015). In fact, some other well-designed meta-analyses were conducted showing a small but positive relationship (Martin, McNally, and Kay, 2013; Bae et al, 2014). However, it provided little insight into the conditions under which entrepreneurship education is more or less likely to be associated with EIs. Moreover, regarding the investigation of entrepreneurship education impacts, many studies have reported diverse methodologies (from the study of a compulsory course to the inclusion of a control group, or the use of pre- and post-measures with Liñán and Fayolle, 2015) and showed inconsistent and ambiguous findings (Lorz et al, 2013). In fact, in some studies, positive impacts are found (Fayolle et al, 2006; Souitaris et al, 2007; Pittaway and Cope, 2007), but in others, evidence showed that the effects are negative (Oosterbeek et al, 2010). In this sense, von Graevenitz et al (2010) consider it beneficial that the general intention level decreases as a result of the realistic information received.

The literature review showed also diversity in choosing the type of variable to measure entrepreneurship education varying from seeing it as binary variable (e.g., Byabashaija and Katono, 2011; Gerba, 2012; Heuer and Kolvereid, 2014), to the use of a pretest–posttest design or using an ex ante and ex post measurement (e.g., Chen et al, 2015; Fayolle and Gailly, 2008; 2009; 2015; Fretschner and Weber, 2013; Hattab, 2014; Karimi et al, 2012; 2016; Karlsson and Moberg, 2013 ; Maresch et al, 2015; Mueller, 2011; Rauch and Hulsink, 2015; Sánchez, 2013; Souitaris et al, 2007; Zhang et al, 2014). In reviewing these methodological perspectives, some researchers have found numerous weaknesses and called for analyses of a more precise nature (Lorz et al, 2013; Rideout and Gray, 2013; Rauch and Hulsink, 2015).

2.3 The rationale of using TPB as chosen theoretical framework for prediction and evaluation

The TPB has become one of the most influential theories applied to understand some type of human behavior (Armitage and Conner 2001), and especially entrepreneurial behavior (Krueger and Carsrud 1993; Krueger et al, 2000; Kautonen et al, 2013; 2015; Lortie and Castogiovanni, 2015). The theory is supported as a widely accepted tool for predicting intentions and behavior because of its coherence, parsimony, generalizability, and theoretical robustness for understanding and predicting intentions (Krueger et al, 2000).

The TPB provides a general framework to analyze the EI of a person (Ajzen, 1991). In the TPB framework, intention is a function of three antecedents: attitude toward behavior, subjective norm and perceived behavioral control. These theoretical antecedents should be sufficient to predict intentions. Their relative importance in the prediction of intention is expected to vary across behaviors, situations and contexts (Ajzen, 1991). According to the TPB, the *attitude towards behavior* (ATB) is a person's judgments about the impact of the desired behavior; *subjective norm* (SN) refers to what the social group that is important to that person thinks about performing the intended behavior; and *perceived behavioral control* (PBC) is an individual's perception of the ease or difficulty of performing the intended behavior (Ajzen, 1991). The TPB predicts as a general rule that the more favorable the ATB and SN are with respect to the behavior, and the greater the PBC is, the stronger an individual's intention to perform the behavior in question will be (Ajzen, 1991).

As a research field and a powerful theoretical framework, EI is rapidly evolving with different areas of specializations (Liñán and Fayolle, 2015). We mainly focus on a core EI model based on the TPB in order to test students' intention to start a new business in a Saudi context. Literature on EI is evolving with different major contributions (Krueger and Carsrud, 1993; Engle et al, 2010; Fayolle and Liñán, 2014; Liñán and Fayolle, 2015), our understanding of EIs is guided by the TPB of Ajzen's (1991). During the last few years, some researchers have started applying the TPB to investigate intention in a wide range of entrepreneurial scenarios (Fayolle and Liñán, 2014). In this context, the TPB contributes to our understanding of the entrepreneurial behavior emergence prior to the onset of any observable action (Liñán and Chen, 2009; Kautonen et al, 2013; 2015). Its validity has been proven in the domain of entrepreneurship (Krueger et al, 2000; Schlaegel and Koenig, 2014). Many studies have applied the TPB to predict the intention to start a business among university students in different contexts and countries (Aloulou, 2015a; 2015b; 2016; Autio et al 2001; Engle et al 2010; Fayolle et al, 2006; Fayolle and Gailly, 2015; Kolvereid, 1996; Krueger et al, 2000; Liñán and Chen, 2009). The TPB is also used to predict behavior as the final criterion (Ajzen, 1991). In our study, the entrepreneurial behavior is corresponding to measure the actual commitment in starting a new business. This theory is probably particularly useful in addressing processes that can be influenced by way of an entrepreneurship education program (Liñan et al, 2011; Rauch and Hulsink, 2015). From the TPB perspective, the link between intentions and behaviors depends on the extent to which behavior is under volitional control (Ajzen, 1991). But, it is revealed that there is a gap between intentions and behaviors in sense that not every intention is eventually transformed into actual behavior (Armitage and Conner, 2001; Sheeran, 2002; Sutton, 1998). This link intention – behavior began relatively to be explored in entrepreneurship literature (Kautonen et al, 2013; Kautonen et al, 2015; Nishimura and Tristán, 2011; Varamäki et al., 2016). As theoretical framework, the TPB has been used to evaluate the effects of entrepreneurship education on attitudes, intentions and behaviors (Bae et al, 2014; Fayolle et al, 2006; Fayolle and Gailly, 2009; 2015; Fayolle and Liñán, 2014; Fretschner and Weber, 2013; Karimi et al, 2012; 2016; Liñán and Fayolle, 2015; Mueller, 2011).

2.4 Research model for prediction and evaluation

These studies indicated the potential international use of Ajzen's model to predict entrepreneurial intent of university students. Although the TPB has successfully predicted students' EIs in different contexts as presented below, its utility at predicting intentions and especially at assessing entrepreneurship education impact in Arab countries has not been well established (e.g., Hattab, 2014). Our attention turns to applying the TPB to Saudi Arabia context. A research model of EIs based on TPB is shown in figure 1.

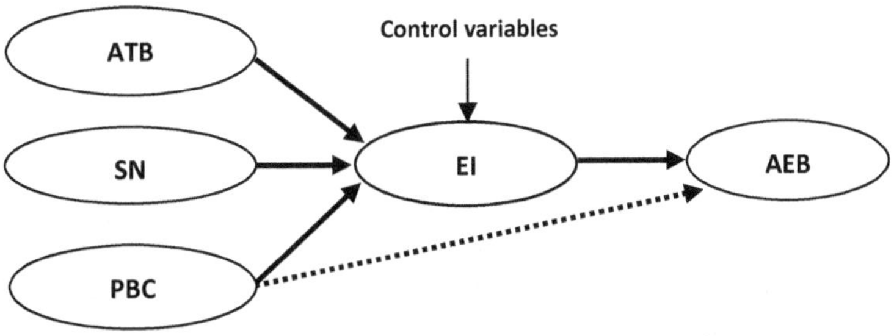

Figure 1: Research model linking TPB antecedents, EI and AEB

Overall, the theory has received strong empirical support in explaining entrepreneurial career choices. Most of the published empirical studies that have applied the TPB to predict entrepreneurial intention and behavior found that ATB, SN and PBC contributed significantly to the explanation of intentions (Kolvereid 1996; Krueger et al, 2000; Autio et al, 2001). However, the strength of the influence of these antecedents varies from one study to another. Previous studies showed the significant contribution of ATB and PBC to the explanation of intentions, but a controversial influence of SN (Armitage and Conner 2001; Krueger et al, 2000; Autio et al, 2001; Aloulou, 2015a; 2015b; 2016b; Kolvereid 1996; Engle et al, 2010). Prior applications of the TPB in the entrepreneurship literature suggest that attitude, subjective norms, and PBC typically explain 30%–45% of the variance in intentions (Kolvereid, 1996; Krueger et al, 2000; Autio et al, 2001; Liñán and Chen, 2009). Therefore, in previous studies, intentions explain up to 15-30% of the variance in actual or subsequent behaviours (Ajzen, 1991; Kautonen et al, 2015; Kautonen et al, 2013; Krueger et al, 2000; Sheeran, 2002).

Based on the literature review and previous studies, the hypotheses of this study are stated as follows. In the first set of hypotheses (1 to 3), we suppose that:

H1: ATB is positively related to EI before (H1a) and after (H1b) the completion of EC.
H2: SN is positively related to EI before (H2a) and after (H2b) the completion of EC.
H3: PBC is positively related to EI before (H3a) and after (H3b) the completion of EC.

In the second set of hypotheses (4-5), the TPB supports that:

H4: EI is considered as the main direct predictor of AEB in the 1st wave (H4a) and in the 2nd wave (H4b).
H5: PBC is considered as the main direct predictor of AEB in the 1st wave (H5a) and in the 2nd wave (H5b).

In the third set of hypotheses (6-7), we suppose that:

H6: there is an Impact of the EC on EI and Its Antecedents and AEB after the completion of the EC. Students will have higher ATB (H6a), SN (H6b), PBC (H6c), EI (H6d), and AEB (H6e) after the EC than before.
H7: Students, who have increased their ATB, their SN, and their PBC, will have increased their EI and will also be more engaged in their AEB.

3. Methodology

3.1 Data collection process

More attention is paid to the research design especially in terms of theoretical framework, structured sampling procedures, adequate sample size, time of measurement (utilization of an ex ante/ex post measurements), validity and reliability procedures. This study attempts to examine the impacts of the EC on attitudes, intentions and behaviors from the beginning to the end of the course using a pretest-posttest longitudinal quasi-experimental design (following Lorz et al, 2013; Rauch and Hulsink, 2015; Rodrigues et al, 2009; Sanchez, 2013; Souitaris et al, 2007). Only a matched sample was under treatment in order to take into account self-selection bias. However, a control group was not adopted in this study.

3.2 Sample characteristics and EC description

3.2.1 Sampling procedure and characteristics

To test our hypotheses, we used a questionnaire initially developed by Kolvereid (1996) and adapted by Fayolle and Gailly (2015). The questionnaire was designed in English and then translated into Arabic and back-translated to ensure the accuracy and appropriateness of language. A first version of the questionnaire was drafted and, then reviewed by 2 academics and pilot-tested on 10 university students (not included in the sample). Some changes were made on questionnaire to improve its readability, format and relevance of its instruments. The questionnaire consisted of three parts: items of the antecedents of EI; items of EI as a main dependent variable to measure the likelihood of starting a new business; and two questions about the AEB; and items about demographic characteristics' information (gender, parents as owners, relatives as owners, entrepreneurship and social prior experiences, entrepreneurship training). The target population of the study was 330 Business college students (male and female) enrolled in the EC in their last year of study in the College of Economics and Administrative Sciences (CEAS). Among 330 students to whom the questionnaires administered, 151 (45.76%) completed and matched properly the two questionnaires (at wave 1 and at wave 2), and their answers were included in the study. The data collected were then analyzed using standard statistical procedures (SPSS software, version 21). It is worth noting here that 177 students participated in the first survey and 160 students in the second survey. We used descriptive statistics for describing relevant sample's demographic characteristics (see table 1).

The final sample of 151 students was yielded, 109 men (72.2%) and 42 women (27.8%), aged between 23 and 25 years for 83.4% of them. As regards family and relatives ownership background, 22.5% were parents as owners and 55.6% relatives as owners. In the case of experiences, at least 38.4% of students had experience in business, entrepreneurship or social activities. Only 23.2% of them were trained in entrepreneurship.

Table 1: Demographic Characteristics of the Sample' respondents (N = 151)

Variable	Demographics	Frequency (n)	Valid percent (%)
Gender	Male	109	72.2
	Female	42	27.8
Age (years)	+ 23 and - 25	126	83.4
	+ 25	25	16.6
Parent Owner	Yes	34	22.5

Variable	Demographics	Frequency (n)	Valid percent (%)
Relatives Owners	Yes	84	55.6
Business experience	Yes	58	38.4
Entrepreneurship Prior Experience	Yes	18	11.9
Entrepreneurship Training	Yes	35	23.2
Social Experience	Yes	57	37.7

3.2.2 'Riyadah al-A'mal': The EC at IMSIU

A thorough descriptions of the respective entrepreneurship program and intervention under scrutiny are provided (learning objectives, duration, and pedagogical methods). In fact, our EC, called "Riyadah al-A'mal", is a 8th level course, which is common course in the bachelor program for business administration specializations, and as optional course for Finance and Investment specialization in the College of Economics and Administrative Sciences. The course is organized into two aspects: a conceptual aspect introduces the student to the basic concepts of entrepreneurship, entrepreneur, creativity and innovation, SME, business plan, entrepreneurial team and the funding of the entrepreneurial project (see table 2 for the covered topics); and a practical aspect requires students to apply these concepts following a 5 steps – entrepreneurial methodology: evaluating the entrepreneurial personality of students; selecting the business idea/opportunity; checking for the coherence between student and project idea; feasibility study; and elaboration of business plan.

Table 2: Timeline and contents of the EC

Week	Content	Week	Content
1	Enrollment to the course	9	Business plan
2	Introducing the course	10	Entrepreneurial teams
3	Basics of entrepreneurship	11	Funding the project
4	Characteristics and attributes of entrepreneur	12	Business plan writing
5	Creativity, innovation and entrepreneurship	13	Forum for students on entrepreneurship
6	Turning ideas into projects	14	Business plan presentation and evaluation
7	Entrepreneurship and SMEs	15	Week review
8	Success and failure Factors of SMEs	16	Final exams

The course meets twice a week (3 hours) during a semester of 14 weeks. Each class has roughly 25 – 35 students. The teaching means used in the course include lectures and case studies in order to enrich the students' knowledge with the experiences of others, attitudes and necessary skills for entrepreneurship. The project- and team-work based approaches are chosen in this course to encourage both individual and group learning. The process of learning how to draft a business plan is intended to instill the knowledge and skills and to strengthen one's EIs (e.g., Bae et al, 2014; Fayolle et al, 2006; von Graevenitz et al, 2010). For our research, It was the chosen approach for experiential learning in this EC to prepare students to an entrepreneurial career, specifically for starting their own businesses.

3.3 Data analysis

3.3.1 Measures of variables and reliability

Based on previous studies (Kolvereid, 1996; Fayolle and Gailly, 2015; Liñán, 2008), all variables related to EI and TPB antecedents were measured using a seven point Likert scale with extremes "Strongly disagree" and "Strongly agree". Demographic characteristics were measured using a binary statement (male/female; yes/no). We used some items expressed in a positive sense and others in reverse directions according to Liñán et al (2011) to avoid acquiescence bias.

(a) EI: 3 items concerned the measurement of EI. An index of intention to become self-employed was created by averaging the scores of these items. The reliability coefficient of EI was checked (table 4, for reliability, means, standard deviations and Person correlation among the analysis variables, is available on request).

(b) ATB: According to Kolvereid (1996), 32 items were used to measure ATB, and concerned assertions were linked to 11 reasons: 5 reasons assumed to favour employment; and 6 reasons assumed to favour self-employment. Indexes of the 11 reasons were created, and a score was obtained for each index by averaging the item scores. The reliability coefficients of indexes and a principal component analysis were checked (Table 3, for reliability and Spearman correlation coefficients, N = 151; and Table 4 are available on request). Then, measures of employment and self-employment attitudes were obtained by adding the index scores of the respective reasons. Finally, an indicator of employment status choice attitude was calculated as a numerical difference between self-employment and employment attitudes measures. Table 3 shows the Spearman correlations between attitude indexes and intentions to become self-employed. Eight and nine of the 11 correlations are statistically significant at 5% respectively in the 1st and 2nd wave. Similar to Kolvereid (1996), seven and eight of the 11 correlations are in the expected direction respectively for the 1st and 2nd waves.

(c) SN: is the product of two sets of measures, following Kolvereid (1996). The first set contains three items measuring the individual's beliefs about whether their family, friends or other important people think that they should (not) become an entrepreneur. The second set contains three other items and represents the degree to which those opinions affect the individual's decision as to whether or not to go ahead and start a business. After multiplying the corresponding pairs of the belief and motivation-to-comply items, three products were added up to create a final index. The reliability coefficient of SN was checked (table 4).

(d) PBC: Following Kolvereid (1996), six items concern PBC. After recodification, the scores of the items were averaged to obtain an overall measure of PBC. The reliability coefficient of the variable was checked (table 4).

(e) Actual Entrepreneurial Behaviour (AEB). It refers to making an effort to start a business rather than achieving the outcome of having started a business (Kautonen et al, 2013). To operationalize the AEB in terms of different engagement levels in line with the TPB (Ajzen, 1991), two questions were chosen, according to Kautonen et al (2013). In the 1st question, we ask the distance learner: '*in the last semester up to now, have you started a business or thought about starting a business alone or together with others?*'. In 2nd question, the respondent could choose between four options: (1) have not thought about starting a business; (2) thought about it but have not taken any action; (3) have not started a business but have commenced preparations and intend to start up in the near future; and (4) have started a business. These options can measure in one item the AEB performed by the individual at the time of survey (scaled 1 to 4 for the 1st to the 4th option).

f) Demographic characteristics: were chosen to be tested if they are predictors of entrepreneurial intention (Kolvereid, 1996; Fayolle and Gailly, 2015; Ozyilmaz, 2011). The present study employed a subset of them which were measured in the following way: gender as a dummy variable: gender = 1 if the student is male, 2 if female; age: 1 = (less than 23 years); 2 = (from 23 and to 25 years); 3 = more than 25 years; parents as owners and relatives as owners: Yes = 1 (exists); No = 2 (doesn't exist); entrepreneurship experience and training: Yes = 1 (have); No = 2 (doesn't have); social experience: Yes = 1 (have participated in); No = 2 (if not).

Table 4 provides the attitude's indexes, the number of items, and their reliability (Cronbach' alpha which varies from 0.548 to 0.897 in wave 1 and from 0.556 to 0,911 in wave 2. For the attitude antecedent, a PCA was checked as suggested by Kolvereid (1996) and 8 factors were found to explain 71.25 % of the variance in the 1st wave and 7 factors with 71.52% in the 2nd wave. The reliability of EI and its antecedents was checked. Cronbach's alphas are higher than 0.737 in the two waves. Descriptive statistics among AEB, EI, ATB, SN, PBC and the Pearson correlation among them were showed. It has been noted that there are significant bivariate correlations between most of the variables: the largest correlation coefficient between variables (SN and EI) is 0.534 and the lowest one (SN and PBC) is 0.046. EI are found to have statistically significant correlations with ATB, and SN in the 1st wave and with all TPB antecedents in the 2nd wave. In addition, SN has a statistically significant correlation with ATB. EI are also found to have a significant correlation with AEB in the two waves.

3.3.2 Data analysis

A SPSS software (V. 21) was used to assess validity and reliability and to test the research hypotheses with linear regression modeling and Student' t-test for regression estimates. In fact, assumptions in regression analysis were checked about normality, linearity and multicollinearity. Therefore, regressions were used to assess the relative contribution of each predictor variable by controlling the effects of other predictor variables in the prediction equation. Data was analyzed by using hierarchical multiple regression in order to test linkages between TPB antecedents as independent variables and EI as dependent variable. Before that, control variables were entered first followed by the second regression that included control variables and independent variables. The last regression consisted of PBC, EI and AEB. The same hierarchical regression modeling was applied for the two waves (before and after the completion of EC).

4. Results

H1, H2 and H3 stated that the more favorable the ATB and SN with respect to becoming self-employed, and the greater the PBC, the stronger the individual's intention to become self-employed before and after the completion of an entrepreneurship course. Table 5 showed the results for models 1b and 2b. In wave 1, two main variables contribute significantly to the explanation of the variance in intentions (F=11.131, *p*<0.01, R^2=0.443). The SN explained the highest value of 42.1 percent (β=0.421, *p*<0.01) of EI variance, followed by the ATB with 27.0 percent (β=0.218, *p*<0.01). However, PBC is positively but not significantly related to EI. In wave 2, all variables contribute significantly to explain the variance in EI (F=21.149, *p*<0.01, R^2=0.573). These variables explained the respective percentages of EI variance: for PBC (β=0.462, *p*<0.01); For SN (β=0.261, *p*<0.01), and for ATB (β=0.180, *p*<0.01). H1a, H1b, H2a, H2b, H1c, and H3b are supported, but H3a was not supported. H4 and H5 stated that EI and PBC are the main direct predictor of AEB in the two waves. The results in table 5 for models 3 and 4 showed that in wave 1, these variables are related significantly to AEB and contribute to the explanation of AEB (F=10.405, *p*<0.01, R^2=0.123) with the respective regression estimates: for EI (β=0.257, *p*<0.01) and for PBC (β=0.196, *p*<0.05). But, in wave 2, only EI contribute to the explanation of AEB (F=10.405, *p*<0.01, R^2=0.123) with a regression estimate of (β=0.339, *p*<0.01). H4a, H5a and H4b were supported, but H5b not supported. The set of hypotheses 6 stated that there is an impact of the EC on EI and its antecedents and on AEB and its antecedents. The results of regression in table 5 when comparing the model 1b and model 2b for EI as dependent variable, and when comparing models 3 and 4 for AEB as dependent variable, the regression estimates were changed. ATB did not exerts a stronger effect on EI after the EC completion of than before, SN exerts a weaker effect on EI after the EC completion than before, and PBC exerts a stronger effect on EI after the EC completion than before.

Table 5: Hierarchical regression models for predicting EI and EAB (N = 177)

Dependent variable	EI				AEB	
Wave	Before		After		Before	After
Model	1a	1b	2a	2b	3	4
Independent variables	(β)	(β)	(β)	(β)	(β)	(β)
Sex	.231**	.151*	.010	.029	-	-
ParentOwner	.195*	.185**	.078	.151**	-	-
RelativeOwner	-.091	-.025	-.077	-.019	-	-
BusinessExperience	-.106	-.007	-.200*	-.014	-	-
EntrepreneurshipExperience	-.161	-.153*	.034	-.057	-	-
EntrepreneurshipTraining	-.161	-.098	-.142	-.104	-	-
SocialExperience	-.051	-.063	.002	.035	-	-
ATB	-	.270**	-	.180**	-	-
SN	-	.421**	-	.261**	-	-
PBC	-	.076	-	.462**	.196*	.07
EI	-	-	-	-	.257**	.339**
R Square (R^2)	.175	.443	.077	.573	.123	.153
Adjusted R Square (R^2)	.135	.403	.032	.573	.111	.137
F	4.335	11.131	1.706	21.149	10.405	12.890
F Change (ΔF)	4.335	22.441	1.706	61.465		
Significance of F	.000**	.000**	.112	.000**	.000**	.000**
Hypotheses	H1a and H2a supported H3a non supported		H1b, H2b and H3b supported		H4a and H5a supported	H4b supported H5b non supported

** $p < 0.01$. ; * $p < 0.05$. ; † $p < 0.1$

In order to test the hypotheses 6 and 7 and check the main variables that are affected by the EC, the impact of EC is considered when measuring change in ATB, SN, PBC, EI and AEB. To assess this impact, we computed for each participant the difference between the measures of all main variables before and after taking the EC. The results are showed in Table 6, in terms of the average difference between the measures of variables after and before the taking the EC, as well as the standard deviation, significance of those differences and the Pearson correlation between them. We conducted a paired t-test to compare the mean values of the measures of intention, its antecedents and AEB in the two waves.

Table 6: Impact of the EC: Paired T-tests (difference between means) and Pearson Correlation (N=151)

Observed difference	Mean (before – after)	Std. Dev.	*SE*	*P*	(1)	(2)	(3)	(4)	(5)
in ATB (1)	-.359	5.67	.46	.44	1				
in SN (2)	.618	10.06	.82	.45	.072	1			
in PBC (3)	.143	.98	.08	.07†	.045	.357**	1		
in EI (4)	-.011	1.35	.11	.92	**.233****	**.476****	**.258****	1	
in AEB (5)	.433	.87	.07	.00**	.143	.335**	**.203***	**.212****	1

** $p < 0.01$. ; * $p < 0.05$. ; † $p < 0.1$.

It should be noted that there was no significant difference or change ATB, SN and EI, but a slightly significant difference in PBC (mean=0.143, *p*<0.1) and a strong significant difference in AEB (mean=0.433, *p*<0.01). The three antecedents of EI have, on average, been affected by the EC. Even though there seems to be a globally slightly negative impact on the level of intention (mean=-0.011) and attitudes (mean=-0.359), but more impact on SN, AEB and PBC. This impact did not appear to be significant for the whole sample, except for PBC and AEB. Only hypotheses H6c and H6e were supported while H6a, H6b and H6d were not supported. So, H6 was partially supported. In order to test the hypothesis 7, we used a correlation analysis, as shown in table 6. A change in ATB, SN, PBC was significantly related to increased EI. Moreover, a change in EI and PBC was significantly related to increased AEB. Therefore, H7 was supported.

5. Discussion and conclusion

This study elucidates that the TPB is validate tool used to predict EI and actual behaviors and assess the impact of entrepreneurship course on attitudes, intentions and behaviors. On one hand, the findings provide a strong evidence that the main antecedents of the TPB contribute significantly to the explanation of intentions and behaviors. The findings support previous studies (Aloulou, 2015; 2016; Engle et al., 2010; Iakovleva and Solesvik, 2014; Kautonen et al, 2013; 2015; Kolvereid, 1996; Liñán et al, 2011a; 2011b). On the other hand, the findings provide some evidence that EC has an impact of attitudes, intentions and behaviors, but with reserve. This is due to the mitigated results found in previous studies (Fayolle and Gailly, 2015; Karimi et al, 2012; Souitaris et al, 2007). The interesting fact identified in this study is that the PBC played a role in explaining EI after the completion of the EC, and, in return, EI played a main role (solely) in explaining AEB. This can confirm the mediating role of EI between PBC and AEB (e.g., Bagozzi et al, 1989). That's mean that after taking the EC, students were committed into starting a business (going from one engagement level to another) after thinking about it (stable intentions), and perceiving that they have the needed skills to accomplish more entrepreneurial tasks that are critical to the performance of the AEB. The nature of the EC and the adopted process of learning (through the drafting of business plans) as seems to have an influence on their actual behaviors (Bae et al, 2014; Fayolle et al, 2006; von Graevenitz et al, 2010).

This study has followed most of the recommendations suggested by several authors about the conducting the research, its procedure of utilization of the ex-ante/ex-post measurements (Bae et al, 2014; Fretschner and Weber, 2013; Lorz et al, 2013; Rodrigues et al, 2009; Sánchez, 2013; Rauch and Hulsink, 2015). However, this study has some limitations that affects the generalizability of the findings due to the small size of the sample which was related to one university. Other limitation is related to the investigation of the impact of EC in short term. Future research study should take into account the long term. Entrepreneurship scholars, accordingly, call for testing intentions models such as TPB on samples of subjects in different stages of life as made by Kautonen et al (2013) and after participating in entrepreneurship courses (Rauch and Hulsink, 2015).

References

Ajzen, I. (1991) "The theory of planned behavior", *Organizational Behavior and Human Decision Processes*, Vol. 50, No. 2, pp. 179-211.

Aloulou, W.J., (2015a), "The Prediction of Entrepreneurial intention among Preparatory Year' Saudi Students: Testing an intent model", *in ICIE 2015 3rd International Conference on Innovation and Entrepreneurship*, 19 – 20 March, Durban, South Africa.

Aloulou, W.J. (2015b) "Entrepreneurial Intention among Freshmen Students - Application of the Theory of Planned Behaviour in Saudi Context". *Journal of Enterprising Culture*, Vol. 23, No. 04, pp. 473-500.

Aloulou, W.J. (2016) "Predicting the Entrepreneurial intentions of Final Year Business Students Applying the Theory of Planned Behavior in Saudi context", the *Journal of Small Business and Enterprise Development*, Vol. 23, No. 4, pp. 1142-1164.

Armitage, C.J., and Conner, M. (2001) "Efficacy of the theory of planned behaviour: a meta-analytic review", *British Journal of Social Psychology*, Vol. 40, No. 4, pp. 471-99.

Autio, E., Keeley, R.H., Klofstein, M., Parker, G.G.C. and Hay, M. (2001) "Entrepreneurial intent among students in Scandinavia and in the USA", *Enterprise and Innovation Management Studies*, Vol. 2, No. 2, pp. 145-60.

Bae, T.J., Qian, S., Miao, C., and Fiet, J.O. (2014) "The Relationship Between Entrepreneurship Education and Entrepreneurial Intentions: A Meta-Analytic Review". *Entrepreneurship Theory and Practice*, Vol. 38, No. 2, pp. 217-254.

Bagozzi, R.P., Baumgartner, J., and Yi, Y. (1989) "An investigation into the role of intentions as mediators of the attitude-behavior relationship". *Journal of Economic Psychology*, Vol. 10, No. 1, pp. 35-62.

Bird, B. (1988) "Implementing entrepreneurial ideas: The case for intention". *Academy of management Review*, Vol. 13, No. 3, pp. 442-453.

Byabashaija, W., and Katono, I. (2011) "The impact of college entrepreneurial education on entrepreneurial attitudes and intention to start a business in Uganda". *Journal of Developmental Entrepreneurship*, Vol. 16, No. 01, pp. 127-144.

Chen, S.C., Hsiao, H.C., Chang, J.C., Chou, C.M., Chen, C.P., and Shen, C.H. (2015) "Can the entrepreneurship course improve the entrepreneurial intentions of students?". *International Entrepreneurship and Management Journal*, Vol. 11, No. 3, pp. 557-569.

Duval-Couetil, N. (2013) "Assessing the impact of entrepreneurship education programs: Challenges and approaches". *Journal of Small Business Management*, Vol. 51, No. 3, pp. 394-409.

Engle, R.L., Dimitriadi, N., Gavidia, J.V., Schlaegel, C., Delanoe, S., Alvarado, I., He, X., Buame, S., and Wolff, B. (2010) "Entrepreneurial intent: A twelve-country evaluation of Ajzen's model of planned behavior". *International Journal of Entrepreneurial Behavior* and *Research*, Vol. 16, No. 1, pp. 35-57.

European Commission, (2012) *Effects and impact of entrepreneurship programmes in higher education*, Report of the Directorate-General for Enterprise and Industry, 87p. Accessed January 17, 2016: http://ec.europe.eu/DocsRoom/documents/375/attachments/1/translations/en/renditions/native.

European Commission, (2013) *Entrepreneurship 2020 Action Plan*. Communication from the Commission to the European Parliament, The Council, The European Economic and Social Committee and the Committee of the Regions, Reigniting the entrepreneurial spirit in Europe. Brussels: European Commission.

Fayolle, A., and Gailly, B. (2015) "The impact of entrepreneurship education on entrepreneurial attitudes and intention: Hysteresis and persistence". *Journal of Small Business Management*, Vol. 53, No. 1, pp. 75-93.

Fayolle, A., Gailly, B., and Lassas-Clerc, N. (2006) "Assessing the impact of entrepreneurship education programmes: a new methodology". *Journal of European industrial training*, Vol. 30, No. 9, pp. 701-720.

Fayolle, A., and Liñán, F. (2014) "The future of research on entrepreneurial intentions". *Journal of Business Research*, Vol. 67, No. 5, pp. 663-666.

Fretschner, M., and Weber, S. (2013) "Measuring and understanding the effects of entrepreneurial awareness education". *Journal of Small Business Management*, Vol. 51, No. 3, pp. 410-428.

Gerba, D.T. (2012) "Impact of entrepreneurship education on entrepreneurial intentions of business and engineering students in Ethiopia". *African Journal of Economic & Management Studies,* Vol. 3. No. 2, pp. 258-277.

Hattab, H.W. (2014) "Impact of Entrepreneurship Education on Entrepreneurial Intentions of University Students in Egypt". *Journal of Entrepreneurship*, Vol. 23, No. 1, pp. 1-18.

Heuer, A., and Kolvereid, L. (2014) "Education in entrepreneurship and the Theory of Planned Behaviour". *European Journal of Training and Development*, Vol. 38, No. 6, pp. 506-523.

Iakovleva, T., and Solesvik, M. Z. (2014) "Entrepreneurial intentions in post-Soviet economies". *International Journal of Entrepreneurship and Small Business*, Vol. 21, No. 1, pp. 79-100.

Jonathan, P. (Ed.) (2008) *Entrepreneurship and Higher Education. Local Economic and Employment Development (LEED)* OECD Publishing.

Karimi, S., Biemans, H. J., Lans, T., Mulder, M., and Chizari, M. (2012) "The Role of Entrepreneurship Education in Developing Students' Entrepreneurial Intentions". Available at SSRN 2152944.

Karlsson, T., and Moberg, K. (2013) "Improving perceived entrepreneurial abilities through education: Exploratory testing of an entrepreneurial self-efficacy scale in a pre-post setting". *The International Journal of Management Education*, Vol. 11, No. 1, pp. 1-11.

Kautonen T., Van Gelderen, M., and Fink, M. (2015) "Robustness of the theory of planned behavior in predicting entrepreneurial intentions and actions". *Entrepreneurship Theory and Practice*, Vol. 39, No. 3, pp. 655-674.

Kautonen T., Van Gelderen, M., and Tornokoski E.T. (2013) "Predicting entrepreneurial behavior: a test of the theory of planned behaviour", *Applied Economics*, Vol. 45, No. 6, pp. 697-707.

Kelley, D., Bosma, N. and Amoros, J.E. (2011) "Global entrepreneurship monitor", Global report 2010, 85p.

Kolvereid, L. (1996) "Prediction of employment status choice intentions", *Entrepreneurship Theory and Practice*, Vol. 21, No. 1, pp. 47-57.

Krueger, N.F., and Carsrud, A.L. (1993) "Entrepreneurial intentions: applying the theory of planned behaviour". *Entrepreneurship & Regional Development*, Vol. 5. No. 4, pp. 315-330.

Krueger, N.F., Reilly, M.D., and Carsrud, A. L. (2000) "Competing models of entrepreneurial intentions", *Journal of Business Venturing*, Vol. 15, No. 5, pp. 411-32.

Kuratko, D.F., (2005) "The emergence of entrepreneurship education: Development, trends, and challenges". *Entrepreneurship Theory and Practice*, Vol. 29, No. 5, pp. 577-597.

Liñán, F., (2004), "Intention-based models of entrepreneurship education", *Piccolla Impresa/Small Business*, Vol. 3, No. 1, pp.11-35.

Liñán, F., and Chen, Y.W. (2009) "Development and Cross-Cultural Application of a Specific Instrument to Measure Entrepreneurial Intentions". *Entrepreneurship Theory and Practice*, Vol. 33, No. 3, pp. 593-617.

Liñán, F., and Fayolle, A. (2015) "A systematic literature review on entrepreneurial intentions". *International Entrepreneurship and Management Journal*, Vol. 11, No. 4, pp. 907-933.

Liñán, F., Rodríguez-Cohard, J.C., and Guzmán, J. (2011a) Temporal stability of entrepreneurial intentions: a longitudinal study. In Borch, O.J., Fayolle, A., Kyro, P., Ljunggren E., (eds.), *Entrepreneurship Research in Europe: Evolving Concepts and Processes*, chapter 2 (pp. 34-55).

Liñán, F., Rodríguez-Cohard, J.C., and Rueda-Cantuche, J.M. (2011b) "Factors affecting entrepreneurial intention levels: a role for education". *International Entrepreneurship and Management Journal*, Vol. 7, No. 2, pp. 195-218.

Lortie, J., and Castogiovanni, G. (2015) "The theory of planned behavior in entrepreneurship research: what we know and future directions". *International Entrepreneurship and Management Journal*, Vol. 11, No. 4, pp. 935-957.

Lorz, M., Mueller, S., and Volery, T. (2013) "Entrepreneurship education: a systematic review of the methods in impact studies". *Journal of Enterprising Culture*, Vol. 21, No. 02, pp. 123-151.

Maresch, D., Harms, R., Kailer, N., and Wimmer-Wurm, B. (2015) "The impact of entrepreneurship education on the entrepreneurial intention of students in science and engineering versus business studies university programs". *Technological Forecasting and Social Change*. Online 23 December 2015.

Martin, B.C., McNally, J.J., and Kay, M.J. (2013) "Examining the formation of human capital in entrepreneurship: A meta-analysis of entrepreneurship education outcomes". *Journal of Business Venturing*, Vol. 28, No. 2, pp. 211-224.

Matlay, H. (2008) "The impact of entrepreneurship education on entrepreneurial outcomes". *Journal of Small Business and Enterprise Development*, Vol. 15, No. 2, pp. 382-396.

McKinsey and Company, (2015) Saudi Arabia Beyond oil: the investment and productivity transformation, *McKinsey Global Institute report*. Retrieved December 20, 2015 from http://www.mckinsey.com/.

Mueller, S. (2011) "Increasing entrepreneurial intention: effective entrepreneurship course characteristics". *International Journal of Entrepreneurship and Small Business*, Vol. 13, No. 1, pp. 55-74.

Nishimura, J.S. and Tristán, O.M. (2011) "Using the theory of planned behaviour to predict nascent entrepreneurship". *Academia, Revista Latinoamericana de Administración*, Vol. 46, pp. 55-71.

Oosterbeek, H., van Praag, M. and Ijsselstein, A. (2010) "The impact of entrepreneurship education on entrepreneurship skills and motivation", *European Economic Review*, Vol. 54, No. 3, pp. 442-454.

Ozyilmaz, A. (2011) The effects of demographic characteristics on entrepreneurial intention in the pre-venture stage of entrepreneurship. *International Journal of Entrepreneurship and Small Business*, *14*(3), 406-424.

Pittaway, L. and Cope, J. (2007) "Entrepreneurship education – a systematic review of the evidence", *International Small Business Journal*, Vol. 25, No. 5, pp. 477-506.

Porter, M. (2012) *Entrepreneurship and Competitiveness: Implications for Saudi Arabia*. Global Competitiveness Forum, Riyadh, Saudi Arabia, 24 January.

Rauch, A., Hulsink, W. (2015) "Putting entrepreneurship education where the intention to act lies: An investigation into the impact of entrepreneurship education on entrepreneurial behavior", *Academy of Management Learning & Education*, Vol. 14, No. 2, pp. 187–204.

Rideout, E.C., and Gray, D.O. (2013) "Does entrepreneurship education really work? A review and methodological critique of the empirical literature on the effects of university-based entrepreneurship education". *Journal of Small Business Management*, Vol. 51, No. 3, pp. 329-351.

Rodrigues, R.G., Raposo, M., Ferreira, J., and Do Paco, A. (2009) "Entrepreneurship education and the propensity for business creation: testing a structural model". *International Journal of Entrepreneurship and Small Business*, Vol. 9, No. 1, pp. 58-73.

Sánchez, J.C. (2013) "The impact of an entrepreneurship education program on entrepreneurial competencies and intention". *Journal of Small Business Management*, Vol. 51, No. 3, pp. 447-465.

Saudi Council of Economic and Development Affairs, (2016, April 24), *Saudi Vision 2030*, April, Retrieved June 02, 2016 from http://vision2030.gov.sa/download/file/fid/417.

Schlaegel, C., and Koenig, M. (2014) "Determinants of Entrepreneurial Intent: A Meta-Analytic Test and Integration of Competing Models". *Entrepreneurship Theory and Practice*, Vol. 38, No. 2, pp. 291-332.

Sheeran, P. (2002) Intentions-behavior relations: a conceptual and empirical review. In W. Strobe, and M. Hewstone (Eds.), *European Review of Social Psychology*, Vol. 12, pp. 1-36.

Souitaris, V., Zerbinati, S., and Al-Laham, A. (2007) "Do entrepreneurship programmes raise entrepreneurial intention of science and engineering students? The effect of learning, inspiration and resources". *Journal of Business venturing*, Vol. *22, No.* 4, pp. 566-591.

Sutton, S. (1998) "Predicting and explaining intentions and behaviour: how well are we doing?", *Journal of Applied Social Psychology*, Vol. 28, No. 15, pp. 1317-1338.

von Graevenitz, G., Harhoff, D. and Weber, R. (2010) "The effects of entrepreneurship education", *Journal of Economic Behavior & Organization*, Vol. 76, No. 1, pp. 90-112.

Varamäki, E., Tornikoski, E., Viljamaa, A., and Ristimäki, K. (2011) "Entrepreneurial intentions of higher education students in Finland - A longitudinal study". In *ICSB World Conference Proceedings*, Stockholm, Sweden.

Weber, R. (2012) *Evaluating entrepreneurship education*. Springer Science & Business Media.

Schwab, K., Sala-I-Martin, X. (2015) *Global Competitiveness Report 2015-2016*. WEF, Retrieved September 23, 2016, from http://www3.weforum.org/docs/gcr/2015-2016/Global_Competitiveness_Report_2015-2016.pdf.

Zhang, Y., Duysters, G., and Cloodt, M. (2014) "The role of entrepreneurship education as a predictor of university students' entrepreneurial intention". *International Entrepreneurship and Management Journal*, Vol. 10, No. 3, pp. 623-641.

Biopesticides: Future State of Art and Opportunities for Entrepreneurship Alternatives in India

Mamoni Banerjee
Indian Institute of Technology, Kharagpur, West Bengal, India
mamoni@see.iitkgp.ernet.in

Abstract: The botanical pesticides are playing an increasing role in pest management and a alternative to chemical pesticides. In this study, rhizome of Sweet flag (*Acorus calamus*) are utilized for development of botanical pesticides against pests: *Spodoptera litura*, *Corcyra cephalonica* and *Spilosoma oblique*. The rhizome of *Acorus calamus* was extracted by Soxhlet extraction unit using Petroleum ether and methanol as solvent. The extracts thus prepared were fractionated by using chromatography. Emulsifiable concentrated formulations were prepared in different concentrations. Bio assay of different solvent extracts and botanical formulations against three pests were conducted at laboratory condition.
The chromatographic study revealed that the active compounds in *A. calamus* rhizomes were α-asarone (39.7%), (E)-methylisoeugenol (15.02%), methyleugenol (9.36%) ,β-asarone (4.51%), α-cedrene (3.07%) and camphor (1.89%). The extract of *Acorus calamus* exhibited contact toxicity against *Spodoptera litura*, *Corcyra cephalonica* and *Spilosoma obliqua* with an LD_{50} value of 0.91 μg/cm2 , 0.69 μg/cm2 and 1.53 μg/cm2 respectively. *A. calamus* extract with Sunflower oil based Formulation showed higher efficacy against *Spodoptera litura* and *Corcyra cephalonica*. The cost of return per ha of botanical pesticides was improved as 14.3% as compared with chemical pesticides. It is indicative cost efficiency ratio during vegetable production at field.

Keywords: Sweet flag (*Acorus calamus*), Lepidopteran pests, Entrepreneurship, Botanical pesticides

1. Introduction

India is the second largest producer of vegetables after China and accounts for 13.4 % of world production. The insect pests inflict crop losses to the tune of 40 per cent in vegetable production (Dhandapani *et all*,2003). To control those pests, around 13 per cent of the total chemical pesticides in India are used on vegetables & fruits (Nigam and Murthy, 2000). As a consequence, 50 -70 % of the vegetables are contaminated with chemical insecticide residue may directly or indirectly affect human and animal health. Use of botanical pesticides are playing an increasing role in pest management. Scientists in different parts of the world are working for the development and establishment of plant based pesticide, usually called as phytopesticide, botanical pesticide, biopesticide or natural pesticides (Siddiqui et al., 2009).The natural resources which are known to use as botanical pesticides at research site are Sweet flag (Acorus calamus), yam bean (*Pachyrrhizus erosus*), sweetsop (*Anona squamosa*), kuchla seed (*Strychnos nuxvomica*), Mahua (*Madhuca latifolia*), Arjun tree (*Terminalia arjuna*), Marigold (*Tagetes sp*) etc. Author's perspective in this study was to develop botanical pesticides from rhizome of Sweet flag (Acorus calamus) against lepidopteran pest. The research has been leaded to (i) protect vegetable with botanical pesticides and (ii) Implementation of the technology for exploiting local and natural botanical plant resources through regional entrepreneurship model.

2. Methodology

Rhizome of *Acorus Calamus* were collected from different parts of Bankura and Burdwan district of West Bengal, India. The rhizome was washed thoroughly and dried under shade for a week. It was then grinded using mixer Grinder. The powder of rhizome of *Acorus calamus* was extracted using Soxhlet extraction unit. Petroleum ether and methanol were used as solvents. The Petroleum ether and methanol were then evaporated using rotary Evaporator to get the crude extract. The crude extracts were stored in refrigerator until use. The extracts thus prepared were analyzed by using Gas chromatography–mass spectrometry (GC-MS). To prepare the different concentrations, different amount of crude extract were diluted with ethanol and water containing emulsifier 1 % Triton X-100 for conducting the bio-efficacy study against *Spodoptera litura, Corcyra cephalonica* and *Spilosoma obliqua* at laboratory condition. To compare the efficacy of the extract with chemical pesticides, Monocrotophos was used. Water containing 0.75% ethanol and 1 % emulsifier served as control. The measured amount of each concentration of plant product, synthetic pesticide and control treatment were topically applied on the third instar larvae of *S. Litura and S.obliqua* and fifth instar larvae of *C. cephalonica* through potter's tower. Emulsifiable concentrated formulations were prepared incorporating Tween-80 and Span 80 as surfactants and sunflower oil, Rice burn oil and palm oil as solvent.

3. Results and Discussion

A. calamus essential oil was 1.12% + 13% (V/W) and the density of the essential oil was determined to be 0.98 g/ml. The GC-MS analysis revealed that active compounds in *A. calamus* rhizomes were α-asarone (39.7%), methyleugenol (9.36%) , (E)-methylisoeugenol (15.02%), β-asarone (4.51%), α-cedrene (3.07%) and camphor (1.89%) etc. Liu *et al* (2013) also noted that principal compounds in the essential oil of *A. calamus* were determined to be α-asarone (50.09%), (E)-methylisoeugenol (14.01%), and methyleugenol (8.59%), followed by β-asarone (3.51%), α-cedrene (3.09%) and camphor (2.42%).

The different concentrations of each crude extract of rhizome of *A calamous* and Monocrotophos were used against *Spodoptera litura, Corcyra cephalonica* and *Spilosoma obliqua* at laboratory condition. The results have been presented at Table 1.

Table 1: Bio-efficacy of Petroleum ether of *A. Calamus* and Monocrotophos on larval mortality in *C. Cephalonica, S. litura and S. obliqua*

Treatment	% Concentration	% Larval mortality of *C. Cephalonica* (hour after Treatment)				% Larval mortality of *S. litura* (hour after Treatment)				% Larval mortality of *S. obliqua* (hour after Treatment)			
		24hrs	48hrs	72hrs	96hrs	24hrs	48hrs	72hrs	96hrs	24hrs	48hrs	72hrs	96hrs
Extract of *A. Calamus*	1.00	10.00	23.33	40.00	50.00	20.00	26.66	40.00	53.33	10.00	30.00	46 .66	60.00
	2.00	13.33	26.66	46.66	63.33	23.33	40.00	53.33	60.00	10.00	33.33	50.00	63.33
	3.00	13.33	30.00	56.66	73.33	33.33	53.33	63.33	70.00	13.33	33.33	60.00	66.66
Monocrotophos	0.05	30.00	53.33	76.66	96.66	36.66	66.66	93.33	96.66	20.00	60.00	83.33	90.00
	0.06	40.00	66.66	86.66	100.00	43.33	80.00	93.33	96.66	23.33	70.00	93.33	96.66
	0.07	50.00	73.33	86.66	100.00	43.33	93.33	100.00	100.00	30.00	80.00	96.66	100.00
Control		00	00	00	00	20.00	26.66	40.00	53.33	00	00	00	00

The extract of rhizome of *A. calamus* was found to produce 63.33% and 73.33 % larval mortality in *C. Cephalonica* at 96 hrs after treatment when used at 2.00% and 3.00 % concentrations respectively. It was also observed that with the increasing concentrations of plant extracts, there was a corresponding increase in larval mortality. Morya *et al* (2010) also noted that there was a dose dependent increase in mortality of *C. Cephalonica* after treatment with *L. camara*, and *C. inerme*. Larval stage was found to be more sensitive to the toxic effect than pupae and adults. The higher concentrations of . It was also noted by Morya *et al that* 1.5 and 2.0 g were highly effective as they produced 100% mortality in the larval stage itself. Monocrotophos , the most commonly pesticides used by farmers against various crop was included as a check against *A. Calamus*. 100 % mortality was found at 96 hrs after treatment when used 0.06% and 0.07 % concentrations respectively against *C. Cephalonica*. The larval mortality of *S. litura* was recorded to be 53.33 %, 60.00 % and 70 % when treated with 1.00 %, 2.00% and 3.00 % concentrations of *A. Calamus* extract respectively at 96hrs after treatment. Baskar et al also reported that in case of Spodoptera litura Fab. (Lepidoptera: Noctuidae), a total mortality of 68.06% was observed in ethyl acetate leaf extract of *Aristolochia tagala* at 5% concentration

The larval mortality of S. obliqua was found to be 60.00 % when treated with 1.00 % concentration of plant extract at 96hrs after treatment. However, a corresponding increase in larval mortality was observed with increasing concentrations of plant extract and as high as 66.66 % larval mortality was recorded at 96hrs after treatment with 3.00 % concentration. Meena and Divender (2013) also noted that the oviposition deterrent effect increased with an increase in concentration; being maximum at 3 percent against both Bactrocera Tau (85.3 %) and B. Cucurbitae. Both for *S. litura* and *S. obliqua*, 100 % larval mortality was recorded at 96hrs after treatment with 0.07 % concentration of Monocrotophos.

It was also reveled from this experiment that the plant extract has contact effect on all three lepidopteran pest. Yao *et al* (2008) noted the ethanol extract of *A. calamus* having strong repellency and contact effect to *S. zeamais* .

The mortality as obtained through topical application of herbal product and synthetic pesticides on *C. cephalonica, S. litura* and *S. obliqua* were subject to probit analysis to find out the LC50 values and comparative toxicity on the basis of LC50 value. The same has been presented in Table 2.

Table 2: Comparative toxicity of Petroleum ether and methanol extract of *A. Calamus*, Monocrotophos on larval mortality in *C. Cephalonica, S. litura* and *S. obliqua*

Treatment	*C. Cephalonica*				*S. litura*				*S. obliqua*			
	Hetero geneity	Regression Equation	LC_{50} (mg/lit)	Fiducial Limits	Heteroge neity	Regression Equation	LC_{50} (mg/lit)	Fiducial Limits	Heteroge neity	Regression Equation	LC_{50} (mg/lit)	Fiducial Limits
Extract of *A. Calamus*	0.031	1.45717+ 1.28197x	0.69823	+0.7820178 -0.425902	0.345	0.07810+ 0.62318x	0.91250	+1.022 -0.5475	0.05	0.27348+ 0.39690x	1.53399	+1.74049 -0.926500
Monocrot ophos	0.88	2.75803+ 3.60456x	0.0051	+00.005712 -00.003111	0.88	3.18007+ 3.60456x	0.00519	+0.00790 -0.0001	1.617	3.24763+ 2.39492x	00.0058	+0.0065 -0.0035

It was revealed from the analysis that monocrotophos was the most toxic with LC_{50} Values of 0.0051mg/lit, 0.00519mg/lit and 00.0058mg/lit respectively against *C. Cephalonica*, *S. litura* and *S. obliqua* but the LC50 value of *A. Calamus* against *C. Cephalonica* and *S. litura* is also low and it may be effective to minimize the pest population of *C. Cephalonica* and *S.litura*. Kumar *et al* (2015) noted that Lethal concentration 50 (LC_{50}) values of ethanolic extract of rhizome *Acorus Calamus* against larvae, adult males and females of D. melanogaster were 109.54, 52.51 and 41.11 mg/L respectively.

Three formulations of *A. Calamus* were prepared and were tested against *C. Cephalonica* and *Spodoptera litura*. The bio-efficacy data of different formulations of *A. Calamus* against *C. Cephalonica* and *Spodoptera litura* are presented at Table 3

Table 3: Bio-efficacy of different Emulsifiable concentrated formulations of *A. Calamus* against *C. Cephalonica and S. litura*

Formulation	% Larval mortality of C. Cephalonica (hour after Treatment)				% Larval mortality of S. litura (hour after Treatment)			
	24hrs	48hrs	72hrs	96hrs	24hrs	48hrs	72hrs	96hrs
Sunflower oil based Formulation	14.12	32.00	57.36	72.15	32.26	49.02	58.29	72.56
Rice burn oil based Formulation	15.12	31.00	56.48	70.15	33.21	48.26	59.29	69.39
palm oil based Formulation	13.12	32.00	58.29	69.23	33.89	52.26	62.32	68.69
Control	00	00	00	00	00	00	00	00

The larval mortality of *C. Cephalonica* and *Spodoptera litura* were more or less similar in different formulations in different hours after treatment. The highest mortality was found with Sunflower oil based Formulation at 96 hrs after treatment.

Sunflower oil based Formulation was applied in farmer's field for cabbage crop. The cost of return per ha of botanical pesticides as compared with chemical pesticide is at Table 4:

Table 4: The cost of return per ha of botanical pesticides as compared with chemical pesticide (Rs/ ha)

Particulars	Return using Sunflower oil based Formulation	Return using Chemical pesticide	Difference
Cabbage	54,356	46,583	7773

The cost of return per ha of botanical pesticides was improved as 14.3% as compared with chemical pesticides. It is indicative cost efficiency ratio during vegetable production at field. The indirect benefits are human health improvement, soil health improvement, increase of parasite, predators in the field. Amoabenga *et* al also demonstrated that the use of locally available plant materials as crop protectants could be less expensive and give financial benefits that are higher or comparable to synthetic insecticides

4. Conclusion

It emerged out that locally available indigenous plant species can profitably be utilized for protection of noxious pest which may open the opportunities for Entrepreneurship at regional level in different ways Such as Entrepreneur for cultivation of *A. Calamus*, Entrepreneur for development of botanical pesticide, Entrepreneur for cultivation of organic Vegetable using the botanical pesticides etc.

References

Arvind Kumar, Sunita Sharma, Gaurav Verma (2015) Insecticidal and Genotoxic Potential of *Acorus Calamus* rhizome extract against *Drosophila melanogaster* Asian J Pharm Clin Res, 8(4): 113-116

Blankson W. Amoabenga, Geoff M. Gurr, Catherine W. Gitauf, Philip C. Stevenson (2013) Cost: benefit analysis of botanical insecticide use in cabbage: Implications for smallholder farmers in developing countries. Crop Protection. 57: 71- 76

Baskar, K., Maheshwaran, R., Kingsley, S. and Ignacimuthu, S. (2011) Bio-efficacy of plant extracts against Asian army worm *Spodoptera litura* Fab. (Lepidoptera: Noctuidae). Journal of Agricultural Technology 2011 (7(1): 123-131

Dhandapani, N., Shelkar, U. R. and Murugan, M. 2003. Bio-intensive pest management in major vegetable crops: An Indian perspective. Journal of Food, Agriculture and Environment, 1(2): 330-339

Kiran MORYA, Sujatha PILLAI, Prabhudas PATEL (2010) Effect of powdered leaves of *Lantana camara, Clerodendrum inerme* and Citrus limon on the rice moth, *Corcyra cephalonica*. Bulletin of Insectology 63 (2): 183-189, 2010

Meena and Divender (2013) Plant extract as Oviposition Deterrents against Fruit Flies, *Bactrocera Spp* infesting vegetable crops Pesticide Research Journal 25 (1) : 24-28

Nigam, G.L. and Murthy, K.S.2000. An optimum use of pesticides in integrated pest management technology. Pesticides information., 25 (2): 145- 48.

Siddiqui, B.S., S.T. Ali, R.M. Tariq, T. Gulzar, M. Rasheed and R. Mehmood. 2009. GC-based analysis of insecticidal constituents of the flower of *Azadirachta indica* A. Juss. Natural Product Research, 23(3): 271-283.

Xin Chao Liu , Li Gang Zhou , Zhi Long Liu and Shu Shan Du, (2013). Identification of Insecticidal Constituents of the Essential Oil of *Acorus calamus* Rhizomes against *Liposcelis bostrychophila Badonnel*. Molecules 18(5), 5684-5696

Yingjuan Yao, Wanlun Cai, Changju Yang, Dong Xue, Yanzhang Huang (2008). Isolation and characterization of insecticidal activity of (Z)-asarone from *Acorus calamus* L. Insect Science,15:229-236

Freshmen Students' Entrepreneurial intentions in the College of Economics and Administrative Sciences (CEAS) at Al-Imam Mohammad bin Saud Islamic University (IMSIU)

Jamel Choukir, Wassim Aloulou, Faouzi Ayadi, Slim Mseddi and Falah Subaie
CEAS, Al Imam Muhammad Bin Saud Islamic University (IMSIU), Riyadh, KSA
jchoukir1@gmail.com
wassim.aloulou@gmail.com
fayadi2000@yahoo.fr
slim_mseddi@yahoo.fr
falsubaie@yahoo.com

Abstract: This explanatory research focuses on entrepreneurial intention. It investigates the main factors determining entrepreneurial intention in higher education institution. The research aims are to highlight students' entrepreneurial intention, and to test an extended Theory of Planned Behaviour. A quantitative survey was conducted on a sample of 2778 Saudi freshmen students. The research findings reveal that the TPB is a validated tool to predict entrepreneurial intentions of Freshmen Students. The results provide a strong support for the TPB antecedents which contributing to the intention explanation. The findings confirm the idea that the control variables influence indirectly the TPB antecedents, and the explanation of entrepreneurial intentions. The results show also many significant relationships such as between students' entrepreneurial intention and social norms, and between career choice intention and gender. Furthermore, it was found that there was a Saudi entrepreneurial student profile. The findings reveal also that the entrepreneurship socialization in Saudi context operated throughout relatives and friends for both male and female students. They allowed to compare College Economics and Administrative Sciences students' entrepreneurial intention with GUESSS international standard.

Keywords: Entrepreneurship, Entrepreneur Intention, Attitude, Social Norms, Freshman student's

1. Introduction

According to many recent Studies and Reports (Global Entrepreneurship Monitor – GEM, 2009-2010, Saudi McKinsey Report, 2015; Porter Saudi Report, 2012) the most indicators regarding to entrepreneurial activity in Kingdom Saudi Arabia (KSA) are positive and higher than the international average, excepted entrepreneurial effective action, for example, the percent of people between 18-64 who desire to become an entrepreneur is under the International Standard despite the availability of opportunities and resources. The Saudi entrepreneurial environment seemed favourable but tangible actions are still timid. Based on this evidence, the idea to explore entrepreneurial intention from student perspective emerged.

This research issue is related to an institutional entrepreneurial project namely *"Unleashing your potential for entrepreneurship"* that responds to the National Reform Plan *"Saudi Arabia 2030 Vision"* and focuses on human resources considered as the main mechanism for development. This research tries to answer to the following questions *"Which are the main antecedents that determine freshmen students entrepreneurial Intention"; "Do the students enrolled in the college are entrepreneurial in their mindsets?"*

Moreover, in a complex, uncertain, and a competitive context, the University should equip students with more than knowledge but skills and behaviours (European Commission, 2013) in order to overcome the new challenges. According to many studies (Garavan *et al.*, 1999; Gardner, 2008), the University, particular the Business School, performance could not have been measured only through undergraduate, graduate, postgraduate outcomes, or research outcomes but also through its capabilities to shape students with entrepreneurial mindsets.

This research focused on an empirical questionnaire-based survey and investigated the main factors determining entrepreneurial intention of freshmen students by applying an extended Theory of Planned Behaviour. From a targeted population of 2778 students, all CEAS students enrolled in first year and first term were concerned.

The objective of this research are threefold. First, we test the TPB in Saudi Higher Education Institutions precisely on freshmen student in fields of economics, finance, insurance, business administration, accounting and banking, representing 20 % of enrolled students at IMSIU in order to determine the Saudi freshman students' entrepreneurial profile. Second, we explore extended TPB including control and contextual variables both to determine their predictive power, and to understand the weight of context effect on Entrepreneurial Intention. Therefore, our third objective, the extended TPB Model could allow us to explore whether findings differences are due to the context or to others variables.

This paper is structured as follows. The second section reviews the literature on different entrepreneurial intention research focused on student perspective. The third section presents the appropriate framework and methodology to explore the freshmen student's entrepreneurial intentions. The fourth section discusses the main findings regarding to previous researches. Finally, a conclusion with the implications, limitations, and perspectives was included in the fifth section.

2. Theoretical foundations, Framework and Hypotheses development

A survey of the literature review on the entrepreneurial intention showed that the literature was very abundant. Moreover, this research topic is not ostensibly new. It dates back to 1970s: Shapero (1975); followed by Shapero & Sokol (1982), and Bird, (1988). A several studies appeared in 1990s and 2000s have focused on entrepreneurial intention (Davidsson, 1995; Kolvereid, 1996; Krueger *et al.*, 2000; Kautonen *et al.*, 2013, 2015; Malebana, 2014, Küttim *et al.*, 2014; Fayolle and Linan, 2014, Schlaegel & Koenig, 2014; Zhang *et al.*, 2015). These different researches were characterized by using a variety of framework in order to explain why some individual are more entrepreneurial than others.

The Theory of Planned Behavior (Ajzen, 1991) has been emerged in order to bring a consistent response to the behavioral prediction issue. The main premise of the TPB consists of that individual act according a given intention (Ajzen, 1991). According to TPB, intentions could be predicted through three main cognitive constructs such as attitude toward behavior which referred to the degree to which a person has a favorable or unfavorable evaluation, subjective norm referred to the perceived social pressure to perform or not about a particular behavior (Kruger & Carsrud, 1993; Krueger *et al.*, 2000), and perceived behavioral control which referred to a person's perception of the ease or difficulty of performing an appropriate act. Based on a literature review on entrepreneurial intentions, these three antecedents have significant relationship with intentions, but, vary from context to another (Ajzen, 1991; Armitage & Conner, 2001). The mixture of these constructs with available opportunities and required resources translated the intentions into actions and tangibles behaviour.

In entrepreneurial literature the TPB framework has been used widely (Kruger & Carsrud, 1993; Krueger *et al.*, 2000; Liñán & Chen, 2009; Moriano *et al.*, 2012; Carr & Sequeira, 2007). In order to increase The TPB efficiency as a tool to explain and to predict entrepreneurial intention, we added, other independent variables that could determine the individual intentions concerned with student personal, family, and social backgrounds, and the extra-curriculum activities (Scherer et al., 1989; 1990; Ozyilmaz, 2011; Van Auken et al., 2006; Strobl et al., 2012; Zellweger et al., 2011).

Consequently, the entrepreneurial intention as a social construct is a result of social context and socialization process. Socialization is ensured by multiple institutions conditioning the individual behavior. The multiplicity of socializing agents is causing the difficulty of identifying provisions and entrepreneurial interest (Starr & Fondas 1992; Nabli 2009). The family as the primary socialization instance is a place of social structuring; it is accepted by psychologists and sociologists that childhood remains a prime socialization period.

To illuminate more globally the family footprint that individuals receive during their socialization, Bourdieu (1977) advances the concept of "habitus". Habitus is the set of tastes, behaviors, ways of perceiving, feeling and saying that an individual receives from his family and social environment. It is with respect to this inherited set of habits that every man acts in society.

For example, an individual who is brought up in a family of entrepreneurs and who gets involved at a very young age in activities related to business is more likely to incorporate entrepreneurial predispositions. In fact, the entrepreneurship frame of mind is partly the result of a form of inheritance transmitted by the family, and the environment (Lahire, 2002; Klyver & Hindle 2007).

We consider that the entrepreneurship intention depends on the modalities of its socialization. The socialization of entrepreneurship involves learning professional knowledge, standards and conventions regarding to a specialized field of activities (Starr & Fondas 1992). It consists of learning behaviors, roles, values, and social norms. In other words, it is a process of acquiring knowledge, models, values, symbols, in short the 'ways of seeing the world, of acting, thinking feeling typical of groups and the society in which the individual is called upon to live.' (Starr & Fondas 1992).

A few researches (Al-Harrasi & Salti, 2014; Hammami & Affes, 2013; Ben Ali; 2016, Aloulou, 2015, 2016) were related to student's Entrepreneurial intention in Arab Higher Education Institutions from TPB Model and through different angles such as eLearning students, information systems students, and final year university student.

The Research Model is presented below:

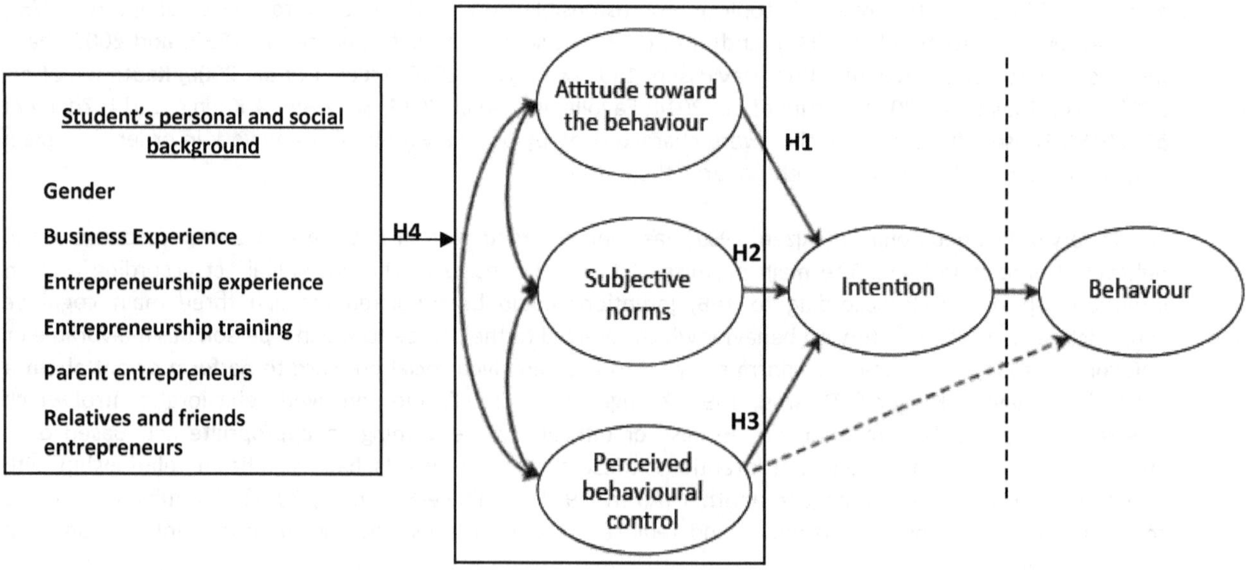

Figure 1: Hypothesized Research model

Previous studies related to the application of the TPB in the entrepreneurship fields found that the TPB antecedents contributed significantly to the explanation of entrepreneurial intentions. Several studies found that the control variables such as gender, prior experience, roles models, prior family business (Strobl et al., 2012; Carr & Sequeira, 2007) influence indirectly the entrepreneurial intentions through the TPB antecedents. Hence, the following hypotheses:

H1: There is a positive relationship between attitude toward the behaviour and entrepreneurial intentions of freshmen students.

H2: There is a positive relationship between subjective norms and entrepreneurial intention of freshmen students.

H3: There is a positive relationship between perceived behavioural control and entrepreneurial intention of freshmen students.

H4: There is a significant relationship of student's personal and social background and TPB's antecedents (Attitude toward the behaviour, H4a; Subjective norms, H4b; Perceived behavioural control, H4c).

3. Methodology

3.1 Data collection

The population for this study was CEAS's freshmen student in IMSIU, located in Riyadh city, capital of Kingdom Saudi Arabia (KSA). These students were chosen because they were suitable to the study about students' entrepreneurial intention before receiving any official curriculum or ex-curriculum entrepreneurial course. The global survey consists of 2778 students enrolled in the first term and first year in CEAS.

The Questionnaire structure design was based mostly on the Global University Entrepreneurial Spirit Students' Survey (GUESSS) in which the TPB (Ajzen, 2002; Fishbein & Ajzen, 1975) was the main theoretical construct. This may be the first data collection in KSA, with the participation of Al-Imam Mohamed bin Saud Islamic University (IMSIU).

Based on the works of Linan and Chen (2009), we have built the survey questionnaire which is consisted of scale questions that were based on the seven-point Likert scale (strongly disagree 1; disagree 2; tend to be different 3; neutral 4; agree 6 and strongly agree 7) nominal and ordered ones. Likert scale type questions were used for entrepreneurial intentions (6 items); attitudes (5 items); subjective norms (3 items) and behavioural control (6 items), whereas nominal scales were used for demographic social and academic variables and ordinal for preferences one. The instrument was reviewed twice to guarantee that the respondents understood all research statements and the measurement scales used in study easily. Based on the feedback provided, the instrument was adjusted. The Study adopted the hand-and-pencil questionnaire which was managed by faculty members and filled by students in class. The response rate was 70%; which could be considered as interested (Faria & Wellington, 2004). The data collection was conducted from September to the end of October 2016.

3.2 Sample characteristics

The study involved 1964 first term CEAS students. Of the 1964 respondents 64.1% were male (41.6% in the international sample), 35.9% female (58.4%). 67.2% of the respondents were in the age between 20-24, 29% were in the age category under the age of 20, followed by the category more than 24 years old representing 2,7%. The student sample was homogeneous with regard to marital status, with 93.6% of respondents indicating they were single (81.5% in the international sample). Respondent characteristics were different compared to the international sample with regard to age, gender, and marital status (Dawson *et al.*, 2014 – GUESSS, 2014).

64.4% of the respondents reported that they did not run a business, 89% and 77.6% of the respondents did not have entrepreneurship experience neither entrepreneurship training. However, 33.7% of respondents mentioned that they had a business experience against 21.4% of participants whose participated in entrepreneurship training. 63.3% of the respondents (male) reported that they held a professional occupation, which represented three times more than female (20.8%). 30.5% of the respondents said that one or both of their parents had their own business. More than half of the respondents reported that they had a relative as an entrepreneur. 29.6% of the respondents reported that they had a friend as an entrepreneur.
Upon graduation, over 32.8% of the respondents indicated their intention to work as an employee in public sector. 29.2% of the respondents have the intention to start their own business which is closer to the international sample (30.7%). A few respondents indicated that they intended to work in charitable sector. The third highest response was the intention to work in private sector. We detected some difference with regard to gender. Career choices clearly differed from male to female students: for male students we obtained the following order: the private sector (1), public sector (2), and entrepreneurship (3), contrarily for female students: the public sector (1), entrepreneurship (2), the private sector (3). Globally, entrepreneurship choice occupied the second rank as career choice. The following figure 2 describes this difference between male and female. Finally, figure (3) represented the career intention choice for both male and female students.

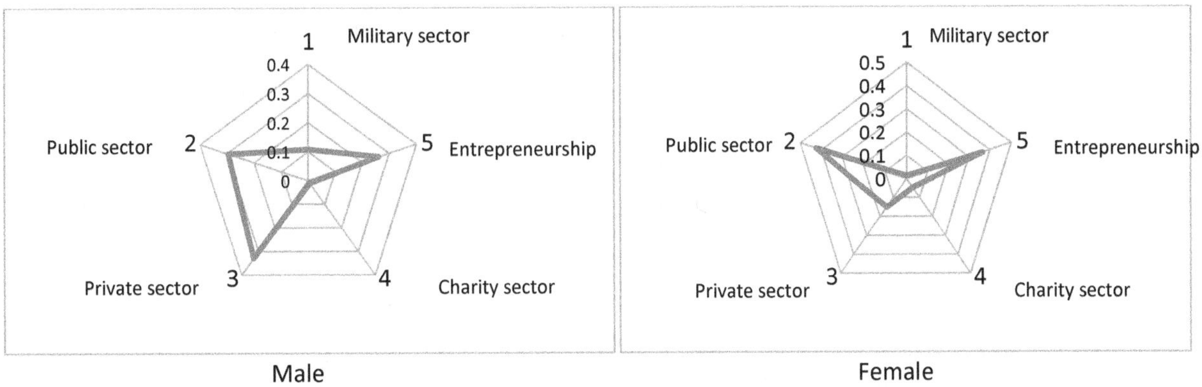

Figure 2: Career intentions by gender

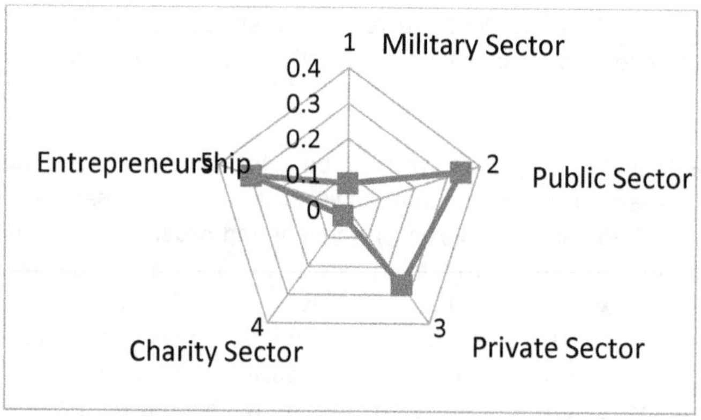

Figure 3: Career Choice Intention

3.3 Data analysis strategy

Data were analyzed by means of the SPSS using descriptive statistics. This study was mainly concerned with the relationship between the antecedents of entrepreneurial intention as the independent variables (Attitudes Toward Behaviour, Subjective Norms, and Perceived Behavioural Control) and freshmen student entrepreneurial intention as dependent variable. The factor loadings were tested with the KMO index. The reliability of the measuring instruments was tested by means of Cronbach's Alpha (Table 1).

Table 1: Measures of TPB variables

TPB variables	Mean	Std. Deviation	# of items	Factor Loading and KMO	Cronbach's Alpha
Attitudes Toward Behaviour (ATB)	5.62	1.13	6 items	FL = 60.163%, KMO = 0.832	0.824
Subjective Norms (SN)	5.12	1.48	3 items	FL = 76.884%, KMO = 0.726	0.850
Perceived Behavioural Control (PBC)	4.67	1.30	5 items	FL = 61.681%, KMO = 0.845	0.874
Entrepreneurial Intention (ENTINT)	5.68	1.26	6 items	FL = 66.240%, KMO = 0.861	0.896

The results show that most respondents have a positive attitude and intention towards entrepreneurial behavior. Subjective norms (family and friends) also influence their entrepreneurial intentions. The standard deviations, measuring the uncertainties and the concentration of data around the mean, are low (1.13-1.48 see table 3) and indicate that they are grouped around the mean. In order to determine the discriminant validity of the variables measuring the independent variables (TPB antecedents: Attitudes, subjective norm and perceived behavioral control), we have to analyze the correlations between the attributes defining these variables. Correlations between these four variables (Table 2) show the existence of a correlation structure for each variables considered. This analysis verifies the principle of interdependence of the measured concepts. It has been noted from the table that the TPB antecedents are significantly correlated with the entrepreneurial intentions and major of them correlated with control variables.

Table 2: Spearman's rho Correlations between TPB variables and control variables (N = 1713)

	1	2	3	4	5	6	7	8	9	10	11
1 Gender	1										
2 Business Experience	.284**	1									
3 Entrepr. Experience	.133**	.292**	1								
4 Entrepr. Training	.101**	.293**	.202**	1							
5 Parents Businessmen	-.005	.149**	.172**	.154**	1						
6 Relatives Businessmen	.062**	.151**	.169**	.219**	.224**	1					
7 Friends Businessmen	.091**	.201**	.199**	.189**	.135**	.358**	1				

	1	2	3	4	5	6	7	8	9	10	11
8 ATB	.074**	-.074**	-.102**	-.088**	-.089**	-.096**	-.113**	1			
9 SN	.118**	-.093**	-.104**	-.099**	-.080**	-.125**	-.156**	.467**	1		
10 PBC	.070**	-.139**	-.190**	-.148**	-.123**	-.140**	-.175**	.500**	.491**	1	
11 ENTINT	.043	-.125**	-.194**	-.167**	-.159**	-.173**	-.214**	.634**	.523**	.583**	1

**. Correlation is significant at the 0.01 level (2-tailed).

Data were also analyzed by using hierarchical multiple regression analysis with student's t-test for regression estimates in order to test the linkage between ATB, PBC and SN as independent variables and entrepreneurial intention (ENTINT) as dependent variable. Before testing the linkage between the independent and dependent variables, control variables were entered first, followed by the second regression that included control variables and independent variables. Another analysis using linear regressions was also done between the antecedents of the TPB as dependent variables and control variables as independent ones.

All the dimensions of the TPB model obtained a higher percent (more than 70%) which revealed a higher degree of the homogeneity of the respective items.

4. Results and discussion

These hypotheses 1, 2 and 3 stated that the TPB antecedents have positive relationship with entrepreneurial intentions. The results as shown in Table 3 revealed that all antecedents contribute significantly (β=0.436, $p<0.01$ for attitudes as having the higher value of β, then, β=0.254, $p<0.01$ for perceived behavioral control, and β=0.204, $p<0.01$ for subjective norms) to the explanation of the variance in intentions (F =668.063, $p<0.01$, R2=0.589). Hypotheses H1, H2 and H3 have received strong significance.

Moreover, as showed in table 3, regression models concerned a relationship between control variables and TPB antecedents as dependent variables. The findings showed that some of the control variables influence attitudes, norms and perceived control: gender having positive relationship with all the TPB antecedents; relatives as businessmen having positive relationship only with subjective norms; and most of the other control variables having negative relationship with more than one antecedent. These findings support hypothesis H4 for most of the variables.

According to Fisher Test our theoretical model is significant (Table 3). The control variables, from gender to friend businessmen, were statistically significant excepted business experience in relation with the dependent variable EI. However, this significance will change when we include the TPB model. Only parent entrepreneurs, and relatives and friend entrepreneurs remained significant. This difference was due to the socialization mechanism. Some significant cultural change seemed operating in Saudi society. Besides the family effect, the relatives and friends for both at the same time male and female student have a determinant effect on the entrepreneurial intention.

Table 3: Hierarchical regression modelling for predicting entrepreneurial intentions and TPB antecedents

Dependent variable	Model with control variables	TPB Model	ATB model	SN model	PBC model
	Standard β	Standard β	Standard β	Standard β	Standard β
Gender	.110**	-.008	0.116**	0.149**	0.126**
Business Experience	-.025	.017	ns	-.062*	-.073**
Entrepreneurship Experience	-.082**	-.018	ns	-.060*	-0.120**
Entrepreneurship Training	-.052*	-.022	ns	ns	-0.075**
Parents Businessmen	-.074**	-.042*	ns	ns	-0.049†
Relatives Businessmen	-.067*	-.024	ns	0.057*	ns
Friends Businessmen	-.109**	-.035†	-.052*	-.115**	-.103**
ATB	-	.436**	-	-	-
SN	-	.204**	-	-	-
PBC	-	.254**	-	-	-
R^2	0.064	0.589	0.025	0.056	0.079
ΔR^2	0.064	0.525	-	-	-
F	15.427**	668.063**	5.994**	14.315**	20.100**
%	0.000	0.000	0.000	0.000	0.000

**. significant at the 0.01 level ($p < 0.01$).
*. significant at the 0.05 level ($p < 0.05$).
†. significant at 0.1 level ($p < 0.1$).

5. Conclusion, limitations and perspectives

Despite the high number of studies on entrepreneurial intention formation, some conclusive facts have been reached about the most widely utilized TPB model. Using extended TPB framework, this research presented some significant relationships. The findings illustrate that the TPB is an accepted and validated tool to predict entrepreneurial intentions of Saudi Freshmen students. They provide strong support for the TPB antecedents as contributors to the intention explanation. The results support the idea that the control variables influence indirectly the TPB antecedents to the explanation of entrepreneurial intentions.

The main control variables have a significant effect on student entrepreneurial intention. The entrepreneurial family background and social norms had also an effect on entrepreneurial intention. Otherwise, the entrepreneurial background acted differently for male and female students. Contrarily to female students, the entrepreneurial training, business background, and enterprise creation experience seemed to be more determinant for male students. Finally, these research findings confirmed the existence of entrepreneurial potential among all students beyond the academic major (Economics, Insurance, Business Administration, Finance, Banking, and Accounting).

This research offered the preliminary results about the main determinants of freshman student's entrepreneurial intentions. As revealed that all the constructs were reliable and valid (Tab. 1 and 2). The results exploration revealed several significant construct which need further investigation such as: relationship between career intention and gender, intention and gender, and entrepreneurship and role models.

The limitations of this research are threefold. First, among a few researches on student entrepreneurial intention in higher education institution this paper could be insert. However, this research is limited to student in particular geographic area, and discipline. Second, this research has a methodological limitation. It consisted of studying student entrepreneurial intention in static perspective at a given moment (level one and first term in a university teaching process). Third, a theoretical limitation could be mentioned regarding to entrepreneurship explanation from exclusively intention perspective.

Furthermore, the relationship between the intermediate variables and control variables regarding to entrepreneurial intentions require more investigation, especially gender variable, and student previous background. Using Structural Equation Model (SEM) will allow us to investigate relationships between different constructs. It seems that no research has included all constructs during the exploration of the student entrepreneurial intention formation. The entrepreneurial intention leading to effective behavior for CEAS's freshmen students requires more insight. Moreover, the student entrepreneurial intention will be explored based on longitudinal perspective in order to define the curriculum and extra curriculum impact. Longitudinal perspective ensures comparison between different stages.

References

Ajzen, I. (1991). The theory of planned behaviour. *Organizational Behaviour and Human Decision Processes*, *50*, 179–211.

Ajzen, I. (2002). 'Perceived behavioural control, self-efficacy, locus of control, and the theory of planned behaviour', *Journal of Applied Social Psychology*, 32(4): 665–84.

Al-Harrasi, S., & Al-Salti, Z. S. (2014). Entrepreneurial Intention among Information Systems (IS) Students at Sultan Qaboos University: An Exploratory Study. *Global Journal of Management and Business Research*, 14(9), pp 31-34.

Aloulou, W., (2015a), "The Prediction of Entrepreneurial intention among Preparatory Year' Saudi Students: Testing an intent model", *in ICIE 2015 3rd International Conference on Innovation and Entrepreneurship*, 19 – 20 March, Durban, South Africa. (http://academic-conferences.org/)

Aloulou, W., (2015b), "Entrepreneurial Intention among Freshmen Students: Application of the Theory of Planned Behaviour to Saudi Context". *Journal of Enterprising Culture,* Vol. 23, No 4, pp. 473-500. (*World Scientific Publishing*) DOI: 10.1142/S0218495815500168.

Aloulou, W., (2016a), "Predicting entrepreneurial intentions of university freshmen students from EAO modelling and personal background in Saudi Arabia". *Journal of Entrepreneurship in Emerging Economies*, Vol. 8, No 2, pp. 180 -203. (*Emerald Publishing*)

Aloulou, W., (2016b), "Predicting the Entrepreneurial intentions of Final Year' Business Students Applying the Theory of Planned Behavior in Saudi context", in the *Journal of Small Business and Enterprise Development,* Vol. 23, No 4, pp. 1142 - 1164. (*Emerald Publishing*)

Armitage, C. J., and Conner, M. (2001), "Efficacy of the theory of planned behaviour: A meta-analytic review", *British Journal of Social Psychology*, Vol. 40, pp. 471-499.

Ben Ali, Tarek (2016). Explaining the Intent to Start a Business among Saudi Arabian University Students. *International Review of Management and Marketing*. 6(2), 345-353.

Bird, B. (1988). Implementing entrepreneurial ideas: The case for intention. *Academy of management Review*, 13(3), 442-453.

Bourdieu, P., (1977**)**, "Outline of a theory of practice", Cambridge, U.K: Cambridge University Press.

Carr, J. C., and Sequeira, J. M. (2007), "Prior family business exposure as intergenerational influence and entrepreneurial intent: A Theory of Planned Behavior approach", *Journal of Business Research*, Vol. 60 No. 10, pp. 1090-1098.

Davidsson, P. (1995), "Determinants of entrepreneurial intentions", paper presented at the *RENT IX*, 23–24 November 1995, Piacenza, Italy.

Dawson, A., Sharma, P., Reda, B., (2014), Global University Entrepreneurial Spirit Students' Survey, Guesss Report 2013-2014.

European Commission, (2013) Entrepreneurship as a main driver for economic growth. Memo, Brussels.

Faria, A. J. & Wellington, W. J. (2004). A Survey of Simulation Game Users, Former Users and Nevers Users, *Simulation and Gaming*, 35(2), 178-207.

Fayolle, A., & Liñán, F. (2014). The future of research on entrepreneurial intentions. *Journal of Business Research*, 67(5), 663-666.

Fishbein, M., & Ajzen. I. (1975), *Beliefs, Attitudes, Intentions, and Behavior: An Introduction to Theory and Research*, Reading, MA: Addison-Wesley.

Garavan, T. N., Barnicle, B., & O'Suilleabhain, F. (1999). Management development: contemporary trends, issues and strategies. *Journal of European Industrial Training*, 23(4/5), 191-207.

Gardner H. (2008). Five Minds for the Future. Boston Mass. Harvard University Press.

GEM (2009-2010). Global Entrepreneurship Reports. Babson and Universidad del Desarrallo.

Hammami, H., Affes, H., (2013), Factors of Entrepreneurial Intention of the Public Civil Servant: Empirical Evidence in the case of Tunisia, *International Journal of Business Management & Economic Research*, 4(1), pp. 673-687.

Kautonen, T., Gelderen, M., & Fink, M. (2015). Robustness of the theory of planned behavior in predicting entrepreneurial intentions and actions. *Entrepreneurship Theory and Practice*, 39(3), 655-674.

Kautonen, T., Van Gelderen, M., & Tornikoski, E. T. (2013). Predicting entrepreneurial behaviour: a test of the theory of planned behaviour. *Applied Economics*, 45(6), 697-707.

Klyver, K., & Hindle, K. (2007). Entrepreneurship and mass media: audiences' perceptions of entrepreneurship stories in mass media. In *AGSE 2007: Regional frontiers of entrepreneurship research 2007: Proceedings of the 4th Regional Frontiers of Entrepreneurship Research conference, 2007* January, (pp. 1083-1095). AGSE.

Kolvereid, L. & Isaksen, E. (2006), New business start-up and subsequent entry into self-employment", *Journal of Business Venturing,* Vol. 21 No. 6, pp. 866–885.

Kolvereid, L. (1996), Prediction of employment status choice intentions, *Entrepreneurship Theory and Practice*, *21*(1), 47–57.

Krueger, N. (1993), "The impact of prior entrepreneurial exposure on perceptions of new venture feasibility and desirability", *Entrepreneurship Theory and Practice*, Vol. 18 No. 1, pp. 5-21

Krueger, N. F. Jr., and Carsrud, A. L. (1993), "Entrepreneurial intentions: Applying the theory of planned behaviour", *Entrepreneurship and Regional Development*, Vol. 5, pp. 351-330

Krueger, N.F., Reilly, M.D., & Carsrud, A.L. (2000), Competing models of entrepreneurial intentions, *Journal of Business Venturing, 15*, 411–32.

Küttim, M., Kallaste, M., Venesaar, U., & Kiis, A. (2014). Entrepreneurship education at university level and students' entrepreneurial intentions. *Procedia-Social and Behavioral Sciences*, 110, 658-668.

Lahire, B. (2002), Portraits sociologiques : dispositions et variations individuelles, Nathan.

Liñán, F., & Chen, Y.-W. (2009). Development and cross-cultural application of a specific instrument to measure entrepreneurial intentions. *Entrepreneurship Theory and Practice*, 33.

Liñán, F., Urbano, D., & Guerrero, M. (2011). Regional variations in entrepreneurial cognitions: Start-up intentions of university students in Spain. *Entrepreneurship and Regional Development, 23*(3-4), 187-215.

Malebana, J. (2014). Entrepreneurial intentions of South African rural university students: A test of the theory of planned behaviour. *Journal of Economics and behavioral studies*, 6(2), 130.

MGI (2015). Saudi Arabia Beyond oil: the investment and Productivity transformation. Executive Summary.

Moriano, J., Gorgievski, M., Laguna, M, and Zarafshani, K. (2012). A cross-cultural approach to understanding entrepreneurial intention. *Journal of Career Development*, 39 (2), 162-185.

Nabli R., (2009), "Les paradoxes de l'entrepreneuriat familial : le cas des entrepreneurs sfaxiens", Colloque international « La vulnérabilité des TPE et des PME dans un environnement mondialisé », *11es journées scientifiques du Réseau Entrepreneuriat, INRPME, AUF, AIREPME*, Canada, 27-29.

Ozyilmaz, A. (2011). The effects of demographic characteristics on entrepreneurial intention in the pre-venture stage of entrepreneurship. *International Journal of Entrepreneurship and Small Business, 14*(3), 406-424.

Porter, M. (2012). Entrepreneurship and Competitiveness: Implications for Saudi Arabia. Global Competitiveness Forum, Riyadh, KSA.

Scherer, P.D., Adams, J., Carley, S., and Wiebe, F. (1989), "Role model performance effects on development of entrepreneurial career preference", *Entrepreneurship Theory and Practice*, Vol. 13 No. 3, pp. 53-81.

Scherer, R., Brodzinski, J., and Wiebe F. (1990), "Entrepreneurial career selection and gender: A socialization approach", *Journal of Small Business Management*, Vol. 28 No. 2, pp. 37-44.

Schlaegel, C., & Koenig, M. (2014). Determinants of entrepreneurial intent: a meta-analytic test and integration of competing models. *Entrepreneurship Theory and Practice*, 38(2), 291-332.

Shapero, A. & Sokol, L. (1982),"The Social Dimensions of Entrepreneurship", In The Encyclopedia of Entrepreneurship, Eds. C. Kent, D. Sexton & K. Vesper, Englewood Cliffs: Prentice-Hall.

Shapero, A. (1975). The displaced, uncomfortable entrepreneur. Psychology Today, 9 (November), 8388, 133.

Starr, J. A., & Fondas, N. (1992). A model of entrepreneurial socialization and organization formation. *Entrepreneurship: Theory and Practice*, 17(1), 67-77.

Strobl, A., Kronenberg, C., and Peters, M. (2012), "Entrepreneurial attitudes and intentions: assessing gender specific differences", *International Journal of Entrepreneurship and Small Business*, Vol. 15 No. 4, pp. 452-468.

Van Auken, H., Stephens, P., Fry, F. L., and Silva, J. (2006), "Role model influences on entrepreneurial intentions: A comparison between USA and Mexico", *International Entrepreneurship and Management Journal,* Vol. 2 No. 3, pp. 325–336.

Zhang, P., Wang, D. D., & Owen, C. L. (2015). A study of entrepreneurial intention of university students. *Entrepreneurship Research Journal*, 5(1), 61-82.

Zellweger, T., Sieger, P. and Halter, F. (2011), "Should I Stay or Should I go? Career Choice Intentions of Students with Family Business Backgrounds", *Journal of Business Venturing*, Vol. 26 No. 5, pp. 521-536.

What Hampers Innovation of Indonesian Manufacturing Firms? Insight from the Indonesia Innovation Survey

Arif Hartono
Management Department, Faculty of Economics, Universitas Islam Indonesia, Yogyakarta, Indonesia
arif.hartono@uii.ac.id

Abstract: The main objective of this study is to provide new empirical evidences on obstacles that hamper innovation activities performed by Indonesian manufacturing firms. The empirical analysis in this study is derived from the second Indonesia Innovation Survey (IIS) 2011 that covers 2009-2010 periods. The findings show that constraints related to financial and risk is the most important perceived by the firms. Innovators and non-innovators perceived the barriers differently. Based on factor analysis, the innovation barriers can be grouped and labelled as: "market and institution", "employee and organization", "financial and risk", and "knowledge and cooperation". The first two groups of barrier tend to have positive direction of influence on types of innovation and innovation success; by contrast, the last two groups of barrier are more likely have negative direction of impact. Based on the study findings, recommendations are proposed.

Keywords: innovation barrier, manufacturing firms, Indonesia

1. Introduction

A number of innovation barriers studies in different developing countries have been conducted, for examples, *Brazil* (e.g. Kuhl and da Cunha, 2013), *Cyprus* (e.g. Hadjimanolis, 1999), *China* (e.g. Fu et al., 2015, Savitskaya et al., 2010, Xie et al., 2010, Zhu et al., 2012), *Malaysia* (e.g. Shiang and Nagaraj, 2011), and *Turkey* (e.g. Demirbas et al., 2011). Surprisingly, there is no empirical evidence that focusses on innovation barriers faced by Indonesian firms. More specifically, there is no previous innovation barrier study that exploits Indonesia innovation survey data, therefore this study intends to address this gap. In the case of Indonesia, innovation barrier tend to be linked to various study's themes, for instances, Indonesian furniture SMEs strategy in accessing knowledge (e.g. Van Geenhuizen and Indarti, 2005); technological development in Indonesia (e.g. Okamoto and Sjoholm, 2001); technology transfer in an Indonesian turbine industry (e.g. Soekarno et al., 2009); and challenges in attracting foreign direct investment to Indonesia (Lipsey and Sjoholm, 2011).

This study is the first study that investigates innovation barriers on the basis of the Indonesia Innovation Survey (IIS) 2011 that covers 2009-2010 periods. The main objective of this study is to provide new empirical evidences on obstacles that hamper innovation activities performed by Indonesian manufacturing firms. More specifically, this study aims to: investigate the innovation barriers perceived by Indonesian manufacturing firms based on the firms' innovativeness i.e. innovators versus non-innovators; investigate the nature of any factors that hamper innovation faced by Indonesian manufacturing firms; link different innovation barriers with different types of innovation adopted by Indonesian manufacturing firms; and investigate the influence of innovation barriers on innovation success.

This study attempts to address the following research questions: (1) To what extent innovation barriers are perceived by Indonesian manufacturing firms? (2) What is the nature of innovation barriers encountered by Indonesian manufacturing firms? To what extent innovation barriers effect different types of innovation and innovation success of Indonesian manufacturing firms? Addressing the research questions is essential with the hope that the finding sheds the light on innovation barriers issues of Indonesian firms as well as enriches the innovation barriers literature in the context developing countries.

2. Literature Review & Hypotheses Development

2.1 Innovation barriers and firm innovativeness

According to Hueske and Guenther (2015), previous studies show ambiguous findings on the relationship between the firm innovativeness and the perception of innovation barriers and only a minority of the studies that disclose that the innovativeness might influence innovation barriers' perception (e.g. Baldwin & Lin, 2002; D'Este *et al.*, 2012; Galia & Legros, 2004). This means that the relationship between innovation barriers and the firm innovativeness shows different ways of directions. The positive relationship may indicates revealed barriers and on the contrary, the negative relationship shows deterring barriers (D'Este *et al.*, 2012).

Referring to revealed barriers, when innovators face barriers in the innovation activities engagement, this does not prevent them from performing the innovation activities, but this increases their consciousness and knowledge through the direct experiences in overcoming the barriers (D'Este *et al.*, 2012). Previous studies that support this view found that the greater the firm's involvement in innovation activities, the greater the importance attached to the constraints to innovation or it shows positive association between innovation barriers' perceptions and innovation propensity (Baldwin & Lin, 2002; Galia & Legros, 2004; Hadjimanolis, 1999; Iammarino *et al.*, 2009). Further interpretation on the positive association between innovation obstacles and innovation propensity on the studies that use innovation surveys (e.g. CIS) is that such association cannot be interpreted as preventing innovation but rather as a sign of how successful the firm (Baldwin & Lin, 2002; Tourigny & Le, 2004). While, deterring effect exists when there is a reverse causality between the innovation barriers' perception and innovation; therefore innovation activity is significantly reduced by the existence of obstacles (e.g. Mohnen & Röller, 2005; Savignac, 2006; Tiwari *et al.*, 2007).

Using Canadian firms data, previous scholars, such as Mohnen and Rosa (2000) and Baldwin and Lin (2002), examine innovation constraints between innovators and non-innovators. Mohnen and Rosa (2000) use R&D activities as a proxy of innovation intensity and their study reveals that the more firms involve in R&D activities, the greater important attach to the innovation barriers. The later study also found a similar finding. On the basis of data from the UK CIS, a recent study conducted by D'Este et al., (2012) shows a positive relationship between innovation-active firms and barriers related to cost, knowledge, and regulation. The more firms engage heavily in innovation activities are more likely to perceive the three barriers are more important than firms do not engage in innovation activities, with the exception of constraints related to market. The second stream of literature shows negative association between the perception of innovation obstacles and firms' effort to innovate. For instances, using innovation data on French manufacturing firms, Savignac (2006) found that the likelihood that a firm will perform innovation activities is significantly reduced by the existence of financial obstacles. Based on the Dutch CIS data, Tiwari et al., (2007) found a strong and significant detterant impact on the presence of financial constrainst on R&D investment.

In the case of developing countries, revealed effects of innovation barriers on the propensity to innovate were found on the studies conducted by Hadjimanolis (1999) and Shiang and Nagaraj (2011). On the basis of innovation data on Cypriot small medium firms, Hadjimanolis (1999) found that the higher the importance of external barriers perceived by the SMEs' owner/manager, the higher is the innovativeness. A possible reason is because the innovative firms despite facing important barriers, they tend able to find ways to overcome the barriers. The same finding also can be found in Malaysian manufacturing firms i.e. the firms that engage in innovation activities are more likely to face greater barriers (Shiang & Nagaraj, 2011). Based on this, a hypothesis may be proposed:

H1 Innovative firms perceive innovation barriers more important than non-innovative firms

2.2 Innovation barriers, innovation and performance

Financial constraints and its impact on innovation performance (e.g. Canepa & Stoneman, 2002; 2008; Efthyvoulou & Vahter, 2012; Mohnen *et al.*, 2008; Savignac, 2006) and the factors influencing perceptions of constraints (e.g. Baldwin & Lin, 2002; Galia & Legros, 2004; Iammarino *et al.*, 2009) have been discussed in the majority of innovation barriers literature. However, the link between innovation barriers and different types of innovation adopted by firms tend to be less studied. The impact of innovation barriers on different types of innovation in the Spanish firms was studied by Guijarro et al., (2009). The study suggests that individual barrier have varying levels of impact on different types of innovations. The study found that process and management innovation are negatively affected by financial and human resources, while barriers related to external environment is positively affected the two types of innovation. Silva et al., (2007) linking a diverse of innovation barriers to the Portuguese firms' propensity for innovating the product or process innovation. The study found that high cost of innovation, lack of financing sources, lack of skilled personnel, and lack of customers' responsive to new products significantly affect the propensity for innovating the product or process innovation (Silva *et al.*, 2007).

In the context of Indonesia, previous studies have linked innovation barriers to a wide range of Indonesia's development issues. Financial constraint found to be the most important barrier that hinder Indonesian furniture SMEs in accessing knowledge to be used in innovation process (Van Geenhuizen and Indarti, 2005) and also found to be the main constraint faced by majority of Indonesian SMEs owners (OECD, 2010).

Knowledge and skills related barriers also hamper technological development in Indonesia. According to Okamoto and Sjoholm (2001) Indonesia suffers from lack of technological development driven by the low level of R&D budget and education and it affected the country to rely on foreign firms on the enhancement its technological capability. The low level of the following conditions, e.g. scientific cooperation among Indonesian technology producers, internal R&D activities and technology absorptive capacity, hamper Indonesian firms from performing innovation activities (Lakitan, 2013).

Previous studies that investigate the impact of innovation barriers on innovation and firm performance have been conducted. Hewitt-Dundas (2006) found that different innovation barriers effects innovation success differently during two periods of innovation survey in Ireland. Lack of market opportunities in the former innovation survey significantly affected innovation success in the later period of innovation success. Lack of information on new technologies significantly influences innovation sales in both periods of surveys. The changes in the strength of certain obstacles (e.g. high risk of innovation, managerial expertise) over the two periods also affect the innovation success. Financial constraint found significantly and negatively affects: labour productivity across SMEs in European countries (Ferrando & Ruggieri, 2015); innovation performance of innovative firms in Western and eastern European countries (Efthyvoulou & Vahter, 2012); and innovation activities in various European countries (e.g. Canepa & Stoneman, 2002; Mohnen *et al.*, 2008; Savignac, 2006).

In developing countries context a diverse of innovation barriers also found negatively affect different types of firms' performance. Constraints such as high cost of innovation, lack of appropriate source of finance, and lack of government's R&D and technology found negatively and significantly affect managers of Turkish SMEs (Demirbas *et al.*, 2011). Using panel data of start-ups in 61 developing countries, Doruk and Soylemezoglu (2014) find that start-ups and new business registration (bureaucratic barriers) and costs are main constraints that impede start-ups development. Based on this, the following hypotheses are proposed:

H2 *Different innovation barriers negatively influence different types of innovation.*
H3 *Different innovation barriers negatively influence innovation success.*

3. Data and Methods

3.1 Data

The empirical analysis in this study is derived from the second Indonesia Innovation Survey (IIS) 2011 that covers 2009-2010 periods. The surveyed firms' classification is based on International Standard Industrial Classification (ISIC) Rev. 3.1. The IIS 2011 used Oslo Manual (OECD/Eurostat, 2005) as the guidelines for collecting and interpreting innovation data.

3.2 Methods

T test is used in this study "for evaluating the difference between two groups of sample respondents on a single dependent variable" (Cooksey, 2007, p.194). In this case, the innovation barriers difference between two groups of innovators and non-innovators is assessed. Factor analysis (i.e. principal component analysis) is also employed in order to identify and to combine innovation barriers variables in "a weighted fashion to form components which account for the maximum amount of variability in the variables' scores" (Cooksey, 2007, p.138). Logistic regression is performed to handle predictions of and modelling responses to a categorical dependent variables i.e. innovation decisions. The firm that performs a type of innovation (product, process, organisational, or marketing) is coded 1, 0 otherwise. Finally, Tobit regression is employed to test the influence of innovation barriers on innovation success. Innovation success is indicated by sales of innovative products that new to the market and new to the firms that consists of 0 and positive proportion.

4. The Study Results

4.1 Descriptive statistics

Table 1 reports the descriptive statistics of the study. On average, it can be observed that the highest proportion types of innovation adopted by Indonesian manufacturing firms is marketing innovation (42.8%) and the lowest proportion is organisational innovation (31%). The fact that proportion of non-technological innovation (i.e. marketing innovation) is the highest among the adopted innovation is typically innovation activities in developing countries that tend to focus on the market rather than on the technology (Wamae, 2009). Technological innovation (i.e. product and process innovations) is accounted for around 38% and 32%, respectively. In terms of innovation success, on average, the proportion of product innovation new to the market is greater than product innovation new to the firm i.e. 15.37% versus 8.43%.

Turning to innovation barrier variables, the range of the responses related to innovation barrier questions is from 0 (not important) to 4 (very important). On average, the score of each barrier related to *financial and risk* (i.e. INFUND, EXFUND, COST and RISK) accounted nearly 3 and this indicates the top four mean scores compared to other types of barriers. This supports a previous innovation activities study stating that "firms in developing countries report that dominant barrier to innovation is the lack of funds – due either to the high costs of innovation or to the lack of internal or external funds available" (Bogliacino *et al.*, 2012, p.238). Then, it is followed by the mean scores of constraints related to *knowledge and market* (i.e. MKT_DOMINATION, COOPERATION, DEMAND_UNCERTAINTY, and TECH_INFO) accounted for 2.642, 2.598, 2.558, and 2.501 respectively. By contrast, the mean scores of the obstacles related to *employee and organisation* (i.e. ORGRIGID and MGR_RESIST) are the lowest among innovation barriers i.e. 1.789 and 1.732 respectively.

In regards to firm resources, the mean of firm size is nearly 175 people. Mature firms (more than 20 years) dominate in the IIS 2011 data set. During 2009-2010 periods, on average exporters that sell their products to overseas is nearly 10%. The proportion of national firms is significantly higher compared to multi nationals and joint ventures. In relation to labour education, a majority of employees hold low level of education. Proportion of employees that hold education degrees lower than high school is around 56%. Percentage of labour that holds high school degree is around 36%. While, less than 5% of employee holds diploma and under graduate degree. In the case of technology intensity, there is a big gap between the proportions of low- and high-technology firms i.e. 7.35% versus 0.9%.

Table 1: Descriptive Statistics Outputs

VARIABLES	OBS.	MEAN	SD	MIN.	MAX.
Innovation Decision					
PRODINOV	1179	.377	.485	0	1
PROCINOV	1179	.322	.468	0	1
ORGINOV	1179	.310	.463	0	1
MKTGINOV	1179	.428	.495	0	1
Innovation Success					
INNSUCCESS_MARKET (%)	1179	8.429	16.985	0	100
INNSUCCESS_FIRMS (%)	1179	15.368	26.131	0	100
Innovation Barriers					
COST	1179	2.936	1.312	0	4
RISK	1179	2.880	1.313	0	4
INFUND	1179	2.847	1.381	0	4
EXFUND	1179	2.657	1.513	0	4
MKT_DOMINATION	1179	2.642	1.390	0	4
COOPERATION	1179	2.598	1.410	0	4
DEMAND_UNCERTAIN	1179	2.558	1.356	0	4
TECH_INFO	1179	2.501	1.360	0	4
PERSONNEL	1179	2.421	1.403	0	4
INFRASTRUCTURE	1179	2.385	1.436	0	4
MARKET_INFO	1179	2.342	1.342	0	4
LABOUR	1179	2.335	1.426	0	4
IND_STANDARD	1179	2.289	1.464	0	4
GOVREG	1179	2.254	1.480	0	4
CUSTOMER_ACC	1179	2.248	1.348	0	4
STAFF_RESIST	1179	2.000	1.436	0	4
ORG_RIGID	1179	1.789	1.400	0	4
MANAGER_RESIST	1179	1.732	1.395	0	4
Firm Resources					
SIZE	1179	174.61	1318.08	20	32977
AGE	1179	21.077	12.704	0	84
EXPORT	1179	9.726	25.106	0	100
OWN_NATIONAL	1179	0.899	.301	0	1
OWN_MULTINATIONALS	1179	0.059	.235	0	1
OWN_JOINT VENTURE	1179	0.042	.202	0	1
OPERATION_PLANT	1179	0.092	.289	0	1
OPERATION_HQ	1179	0.908	.289	0	1
EDU_UNDERHS	1179	56.247	36.423	0	100
EDU_HIGHSCHOOL	1179	36.430	31.492	0	100
EDU_DIPLOMA	1179	3.246	6.779	0	55
EDU_UNDERGRAD	1179	4.077	8.623	0	90
LOW TECH	1179	0.735	.442	0	1

VARIABLES	OBS.	MEAN	SD	MIN.	MAX.
MID-LOW TECH	1179	0.174	.379	0	1
MID-HIGH TECH	1179	0.082	.275	0	1
HIGH-TECH	1179	0.009	.096	0	1

Outputs of correlation between innovation barriers variables are presented in table 2. All the correlation among innovation barrier variables indicates positive and significant direction of relationships. It can be seen that in general, correlation coefficients show low and moderate relationships.

Table 2: Correlation of Innovation Barriers (1179 firms)

	1	2	3	4	5	6	7	8	9	10	11	12	13	14	15	16	17	18
1.INFUND	1																	
2.EXFUND	.75	1																
3.COST	.61	.58	1															
4.RISK	.54	.51	.68	1														
5.STAFF_RESIST	.35	.33	.34	.29	1													
6.MGR_RESIST	.32	.31	.30	.26	.69	1												
7.ORGRIGID	.31	.28	.27	.20	.60	.73	1											
8.PERSONNEL	.40	.38	.35	.30	.50	.45	.46	1										
9.TECH_INFO	.45	.42	.38	.33	.32	.31	.31	.50	1									
10.MKT_INFO	.40	.37	.34	.28	.35	.34	.37	.44	.57	1								
11. COOP	.49	.50	.41	.40	.31	.27	.30	.38	.49	.50	1							
12. LABOUR	.43	.39	.39	.37	.47	.44	.46	.52	.46	.44	.50	1						
13. MKT_DOMINATE	.30	.30	.36	.37	.25	.27	.29	.32	.29	.33	.30	.38	1					
14. DEMAND	.40	.37	.40	.39	.33	.34	.34	.33	.37	.38	.40	.45	.51	1				
15. CUSTOMER_ACC	.32	.31	.32	.33	.27	.30	.31	.27	.33	.44	.35	.37	.43	.56	1			
16. INFRA	.42	.41	.42	.41	.36	.35	.35	.42	.40	.37	.43	.51	.38	.45	.44	1		
17. STANDARD	.43	.43	.42	.39	.40	.41	.41	.39	.38	.39	.44	.50	.40	.44	.40	.59	1	
18. GOVREG	.41	.39	.40	.38	.39	.42	.42	.36	.36	.39	.43	.48	.38	.45	.40	.57	.85	1

All significant levels are at 1% (p<0.01).

4.2 Empirical Results

Table 3 clearly shows that the overall mean of the barriers related to *financial and risk factors* (i.e. COST, RISK, INFUND, and EXFUND) for all firms, non-innovators and innovators outnumbered the mean of other barriers (greater than 2.6). It means that cost and financial related barriers to be perceived as the most important barriers than other barriers. This finding supports a majority of previous studies on innovation barriers. While, barriers associated to manager and organisation behaviour towards innovation are the lowest mean (lower than 2.0). It applies for all firms, non-innovators and innovators. It means that such barriers perceived to be least important by the Indonesian manufacturing firms.

Table 3: T-test of innovation barriers between non-innovators and innovators firms (1179)

INNOVATION BARRIERS	OVERALL MEAN	NON-INNOVATORS	INNOVATORS	t Test
COST	2.936	2.952	2.926	.325
RISK	2.880	2.891	2.872	.235
INFUND	2.847	2.856	2.842	.170
EXFUND	2.657	2.697	2.632	.708
MKT_DOMINATION	2.642	2.631	2.649	-.218
COOPERATION	2.598	2.587	2.605	-.206
DEMAND_UNCERTAIN	2.558	2.570	2.551	.238
TECH_INFO	2.501	**2.592**	2.444	1.822*
PERSONNEL	2.421	2.397	2.436	-.455

INNOVATION BARRIERS	OVERALL MEAN	NON-INNOVATORS	INNOVATORS	t Test
INFRASTRUCTURE	2.385	2.404	2.373	.359
MARKET_INFO	2.342	2.408	2.300	1.356
LABOUR	2.335	2.397	2.295	1.197
STANDARD	2.289	2.352	2.250	1.164
GOVREG	2.254	2.279	2.237	.478
CUSTOMER_ACC	2.248	2.279	2.227	.645
STAFF_RESIST	2.000	1.782	**2.139**	-4.189***
ORGRIGID	1.789	1.642	**1.882**	-2.880***
MANAGER_RESIST	1.732	1.563	**1.839**	-3.324***

$^{*}p<0.10$; $^{**}p<0.05$; $^{***}p<0.01$

It can be observed that in general, non-innovators face greater obstacles than innovators. However, based on the t test results, innovators and non-innovators are significantly different on the four barriers related to knowledge (i.e. TECH_INFO, STAFF_RESIST, ORGRIGID and MANAGER_RESIST). Surprisingly, non-innovative firms only perceive (at marginal level) one type of barrier i.e. TECH_INFO that is more important than innovative firms. While innovators significantly perceive the rest of the three barriers are more important than non-innovators. Based on this, hypothesis 1 is accepted. The findings support previous studies of revealed barriers to innovation (e.g. Baldwin & Lin, 2002; Galia & Legros, 2004; Iammarino *et al.*, 2009) that state innovators reporting more likely to have experienced the barriers to innovation than non-innovators. This means that the more the innovators perform innovation activities, the greater they will experience impediments related to knowledge (i.e. STAFF_RESIST, ORGRIGID and MANAGER_RESIST). Despite the innovators face greater levels of knowledge obstacles; however it does not stop them to perform innovation activities.

4.3 Factor Analysis

Table 4 displays the results of varimax rotated factor analysis of the 18 innovation barrier variables. Factor loadings above 0.3 were used for factor grouping. Bartlett test of sphericity: 12000, significance=0.000. The Kaiser-Meyer-Olkin measure of sampling adequacy =0.917 is well above the acceptable range (0.50) (Hair *et al.*, 2014). The scale reliability value for each factor (coefficient alpha) is 0.924. The factors from the principal components analysis are grouped and labelled into four groups of barriers related to "market and institution", "employee and organisation", "financial and risk", and "knowledge and cooperation".

Table 4: Component Loadings for Innovation Barriers

VARIABLE	FACTOR1	FACTOR2	FACTOR3	FACTOR4
INFUND	-.067	.015	**.476**	.099
EXFUND	-.065	.005	**.476**	.087
COST	.033	.002	**.502**	-.066
RISK	.090	-.045	**.487**	-.118
STAFF_RESIST	-.040	**.519**	.051	-.004
MANAGER_RESIST	.009	**.564**	-.002	-.054
ORGRIGID	.039	**.520**	-.072	.017
PERSONNEL	-.073	.251	.019	**.336**
TECH_INFO	-.052	-.035	.030	**.557**
MARKET_INFO	.048	-.020	-.086	**.543**
COOPERATION	.048	-.073	.141	**.366**
LABOUR	.129	.163	.015	.223
MKT_DOMINATION	**.400**	-.067	-.021	.014
UNCER_DEMAND	**.394**	-.063	-.013	.084
CUSTOMER	**.413**	-.108	-.107	.150
INFRASTRUCTURE	**.334**	.023	.067	.023

VARIABLE	FACTOR1	FACTOR2	FACTOR3	FACTOR4
STANDARD	**.413**	.102	.058	-.111
GOVREG	**.427**	.111	.040	-.132
Eigenvalue	7.866	1.226	1.632	1.063
Cronbach's alpha		.924		
Kaiser-Meyer-Olkin		.917		
Percentage of total variance explained		65.50		

Factor 1: "market and institutions" barriers; Factor 2: "employee and organisation" barriers; Factor 3: "financial and risk" barriers; Factor 4: "knowledge and cooperation" barriers.

4.4 Logistics Regression

Table 5 presents the logistic regression outputs that consist of six models. Market and institution related barriers have no significant relationship with any types of innovation. Barriers related to employee and organisations positively and strongly influence all types of innovation (except ORGINN). Financial and risk and knowledge and cooperation constraints tend to have negative direction of influence on types of innovation. Financial and risk barriers negatively and significantly influence all types of innovation except MKTGINN. Constraint related to knowledge and cooperation is more likely to have negative direction of influence on types of innovation. Such barriers negatively and significantly influence both PRODINN_NEW2MARKET and PROCINN. This finding support a previous study that shows innovation barriers affected types of innovation differently (Guijarro *et al.*, 2009). Based on this hypothesis 2 can be answered.

Table 6: Logistic regression outputs

INDEPENDENT VARIABLES	Model 1 PRODINN	MODEL 2 PRODINN_NEW2MKT[1]	MODEL 3 PRODINN_NEW2FIRMS[2]	MODEL 4 PROCINN	MODEL 5 ORGINN	MODEL 6 MKTGINN
Market & institution	.013 (.019)	.022 (.018)	.008 (.019)	.031 (.019)	-.023 (.018)	-.009 (.019)
Employee & organisation	**.078***** (.013)	**.083*****(.013)	**.074***** (.013)	**.045*****(.013)	.017 (.013)	**.061*****(.014)
Financial & risk	**-.034**** (.016)	**-.047*****(.015)	**-.031***(.016)	**-.038****(.015)	**-.050*****(.015)	-.014 (.016)
Knowledge & cooperation	-.028 (.019)	**-.043****(.017)	-.013 (.018)	**-.034***(.018)	-.016 (.017)	-.017 (.019)
Size	-.00002 (.00002)	-.00001 (.00002)	-.00001 (.00002)	.000 (.000)	-.00002 (.00002)	-.00002 (.00002)
Firm age	.0003 (.001)	-.0004 (.001)	-.00003 (.001)	-.001 (.001)	.00001 (.001)	-.001 (.001)
Export	**.001***(.001)	**.0009***(.0005)	**.001****(.001)	.001 (.001)	.0001 (.0005)	.001 (.001)
Operation (Plant)	-.049 (.051)	-.039 (.048)	-.023 (.050)	-.060 (.051)	-.051 (.051)	-.031 (.053)
Operation (Head Quarter)	-	-	-	-	-	-
Ownership (National)	.043 (.073)	-.001 (.067)	.052 (.073)	.078 (.074)	.002 (.069)	.087 (.076)
Ownership (Multinational)	.035 (.091)	-.045 (.085)	.027 (.091)	.093 (.092)	-.035 (.089)	.081 (.094)
Ownership (Join Venture)	-	-	-	-	-	-
EDU (Under High School)	-.002 (.002)	-.002 (.002)	-.002 (.002)	-.001 (.002)	-.001 (.002)	-.002 (.002)
EDU (High School)	-.002 (.002)	-.002 (.002)	-.003 (.002)	-.001 (.002)	-.001 (.002)	-.003 (.002)
EDU (Diploma)	-.002 (.003)	-.002 (.003)	-.003 (.003)	-.004 (.003)	-.002 (.003)	-.001 (.003)
EDU (Undergrad)	-	-	-	-	-	-
Low-Tech	-.099 (.141)	-.170 (.124)	-.121 (.138)	.181 (.170)	-.042 (.135)	-.027 (.148)
Med-Low Tech	-.115 (.144)	-.194 (.127)	-.127 (.141)	.097 (.173)	-.086 (.138)	-.097 (.151)
Med-High Tech	-.044 (.148)	-.111 (.130)	-.062 (.144)	.187 (.175)	-.101 (.142)	.035 (.154)
High-Tech	-	-	-	-	-	-
Observation	1179	1179	1179	1179	1179	1179
Log likelihood	-756.53	-674.75	-744.35	-725.18	-708.92	-787.70

* p<0.10, ** p<0.05, *** p<0.01, all coefficients are presented in marginal, standard errors are in the parentheses
[1]Product innovation that new to the market; [2]Product innovation that new to the firms

Turning to control variables, a majority of the variables have no significant effect on all types of innovation. Positive and significant effect can only be found in the influence of exporters on PRODINN, PRODINN_NEW2MARKET, and PRODINN_NEW2FIRMS. However the impact level was found very weak. The rest of the control variables, such as firms' size, age, labour quality (employee education levels), and technology intensity variables have negative association with types of innovation.

4.5 Tobit Regression

Table 7 reports output of the Tobit regression and it can be observed that barriers related to market and institution and employee and organisation have positive direction of influence on innovation success variable. Employee and organisation barriers strongly and significantly impact both innovation success new to the market and firms. In contrary, financial and risk as well as knowledge and cooperation barriers negatively associate to innovation success. Both groups of barriers negatively and significantly influence innovation success new to the market. Based on the study findings, therefore, hypothesis 3 is supported. In terms of firm resources, only exporters that positively and significantly impact innovation success that new to the firms.

Table 7: Tobit regressions outputs

INDEPENDENT VARIABLES	MODEL 1 INNSUCCESS_MARKET	MODEL 2 INNSUCCESS_FIRMS
Market & institution	.663 (.644)	.166 (1.016)
Employee & organisation	**2.868***** (.466)	**3.651***** (.728)
Financial & risk	**-1.243**** (.518)	-.924 (.835)
Knowledge & cooperation	**-1.799***** (.614)	-.509 (.979)
Size	-.0003 (.001)	-.001 (.001)
Age	-.009 (.036)	.011 (.057)
Export	.026 (.017)	**.065**** (.028)
Operation (PLANT)	-1.515 (1.662)	-2.712 (2.669)
Operation (Head Quarter)	-	-
Ownership (National)	-.309 (2.300)	1.261 (3.800)
Ownership (Multinational)	-1.724 (2.943)	1.195 (4.763)
Ownership (Join Venture)	-	-
EDU (Under High School)	-.080 (.054)	-.055 (.092)
EDU (High School)	-.082 (.058)	-.104 (.097)
EDU (Diploma)	-.053 (.105)	-.097 (.176)
EDU (Undergrad)	-	-
Low-Tech	-5.187 (4.295)	-2.861 (7.289)
Med-Low Tech	-5.969 (4.398)	-3.236 (7.439)
Med-High Tech	-3.688 (4.502)	.778 (7.613)
High-Tech	-	-
Observation	1179	1179
Log likelihood	-2139.37	-2715.71

*p<0.10, **p<0.05, ***p<0.01, *all coefficients are presented in marginal, standard errors are in the parentheses*

5. Conclusion and Implications

Innovative and non-innovative firms only perceive the innovation barriers related to knowledge differently. Non-innovators perceive lack of information on technology is more important than the innovators. While the innovators perceive barriers related to employee and organisation (i.e. staff and manager resistance toward change and organisational rigidity) are more important than non-innovators. The fact that innovators experience such barriers greater or more important than non-innovators cannot be assumed that the barriers automatically prevent the innovators from performing innovation activities and this so called revealed barriers. The awareness towards the barriers may be gained through learning and experience during the firms performing innovation activities (see D'Este *et al.*, 2012 for review). The more the innovative Indonesian manufacturing firms perform innovation activities, the greater their level of awareness and experiences toward barriers related to employee and organisation.

The direction of the barriers' impact on innovation success is in line to the barriers impact on types of innovation. The first two constraints have positive association to innovation success; conversely the last two barriers show negative direction. Market and institution constraints have no significant impact on both innovation successes. Employee and organisation barriers positively and significantly influence both innovation successes. Constraints related to financial and risk, and knowledge and cooperation significantly and negatively influence the innovation success that new to the markets. However both groups of barriers have no significant impact on the innovation success that new to the firms.

Based on the aforementioned findings, recommendation to overcome innovation barriers may be proposed. From the firms' perspective, innovative firms that face revealed barriers related to employee and organisation is the necessity to implement better management of innovation activity e.g. education, training and workshop in order to minimise the impacts of the obstacles. Financial development or appropriate fiscal policy to provide the required finance to innovation activity may relevant to overcome financial and risk barrier, for instance the easiness access to financial intermediaries (e.g. banks, venture capital, etc.). In this case, the involvement from government is crucial.

References

Baldwin, J. & Lin, Z. (2002) Impediments to Advanced technology Adoption for Canadian Manufacturers. *Research Policy*, 31 (1): pp. 1-18.

Bogliacino, F., Perani, G., Pianta, M. & Supino, S. (2012) Innovation in Developing Countries: The Evidence from Innovation Surveys. *Latin American Business Review*, 13 pp. 219-261.

Canepa, A. & Stoneman, P. (2002) *Financial constraints on innovations: a European cross country study*.

Canepa, A. & Stoneman, P. (2008) Financial constraints to innovation in the UK: evidence from CIS2 and CIS3. *Oxford Economic Paper*, 60 pp. 711-730.

Cooksey, R. W. (2007) *Illustrating Statistical Procedures for Business, Behavioural and Social Science Research*. Victoria, Australia: Tilde University Press.

D'Este, P., Iammarino, S., Sanova, M. & Tunzelmann, N. V. (2012) What hampers Innovation? Revealed Barriers Versus Deterring Barriers. *Research Policy*, 41 (2): pp. 482-488.

Demirbas, D., Hussain, J. G. & Matlay, H. (2011) Owner-managers' perceptions of barriers to innovation: empirical evidence from Turkish SMEs. *Journal of Small Business and Enterprise Development*, 18 (4): pp. 764-780.

Doruk, O. T. & Soylemezoglu, E. (2014) The constraints of innovation in developing countries: Too many barriers to start ups? *Procedia-Social and Behavioral Sciences*, 150 pp. 944-949.

Efthyvoulou, G. & Vahter, P. (2012) *Financial constraints, innovation performance and sectoral disaggregation*. Sheffield, UK:

Ferrando, A. & Ruggieri, A. (2015) *Financial constraints and productivity: evidence from Euro area companies*.

Galia, F. & Legros, D. (2004) Complementarities Between Obstacles to Innovation: Evidence from France. *Research Policy*, 33 (8): pp. 1185-1199.

Guijarro, A. M., Garcia, D. & Auken, H. V. (2009) Barriers to innovation among Spanish manufacturing SMEs. *Journal of Small Business Management*, 47 (4): pp. 465-488.

Hadjimanolis, A. (1999) Barriers to Innovation for SMEs in a Small Less Developed Country (Cyprus). *Technovation*, 19 (9): pp. 561-570.

Hair, J. F., Black, W. C., Babin, B. J. & Anderson, R. E. (2014) *Multivariate Data Analysis*. the USA: Pearson Education Limited.

Hewitt-Dundas, N. (2006) Resource and capability constraints to innovation in small and large plants. *Small Business Economics*, 26 pp. 257-277.

Hueske, A. K. & Guenther, E. (2015) What hampers innovation? External stakeholders, the organization, groups and individuals: a systematic review of empirical barrier research. *Management Review Quarterly*, 65 pp. 113-148.

Iammarino, S., Sanna-Randaccio, F. & Sanova, M. (2009) The perception of obstacles to innovation foreign multinationals and domestics firms in Italy. *Revue d'Economie Industrielle*, 125 pp. 75-104.

Mohnen, P. A., Palm, F., Loeff, V. D., Schim, S. & Tiwari, A. (2008) *Financial Constrains and Other Obstacles: Are They a Threat to Innovation Activity?*

Mohnen, P. A. & Röller, L. H. (2005) Complementarities in Innovation Policy. *European Economic Review*, 49 (6): pp. 1431-1450.

OECD (2010) Indonesia. In: *SMEs, Entrepreneurship and Innovation*. Paris, France: OECD Publishing:

OECD & Eurostat (2005) Oslo Manual: Guidelines for Collecting and Interpreting Innovation Data 3rd Edition.

Savignac, F. (2006) The impact of financial constraints on innovation: evidence from French manufacturing firms. *Cahiers de la Maison des Sciences Économiques v06042*,

Shiang, L. E. & Nagaraj, S. (2011) Impediments to Innovation: Evidence from Malaysian Manufacturing Firms. *Asia Pacific Business Review*, 17 (2): pp. 209-223.

Silva, M., Leitao, J. & Raposo, M. (2007) *Barriers to innovation faced by manufacturing firms in Portugal: How to overcome it?*

Tiwari, A. K., Mohnen, P., Palm, F. C. & van der Loeff, S. S. (2007) *Financial constraints and R&D investment: Evidence from CIS*. United Nations University:

Tourigny, D. & Le, C. D. (2004) Impediments to innovation faced by Canadian manufacturing firms. *Economics of Innovation and New Technology*, 13 (3): pp. 217-250.

Wamae, W. (2009) Enhancing the role of knowledge and innovation for development. *International Journal of Technology Management and Sustainable Development*, 8 (3): pp. 199-220.

Wastyn, A. & Hussinger, K. (2011) *In Search for the Not-Invented Here Syndrome: The Role of Knowledge Sources and Firms Success*. IN: The DRUID Conference 2011. Conference:Location.

Zhu, Y., Wittmann, X. & Peng, M. W. (2012) Institution-based barriers to innovation in SMEs in China. *Asia Pacific Journal of Management*, 29 pp. 1131-1142.

The Effect of Innovations to Brand Equity: The Role of Customers Satisfaction on Postal Service

Salmi Mohd Isa, Shayan Kiumarsi and Neoh Boon Ping
Graduate School of Business, Universiti Sains Malaysia, Penang, Malaysia.
salmi.mohd.isa@usm.my
kiumarsi78@gmail.com
bpstation8874@gmail.com

Abstract: The postal services have evolved steadily and play a vital role to deliver communication over many centuries. A successful innovation will help postal industry to create strong brand equity. From the marketing standpoint, brand equity and innovation play a critical role to aid elasticity for long-term growth. Innovation is the basic of all competitive advantages and the key to aid an organization to stay highly competitive, winning new customers and remain relevant in today's business world. This study examines the effect of innovations to brand equity with the role of customer satisfaction to postal service in Malaysia. A closed-ended self-administered questionnaire was designed. Two high density states namely Penang and Kuala Lumpur were targeted as area of study focus. A total of 116 valid sets of data were collected from POS Malaysia (POSM) customers within 12 weeks through convenient sampling. Both Statistical Package for Social Science (SPSS) and Partial Least Square (PLS) software were used for data analysis. The results of the analysis show that both product innovation and service innovation contributes to brand equity. However, the marketing innovation does not affect the brand equity. Customer satisfaction do partially mediate the effect of product innovation and service innovation to brand equity of POSM. The study has some limitations where the responds represent the rural area are not collected. Also, the in-depth need of customers which leads to brand equity is not yet explored. The future research may include the responds from rural area. Also, the perceptive of POSM's employees regarding the POSM's innovation and brand equity is worthwhile to obtain. Regardless of the limitations, this study provides an in-depth understanding of innovation and brand equity from the perspective of postal service industry.

Keywords: Innovation, brand equity, customer satisfaction, postal service, Malaysia

1. Introduction

Branding was developed since 18th century where producers used names and images to strengthen brand association (Farquhar, 1989). Brand aids to build up long-term relationship and mental association among customers (Kapferer, 2008). On the other hand, innovation is a key weapon used in marketing strategies to win customers and to gain market share which helps in firm success and develop sustainable competitive advantage in an organization. Innovation helps to reinforces and broaden brand meaning (Beverland, Napoli and Farrelly, 2010) and thus being a key determinant of brand equity. Therefore, both innovations and brand equity does play a vital role to aid in the success and growth of a company (Slotegraaf and Pauwels, 2008). However, innovation needs to be able to solve complex customer requirements, demands or fulfill the unmet market needs (Kanagal, 2015). An organization's brand equity will positively increase when the customers are satisfied with the innovation implemented (Liao and Cheng, 2014).

POSM is Malaysia's sole postal service provider since 1800s. This giant service provider which started operations in conventional form does face challenges during the boom of digital society with the advancement of internet services, rapid growth of the e-commerce businesses, the growth of e-services and digital services. Therefore, building strong brand equity is essential for POSM in order to stay sustainable in the industry, pursue long-term relationships with consumers and differentiate themselves from other competitors. POSM puts tremendous efforts on innovative activities in order to achieve stronger brand equity. They have performed rebranding in order to remain relevant and at the same time position themselves at a competitive leverage in the technological advancement century. This research study the in depth role of customers' satisfaction on innovation and brand equity in order to allow POSM to accurately focus on the areas for brand equity improvement and thus contribute to the increase of profit and net income in the near future.

2. Literature review

2.1 Brand Equity

The brand equity topic has been the growing interest since the emerged in the 1980's. Brand equity plays an important role to business sustainability. Consumers will be able to differentiate a company with strong brand and thus leading to higher consumer preference and purchase intension (Cobb-Walgren, Ruble and Donthu,

1995). When consumers are overloaded with information gain through the cyber world, brand equity will aid the consumers in information processing (Krishan and Hartline, 2001). Aaker (1992) stated that there are 5 assets created by brand equity: brand loyalty, brand awareness, perceived brand equity, brand association based on perceived quality and other proprietary brand assets. The customer-based brand equity is dominant perspective. The reason for this is that a brand that brings value to customers will eventually bring impact to investors, manufacturer, or retailers (Cobb-Walgren et al., 1995). Hence, a consumer who favour the brand and have strong and unique brand association will contribute to customer-based brand equity.

2.2 Innovation

Innovation is where new idea being exploited and transform into value which creates sustainable profits to an organization (Sciences, 2007). Since year 1986, Tushman and Nadler mentioned that an organization has to manage today's business effectively and simultaneously creating innovation for tomorrow in order to gain competitive advantage. Innovation aid to conquer and sustain the fast evolving business world and critical drive of economic performance (Urbancova, 2013). Innovation is being describe as the focal point of an organization strategy which an organization develop to aid the company to adapt external environment and reach to perceived changes from the inside out of the organization (Milling and Stumpfe, 2000). Innovation can be implemented in many perspectives of the organization; the organization's structures, outcomes, and processes. This will help to maintain or improve the level of company performance and effectiveness (Damanpour and Gopalakrishnan 1999).

2.3 Customers Satisfaction

Customers satisfaction is the fundamental indicator of the organization's performance as it is linked to behavioral and economic consequences of the firm (Anderson, Fornell and Mazvancheryl, 2004). Creating high degree of satisfaction is important for today's business world as it helps in product differentiation and building a strong customer relationship (Deng, Lu, Wei and Zhang, 2010). It helps to build long and profitable relationships between organization and consumers (Eshghi, Haughton and Topi, 2007). The consumer purchase intention was influenced by customer satisfaction (Cronin and Taylor, 1992). Customer satisfaction aid in repeat purchase behavior as well (LaBarbera and Mazursky, 1983; Wilson, 2002). Customers with good satisfaction experience are more willing to pay higher price (Huber, Herrmann and Wricke, 2001). Many companies spend significant budgets to measure customer satisfaction (Sivadas and Baker-Prewitt, 2000). Today, achieving high levels of customer satisfaction has become major goal for many companies (Homburg and Giering, 2001).

3. Diffusion of Innovation Theory

Diffusion of innovation theory is a theory that details specific factors for a populous to adopt a particular idea or technology for this instance, innovation from thriving businesses. First popularised by Rogers (1962) the theory classifies consumers into five distinct segregations. The five distinct categories are innovators, early adopters, early majority, late majority and laggards. An illustration is provided below along with corresponding percentile that the consumer groups will occupy.

The diffusion of innovation theory also explains the life cycle of an innovation in the same time vs. percentile of commanding market share. This innovation life cycle is termed the S-curve, which can be sub-divided into 4 phases namely, start-up phase, scaling phase, maturation phase and transition phase. The S-curve is presented below which also observes these four phases of introduction through to decline. Furthermore, it is imperative to identify with key elements which aid the progression of diffusion of innovations which is firstly innovation itself or the quality and relevance of the intended design of the product/service for the intended user. Next is identifying the potential target consumers or users of the said product or service. Thirdly, is identifying the communication channels where these innovations can be accurately communicated. Fourth is the element of time which details the relative time for the target consumers to adopt the innovation. Finally, there is the aspect of the social system whereby a combination of external influences such as mass media or governmental policies which require the masses to comply or internal influences such as social media, inputs from opinion leaders (innovators and early adopters).

The processes typically employed by companies to assess the transitional period of adoption of a particular innovation occur in five stages which are the knowledge, persuasion, decision, implementation and confirmation. The potential consumer if first exposed to knowledge of the innovation but it is not a compressive picture of the product. Consequently, the individual exposed to said information will gain interest towards the innovation and be persuaded to likely seek more relevant in depth details. Ascertaining sufficient details, the consumer will then be able to make a sensible decision whether they should adopt the innovation by weighing the pros and cons of using the innovation. Obtain their buy-off, the consumer then will conduct an individual assessment of the innovation from first-hand experience, determine the usefulness and benefit from of said innovation. Finally, a confirmation can be seen here by the continual usage of the innovation as a sign of a complete integration into their lifestyle as a sign of satisfaction and that they have made the right decision.

4. Brand Equity Theory

Brand equity typically can be described as a point of leverage or shortcoming a specific brand name has over others (their competitors) in their particular line of business. Analogously Aaker (1992) outlines it as an intangible asset and/or liabilities which are tied to an explicit brand name or symbol which either add to or subtract any value to the particular product or service.

The effectiveness of brand equity is visible when consumers of a service or product are willing to bear the price premium that the companies charges due to their command of brand equity over unbranded or unnamed products of services. Moreover, such brands can typically command higher sales volumes relative to other brands in the same market segment. Consequently, this drives their share prices positively due to this bias. Subsequently a good measure of brand equity can also be seen in their positive returns to their shareholders or stakeholders and their promising successive sales forecasts.

Aaker also outlined a brand equity model detailing 5 key elements; Brand loyalty, brand awareness, perceived quality, brand associations and finally other propriety assets. Brand loyalty can be closely linked to the reduced marketing costs as it consumers require less persuasion to make the purchase. This puts one at trade leverage with the ease of attracting new customers and the capability to respond to other competitive threats. Brand awareness relates to the customer's familiarity to the particular brand and their appreciation towards the company's commitments to their business model. Perceived quality is associated with the customers' justification to patronise the product or service either due to clear differentiation or product superiority regardless of pricing. Brand association aims to channel emotional responses for instance inducing feelings of optimism and pleasantness when showcasing the brand name. Proprietary brand assets include legislative road blocks such as patents and trademarks which prevent competitive attacks that would otherwise erode their competitive edge.

5. Theoretical Framework

Based on the literature carried out, three independent variables of innovations comprise of product innovation, service innovation and marketing innovation were used in this study. The brand equity is used as the dependent variable and the customers' satisfaction is used as the mediator.

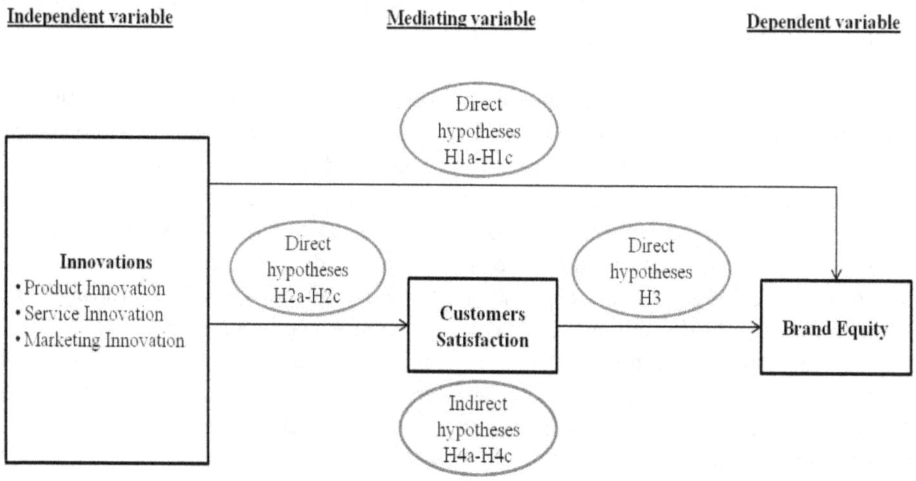

Figure 1: Theoretical Framework

6. Hypotheses Development

A framework was developed to guide research efforts and provide insight for management practices, establish the relationship among the innovations (product innovations, service innovations and marketing innovations), brand equity and customer satisfaction.

6.1 Innovation to Brand Equity

According to the finding of Zhang et al. (2013), brand equity can be greatly affected by innovations. The relationship is found to have a positive impact between variables by Sriram et al. (2012) where product innovation enhances the brand equity and reputational capital of an organization. Innovation helps in positive brand evaluation and thus leading to significant positive effect on brand equity in both long term and short term. A customized service and technology leadership are innovations. These innovations directly impact the brand equity (T, 2014).

The overall innovations of POSM are studied in this context. The innovations include product innovation, service innovation and marketing innovation. The process innovation, new markets innovation, supply chain innovation and organisation innovation are not included in this research study as these innovations are mainly focus on company employee as the respondent. Therefore, they are not included in the study because the focus respondent of the study is POSM customer and it will be impossible for the customers to access the innovation level of the internal process flow and organization of POSM. Hence, the following hypotheses are constructed:

H1a: Product innovation has positive relationship with brand equity.

H1b: Service innovation has positive relationship with brand equity.

H1c: Marketing innovation has positive relationship with brand equity.

6.2 Innovation to Customers Satisfaction

Innovation improves the efficiency of an organization, add value, delights the customers and leads to customer satisfaction (O'Dwyer et al., 2009) . Also, Naveed, Akhtar, & Cheema, (2012) research study states that innovation has a positive relationship with customer satisfaction especially when the customer needs is fulfilled. Consequently, the following hypothesis is tested:

H2a: Product innovation has positive relationship with customers' satisfaction.

H2b: Service innovation has positive relationship with customers' satisfaction.

H2c: Marketing innovation has positive relationship with customers' satisfaction.

6.3 Customers Satisfaction to Brand Equity

Aaker (1992), Blackston (2000) and Keller (1993) mentioned that there are positive connections between customers satisfaction to brand equity. Good customers satisfaction leads to strong brand associations (Keller, 1993; Keller, 2003) and thus improving the brand knowledge and contributes to brand equity (Torres and Tribó, 2011). Consumers are highly involved in the formation of brand equity (Blackston, 2000). The hypothesis tested as below:

H3: Customers satisfaction has positive relationship with brand equity.

6.4 Mediating Effect of Innovation to Brand Equity

Being creative is insufficient to create brand equity. Therefore, innovation has to be able to solve the customers' problem or fulfill the unmet market needs (Kanagal, 2015). The fulfillment of customers needs which leads to customers' satisfaction is vital to achieve long-term business success. Customers whom are satisfied with the implemented innovation by an organization will have a positive effect the organization brand equity and the organization's valuable asset (Liao and Cheng, 2014). Hence, the following hypotheses are constructed:

H4a: Customers satisfactions mediate the relationship between product innovation and brand equity.

H4b: Customers satisfactions mediate the relationship between service innovation and brand equity.

H4c: Customers satisfactions mediate the relationship between marketing innovation and brand equity.

7. Methodology

7.1 Research design

This research study utilizes a quantitative approach with the aid of questionnaire as data collection method as the major research instrument. A validated construct of questionnaire was adapted from the literature of past researcher framework. This is a cross-sectional study and the data were all collected at specific period (from early September to early October - 6 weeks). A total of 500 copies of questionnaire were distributed by convenient sampling to POSM customers and then snowballing sampling method to other POSM users. The population of interest in this research study is the POSM customers. The relationship among variables in the theoretical framework was tested with hypothesis testing method. Specific validated measurements were used to certify the construct which consists of previously mentioned innovation types (i.e. product innovation, service innovation and marketing innovation); with the addition of customers' satisfaction as the moderator and brand equity. A total of 161 questionnaires were received. However, only 116 data were usable after performing a data screening with focus to the population of interest (Sekaran and Bougie, 2016).

7.2 Data Analysis

The descriptive analysis of the research study was analysed using SPSS (Statistical Package of Social Science) version 22 where the demographic profile and the standard deviation of variables to confirm the data accuracy were obtained. The customers' degrees of acquaintance to POSM were analysed using SPSS software as well. The measurement models of construct in this research framework were tested with confirmatory factor anaylsis (CFA) with the aid of Partial Least Square (PLS) software version 3.0. The number of factors and measurement items were identified before the analysis began. The fitting of factors and loading of measured item were tested with CFA. The construct validity, reliability test and goodness-of –fit measurement results were obtained. After obtaining the measurement model result, the research proceeded with Structural Modelling. The strength of the prediction or the association of the model with multiple dependent variables were gauged with path analysis method where a one tailed test was applied. Then the analyses continue with Q2 assessment using blindfolding procedure when the contrasts were tested to be endogenous. The last test was mediation effect assessment using bootstrapping procedure. The following tabulate and describe the finding of this research. The respondents' demographic profile, consumers' degree of acquaintance to POSM, the Goodness of data and hypotheses were presented.

7.3 Respondent Profile

A total of 64 respondents were female. The young consumers' feedback rates were at 69.8%. The young consumers of the respondents were from the age group of 18-27 and 28-37. The respondents of this study came from various education backgrounds. The majority of the respondents received tertiary education ranging from Bachelors' Degree to Philosophy Doctorate and Professional Certificate. Bachelor Degree holders were the major respondent (70.7%). Besides, majority of the respondents were employees (87.9%). Lastly, the respondents from Penang contributed 51.7% to the overall usable data collected and respondent from Kuala Lumpur contributed 48.3%.

7.4 Consumers degree of acquaintance to POSM

Only 22.4% of the respondents were aware of the new logo implemented. This indicates that most of the respondents are not aware of the POSM currently brand logo where the customers' acknowledgement on the logo were still at the year 2014. Most of the respondents had experience with POSM within the year (64.7%). There are 5 key businesses under POSM. Most of the customers were aware of POSM supply chain solution (SCS) key business (76.7%) followed by one-stop solution (OSS) (62.9%). The communication and distribution solution was the next most acknowledge key business with 47.4% respondents knowing this key business. The least acknowledge key business were international business solution (26.7%) followed by digital solution 12.9%.

7.5 Goodness of Data

The below table shows the main loading value were above 0.5 which exceeding the cut off point suggested by Hair et al. (2010). The Composite Reliability (CR) value were above 0.7 (Hair et al., 2010) which indicates a strong reliability of the measurements. The Average Variance Extracted (AVE) values were in the range of 0.633 to 0.886 which were greater than the recommended value 0.5 as it indicates that the construct is able to explain more than half to the inconsistency of its measures (Henseler et al., 2009) in convergent validity. The composite reliability values of the study were ranging from 0.851 to 0.959 which verifies that the measurement model were reliable.

Table 1: PLS Result of Construct Validity, Convergent Validity and Reliability Analysis Result

Model Construct	Measurement Items	Loading	CR	AVE
Brand Equity	BE1	0.891	0.880	0.711
	BE2	0.820		
	BE3	0.816		
Customers Satisfaction	CS1	0.959	0.959	0.886
	CS2	0.934		
	CS3	0.931		
Marketing Innovation	MI1	0.772	0.851	0.655
	MI2	0.825		
	MI3	0.830		
	MI4	NA		
Productive Innovation	PI1	0.833	0.887	0.662
	PI2	0.781		
	PI3	0.815		
	PI4	0.826		
Service Innovation	SI1	0.815	0.896	0.633
	SI2	0.766		
	SI3	0.887		
	SI4	0.786		
	SI5	NA		
	SI6	0.714		

The correlations between the measures were examined for potential overlapping constructs. Demonstrated below is a correlation matrix of the correlations between the construct and square root of AVE diagonally in bold. Observing the results, the square root of the AVE of each construct was found to have a greater correlation between any other construct consequently indication adequate validity.

Table 2: PLS Result of Discriminant Validity Measures

Model Construct	BE	CS	MI	PI	SI
Brand Equity (BE)	**0.843**				
Customers Satisfaction (CS)	0.715	**0.941**			
Marketing Innovation (MI)	0.736	0.605	**0.809**		
Product Innovation (PI)	0.804	0.764	0.776	**0.814**	
Service Innovation (SI)	0.722	0.703	0.676	0.740	**0.796**

Note: The presented in bold represents the square root of average variance extracted (AVE).

Table 6 shows the GoF value for this study was 0.689 in which it exceeded the cut-off value of 0.36 (Wetzels, Odekerken and Van, 2009). This adequately shows that this study had acceptable predictive relevance, and that the model was a good-fit.

Table 3: PLS Result of Goodness-of-fit (GoF) Index

Variable	AVE	R Square
Brand Equity	0.711	0.712
Customers Satisfaction	0.886	0.626
Marketing Innovation	0.655	
Product Innovation	0.662	
Service Innovation	0.633	
Average AVE and R Square	0.709	0.669
Average AVE* Average R Square		0.475
Square Root of AVE*R Square		**0.689**

7.6 Hypotheses Testing

The results in Table 6.0 shows that among three dimension tested, only two comprises of product innovative, and service innovative contributes towards the brand equity of POSM. The innovations dimension contribution to customer satisfaction. The customer satisfaction contributes towards brand equity as well. The customer satisfaction does mediate between product innovation and service innovation towards brand equity. However, the customer satisfaction does not mediate between marketing innovation and brand equity.

Table 4: Significance of Direct Effect and The Significance of Direct Effect of Independent Variables to Dependent Variable without Mediating Variable -Path Coefficients (n=116)

Hypothesis	Relationship	Beta value	Sample mean	Standard error	t-value	Result
H1a	PI -> BE	0.178	0.175	0.094	1.891*	Supported
H1b	SI -> BE	0.231	0.236	0.078	2.958**	Supported
H1c	MI -> BE	-0.049	-0.048	0.098	0.503	Not Supported
H2a	PI -> CS	0.359	0.354	0.101	3.535***	Supported
H2b	SI -> CS	0.568	0.564	0.101	5.604***	Supported
H2c	MI -> CS	0.176	0.177	0.067	2.610**	Supported
H3	CS -> BE	0.315	0.321	0.085	3.710***	Supported
H4a	PI -> BE	0.178	0.175	0.094	1.891*	Supported
H4b	SI -> BE	0.231	0.236	0.078	2.958**	Supported
H4c	MI -> BE	-0.049	-0.048	0.098	0.503	Not Supported

Note: *P<0.05, **P<0.01, ***P<0.001

8. Discussion

Hypothesis H1a proposed product innovation have significant impact on band equity. The t-value is 1.891 indicated that the hypothesis is supported. Product innovation was found to have positive relationship with POSM brand equity. This finding was supported by Norskov et al. (2015) who viewed that the product innovation does affect the brand equity. According to Slotegraaf and Pauwels, (2008), the key assets of an organization are product innovation and brand equity. They play a straightforward role in firm development and success. Sriram et al. (2007) proven that product innovation leads to significant positive effect on brand equity in both short and long run. A good product innovation leads to favorable brand evaluation and higher purchase intentions. Hypothesis H1b proposed that service innovation has significant impact on brand equity. The hypothesis is supported with 2.958 t-value. This finding was aligned the other research topic where service innovation is positively related to brand equity by Atashfaraz and Abadi (2016). Hypothesis H1c proposed the marketing innovation significant impact the brand equity. This hypothesis is not supported where the t-value is only 0.503. The finding was absolutely contradicting to previous study from Keller (1993) where innovations affect the service brand equity. However, this finding aligns with (Schroeder, 1990) that the marking innovation has to be contribution to customer satisfaction in order to create brand equity.

The hypothesis of H2a was accepted where product innovation contributed towards customer satisfaction. It carries the meaning that product innovation plays an important role to influence the customers' perception in brand equity of POSM (Kiumarsi, Jayaraman and Isa, 2015). The hypothesis is supported by O'Dwyer et al. (2009) where innovation improves the efficiency of the organization, add value, delights the customers and leads to customer satisfaction. The hypothesis H2b, the contribution of service innovation towards customers' satisfaction was accepted. The hypothesis H2c was accepted where marketing innovation contribution towards customer satisfaction was significant.

The hypothesis H3 was supported where customer satisfaction contributes towards brand equity. This finding was aligned with the justification from Pappu et al. (2006). Customers satisfaction is the fundamental indicator of the organization's performance. A strong relationship is build between customers and the organization with a high level of satisfaction. A satisfied consumer will be able to differentiate the product received (Deng et al., 2010). Customers who are satisfied with the service and product will be able to link the perceive quality of the product. The brand awareness will be created and they will be more loyal towards a service they are satisfied with. Customers satisfaction aid in repeat purchase behavior as well and thus creates a long-term business connection.

The hypothesis H4a proposed that customer satisfaction mediates the relationship between product innovation towards brand equity. The hypothesis H4b proposed that customer satisfaction mediates the relationship between service innovation towards brand equity. Theses two hypothesis H4a and H4b were accepted. Creating high degree of satisfaction is important for today's business world as it helps in product differentiation (Deng et al., 2010). This is supported by Eshghi, Haughton and Topi (2007) where customer satisfaction helps to build long and profitable relationships between organization and consumer. The consumer purchase intention was influenced by customer satisfaction (Cronin and Taylor, 1992). Customer satisfaction aid in repeat purchase behavior as well (LaBarbera and Mazursky, 1983; Wilson, 2002; Reichheld, 1992). This will contribute highly to the element of brand equity; brand association and brand loyalty. Hypothesis H4c proposed that customer satisfactions mediate the relationship between marketing innovation towards brand equity. However, this hypothesis was not supported.

9. Conclusion

This research study provides a better understanding on effect of innovation and customers satisfaction towards brand equity of postal service. The findings are beneficial to provide guidance for POSM to further understand the current situation of the business environment. The impact of innovations namely product innovation, service innovation and marketing innovation on brand equity are empirically tested. Product innovation and service innovation are positively related to brand equity. Between these two innovations, service innovation having higher influence power than the product innovation. On the other hand, marketing innovation is negatively related to brand equity. Besides that, service innovation does influence brand equity followed by product innovation and marketing innovation. Customer satisfaction is mediate both the product innovation and service innovation to brand equity. However, the customer satisfaction does not mediate marketing innovation and brand equity as per expected.

In conclusion, product innovation and service innovation have significant and positive relationship on POSM's brand equity. Hence, POSM as a postal service provider has to implement user friendly service in order to attract and retain the customers. The introduction of wide ranges of product innovation can served as complimentary product at the beginning stage. From this point, the business needs an innovative product that start to grow and leads to maturity with the entering of early majority adopters. Moreover, to build a long term customers association, POSM has to be consistent with their brand promise. The marketing material like logo which represents the brand image has to be standardized in term of colours, font size. Other branding and marketing related tools have to be standardised from the interior design of the kiosk, post office to the parcel sending envelope and the parcel delivery transportation. The innovations will help to increase the customer satisfaction and allow them to have a long term relationship with POSM. Thus, innovations and customer satisfaction can lead to a strong brand equity.

Acknowledgements

This research is under the Fundamental Research Grant Scheme (FRGS) funded by Ministry of Higher Education (MOHE) Malaysia. Thank you to Universiti Sains Malaysia (USM) for the opportunity to conduct the research.

References

Aaker, D. A. (1992). The value of brand equity. Journal of business strategy, 13(4), 27-32.

Anderson, E. W., Fornell, C., & Mazvancheryl, S. K. (2004). Customer satisfaction and shareholder value. Journal of marketing, 68(4), 172-185.

Atashfaraz, M., Abadi, M.H. S. A (2016). Impact Of E-Service Innovation On Brand Equality And Customer Loyality In Samsung International Corporation. Procedia Economics and Finance 36 (2016) 327 – 335.

Beverland, M. B., Napoli, J., & Farrelly, F. (2010). Can all brands innovate in the same way? A typology of brand position and innovation effort. Journal of Product Innovation Management, 27(1), 33-48.

Blackston, M. (2000). Observations: Building brand equity by managing the brand's relationships. Journal of Advertising Research, 40(06), 101-105.

Cobb-Walgren, C. J., Ruble, C. A., & Donthu, N. (1995). Brand equity, brand preference, and purchase intent. Journal of advertising, 24(3), 25-40.

Cronin Jr, J. J., & Taylor, S. A. (1992). Measuring service quality: a reexamination and extension. The journal of marketing, 55-68.

Damanpour, F., & Gopalakrishnan, S. (1999). Organizational adaptation and innovation: The dynamics of adopting innovation types. In The dynamics of innovation (pp. 53-80). Springer Berlin Heidelberg.

Deng, Z., Lu, Y., Wei, K. K., & Zhang, J. (2010). Understanding customer satisfaction and loyalty: An empirical study of mobile instant messages in China. International journal of information management, 30(4), 289-300.

Eshghi, A., Haughton, D., & Topi, H. (2007). Determinants of customer loyalty in the wireless telecommunications industry. Telecommunications policy, 31(2), 93-106.

Farquhar, P. H. (1989). Managing brand equity. Marketing research, 1(3).

Hair, J. F., Black, W. C., Babin, B. J., Anderson, R. E., & Tatham, R. L. (2010). Multivariate data analysis. (7th ed.) New Jersey: Prentice Hall.

Henseler, J., Ringle, C. M., & Sinkovics, R. R. (2009). The use of partial least squares path modeling in international marketing. Advances in international marketing, 20(1), 277-319.

Homburg, C., & Giering, A. (2001). Personal characteristics as moderators of the relationship between customer satisfaction and loyalty—an empirical analysis. Psychology & Marketing, 18(1), 43-66.

Huber, F., Herrmann, A., & Wricke, M. (2001). Customer satisfaction as an antecedent of price acceptance: results of an empirical study. Journal of Product & Brand Management, 10(3), 160-169.

Kanagal, N. B. (2015). Innovation and product innovation in marketing strategy. Journal of Management and marketing research, 18, 1-25.

Kapferer, J. N. (2008). The New Strategic Brand Management: Creating and Sustaining Brand Equity.

Keller, K. L. (1993). Conceptualizing, measuring, and managing customer-based brand equity. the Journal of Marketing, 1-22.

Keller, K. L. (2003). Brand synthesis: The multidimensionality of brand knowledge. Journal of consumer research, 29(4), 595-600.

Krishnan, B. C., & Hartline, M. D. (2001). Brand equity: is it more important in services? Journal of services marketing, 15(5), 328-342.

Kiumarsi, S., Jayaraman, K., & Isa, M. S. (2015). Service Quality and Innovation in Malaysian Post Offices: An Empirical Study. Global Business and Organizational Excellence, 35(1), 55-66.

Liao, S., & Cheng, C. C. (2014). Brand equity and the exacerbating factors of product innovation failure evaluations: A communication effect perspective. Journal of Business Research, 67(1), 2919-2925.

Milling, P. M., & Stumpfe, J. (2000, August). Product and process innovation-a system dynamics-based analysis of the interdependencies. In V Proceedings of the 18th International Conference of the System Dynam& ics Society.

Naveed, T., Akhtar, I., & Cheema, K. U. R. (2012). The impact of innovation on customer satisfaction and brand loyalty: A study of the students of Faisalabad.

Nørskov, S., Chrysochou, P., & Milenkova, M. (2015). The impact of product innovation attributes on brand equity. Journal of Consumer Marketing, 32(4), 245-254.

O'Dwyer, M., Gilmore, A., & Carson, D. (2009). Innovative marketing in SMEs. European Journal of Marketing, 43(1/2), 46-61.

Pappu, R., & Quester, P. (2006). Does customer satisfaction lead to improved brand equity? An empirical examination of two categories of retail brands. Journal of Product & Brand Management, 15(1), 4-14.

Reichheld, F. F. (1992). Loyalty-based management. Harvard business review, 71(2), 64-73.

Roberts, P. W. (1999). Product innovation, product-market competition and persistent profitability in the US

Rogers, E. (1962). Diffusion of Innovations. New York, USA: Free pressof Glencoe, 1, 79-134.

Schroeder, D. M. (1990). A dynamic perspective on the impact of process innovation upon competitive strategies. Strategic Management Journal, 11(1), 25-41.

Sciences, A. (2007). The Dimensions of Innovation and its Dynamics, (May).

Sekaran, U. & Bougie, R. (2016). Research methods for business: A skill building approach (7th ed). John Wiley & Sons, Inc.
Sivadas, E., & Baker-Prewitt, J. L. (2000). An examination of the relationship between service quality, customer satisfaction, and store loyalty. International Journal of Retail & Distribution Management, 28(2), 73-82.
Slotegraaf, R. J., & Pauwels, K. (2008). The impact of brand equity and innovation on the long-term effectiveness of promotions. Journal of Marketing Research, 45(3), 293-306.
Sriram, S., Balachander, S., & Kalwani, M. U. (2007). Monitoring the dynamics of brand equity using store-level data. Journal of Marketing, 71(2), 61-78.
Torres, A., & Tribó, J. A. (2011). Customer satisfaction and brand equity. Journal of Business Research, 64(10), 1089-1096.
Tripathi, S. (2013). An empirical study-awareness of customers on service quality of public sector banks in Varanasi. Journal of Business Management and Social Science Research, 2(1), 24-29.
Trong Tuan, L. (2014). Clinical governance, corporate social responsibility, health service quality, and brand equity. Clinical Governance: An International Journal, 19(3), 215-234.
Tushman, M., & Nadler, D. (1986). Organizing for innovation. California management review, 28(3), 74-92.
Urbancová, H. (2013). Competitive advantage achievement through innovation and knowledge. Journal of Competitiveness, 5(1).
Wetzels, M., Odekerken-Schröder, G., & Van Oppen, C. (2009). Using PLS path modeling for assessing hierarchical construct models: Guidelines and empirical illustration. MIS quarterly, 177-195.
Wilson, A. (2002). Attitudes towards customer satisfaction measurement in the retail sector. International Journal of Market Research, 44(2), 213.
Zhang, H., Ko, E., & Lee, E. (2013). Moderating effects of nationality and product category on the relationship between innovation and customer equity in Korea and China. Journal of Product Innovation Management, 30(1), 110-122.

Open Innovation, R&D Collaboration and Global Strategy in High-tech SMEs: Focused on R&D Collaboration Mode

Rara (Hye-Seong) Jeon[1] and Daniel Dagravel[2]
[1]Doctoral Student, Grenoble Ecole de Management, Grenoble- France
[2]Professor, California States University, Northridge-U.S.A.
rarajeon@gmail.com
daniel.degravel@csun.edu

Abstract: This paper explores which mechanism is involved between firms' global strategy and R&D collaboration mode. Innovation is originally linked to the role of R&D which is the most significant strategy in technological companies (Yip, 1989; Conte & Vivarelli, 2014). To penetrate global markets, firms, especially, SMEs select local partners for R&D to minimize risks and save cost, whereas few firms choose global partners. It would be easy if we could collaborate with global partners who are in the target market and understand their market needs. However, global collaboration is challenging for SMEs, which is why most fail global partnerships. There are certain criteria involved when firms select partners or conduct in-house R&D. To examine this phenomenon, we select high-tech firms who export and collaborate R&D with local and/or global partners. The purpose of our study is to encourage SMEs to achieve globalization and benefit from collaboration with local and/or global partners. The impact of collaborative innovation on SMEs and how it influences globalization is valuable to examine. We used the Upsala model for understanding the steps of globalization, and 'Global Strategy' theory (Laanti, Gabrielsson, & Gabrielsson, 2007) to analyze each firm's global strategies. Our study explores this phenomenon for the first time: How do SMEs leverage globalization successfully through different R&D collaboration modes? At the end of our study, we recommend an appropriate collaboration mode for each firm based on the firms' circumstances and the decision of globalization strategy.

Keywords: Innovation (Open Innovation), Research & Development (R&D), Collaboration, Small Medium Sized Enterprises (SMEs), Global Strategy

1. Introduction

Innovation is essential for an organization's growth (Horibe, 2003) to sustain competitive positioning and to strengthen it (Baregheh, Rowley, & Sambrook, 2009;). At the same time, businesses are forced to find partners to benefit from innovation given rapidly changing global market conditions and increased competition (Vapola, 2011). Thus, the openness in the innovation process is becoming more prominent recently as evidenced in various academic literature (Patra & Krishna, 2015).

Intensive competition in domestic markets give a reason for firms to expand their technology into new markets overseas (Lee & Jeong, 2010; Kang, 2012). However, the uncertainty in the global marketplace has caused a fundamental change in firms' innovation strategies (Lee & Jeong, 2010; Kang, 2012). To mitigate this confusion and secure global markets, collaborative innovation has become commonplace in organizations, and needs to be studied (Zhang, 2011; Qiuyan, 2012).

Globalization could be done simply if firms collaborated with buyers and/or distributors regardless of their size (Kang, 2012). Furthermore, different modes of network relationships have different effects on their performance (Lin & Lin, 2016). International collaboration raises important questions regarding the relationship between R&D and innovation (Ebersberger & Herstad, 2013). Specifically, our study will analyze how high-tech SMEs choose different R&D collaboration modes depending on their circumstances targeting the global markets. We use multiple case analysis to answer these questions. The first part of this paper is an article based on the literature review on open innovation, R&D collaboration, SMEs, globalization, global strategy. Second, we present our contributions at the managerial and theoretical levels.

At theoretical level, our research is based on the most recent literature related to our topic. The recent studies typically use patent data to analyze the impact of foreign knowledge sources on firms' innovations (Peters & Schmiele, 2010), and R&D collaboration with universities, competitors, etc.
In order to explore the phenomenon related to our topic, we divided partnership structures into three scenarios: "Closed", "Open & Local", and "Open & Global". There are potentially great advantages associated with forming global partnerships including expanding markets, improving quality, and enhancing competitiveness (MIT Sloan Management Review, 1989; Pla-Barber and Alegre, 2007; Chetty, Sylvie K., and

Stangl, 2010). The firm's benefit might differ depending on the firm's strategies and situations. However, there are no solid case studies and frameworks for a SMEs to benchmark.

2. Literature Review

2.1 Innovation and Technological Innovation

Innovation is widely considered to play a central role in creating value, sustaining competitive advantage, and representing the evolution in any organization (Baregheh et al., 2009). Firms should actively adapt new technology and create competitiveness for long-term success. Especially, High-tech and rapidly-changing industries require huge amounts of R&D investment and are associated with high risks (Miotti and Sachwald, 2003). Moreover, investing in innovation involve greater risk for firms, especially for SMEs (Kaufmann, Franz, 2002).

Our study focuses on technological innovation, which is critical to globalization (Abdullah and Zain, 2011; Verweij, Pearl, Shelton, Jasmin, Eckert, Parsons, Goddard, Seabrooke-spencer, & White, 2012). Porter (1985), Kang (2012), and various scholars have highlighted that the key success factors for technological innovation are capabilities and management skills. Profiting from technology is imperative and it relates to the management of innovation processes (Rodríguez, Lorenzo, 2011). Therefore, we will explore the process of globalization through different collaboration modes of innovation at this time.

Understanding the process of innovation allows firms to achieve greater efficiency in production and quality (Schumpeter, 1934; Clark and Fujimoto, 1991; Stadler, 2011; Un & Asakawa, 2015).

2.2 Open Innovation and Collaboration R&D

Open innovation highlights "innovation source" which is obtaining ideas or knowledge externally (Salampasis, 2015) while innovation focuses on the process. Open innovation stimulates the increase of diversity of technology and minimizes gaps between technological innovation and consumer needs (Greenstein, 1996; Lichtenthaler, 2011). Short technology life cycles, emerging technologies, rising costs, and risks associated with technology innovation causes attention of external partnership from both practitioners and academics for a number of reasons: (Rigby and Zook, 2002; Christensen et al., 2005; Henkel, Laursen, and Salter, 2006; Enkel, Gassmann, & Chesbrough, 2009; Lee, Park, Yoon, and Park 2010; Vanhaverbeke, 2011; Vrgov, Petar, Vidiki, Predrag, Glassman, and Brian, 2012; Kaisa, 2013).

Firms, especially SMEs need collaboration with external partners to conduct R&D and commercialization (Wynarczyk, Pooran, 2013) because SMEs can benefit from co-investment, or co-marketing, or co-R&D (Diez, 2000; Chesbrough, 2002; Vrgovic, Petar, Vidiki, Predrag, Glassman, Lee & Jeong, 2010; Kang, 2012). However, most SMEs collaborate with their partners at the later stage, marketing or commercialization rather than R&D phase. This is why our study is valuable to explore new phenomenon.

We have divided into two criteria of open innovation based on Openness (Open/ Closed) and geography (Local/ Global) to categorize open innovation. Integrating both concepts of "Open & Global" is an interesting concept to analyze whether or not these collaboration modes can benefit firms for successful globalization (Enkel, Gassmann, and Chesbrough, 2009). However, firms need to be careful in selecting partners, since not all collaborations are equally beneficial (Un & Asakawa, 2015). In this respect, we focus on collaboration mode for R&D, and the strategies on what types of criteria is necessary for firms to determine collaboration modes either local or global partnership as a means to overcome resource constraints and optimize innovation globally.

2.3 Globalization and Global Strategy

SMEs are faced with increasing prices and technological competition from large firms in their local markets (Rammer, Christian, Schmiele, Anja, 2009). This encourages SEMs to challenge and penetrate foreign markets. Globalization tends to benefit large firms compared to SMEs because scaled advantages allow large firms to create new opportunities (Rammer, Christian, Schmiele, Anja, 2009). However, difficulties and uncertainties in foreign markets lead firms to hesitate to penetrate global markets (Cooper, Edgett, and Kleinschmidt 2003; Koufteros, Vonderembse, and Jayaram 2005; Griffiths-Hemans and Grover 2006). Nevertheless, the desire to increase profits is the major reason that firm's move into the global markets (Abdullah and Zain, 2011).

Trade openness is an all-encompassing concept to explain a wide range of activities such as international trade (import & export), foreign direct investment (FDI), and cultural exchange (Archibugi & Iammarino, 2002). Among definitions of globalization, the 'export' is an accurate method to measure globalization rather than using culture, people, technology, and other traits (Chiao et. al. 2006).

In terms of strategy, Porter (1991) and Wasniewski (2010) maintains a successful innovation strategy which involves integrating marketing, production, R&D, procurement, and finance within a firm. Among these, the most influential factors that determines the success or failure of a business and should be employed by all parts of an organization (Porter, 1991; Wasniewski, 2010). In this regard, we need to consider how high-tech SMEs globalize their technology and/or products through different collaboration modes of R&D, and what criteria is involved with both local and global collaboration.

3. Theoretical Foundation

3.1 Globalization theory– *Upsala Model*

Definition of globalization is still ambiguous. The *Uppsala model* explains how firms gradually intensify their activities in foreign markets—it was introduced by Jan-Johansson and Jan-Erik Ahlen in 1977.

According to the Upsala Model, around 75% of the firms utilize "exporting" among globalization procedure, yet very few SMEs were able to open subsidiaries overseas, which is the most expensive method to globalize (Abdullah and Zain, 2011). We used "export" as a filtering SMEs who are qualified as our case firms.

However, several issues remain understudied, such as how firms leverage their globalization through different collaboration mode in R&D.

3.2 Theory of Global Strategy

According to the 'Fundamentals of global strategy' (Cornelis A. de Kluyver, 2010) defined by adaptation, aggregation, and arbitrage (Cornelis A. de Kluyver, 2010). The article 'global strategy' demonstrates the framework of how to evaluate the globalization of individual firms based on the 'corporate strategy': market, cost, environmental, and competitive (Yip, 1989; Laanti et al., 2007). Moreover, Allaire and Firsirotu (1993) built 'Thinking strategy model' which is divided into external and internal variables (factors) and examine a firm's strategies. We integrated both strategies to explore firms' circumstances based on each category.

4. Methodology

We use a multiple case methodology to explore the new phenomenon: key organizational characteristics in the high-tech industry and guided future work in this area (Cousins & Bourgeois, 2014). Descriptive, exploratory, and explanatory analyses are essential to the case study (Cousins & Bourgeois, 2014). Our research provides guidelines for SMEs, practitioners, government agencies, and academics. We explore the conceptual framework related to our theme.

We have chosen high-tech SMEs in South Korea involved in export. The companies exhibit one of the collaboration modes listed above. We use an allonym as a company name to secure their privacy.

Table 1: Descriptive Characteristics of Case firms

Firm	Position	Technology	No. of People	Revenue	Export (%)	R&D team	Overseas sales team	Subsidiary	Types of Collaboration
YL	CEO/ Director	Security Tech.	52	14M	80%	40%	20%	Distributor Overseas	Open & Global
MS	CEO/ Chief of institution	Chemicals for electronics	63	19M	47%	34%	12%	Export through large firms	Open & Global
KC	Director/ Senior researcher	Semiconductor	250	9M	85%	20%	10%	Japan, China	Open & Global
SL	Director/ Manager	Touch panel for Smartphone	300	8M	87%	11%	5%	China, distributors in Japan, USA, Asia	Open & Global
TM	Chairman/ CEO/ Director	VR/ CCTV	210	36M	60%	28%	4%	China, USA, Europe	Open & Global

Firm	Position	Technology	No. of People	Revenue	Export (%)	R&D team	Overseas sales team	Subsidiary	Types of Collaboration
NT	Head of research center/Director	Set-top box	82	15M	100%	80%	15%	Distributors UK, the middle East, S. America	Open & Global
AO	Director	Medical devices	282	90M	45%	15%	20%	USA, China, Japan, etc.	Open & Local
AC	CEO/ Director	AR/VR	51	9M	20%	85%	10%	Export through large firms	Open & Local
ST	Director/ Manager	Set-top box	42	3M	100%	60%	40%	Distributors Europe, S. America	Open & Local
OM	Director/ Head of institution	Medical devices	298	164M	50%	10%	40%	China, USA	Open& Local
SN	Director	Crystal ceramic	210	26M	40%	10%	30%	USA, China	Closed
ST	Director/ Manager	Protection film	53	11M	85%	12%	20%	Distributors in China, S. Ease Asia, Europe	Closed
FR	Chief of institution	Robot	52	4M	30%	60%	20%	Agent in USA, China	Closed
YN	Senior researcher	Visual art equipment	127	40M	60%	60%	14%	USA, UK	Closed

To provide us with a more in-depth understanding of each SME, corporate secondary data was collected ahead of the interviews. During the research period, we were working for the case firms as a participation observation for three years.

In order to compare collaboration modes, we chose SMEs which engage in successful innovation to export with global partners (Open-Global); local partners (Open-Local); and or in-house (Closed). We conducted 24 interviews with 14 firms using different questionnaires depending on collaboration modes. Interviews were audiotaped.

Despite the opportunity of recording each interview, notes were taken in order to collect all the information needed for this study. We applied data triangulation to check for reliability and validity, combining different qualitative methods (i.e. observations, documents, and interviews). Case firms were interviewed once or multiple times (45mins ~ 1h 30mins).

We first gathered all the materials and then wrote a monograph (Eisenhardt, 1989) to synthesize all the events, giving information about the relationships between collaboration mode of R&D and globalization.

We reviewed examined theories and research relevant themes to the current study. From participant observation, we found out the phenomenon related to our theme. The unique experiences afforded us a deep analysis of the phenomenon that may often be invisible to other researchers. From data analysis of the interviews, we translated each interview from Korean to English, and the interview transcripts were analyzed. To analyze the data gathered on the industry level, we have used coding methodologies, using software ATLAS. In the data, we have searched for the process of globalization through the open innovation to analyze them in depth. After the first coding, we searched for the patterns related to our themes in the data, organized the codes, and modified previous conceptual framework. We use the frequency of the codes related to our theme to explore a new phenomenon.

5. Case Study

Following Table 2 demonstrates a firm's global strategy. We examined three cases based on collaboration modes of R&D: Open & Global, Open & Local, and Closed (in-house).

Table 2: Characteristics of Corporate Strategy focusing on Globalization: Open & Global

Internal Strategy	Leadership (Entrepreneurship)	"We have a strong passion about global markets, and the firms have various experiences." (YL/MS/KC/SL) "We targeted global markets from the beginning. (interviews)"
	People	"We hired international staffs from China, Japan, and etc. and they usually communicate with global partners, but it's hard to find people who have engineering backgrounds and achieve language proficiencies." (MS/SL)
	Technology capabilities	"We need a more advanced level of technology." We need to collaborate to obtain comparable technologies which meet the clients' needs." (YL/MS/KC)
	Partners	"We have global partners trust-worthy, and capable of collaborating with each other." (YL/MS)
	Structure	Centralized: Owner of corporations decides global strategies (observations/ interviews)
	Culture	Values: "We understand the significance of global markets." "We obtained global standardization and competitive experiences overseas."
	Strategic process	"We try to find a market need first before developing our technologies." (YL/MS)
External Strategy	Product/ Service	"We tried to minimize the cost of product or services to compete with competitors such as China or other developing countries." (YL/MS/KC)
	Market	"We recognize that markets are the key rather than technology." (YL/MS). "In high-tech industry, the market requires advanced technology continuously." (YL/MS/SL). "We believe that technology can be sourced easily all over the world, but firms cannot survive without markets." (YL/MS)

Partnering with global buyers and/or distributors is the best scenario for firms to cope with the lack of technologies, markets, and funds for innovation, especially targeting overseas markets.

In terms of global collaboration (Open & Global), only very few Korean SMEs export successfully. SMEs collaborate with their buyers, distributors, or university institutions who suggest ideas and are most likely to fit on market trends. However, global collaborations are highly risky for SMEs compared to local collaboration. Although SMEs are capable of globalizing the technologies, it is hard to make a profit in the short-term (YL/MS/KC). Moreover, opening up innovative activity involves substantial business risks with firms accidentally disclosing patented information rendering their competitive advantage obsolete (Henkel, 2006; West, 2003; Alexy et al., 2016). Therefore, those who collaborate with global partners need to have a diverse global background, experiences, and global networks to find the right partners and manage partners well.

Table 3: Characteristics of Corporate Strategy focusing on Globalization: Open & Local

Internal Strategy	Leadership (Entrepreneurship)	"We are more focusing on existing local businesses than global business to avoid risks." (AO/AC/ST) They are more passive than active. (observations/ interviews)
	People	Firm owners, people have experiences overseas, but lack of experience to motivate them to collaborate with others. (observations/ interviews)
	Technology capabilities	Those who supply their technologies to large firms are relatively advanced. (observations/ interviews) "R&D is more intensive than marketing or any other factors since firms are relatively competitive." (AC/AO/ST/OM)
	Partners	"We lack engineers and/or funds for R&D encourage collaboration with universities or institutions." (AC/AC/OM). "References collaborating with conglomerates create opportunities to expand our businesses." (AC/ST/OM).
	Structure	Centralized: Owner has a desire to secure existing businesses rather than taking the risks for global markets. (observations/ interviews)
	Culture	Value: Regular clients (supply to large multinationals), higher level of engineers, fundraising from government. (document analysis/ observations/ interviews)
	Strategic process	"We approach the markets as a second mover rather than first mover to minimize risks." (AC/ST)
External Strategy	Product/ service	"We mainly focused on requirements from large firms." (AC/OM) "We need to consider cost efficiencies to compete with their competitors. (AC/ST/OM)
	Market	"When we supply our technology to large firms, we do not need market survey." (AC/AO) "Other cases, we have brainstormed with experts in either firms, universities, or institutions." (AC/AO/OM)

Those who collaborate with local partners provide their technology to large firms. Challenging leadership and targeting overseas markets encourage these SMEs to be independent from large firms, and create new global markets. However, uncertainly of global markets, lack of experiences overseas, a fear of failure, and lack of exemplary case studies distract a SME to build partnerships in foreign countries.

Table 4: Characteristics of Corporate Strategy focusing on Globalization: Closed

Internal Strategy	Leadership (Entrepreneurship)	Firms are conservative to keep doing in-house in order to secure their technology. Immense pride of their technology. Not enough experience in the global markets. (observations/ interviews)
	People	Hire individuals who have overseas experiences and networks overseas.
	Technology capabilities	"We are leading technology all over the world." Firms tend to collaborate with local or overseas partners who are able to develop the technology which they need. (observations/ interviews)
	Partners	"We do not have external partners." "We do prefer to develop our technology by ourselves to secure our technology." "We are afraid that our competitors emulate our technology." (SN/ST/FR) "We do prefer to collaborate with partners in commercializing and/or marketing phases rather than R&D." (ST/ST/FR/YN)
	Structure	Centralized: Owner of firms are most likely to make a decision in terms of partnership, global strategies, and technology development. (observations/ interviews)
	Culture	Value points: Customer focus, Intensive R&D activities, Higher level of engineers, Top level of technology, Stable revenue from IP and patent. (documents analysis/ observations/ interviews)
	Strategic process	"We focus on future technologies and business models." (SN/ST/FR)
External Strategy	Product/ service	The firms already have competitive technology and services in the world. (observations/ interviews)
	Market	Firms find networks and partners through government agency or participating conventions (exhibitions + conferences). (observations/ interviews)

Compared to the firms which are collaborating with local and/or global partners, those who conduct innovation in-house are relatively capable of developing technology with their own resources. Firms consider that their technology is the top level globally, and they are eager to protect their technology. These firms own the necessary skills to expand markets using their own channels such as agents and/or subsidiaries.

6. Theory Contribution and Discussion

We demonstrate recent literature related to open innovation, R&D collaboration, and globalization. The case studies are primarily directed at high-tech SMEs in South Korea. Our research provides information on what types of collaboration modes are appropriate in each firm and how high-tech SMEs implement open innovation for successful global and local collaboration (*Figure 1*). We implement collaboration theory (Wood, D. J. Gray, 1991) to show how SMEs overcome their constraints through the collaboration R&D.

We create a conceptual framework which other SMEs in a different industry can apply to their firms, and achieve globalization. (Figure 1)

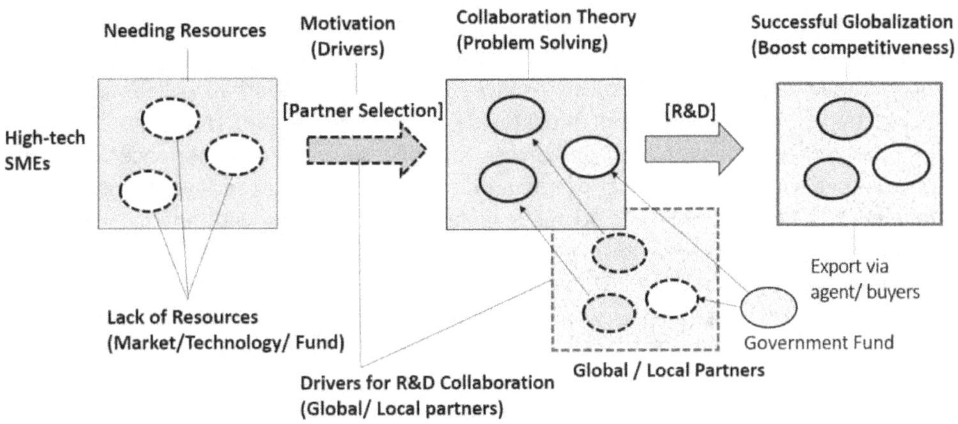

Figure 1: Conceptual Framework: The Process of Open Innovation and Globalization

Following *Figure 2* is the outcome of case studies based on different collaboration mode of R&D. We answer what factors generate firms' decision of R&D collaboration mode.

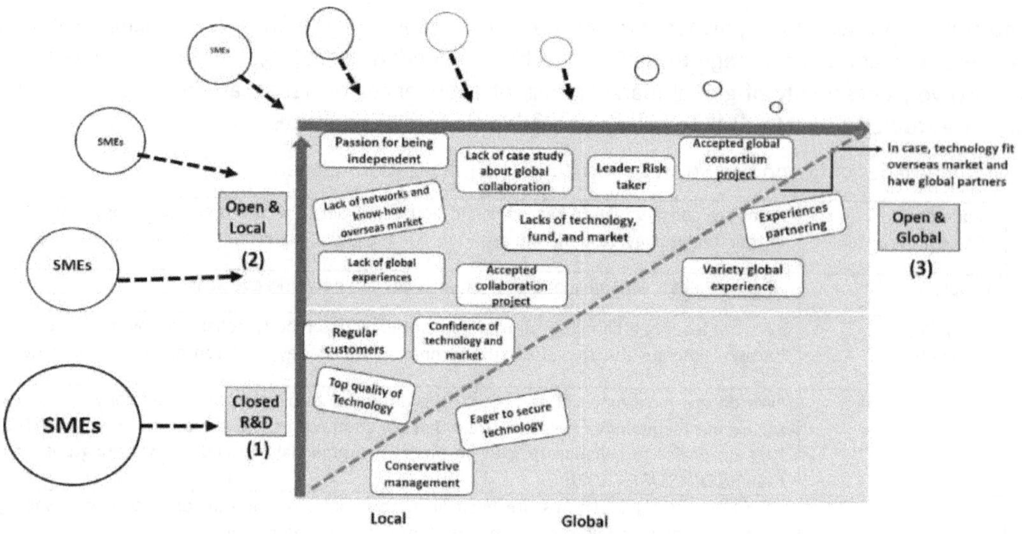

Figure 2: Drivers of R&D Collaboration Mode: Open& Local / Open & Global

Figure 2 represents the phenomenon of each type of R&D, which are Closed, Open & Local, and Open & Global, and demonstrate what types of SMEs are appropriate for which collaboration mode. From these ideas, we create a conceptual framework for academics and practitioners, and suggest a future study for academics as follows (Figure 9). Most case firms who implement Open & Local, are eager to conduct Open & Global after they achieve innovation with local partners. However, "there is no solid case study that SMEs can benchmark know-how implementing open innovation with global partners successfully (AC/ ST)". This is why our case study is valuable and beneficial. Following *Figure 2* are our recommendations and suggestions for beneficiaries on how firms should select collaboration modes to fit their situations to maximize benefits and mitigate risks.

Depending on their circumstances and firms' decision of global strategies, firms can select one or several collaboration modes which are the most appropriate for their goals. We suggest opposite ideas for SMEs, and encourage them to benchmark collaboration modes to benefit from partnerships.

As for the future study, we could examine how different phases of collaboration (between R&D and commercialization phase) influence a degree of globalization, and how government policy impact firms' decision of collaboration modes.

The circle objects (SMEs) represent the number of declining SMEs who engage in increasingly external interactions. The dotted arrow signifies firms who have the appropriate technology targeting global markets from the beginning.

7. Discussion and Conclusion

Each firm's strategy has been analyzed from theoretical and empirical points-of-view in order to explore the phenomenon which types of SMEs successfully collaborate with local and/or global partners. Our outcome shows us that most SMEs conduct R&D by themselves (in-house) rather than collaborating with external partners to protect their technologies and mitigate risks from partnerships. Nevertheless, SMEs need to collaborate with partners to cope with their drawbacks, lack of resources and experiences. Case firms benefit from partnership either with local or global partners unless they have the top level technology and enough budget for conducting R&D. However, once companies fail in collaborating with any partnerships, it impacts the firms' decision not to collaborate with partners any longer. (interviewee /SN/ Director) To increase the success rate of global collaboration for R&D, firms need to cooperate in the same space until the project is finalized such as a joint-lab. This is the best way to minimize risks caused by global partnership and to build a mutual and real-time communication (YL/KC/SL). Otherwise, the time to market will most likely be delayed due to the time difference (YL/KC/SL). Furthermore, to increase the success rate of collaboration, firms need to collaborate with other firms which are in the same industries and have different capabilities.

Our analysis is not to evaluate which collaboration mode has more advantages than others, instead, we recommend what types of SMEs are appropriate to collaborate either with local or global partners. Firms choose different collaboration modes or innovating by themselves based on their circumstances and goals because the measurement of success of globalization is hard to examine in a timeline.

Our case study will implicate SMEs, academic institutions, practitioners, entrepreneurs, and policy makers.Our analysis encourages all of them to understand how to utilize R&D collaboration for their successful globalization based on their situation.

We have concluded that most of the decision-making (such as innovative strategy, the selection of R&D partners, and global strategies) originates from leaders (entrepreneurs). Thus, an enthusiastic and innovative mindset of the leaders and their international experiences are essential for successful collaboration.

Our findings will apply to the SMEs in a variety of industrial categories and countries. Lastly, to increase the successful rate of collaboration among external partners, both parties need to break down strengths and competitive barriers, and create a mutually beneficial relationship.

References

Allaire, Y., & Firsirotu, M. E. (1984). Theories of Organizational Culture. *Organization Studies*. https://doi.org/10.1177/017084068400500301

Archibugi, D., & Iammarino, S. (2002). The globalization of technological innovation: definition and evidence. *Review of International Political Economy*, *9*(1), 98–122. https://doi.org/10.1080/09692290110101126

Baregheh, A., Rowley, J., & Sambrook, S. (2009). Towards a multidisciplinary definition of innovation. *Management Decision*, *47*(8), 1323–1339. https://doi.org/10.1108/00251740910984578

Bok, Lee, Choi, and K. (2012). Open & Global R & D case analysis in S. Korea. *SERI*.

Bougrain, F., & Haudeville, B. (2002). Innovation, Collaboration and SMEs Internai Research Capacities. *Research Policy*, *31*(5), 735–747. https://doi.org/10.1016/S0048-7333(01)00144-5

Buganza, T., & Verganti, R. (2009). Open innovation process to inbound knowledge: Collaboration with universities in four leading firms. *European Journal of Innovation Management*, *12*(3), 306–325. https://doi.org/10.1108/14601060910974200

Burke, G. I., & Jarratt, D. G. (2004). The influence of information and advice on competitive strategy definition in small- and medium-sized enterprises. *Qualitative Market Research: An International Journal*, *7*(2), 126–138. https://doi.org/10.1108/13522750410530039

Chesbrough, H. (2003). Book_Open Innovation.pdf. Havard Business Review.

Conte, A., & Vivarelli, M. (2014). Succeeding in innovation: key insights on the role of R&D and technological acquisition drawn from company data. *Empirical Economics*, *47*(4), 1317–1340. https://doi.org/10.1007/s00181-013-0779-1

Ebersberger, B., & Herstad, S. J. (2013). The relationship between international innovation collaboration, intramural R&D and SMEs' innovation performance: a quantile regression approach. *Applied Economics Letters*, *20*(7), 626–630. https://doi.org/10.1080/13504851.2012.724158

Eisenhardt, K. M. (1989). Building theories from case study research. *Academy of Management Review*, *14*(4), 532–550.

Enkel, E., Gassmann, O., & Chesbrough, H. (2009). Open R&D and open innovation: exploring the phenomenon. *R&D Management*, *39*(4), 311–316. https://doi.org/10.1111/j.1467-9310.2009.00570.x

Henttonen, K. (2013). Open innovation in SMEs – collaboration modes and strategies in commercialisation phase Kaisa Henttonen *. *ISPIM Conference-Innovating in Global Market*, (June).

Horibe, F. (2003). Innovation, Creativity, and Improvement: WORKING THE RIGHT LEVER TO PROSPERITY. *The Canadian Manager*, *28*(1), 20–20: Page count = 3. Retrieved from http://search.proquest.com/docview/213665635?accountid=15297%5Cnhttp://sfx.cbuc.cat/uji?url_ver=Z39.88-2004&rft_val_fmt=info:ofi/fmt:kev:mtx:journal&genre=unknown&sid=ProQ:ProQ%3Aabiglobal&atitle=Innovation%2C+Creativity%2C+and+Improvement%3A+WORKING+THE+RI

Huysmans, J. (2009). Introduction to the Forum on Global Society "' Globalization Theory .'" *Forum American Bar Association*, *3*(1), 2009–2009.

Johnson, J. H., Arya, B., & Mirchandani, D. a. (2013). Global integration strategies of small and medium multinationals: Evidence from Taiwan. *Journal of World Business*, *48*(1), 47–57. https://doi.org/10.1016/j.jwb.2012.06.006

Kaufmann, A., & Tödtling, F. (2002). How effective is innovation support for SMEs? An analysis of the region of Upper Austria. *Technovation*, *22*(3), 147–159. https://doi.org/10.1016/S0166-4972(00)00081-X

Laanti, R., Gabrielsson, M., & Gabrielsson, P. (2007). The globalization strategies of business-to-business born global firms in the wireless technology industry. *Industrial Marketing Management*, *36*(8), 1104–1117. https://doi.org/10.1016/j.indmarman.2006.10.003

Lichtenthaler, U. (2011). Open Innovation: Past Research, Current Debates, and Future Directions. *Academy of Management Perspectives*, *25*(1), 75–93. https://doi.org/10.5465/AMP.2011.59198451

Lin, F. J., & Lin, Y. H. (2016). The effect of network relationship on the performance of SMEs. *Journal of Business Research*, *69*(5), 1780–1784. https://doi.org/10.1016/j.jbusres.2015.10.055

Meissner, D. (n.d.). " Globalization and Open Innovation " - Implications for Innovation and Technology Policy. *Swiss Science and Technology Council*.

Narula, R. (2004). R&D collaboration by SMEs: new opportunities and limitations in the face of globalisation. *Technovation*, *24*(2), 153–161. https://doi.org/10.1016/S0166-4972(02)00045-7

Network, R. S. (2014). Performance Management Collecting and Using Data to Measure Progress , Improve Results. *U.S. Department of Education*, (February).

Nik Ab Halim, N. A., & Zain, M. S. N. (2011). The Internationalization Theory and Malaysian Small Medium Enterprises (SMEs). *International Journal of Trade, Economics and Finance*, *2*(4), 318–322.

Parsons, E., Goddard, E., Seabrooke-spencer, D. J., & White, L. (2012). The Case for a Systems Approach to Manage Technological Innovation. *XXIII ISPIM Conference - Action for Innovation: Innovation from Experience*, (June).

Patra, S. K., & Krishna, V. V. (2015). Globalization of R&D and open innovation: linkages of foreign R&D centers in India. *Journal of Open Innovation: Technology, Market, and Complexity*, *1*(1), 7. https://doi.org/10.1186/s40852-015-0008-6

Peters, B., & Schmiele, A. (2010). The influence of international dispersed vs. home-based R&D on innovation performance. *Centre for European Economic Research*.

Petraite, M. (2013). R & D innovation through networks and collaboration : linking innovation capabilities globally, (June).

Rhee, J., Park, T., & Lee, D. H. (2010). Drivers of innovativeness and performance for innovative SMEs in South Korea: Mediation of learning orientation. *Technovation*, *30*(1), 65–75. https://doi.org/10.1016/j.technovation.2009.04.008

Schneckenberg, D., Velamuri, V. K., Comberg, C., & Spieth, P. (2015). Business model innovation and decision-making : Uncovering mechanisms for coping with uncertainty Business model innovation and decision-making : Uncovering mechanisms for coping with uncertainty. *R&D Management*, (November), 1–35. https://doi.org/10.1111/radm.12205

Su, Y. S., Tsang, E. W. K., & Peng, M. W. (2009). How do internal capabilities and external partnerships affect innovativeness? *Asia Pacific Journal of Management*, *26*(2), 309–331. https://doi.org/10.1007/s10490-008-9114-3

Sung-Wook, K. (2012). An Identification of Unsuccessful, Failure Factors of Technology Innovation and Development in SMEs: A Case Study of Components and Material Industry. *International Journal of Business and Management*, *7*(19), 16. https://doi.org/10.5539/ijbm.v7n19p16

Thorgren, S., Wincent, J., Örtqvist, D., Thomas, N., Network, R. S., Meissner, D., ... Daly, H. E. (2012). How to Drive Innovation and Business Growth: Leveraging Emerging Technology for Sustainable Growth. *Technovation*, *31*(1), 1–10. https://doi.org/10.5465/AMP.2011.59198451

Un, C. A., & Asakawa, K. (2015). Types of R&D collaborations and process innovation: The benefit of collaborating upstream in the knowledge chain. *Journal of Product Innovation Management*, *32*(1), 138–153. https://doi.org/10.1111/jpim.12229

Wasniewski, K. (2010). Corporate strategies - the institutional approach. *Journal of Advanced Research in Management*, (10595).

Wikhamn, W., & Styhre, A. (2016). Open innovation in SMEs : a study of the Swedish bio-pharmaceutical industry. *Journal of Small Business and Enterprreneurship*, *28*(2).

Wynarczyk, P., Piperopoulos, P., & McAdam, M. (2013). Open innovation in small and medium-sized enterprises: An overview. *International Small Business Journal*, *31*(3), 240–255. https://doi.org/10.1177/0266242612472214

Effectuation, Bricolage and the Theory of Planned Behavior: Towards a Conceptual Framework for Inclusiveness

Jule Asikin Julai Poh, Kamarulzaman Ab. Aziz and Intan Soraya Rosdi
Multimedia University, Cyberjaya, Malaysia
jule_poh@live.com.my
kamarulzaman.aziz@mmu.edu.my
soraya.rosdi@mmu.edu.my

Abstract: The Base of the Pyramid (BoP) population refers to the world's four billion people with a daily income of below 4 USD, with most lacking access to basic amenities, and they are largely from the developing economies of Asia, Africa, and Latin America. A firm that adopts inclusive innovation engages in the development of new products or services at significantly low costs with affordable prices that caters to the BoP segment. While many large MNCs have been unsuccessful in addressing the BoP market, many innovative SMEs have shown to do better as they adapt faster to dynamic environments and customer needs. However, more needs to be explored in order to fully understand the factors that influence the decision by firms to behave inclusively and adopt inclusive innovation to meet the needs of those at the BoP. Effectuation is described as a process in which a set of means is taken as given, and the entrepreneur focuses on selecting between possible effects that can be created with that set of means. Bricolage is the concept of making do by applying combinations of the resources at hand to new problems and opportunities. Meanwhile, the theory of planned behavior is one of the major theories used by researchers to explain various behaviors. The objective of the paper is to present a framework capturing how various dimensions of the individual decision-making process impact SMEs' tendencies to engage in the inclusive behavior, specifically in adopting inclusive innovations as their offering to address the BoP consumers. It is believed that the theory of planned behavior, effectuation and bricolage can serve as the underlying models for the framework. The paper presents the reasoning and discussions of this proposed framework. It serves as a valuable reference for researchers, policymakers, SMEs and relevant institutions aspiring to inculcate inclusiveness in their respective spheres.

Keywords: innovation, inclusive innovation, theory of planned behavior, effectuation, bricolage

1. Introduction

Inclusive innovation through opportunity creation approach has been widely discussing as a solution to poverty. The concept is by having private-sector firms create entrepreneurship among the base of pyramid (BoP) segment (Baumol, Litan, and Schramm, 2007) through co-creation (London, 2009) with the collaboration between government and non-governmental organizations (Simanis and Hart, 2009) to improve living standards in developing countries. There is a growth in firms who are exploring ways to produce innovative products and services focused on developing country markets but such innovation is less inclusive (Foster and Heeks, 2016), indicating a lack of inclusive innovation products and services. Therefore, there is a need to examine the inclusion intention in taking action to produce innovative products and services to form opportunities.

According to George, Mcgahan, and Prabhu (2012), Inclusive innovation referred to the development and realization of new ideas which seek to create opportunities that develop social and economic wellbeing for disenfranchised members of society. While Sarasvathy (2008) viewed entrepreneurs as taking actions to exploit opportunities instead of creating profit opportunities by acting experimentally, incrementally and with limited foresight. Taking advantage of resources currently at hand is labeled as bricolage (Baker and Nelson, 2005; Garud and Karnoe, 2003). The Global Research Alliance Organization suggested several key features of inclusive innovation including affordability, sustainability, quality, accessibility for marginalized populations and extensive outreach (GRA,2012).

Most of the previous research on BoP innovation has over-emphasized on innovation models of Multinational Corporations (MNCs) designed for developed countries (Prahalad and Hart, 2002; London, 2008; Williams et al., 2011). Little attention is paid to innovation models involving local actors from emerging markets (Ray and Ray, 2010) particularly, concerning innovation activities in resource-constraint settings leading to a gap in the business activities of local entrepreneurs. Furthermore, the majority of research in this area consists of successful case examples of how the product or new business model innovation improves the life of the poor population by looking at the role of customers, entrepreneurs, or employees. However, there is a lack of theoretical knowledge that shed light on what motivates entrepreneur particularly small, medium enterprises (SMEs) to engage in inclusive innovation.

Socially, governments encourage the poorer communities to participate in SMEs as a mean for income redistribution and poverty alleviation strategies (Suyderhoud, 1999; Chan, 2005). This is due to SMEs are more focused on the low-income groups. The inclusivity is for ensuring accessibility to product and services among the lower income communities in the nation. Big businesses also rely on SMEs to be able to meet the demand for goods and services in an expanding customer base (Katua, 2014).

The question remains as to "What are the determinants of inclusive innovation behaviour among SMEs?" By reviewing studies on individual decision-making and inclusive innovation, this paper aims to construct a model capturing the determinants of inclusive innovation behaviour among SMEs. The following sections review theories that have the potential to explain the determinants of inclusive innovation behaviour and discuss the proposed model.

1.1 Entrepreneurship concept

Business strategy introduced by Prahalad and Hart (2002) and the term evolved to the base of the pyramid (Hammond, Kramer, Katz, Tran, and Walker, 2007; Landrum, 2007) because the people at the BoP are the strength and driving force of the market economy (Reza, 2009). Four billion people are living at the BoP globally. Companies considering BoP as a business strategy need to come up with new products and venture into totally diverse market segments through the components of sustainable development. In order to create anything of value, entrepreneurs need to identify opportunities on which they can act. Initially, individual must undergo a decision process in which action is chosen if market process is to occur (McMullen and Shepherd, 2006). The decision can be made using an inductive, iterative, and incremental process such as effectuation (Sarasvathy, 2001) or bricolage (Baker and Nelson, 2005). An entrepreneur may identify an opportunity for a new product or service, but if resources required are inaccessible or the process of acquiring the resources is challenging (Brush, Greene, and Hart, 2001), he/she can be demotivated to act on the opportunity. Entrepreneurs who focus on the resources under their control when identifying an entrepreneurial opportunity will readily have some of the resources on hand to act on the opportunity, and, therefore, they will more readily take action to create value from the identified opportunity. There have been several theories that have been used to explain entrepreneurship behaviour. However, this study adopts the theory of planned behavior, the theory of effectuation and theory of bricolage in which the concept and framework will be explained in the following sections.

2. Theory of Planned Behaviour (TPB)

Theory of planned behavior (TPB) is a socio-cognitive theory that has been successfully applied in variety of fields (Beck and Ajzen,1991; Harland et al., 1999). In organizational settings, the TPB has been used to understand phenomena such as technology adoption (Sahouly, 2015), worker intention towards an employee participation program (Dawkins and Frass, 2005), and practices of structured interview techniques in staff selection (Van Der Zee, Bakker, and Bakker, 2002). TPB seems to offer an appropriate theoretical framework to understand and predict entrepreneurial intention towards inclusive innovation by taking into consideration of personal and social factors. Intentions have been shown to be the best predictor of planned behaviour. Thus, based on Ajzen (1991), intentions help to understand the act itself, leading to the question of whether the factors that explained the intentions encourage the act of implementing inclusive innovation. There are three components including attitude, subjective norms, and perceived behavioral control (Ajzen, 1991).

2.1 Attitude

The intention of taking inclusive innovation actions should increase if the manager has a positive attitude toward it. This relationship is summarised in the following proposition:

P1: A favourable attitude towards behaviour is positively related to the intention to adopt an inclusive innovation.

2.2 Subjective norms

Subjective norm can also help to explain the intention of implementing inclusive innovation. In particular, the subjective norm is the manager's perception of the inclusive innovation adoption, which is influenced by the company's important reference groups, i.e colleagues, friends, co-worker, employees etc. This lead to the following proposition:

P2: A favourable subjective norm is positively related to the intention to adopt an inclusive innovation.

2.3 Perceived Behavioral Control

Perceived behavioral control denotes to the perception of ease or difficulty of performing the behaviour that the manager desires to perform, and favors an increase in the intention of performing inclusive innovation actions. Furthermore, Ajzen (1991) argues that intention is a sufficient predictor of behaviour in situations where the individual has a very high degree of volitional control over the behaviour. However, in situations where there are problems with volitional control, perceived behaviourial control should be additionally and independently predictive of behaviour. The rationale is that individuals will exert additional effort given increased feelings of control and that action not only depends on intentions but also on non-motivational factors such as the availability of opportunities and resources. This translates into the following relationship:
P3: A favourable perceived behavioural control is positively related to the intention to adopt an inclusive innovation.

2.4 TPB and Behaviour

Behavioural intention is an indication of an individual's readiness to carry out a given behaviour or action. It is perceived to be the immediate antecedent of behaviour. This intention is based on attitude toward the behaviour, subjective norm, and perceived behavioural control with each predictor subjective for its importance about the behaviour and population of interest (Ajzen, 2006). As applied in this study, behavioural intention is an individual's intent to implement inclusive innovation. The context of this study is understood to be SMEs. All the earlier propositions stated regarding the specific context of explaining an individual's decision to adopt an inclusive innovation. As intention is a strong predictor for behaviour, it thus proposed that;
P4: A favourable intention to adopt inclusive innovation is positively related to subsequent inclusive innovation behaviour.

3. Theory of Effectuation

In the context of inclusive innovation, this paper proposes for the components of TPB to be enhanced by including 'effectuation.' Effectuation is described by Sarasvathy (2008) as "a logic of entrepreneurial expertise, a dynamic and interactive process of creating new artifacts in the world." A conceptual model of effectuation in market and venture creation was initially drawn by Sarasvathy (2001) and expanded upon by Sarasvathy and Dew (2005), and by Sarasvathy (2008). The theory suggests that under conditions of uncertainty, entrepreneurs adopt a decision logic that is different to that explicated by a traditional, more rational causation model of entrepreneurship. Effectuation commands that in highly uncertain and dynamic environments, target customers can only be defined ex-post through whoever buys a product or service. Goals change shaped and constructed over time and are sometimes formed by chance. Instead of focusing on goals, the entrepreneur exerts control over the available set of means the things over which the entrepreneur has control (Sarasvathy, 2001). At the firm level, this include physical, human and organizational resources (Barney, 1991). In a study Fisher (2012), provided evidence support for several effectual dimensions including, means, affordable loss, leveraging strategic partnerships and leveraging contingencies.

3.1 Means

Under uncertainty, entrepreneurs focus on the controllable means rather than end-goal and attempt to create any number of successful alternative future outcomes. At the individual level, means include personal knowledge, skills, and social networks. Having a means orientation can help in the evaluation process through visualization of the business as a whole while those with less entrepreneurial experience tend to make remote marketing decisions (Read, Dew, Sarasvathy, Song, & Wiltbank, 2015). At the screening stage, knowing how an idea could fit into the overall picture of the organization is an important skill. The ability to imagine what the final product would look like and work backward given the means such as time, budget, political realities, etc is an improvement to the new product development process (Gary, 2003). The intention is formed by taking one step forward at a time, to learn from that, and to re-evaluate their goals and plans (Valliere, 2015). Lichtenthaler (2009) concluded that the resources and knowledge creation that are based on existing resources and knowledge are essential in uncertain environments because institutions constantly face new challenges.Thus, it is proposed;
P5: Means is positively related to the intention to adopt an inclusive innovation.

3.2 Affordable loss

Affordable loss describes situations where decisions are made with the objective of lessening risk, adhering to budgets and schedules as well as leads to process efficiency (Dew et al., 2009). In other words, rather than investing in calculations about expected returns, potential entrepreneurs are willing to forgo if the actions they engage in happen to not lead to real opportunities to produce new products or services (Sarasvathy,2008). Entrepreneurs who thinks in terms of "how much can I afford to lose in this business" rather than "what rate of return could I anticipate", believe that their company performs better than the businesses of entrepreneurs who don't. It is proposed;

P6: Affordable loss thinking is positively related to the intention to adopt an inclusive innovation.

3.3 Leveraging strategic partnerships

The partner's dimension of effectuation refers to the involvement of partners in the decision-making and innovation process in order to expand means. The construct of cross-functional integration argued that institutions be dependent upon environments for the resources necessary for organizational survival (Olson et al., 2001). Thus, effectuator tries to reduce uncertainty and erect barriers to entry by making strategic partnerships with stakeholders instead of doing external analyses and formal planning. Thus;

P7: Partnership is positively related to the intention to adopt an inclusive innovation.

3.4 Acknowledging the unexpected

Effectuators tend to remain flexible since the structure of the emerging organization is dependent on unexpected opportunities and the particular investments made by stakeholders. Thus, the need for prediction is significantly reduced (Sarasvathy, 2001). Entrepreneurs maintain the flexibility necessary to abandon unfruitful experiments and move to other possibilities.

P8: Acknowledging the unexpected is positively related to the intention to adopt an inclusive innovation.

3.5 Effectuation and Behaviour

Chandler et al. (2011) argued that the specific actions and manifestations of the components including experimentation, affordable loss, flexibility, and pre-commitments be aggregated to form the effectuation construct. Therefore, the degree to which one effectuates is an amalgamation of involvement in each of the sub-dimensions of effectuation. Nelson (2012) found that entrepreneurs with more experience have a greater effectual intent of seeking out pre-commitments before starting a new venture. The results also portrayed the intention of the entrepreneur on the business performance is positively related to the inclination to experiment, be flexible, and to evaluate business opportunities by considering how much one can afford to lose. Corporate entrepreneurs do use effectuation to progress innovative ideas to viable products or services.

P9: Intention mediates the positive effect of effectuation on subsequent inclusive innovation behaviour.

4. Theory of Bricolage

In the context of inclusive innovation, this paper proposes another construct referred to as 'bricolage' as another determinant for inclusive innovation behaviour. Baker and Nelson (2005) defined bricolage as "making do by applying combinations of the resources at hand to new problems and opportunities." Entrepreneurs attempt to overcome resource constraints by engaging in resource-seeking behaviours for instance by engaging in lengthy processes of trying to attract new investments into firms (Brush, Greene, and Hart, 2001). In bricolage, making do includes a bias for action (Baker and Nelson, 2005; Stark, 1989), suggesting that entrepreneurs construct and pursue opportunities without delaying attempts to pursue the right resources for the challenge. Bricolage behaviour generates innovative solutions to social problems of large amplitude and is thus likely to be positively associated with greater scaling of social impact. Indeed, recent research by Senyard et al., (2014) has noted a strong connection between bricolage and innovativeness, considered as a tool that helps entrepreneurs in new ventures become more innovative despite the resource limitations they face. Its is then proposed;

P10: Bricolage is positively related to inclusive innovation behaviour.

5. Inclusive innovation

This study proposes the measure of inclusiveness of the product or service being avail to the markets by the SME as indicator for inclusive innovation behaviour. The measure will be oprationalised based on the dimensions of inclusive innovations; affordable access, sustainable business, high quality, and excluded population as described in the subsections below. Massive outreach is exluded as often market reach of SMEs are rather limited.

5.1 Affordable Access (AA)

"Inclusive innovation will have to be directed at `extreme reduction' in both the production costs and distribution costs." Key elements for this dimension are; I) significant reduction in output costs to allow affordable price, and II) significant reduction in distribution costs to allow reasonable price.

5.2 Sustainable Business (SB)

"After an extended period, the 'affordable access' must not rely on the government financial aid or benevolent government procurement support systems but should work by retaining the market principles with which the private sector works comfortably." Thus, the key elements are; I) not reliant on government subsidies, II) not reliant on significant government procurement, III) not reliant on charity and CSR, and IV) a sustainable business model.

5.3 High Quality (HQ)

"Recognizing the essential rights of the people at the base of the pyramid, who have the same wants should be enjoying almost the same level of quality of utilities as individuals at the top of the pyramid." The key features are; I) meeting quality standards, II) do not lose quality to lower the costs, and III) similar quality level with those of similar products available in the market.

5.4 Excluded Population (EP)

"The excluded population or the disenfranchised, commonly marginalized groups could be referred to the poor, the disabled, the migrants, the women, the youth, the elderly, certain ethnic minorities, and so on." The features are; I) intended for the poor, the disabled, the migrants, the women, the youth, the elderly, certain ethnic minorities, and so on, II) set a price with the poor in mind, and III) distribution intended to make sure ease of access for the poor, the disabled, the migrants, the women, the youth, the elderly, certain ethnic minorities, and so on.

6. Intention and Behaviour

According to Welsch et al. (2013), growth intentions and innovation can contribute to SME outcomes. SME activity makes a significant contribution to economic and social wellbeing as often new small firms will generate jobs, enhance productivity, play a major role in innovation and provide alternative employment opportunities for many subsets of the adult population (Autio, E., 2005). Small firm growth is a consequence of clear, positively motivated business intentions and actions of the owner-entrepreneur, driven by the belief that one's can produce the desired outcomes.

Based on the preceding sections, TPB provides an excellent model to understand the precursors for behaviour. The combination of both TPB and effectuation, as proposed by Jeger, Sušanj and Mijoč (2014), provides a better explanation of entrepreneurial behaviour. Given the nature of inclusive innovation, it thus suggested that inclusive innovation behaviour for business purposes among SMEs might be effectively explained by the theoretical model combining TPB, Effectuation, and Bricolage. Figure 1 below presents the proposed framework. Additionally, it is proposed that the relationship between TPB components and behaviour, the relationship between effectuation and behaviour, and the relationship between bricolage and behaviour, are mediated by intention.

7. Contributions to Theory

To date, the research surrounds inclusive innovation is still relatively under-researched and under-conceptualised. For a better understanding of how SMEs develop the intention to engage in actions that entailed inclusive innovation, it is necessary to analyse the determinants of this intention and the determinants of inclusive innovation. Thus, it should be pointed out that in this type of businesses, the inclusive behaviour is the reflection of the individual entrepreneurial intentions, i.e., innovator-entrepreneur. Thus, this study adopts TPB as a first steps for a better understanding of the significance of the factors in Ajzen's model in explaining SME intentions to engage in inclusive innovation actions and integrating the entrepreneurial theory of effectuation and theory of entrepreneurial bricolage to explain further the logics and actions that underlying the entrepreneur behaviour driving the SMEs. In line with the call for a better development of theory within the field of management on inclusive innovation, this may contribute to the novel findings of inclusive innovation inside organizations.

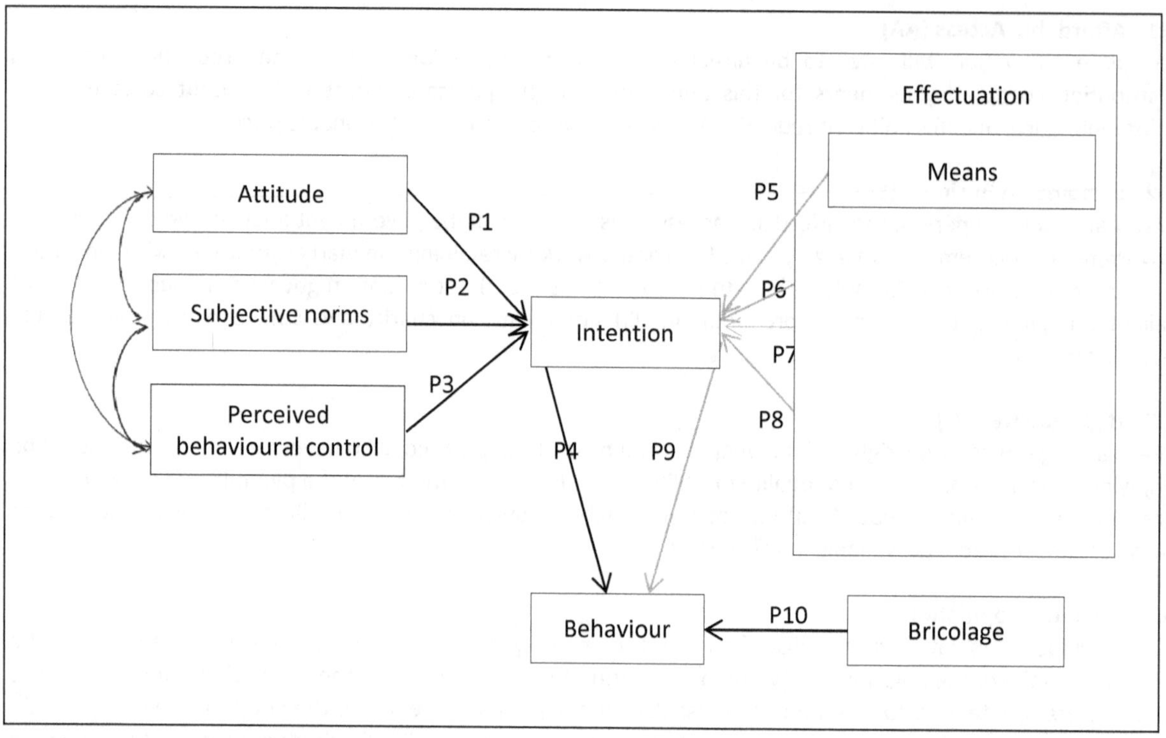

Figure 1: Proposed Framework for Inclusive Innovation in SMEs

8. Implications for Practice

Economic, technological and knowledge resources are not sufficient if the person does not have a positive attitude and the capacity to adopt the necessary actions. Opportunity recognition that focuses on the resources under the control of the people seeking to launch a venture is likely to help entrepreneurs identify opportunities that are actionable. Therefore, encouraging opportunity recognition that orientates on the resources under one's control and then pushes them to find a market gap utilizing these resources will likely lead to entrepreneurial action. Furthermore, this research reinforces the importance of action in the entrepreneurial process. Entrepreneurs who engage in experimentation and who interact early and often with customers will be able to overcome many of the obstacles especially associated with starting a venture.

9. Conclusion

TPB predict entrepreneurial intention by taking into account personal and social factors while the theory of effectuation and bricolage attempt to satisfy the aspiration by considering the limited resources setting. Thus, in the penurious environment, entrepreneur intent to do business at the BoP market need to take into consideration of means, affordable loss, leveraging strategic partnerships and leveraging contingencies in order to achieve sustainable business; ensure affordable access to high quality goods and include the often excluded population.

References

Ajzen, I. (1991) The Theory of Planned Behavior. *Organizational Behavior and Human Decision Processes*, 50, 179–211. http://doi.org/10.1016/0749-5978(91)90020.

Ajzen, I. (2001) "Nature and Operation of Attitudes", *Annual Review of Psychology*, Vol. 52, pp. 27–58. DOI: http://dx.doi.org/10.1146/annurev.psych.52.1.27.

Ajzen, I. (2002) Perceived Behavioural Control, Self-Efficacy, Locus Of Control, and the Theory of Planned Behaviour. *Journal of Applied Social Psychology*, 32(4), 665–683.

Ajzen, I. (2006) Constructing a TPB Questionnaire: Conceptual and Methodological Considerations. Retrieved June 27, 2011 from the World Wide Web: http://www.people.umass.edu/aizen/pdf/tpb.measurement.pdf.

Aziz, K. A. (2016) Convergence and inclusive innovation in the communications sector. International Conference on Advanced Communication Technology, ICACT, 2016–March, 218–222. http://doi.org/10.1109/ICACT.2016.7423336.

Baker, T. and Nelson, R.E. (2005) Creating Something from Nothing: Resource Construction through Entrepreneurial Bricolage. *Administrative Science Quarterly*, 50(3), 329–366.

Barney, J.B. (1991) Firm Resources and Sustained Competitive Advantage. *Journal of Management*, 17(1), 99–120.

Baumol, W., Litan, R., & Schramm, C. (2007). Good capitalism, bad capitalism, and the economics of growth and prosperity. Retrieved from http://papers.ssrn.com/sol3/ papers.cfm?abstract id=985843&download=yes

Beck, L. and Ajzen, I. (1991) 'Predicting Dishonest Actions using the Theory of Planned Behavior.' *Journal of Research in Personality*, 25 (3): 285–301.

Brush, C.G., Greene, P.G., and Hart, M.M. (2001). From initial idea to unique advantage: the entrepreneurial challenge of constructing a resource base. *Academy of Management Executive,* 15 (1), 64-80.

Chandler, G. N., Detienne, D. R., Mckelvie, A., & Mumford, T. V. (2011). Journal of Business Venturing Causation and effectuation processes : A validation study. Journal of Business Venturing, 26(3), 375–390. http://doi.org/10.1016/j.jbusvent.2009.10.006

Chan, S. H. (2005) An Exploratory Study of Using Micro-Credit to Encourage the Setting up of Small Business in the Rural Sector of Malaysia. *Asian Business & Management,* 4(4), 455-479.

Dawkins, C. E., and Frass, J. W. (2005) Decision of Union Workers to Participate in Employee Involvement: An Application of the Theory of Planned Behavior, *Employee Relations,* 27, 511- 531.

Dew, N., Read, S., Sarasvathy, S. D., & Wiltbank, R. (2009) Effectual versus Predictive Logics in Entrepreneurial Decision-making: Differences between Experts and Novices. *Journal of Business Venturing*, 24(4), 287–309. http://doi.org/10.1016/j.jbusvent.2008.02.002.

Dew, N., Sarasvathy, S.D., Read, S., Wiltbank, R., (2009) Affordable loss: behavioral economic aspects of the plunge decision. *Strategic Entrepreneurship Journal* 3, 105–126.

Fisher, G. (2012) E T & P and Bricolage : A of Emerging Theories, 1019–1051. http://doi.org/10.1111/j.1540-6520.2012.00537.x.

Foster, C., and Heeks, R. (2016). Drivers of Inclusive Innovation in Developing County Markets: A Policy Perspective. *Inclusive Innovation for Sustainable Development*, DOI 10.1057/978-1-137-60168-1_4

Garud, R., & Karnøe, P. (2003). Bricolage versus breakthrough: Distributed and embedded agency in technology entrepreneurship. *Research Policy,* 32, 277–300.

Gary, L. (2003) Dealing with a Project's "Fuzzy Front End". *Harvard Management Update*, 8(6), 3.

George, G., Mcgahan, A. M., and Prabhu, J. (2012) Innovation for Inclusive Growth: Towards a Theoretical Framework and a Research Agenda. *Journal of Management Studies*, 49(4), 661–683. http://doi.org/10.1111/j.1467-6486.2012.01048.x.

Global Research Alliance. (2012) "Inclusive Innovation." Available: http://theglobalresearchalliance.org/en/What-we-do/InclusiveInnovation.aspx.

Goyal, A. (2016) Conditions for Inclusive Innovation with Application to Telecom and Mobile Banking. *Innovation and Development*, *9318*(June), 1–22. http://doi.org/10.1080/2157930X.2016.1187845.

Hammond, A. L., Kramer, W. J., Katz, R. S., Tran, J. T., and Walker, C. (2007). The next 4 billion. *Innovations: Technology, Governance, Globalization*, 2(1–2), 147–158.

Harland, P., Staats, H. and Wilke, H. (1999) 'Explaining Pro Environmental Intention and Behavior by Personal Norms and the Theory Of Planned Behavior.'*Journal of Applied Social Psychology*, 29 (2): 505–28.

Halme, M., Lindeman, S., and Linna, P. (2012) Innovation for Inclusive Business : Intrapreneurial Bricolage in Multinational Corporations Minna Halme , Sara Lindeman and Paula Linna. http://doi.org/10.1111/j.1467-6486.2012.01045.x.

Jeger, M., Sušanj, Z. and Mijoč, J. (2014) Entrepreneurial Intention Modeling using Hierarchical Multiple Regression. *Croatian Operational Research Review,* 5, 361–373.

Katua, N. T. (2014) The Role of SMEs in Employment Creation and Economic Growth in Selected Countries. *International Journal of Education and Research*, *2*(12), 461–472.

Krueger, N. F. Jr., Reilly, M. D. and Carsrud, A. L. (2000) Competing Model of Entrepreneurial Intentions. *Journal of Business Venturing*, 15(5-6):411-432.

Landrum, N. E. (2007) Advancing the "base of the pyramid" debate. *Strategic Management Review*, 1(1), 1–12.

Lichtenthaler, U., 2009. Absorptive capacity, environmental turbulence, and the complementarity of organizational learning processes. *Academy of Management Journal 52 (4)*, 822–846.

London, T. (2009).Making better investments at the base of the pyramid. *Harvard Business Review,* 87(5), 106–113.

McMullen, J.S. and Shepherd, D.A. (2006) Entrepreneurial action and the role of uncertainty in the theory of the entrepreneur. *Academy of Management Review*, 31(1), 132–152.

Olson, E., Walker, O., Ruekert, R., Bonner, J., (2001) Patterns of cooperation during new product development among marketing, operations and R&D: implications for project performance. *The Journal of Product Innovation Management 18*, 258–271.

Prahalad, C. K., and Hart, S. L. (2002) The Fortune at the Bottom of the Pyramid. *Strategy and Business,* 20, 1–13.

Ray PK, Ray S. (2010) Resource-constrained Innovation for Emerging Economies: The Case of the Indian Telecommunications Industry. *IEEE Trans Eng Manage* 57(1):144–156.

Read, S., Dew, N., Sarasvathy, S. D., Song, M., & Wiltbank, R. (2015). Marketing Under Uncertainty: The Logic of an Effectual Approach. The Effects of Brief Mindfulness Intervention on Acute Pain Experience: Examination of Individual Difference, 1(503), 1689–1699http://doi.org/10.1017/CBO9781107415324.004

Reza, A. S. (2009) What BoP means for business. Paper presented at the LIRNEasia 5th year anniversary conference, Sri Lanka.

Rebernik et al. (2006) GEM Slovenia 2005: Podjetništvo Med`eljami in Stvarnostjo. IPMMP, Maribor.

Sarasvathy, S.D. (2001) Causation and Effectuation: Towards a Theoretical Shift from Economic Inevitability to Entrepreneurial Contingency. *Academy of Management Review,* 26(2), 243–288.

Sarasvathy, S.D. (2008) Effectuation: Elements of Entrepreneurial Expertise. *New Horizons in Entrepreneurship Research.* Cheltenham, U.K.: Edward Elgar Publishing.

Sarasvathy, S.D. and Dew, N. (2005) New Market Creation as Transformation. *Journal of Evolutionary Economics,* 15(5), 533–565.

Sarasvathy, S., Dew, N., Velamuri, S., and Venkataraman, S. (2003) Three Views of Entrepreneurial Opportunity. In Z. Acs & D. Audretsch (Eds.), Handbook of entrepreneurship research (pp. 141-160). Norwell, MA: Kluwer Academic.

Sahouly, I. Al. (2015) Resurrecting Information Technology Adoption Models : A Theoretic Foundation. *IRACST-International Journal of Research in Management & Technology (IJRMT), 5*(December), 9.

Senyard, J.M., Baker, T., and Davidsson, P. (2009) Entrepreneurial Bricolage: Towars systematic empirical testing. *Frontiers of Entrepreneurship Research*, 29(5), 5–15..

Senyard, J.M., Baker, T., Steffens, P.R., and Davidsson, P. (2014) Bricolage as a Path to Innovativeness for Resource Constrained New Firms, *Journal of Product Innovation Management*, Vol 31, No 2, pp 211–230. http://doi.org/10.1111/jpim.12091

Simanis, E.,&Hart, S. (2006). Expanding possibilities at the base of the pyramid. *Innovations: Technology, Governance, Globalization*, 1(1), 43–51. doi:10.1162/itgg.2006.1.1.43

Širec, K., & Bradač, B. (2009) How does Networking Impact the SMEs Growth. *Organizacija*, 42(2), 59–66. http://doi.org/10.2478/v10051-009-0003-4.

Stark, D. (1989). Bending the bars of the iron cage : bureaucratization and informalization in capitalism and socialism. Notre Dame, Ind.: The Helen Kellogg Institute for International Studies University of Notre Dame.

Suyderhoud, J. P. (1999) The Malaysian Economic Development Challenge: Can Productivity Growth Co-exist with Income Redistribution? 7th Tun Abdul Razak International Conference, Penang.

Valliere, D. (2015) ScienceDirect An Effectuation Measure of Entrepreneurial Intent. Procedia - Social and Behavioral Sciences, 169(August 2014), 131–142. http://doi.org/10.1016/j.sbspro.2015.01.294

van der Zee, K. I., Bakker, A., and Bakker, P. (2002) Why are Structured Interviews so Rarely used in Personnel Selection? *Journal of Applied Psychology,* 87, 176-184.

Van Gelderen, M., Brand, M, Van Praag, M., Bodewes, W., Poutsma, E. and Van Gils, A. (2008) "Explaining Entrepreneurial Intentions By Means of the Theory of Planned Behaviour.

World Resources Institute (2007) The Next 4 Billion: Market Size and Business Strategy at the Base of the Pyramid.

Welsch, H., Price, D. P., and Stoica, M. (2013) Innovation , Performance and Growth Intentions in SMEs. *International Journal of Economics and Management Engineering*, 3(5), 176–18l

Williams, D. R., González, H.M., Williams, S., Mohammed, S. A., Moomal, H. and Stein, D. J. (2008) Perceived Discrimination, Race and Health in South Africa: Findings from the South Africa Stress and Health Study. *Social Science and Medicine*, 67:441-452.

A Framework for Knowledge-Driven Innovation in Small and Medium Enterprises

Jia En Lee, Intan Soraya Rosdi and Chew Kok Wai
Multimedia University, Cyberjaya, Malaysia
en_lee@ymail.com
soraya.rosdi@mmu.edu.my
kwchew@mmu.edu.my

Abstract: Increasingly complex business environments and strong competition from both international and local players place tremendous pressure on small and medium enterprises (SMEs) to improve their innovation performance. A firm's innovative capability refers to its ability to manage its key competences and resources to spur innovative activities, and it is closely linked to the firm's ability to continuously acquire and manage new knowledge. New knowledge from external sources is the key to the success of many innovative SMEs. As employees in SMEs are in fact the firms' knowledge storehouses, the field of human resource management (HRM) becomes relevant. This paper focuses on innovation-centric HRM practices, which are HRM practices designed to stimulate knowledge creation, transfer, and integration processes, which in turn, stimulate innovation. Currently, models of innovation for SMEs which take into account how a firm's knowledge base and innovation-centric HRM practices influence its innovative capability seem limited. Hence, this paper seeks to address the question: How can knowledge sources and innovation-centric HRM practices influence the innovative capability of SMEs? The paper objective is to present a framework on how different types of external knowledge sources and innovation-centric HRM practices contribute to building intellectual capital and the innovative capability of SMEs. Resource-based theory is used as the underlying theory for the framework. The main contribution of this paper is the identification of a specific framework for the development of innovative capability in SMEs. It can be a guide for SMEs as well as for governments and relevant institutions engaged in devising strategies to drive innovation in SMEs.

Keywords: Small and medium enterprises, innovative capability, intellectual capital, human resource management, knowledge sources.

1. Introduction

There is an increasing pressure on SMEs in Malaysia to improve their innovative capability as they face today's volatile and complex business environment. Effective management of knowledge is vital for innovation in firms (De Winne and Sels, 2010) as knowledge is needed in finding opportunities to create new products, processes and services (Van de Ven, 1986). It is important for companies to be innovative in their daily operations so as to gain competitive advantage in the market (Jala, 2013). How a firm utilizes its knowledge base affects its capability to deliver innovation which are either incremental or radical in nature (Subramaniam and Youndt, 2005). According to the study of de Pablos (2004), knowledge is an important resource to enhance the competitiveness of the firm and creates sustain competitive advantage.

A review of literature reveals that models of innovative capability for small and medium enterprises (SMEs) which take into account the influences of a firm's knowledge base on innovative capability seem limited. External sources of knowledge play an important role for SMES as their internal knowledge sources are relatively limited compared to those of large organizations (Henttonen, 2012). Another issue is how the human resources in SMEs could be managed to motivate them to acquire knowledge from outside the firm. Studies on human resource management (HRM) and innovation often refer to this particular type of HRM practice as entrepreneurial HRM practices as they drive employees to seek new knowledge in unchartered territories.

Hence, this study seeks to address the main question: "How can external knowledge sources and entrepreneurial HRM practices influence the innovative capability of Malaysian SMEs?". By reviewing existing studies on external knowledge sources, entrepreneurial HRM practices, intellectual capital and innovative capability, this paper aims to construct a model capturing how the different types of external knowledge sources and relevant human resource management practices contribute to developing the innovative capability of Malaysian SMEs.

2. Literature Review

In this section, literature on SMEs in Malaysia, innovative capability of organizations, intellectual capital, entrepreneurial HRM practices, and knowledge management are discussed as they are relevant to constructing the proposed conceptual framework.

2.1 SMEs in Malaysia

The Small and Medium Enterprise (SME) Corporation Malaysia (SME Corp), previously known as the Small and Medium Industries Development Corporation (SMIDEC), was established in October 2009 to design and develop SME policies and strategies (SME Corporation Malaysia, 2016a). Those SME policies and strategies are aimed to help the growth of the SME industry. SME Corp was appointed by the National SME Development Council (NSDC) to design strategies and monitor the progress of SMEs across all sectors in Malaysia (SME Corporation Malaysia, 2016a).

According to National SME Development Council (2010), the definition of SME in Malaysia is based on two criteria:

a) The number of full-time employees
b) The total sales turnover

SMEs in Malaysia are classified into 3 categories, which are micro, small and medium sized. In Malaysia, SMEs are being classified into 2 broad sectors, which are manufacturing-related and service sectors. These organizations do not have more than 200 full-time employees or their annual sales turnover are not more than RM50 million. SMEs in service sector will not have more than 75 full-time employees or their annual sales turnover are not more than RM20 million (SME Corporation Malaysia, 2016b).

SMEs play an important role in Malaysia's economic development (Saleh and Ndubisi, 2006). Based on a report by the National SME Development Council (2010), the focus of Malaysia's New Economic Model and the Eleventh Malaysia Plan are to unleash the full potential of these SMEs and transform them into more competitive organizations to survive the complex and rapidly changing business environment. 548,267 business establishments are identified as SMEs in Malaysia (National SMEs Development Council of Malaysia, 2010). 86.6% (477,535) of SMEs are in the service sector while 7.2% (40,793) of SMEs are in the manufacturing sector. The remaining 6.2% (34,531) of SMEs are in agriculture sector. Nowadays, SMEs in Malaysia have become crucial in providing 56% of the job opportunities in Malaysia. Furthermore, SMEs in Malaysia contribute 31% to the national GDP. However, this figure is much lower when compared with other Asian counties where their SMEs contribute over 50% of the countries' GDP (Ndubisi, 2008).

2.2 Innovation in SMEs

There are various definitions of 'innovation' in the literature. According to Teece (2010), innovation is the creating of new ideas and the implementation of the new ideas on the product or service. Innovation has also defined as the drastic change of an organization or its existing products and process to gain the sustainable competitive advantage over the competitors (de Leede & Looise, 2005). Researchers like Baregheh, Rowley and Sambrook (2009) defines innovation as the process where firms generate and implement the ideas into improved or new products, services or processes to differentiate themselves and compete in the global market. This study adopts the heavily cited original definition of innovation by Thompson (1965) which defines innovation as "the generation, acceptance and implementation of new ideas, processes, products and services".

According to Baregheh, Rowley and Sambrook (2009), there is no standard and most comprehensive definition of innovation. However, the different definitions of innovation seem to share the common theme which focuses on how knowledge is critical in understanding the needs of customers and obtaining competitive advantage (Gloet & Terziovski, 2004). The continuous pursuit of new knowledge is involved in the process of innovation (Nonaka & Takeuchi, 1995). Hence, the importance of knowledge to the innovation process becomes the focus of this study.

According to Roxas (2008), many studies have stressed the importance of SME sector for the social and economic development of the country. Salim and Sulaiman (2011) has emphasized that there is a positive relationship between organizational innovation and performance of SMEs.

2.3 Innovative Capability

Innovative capability refers to a firm's ability to manage its key competences and resources to spur innovative activities (Fleury, Fleury and Borini, 2013). A firm's key competences and resources involve its administrative, production and operations, marketing, financial, technology, and human resources (Fleury, Fleury and Borini, 2013). A firm's innovative capability is linked closely to its ability for managing, maintaining, and creating knowledge (Camelo-Ordaz, et al., 2011). How a firm utilizes its knowledge base affects its capability to deliver innovation which are either incremental or radical in nature (Subramaniam and Youndt, 2005).

Incremental innovative capability refers to a firm's ability to produce incremental innovations, which involve refining and improving existing products and services (Chandy & Tellis, 2000). Incremental innovative capability leads to minor changes in the firm (Green, Welsh, & Dehler, 2003). Incremental innovation involves improvements on the existing knowledge base (Chang, Gong & Shum, 2011). Radical innovative capability is defined as a firm's ability to create major transformations of existing products, services, or technologies, thus making the existing technologies obsolete (Chandy & Tellis, 2000). Radical innovations disrupt the existing knowledge based or technological pathway to produce something which is significantly new (Gatignon, et al., 2002; Chang, Gong and Shum, 2011).

Based on existing studies, there is only minimal research on innovation characteristics i.e. radical versus incremental innovative capability. Most of the research topics are on innovation outcomes such as technology patents and sales generated from new products, services or process (Subramaniam and Youndt, 2005). In order to enhance market performance, organizations require both incremental and radical innovative capability (Damanpour, 1991).

2.4 Intellectual Capital

Intellectual capital (IC) is defined as the sum of all types of organizational knowledge utilized for the creation of competitive advantage (Youndt, Subramaniam and Snell, 2004). There are three types of intellectual capital within firms (de Pablos, 2004). First is human capital, which is comprised of the knowledge, skills, competencies, and commitment of employees (Edvinsson et al., 1997; Bontis, 1998). Second is social capital, which refers to the knowledge embedded in relationships among employees, current and potential customers, shareholders, suppliers, industry associations, and other parties in the firm's external environment (Daud and Yusoff, 2009). Third is organizational capital, which comprises hardware, software, databases, manuals, policies, strategies, procedures, culture, and other organizational storehouses of knowledge (Bontis, Chua and Richardson, 2000).

All these aspects have complex relationships and are not separable from each other and the absence of either one aspect will result in inefficiency in organizations (Bontis, 1998). There is a possibility that the effectiveness of one aspect of IC depends on the effectiveness of another aspect. For example, one of the researchers has stated that the effectiveness of human capital will be meaningless without the social capital aspect (Bontis, Chua and Richardson, 2000) and that the interaction between human capital and social capital affects the innovative capability of organizations (Subramaniam and Youndt, 2005).

2.5 Human Resource Management (HRM)

Human resource management (HRM) in organizations refers to activities involved in attracting and retaining employees, and managing their performance towards achieving organizational goals (Jones, George & Hill, 2000). In driving people towards innovation, HRM strategies are relevant as HRM focuses on choices made by organizations in their use of the workforce and their impacts on operational and firm performance (Lengnick-Hall, et al., 2009). According to the research of Scarbrough and Carter (2000) and Robertson and Hammersley (2000), HRM plays an important role to develop the intellectual capital of the firm. Within an organization, appropriate HRM practices could help motivate staff to transfer or exchange knowledge with each other (Soliman and Spooner, 2000).

2.5.1 *Entrepreneurial HRM Practices*

The pursuit of new knowledge to replace the existing knowledge base can be done through the access of firm to external knowledge. Scholars refer to this type of HRM approach as 'entrepreneurial' in nature because it encourages firms to explore diverse new ideas in totally unfamiliar territories (Shane & Venkataraman, 2000). New knowledge can be accessed through higher interaction and knowledge exchange between firms' core employees and their external alliance partners (Kang, Morris, and Snell, 2007). This paper focuses on entrepreneurial HRM practices. Having discussed the importance of managing employees to acquire new knowledge, there is a need to properly understand the concept of knowledge management within firms, which is the focus of the following section.

2.6 Knowledge Management and Knowledge Sources

Knowledge management is defined as the process of leveraging the expertise and knowledge in individuals towards value creation for organizations (Scarborough, 2003). It is clear that knowledge in organizations needs to be effectively managed for firms to benefit from them, but a more basic issue would be how to obtain the knowledge in the first place.

Knowledge sources being used by SMEs can come from the firm's internal or external environment (Svetina & Prodan, 2008). Internal sources refer to knowledge within the firm such as employee experience or outcomes of a firm's R&D activities (Kessler, Bierly and Gopalakrishnan, 2000). External knowledge sources refer to the sources of knowledge in a firm's external environment (Bapuji and Crossan, 2004). Examples of external knowledge sources are customers, competitors, alliance partners and universities (Henttonen, 2012).

It has been shown that external knowledge sources are especially important to SMEs as their internal knowledge is relatively limited compared to that of large organizations (Hennttonen, 2012). External knowledge sources can generally be categorized as either scientific-oriented sources or market-oriented sources. Scientific-oriented sources involve scientific actors such as research centers or universities while market-oriented sources include market actors such as competitors and suppliers (Hennttonen, 2012). According to the study of Fleming and Sorenson (2004), scientific knowledge is usually used to enhance technological process and often disconnected from the market. On the other hand, market knowledge is focused on addressing specific customer problems and hence more applicative in nature (Cohen et al., 2002).

2.7 Underlying Theories

This study has identified the resource based theory of the firm and the knowledge based theory of the firm as the underlying theories relevant for the research. The resource-based theory argues that organizations utilize different types of organizational resources to implement their plans or strategies towards obtaining competitive advantage (Grant, 1996). It is the accumulation of organizational resources that creates the unique character of the firm (Kostopoulos et al., 2002). There are four different dimensions of firm resources that could lead to sustainable competitive advantage (Barney, 2000). According to Barney (2000), resources could be classified as physical, human or organizational, but to achieve sustainable competitive advantage, organizations need to have resources which are rare, inimitable, valuable and non-substitutable. Firms will achieve temporary advantage from having rare or valuable resources but the firms would only able to sustain the competitive advantage if they can protect the resource against substitution or resource imitation. Numerous studies have based their work on the resource-based theory.

While the resource-based theory states that valuable resources could help the firm to achieve sustainable competitive advantage while knowledge-based theory states that knowledge is the most influential organizational resource (Nonaka & Takeuchi, 1995). The knowledge-based theory is the extension for the resource-based theory of the firm. Based on these two theories, it seems that the innovative capability of firms is strongly linked to two type of organizational resources, namely employees and knowledge (Egbu, Botterill, & Bates, 2001). According to the work of de Pablos (2004), knowledge is an important resource to enhance the competitiveness of the firm and create sustainable competitive advantage. Both the resource-based and knowledge-based theories are often served as the underlying theories in the organizational innovation study.

In order to have sustained competitive advantage, both employees and knowledge must be managed effectively to enhance the innovative capability of firms (De Winne & Sels, 2010). With all the research constructs duly explained and underlying theories discussed, the next section proposes a research framework.

2.8 Conceptual Framework

This section explains the relationships between each respective construct in this study, namely innovative capability, external knowledge sources, intellectual capital, and entrepreneurial HRM practices. Explanation will then be followed by the relevant hypotheses to be tested in the study.

2.8.1 External Knowledge Sources and Innovative Capability

Utterback (1971) suggests that external knowledge is useful for the whole innovation process, from the idea generation stage to the idea implementation stage. Cohen and Levinthal (1990) then presents that the co-existence of different types of external knowledge will contribute to the innovative activities of the firm. Criscuolo et al. (2005) argue that globally engaged firms tend to be more innovative as they assimilate and exploit the pool of information from different parties, such as suppliers, customers and research centres. Further, Crespi et al. (2008) stresses on the importance of knowledge flow from external parties, especially customers. It is established that different external knowledge sources are important to enhance the innovative capability of organizations (Henttonen, 2012). In existing literature, external knowledge sources are often categorized either as market-oriented knowledge or scientific-oriented knowledge (Schneider, 2009).

Hence, the following propositions are made.

P1a: The use of market-oriented sources of knowledge positively influences a firm's incremental innovative capability.

P1b: The use of market-oriented sources of knowledge positively influences a firm's radical innovative capability.

P2a: The use of scientific-oriented of knowledge positively influences a firm's incremental innovative capability.

P2b: The use of scientific-oriented sources of knowledge positively influences a firm's radical innovative capability.

2.8.2 External Knowledge Sources and Intellectual Capital

In an organization, the development of knowledge and expertise is highly related to the firm's intellectual capital. Interaction with external knowledge sources basically starts with individual employees. Individuals transfer the new knowledge to the group level in the organization when they interact or work with their team or respective departments. Finally, groups will transfer knowledge to the organizational level when it is captured in databases and other methods of organizational documentation (Laine & Laine, 2012). The said processes i.e. individual, group, and organizational levels of knowledge flow can be perceived as contributing to the different types of intellectual capital, namely human, social, and organizational capital. It has been established that different types of external knowledge sources impact a firm's knowledge stocks in different ways (Laine & Laine, 2012).

Thus, the following propositions are made:

P3: The use of market-oriented sources of knowledge positively influences a firm's intellectual capital.

P4: The use of scientific-oriented sources of knowledge positively influences a firm's intellectual capital.

2.8.3 Entrepreneurial HRM Practices and Intellectual Capital

According to previous studies, entrepreneurial HRM practices help to stimulate the individual knowledge acquisition process and hence building human capital. These practices also help improve knowledge exchange between individuals via social networks i.e. social capital. Once the knowledge is transferred into systems or databases in the firm, it becomes organizational capital (Romjin and Albaladejo, 2002; Youndt, Subramaniam and Snell, 2004; Kang, Morris, and Snell, 2007). In this paper, the direct impact of entrepreneurial HRM practices on intellectual capital is reflected via the following proposition:

P5: A firm's entrepreneurial HRM practices positively influence its intellectual capital.

2.8.4 Intellectual Capital and Innovative Capability

The intellectual capital of an organization has direct impacts on both radical and incremental innovation (Rosdi, 2014; Romijn & Albaladejo, 2002; Subramaniam & Youndt, 2005). In terms of human capital, people who are risk takers and open to new experiences will help in developing more radical innovation (Baer, 2007). According to Romijn and Albaladejo (2002), the professional background and skills of employees could help in contributing to both incremental and radical innovations. In terms of social capital, employees who develop relationships with external parties such as suppliers and customers tend to have radical ideas due to their diverse perspective and knowledge (Baer, 2007). According to the study of Romijn and Albaladejo (2002), those firms that interact closely with various external alliances, such as suppliers, funding institutions, research bodies and customers are shown to enhance both radical and incremental innovative capabilities. As for organizational capital, the incorporation of knowledge into operational processes, databases, etc. affects the innovation performance of the firms positively (Gloet & Terziovski, 2004). Hence, the following propositions are made:

P6a: A firm's intellectual capital directly and positively influences its incremental innovative capability

P6b: A firm's intellectual capital directly and positively influences its radical innovative capability

2.8.5 Intellectual Capital as Mediator

While there are studies showing the direct impacts of external knowledge sources on a firm's innovative capability, there are also studies arguing that external knowledge sources impact a firm's innovative capability through its role in building the firm's intellectual capital (Laine and Laine, 2012; Uziene, 2015). As such, additional propositions on the mediated relationships are as follows:

P7a: Intellectual capital mediates the relationship between market-oriented sources of knowledge and a firm's incremental innovative capability.

P7b: Intellectual capital mediates the relationship between market-oriented sources of knowledge and a firm's radical innovative capability.

P8a: Intellectual capital mediates the relationship between scientific-oriented sources of knowledge and a firm's incremental innovative capability.

P8b: Intellectual capital mediates the relationship between scientific-oriented sources of knowledge and a firm's radical innovative capability.

Figure 1 below presents the proposed framework for knowledge-driven innovation in SMEs.

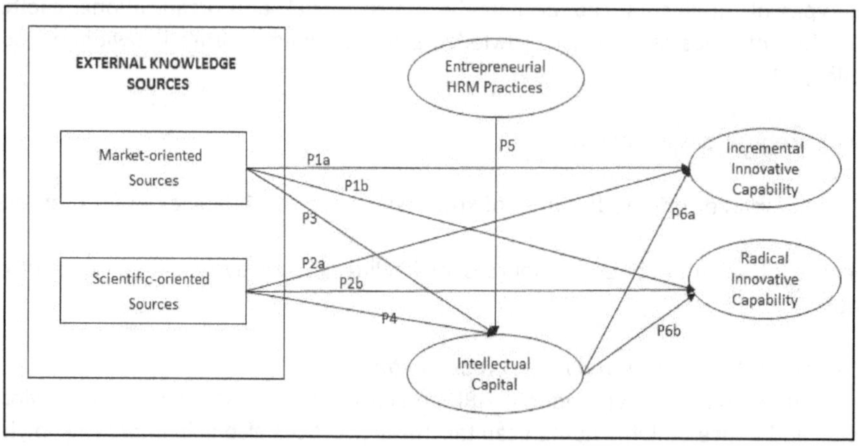

Figure 1: Proposed Conceptual Framework

3. Contributions to Theory

There is a research gap in understanding the relationship between external knowledge sources and organizational innovative capability (Henttonen, 2012). This paper addresses that gap by discussing how different types of external knowledge sources can affect the innovative capability of organizations. It clarifies the links between innovative capability, entrepreneurial HRM practices and external knowledge sources. In addition, this paper provides a different perspective relating to the resource-based theory of the firm, which states that an organization requires different types of resources i.e. human and knowledge resources to create sustainable competitive advantages. Another contribution of this study to the resource-based theory is that evidence is obtained from a multi-disciplinary framework which includes the fields of knowledge management, HRM and innovation.

4. Implications for Practice

The proposed framework is significant for those organizations that place high priorities on the role of external knowledge sources and entrepreneurial HRM practices to enhance the innovative capability of organizations. The importance of managing different types of external knowledge sources to maximize the organizational performance is highlighted. Different external knowledge sources may bring different value to the organizations based on the different type of knowledge that they possess. Furthermore, the proposed framework can be used by SMEs towards building their intellectual capital and innovative capability of firms. It can also be used by the Malaysian government when designing strategies to enhance SME innovative capability.

5. Conclusion

In today's fast changing business environment, firms need to gain competitive advantage by using their innovative capabilities. This paper proposes that SMEs utilizing their external knowledge sources and implementing entrepreneurial HRM practices should be able to build their intellectual capital, which subsequently has a positive impact on their innovative capability. This paper contributes a framework to increase the innovative capability of SMEs to enable them to compete and face the global challenges of the knowledge era.

References

Baer, M., 2007. *Innovation in organizations: The generation and implementation of radical ideas.* Doctoral dissertation. University of Illinois at Urbana-Champaign.

Bapuji, H. and Crossan, M., 2004. From questions to answers: reviewing organizational learning research. *Management Learning*, 35(4), pp.397-417.

Baregheh, A., Rowley, J. and Sambrook, S., 2009. Towards a multidisciplinary definition of innovation. *Management decision*, *47*(8), pp.1323-1339.

Barney, J.B., 2000. Firm resources and sustained competitive advantage. *Advances in Strategic Management*, *17*(1), pp.203-227.

Bontis, N., 1998. Intellectual capital: an exploratory study that develops measures and models. *Management decision*, 36(2), pp.63-76.

Bontis, N., Chua, C.K. and Richardson, S., 2000. Intellectual capital and business performance in Malaysian industries. *Journal of intellectual capital*, 1(1), pp.85-100.

Camelo-Ordaz, C., Garcia-Cruz, J., Sousa-Ginel, E. and Valle-Cabrera, R., 2011. The influence of human resource management on knowledge sharing and innovation in Spain: the mediating role of affective commitment. *The International Journal of Human Resource Management*, 22(07), pp.1442-1463.

Chandy, R.K. and Tellis, G.J., 2000. The incumbent's curse? Incumbency, size, and radical product innovation. *Journal of marketing*, 64(3), pp.1-17.

Chang, S., Gong, Y. and Shum, C., 2011. Promoting innovation in hospitality companies through human resource management practices. *International Journal of Hospitality Management*, 30(4), pp.812-818.

Cohen, W.M. and Levinthal, D.A., 1990. Absorptive capacity: A new perspective on learning and innovation. *Administrative science quarterly*, pp.128-152.

Cohen, W.M., Nelson, R.R. and Walsh, J.P., 2002. Links and impacts: the influence of public research on industrial R&D. *Management science*, *48*(1), pp.1-23.

Crespi, G., Criscuolo, C., Haskel, J.E. and Slaughter, M., 2008. *Productivity growth, knowledge flows, and spillovers* (No. w13959). National Bureau of Economic Research.

Criscuolo, C., Haskel, J.E. and Slaughter, M.J., 2010. Global engagement and the innovation activities of firms. *International Journal of Industrial Organization*, *28*(2), pp.191-202.

Damanpour, F., 1991. Organizational innovation: A meta-analysis of effects of determinants and moderators. *Academy of management journal*, 34(3), pp.555-590.

Daud, S. and Yusoff, W.F.W., 2010. Knowledge management and firm performance in SMEs: The role of social capital as a mediating variable. *Asian Academy of Management Journal*, 15(2), pp.135-155.

De Leede, J. and Looise, J.K., 2005. Innovation and HRM: towards an integrated framework. *Creativity and innovation management*, *14*(2), pp.108-117.

de Pablos, P.O., 2004. Human resource management systems and their role in the development of strategic resources: empirical evidence. *Journal of European Industrial Training*, 28(6), pp.474-489.

De Winne, S. and Sels, L., 2010. Interrelationships between human capital, HRM and innovation in Belgian start-ups aiming at an innovation strategy. *The International Journal of Human Resource Management*, 21(11), pp.1863-1883.

Edvinsson, L., Roos, J., Roos, G. and Dragonetti, N.C., 1997. *Intellectual Capital: Navigating in the new business landscape.* USA: NYU Press.

Egbu, C., Botterill, K. and Bates, M., 2001, September. The influence of knowledge management and intellectual capital on organisational innovations. In *Proceedings of the 17th Annual Conference of the Association of Researchers in Construction Management (ARCOM)* (pp. 5-7).

Fleming, L. and Sorenson, O., 2004. Science as a map in technological search. *Strategic Management Journal*, *25*(8-9), pp.909-928.

Fleury, A., Fleury, M.T.L. and Borini, F.M., 2013. The Brazilian multinationals' approaches to innovation. *Journal of International Management*, 19(3), pp.260-275.

Gatignon, H., Tushman, M.L., Smith, W. and Anderson, P., 2002. A structural approach to assessing innovation: Construct development of innovation locus, type, and characteristics. *Management Science*, 48(9), pp.1103-1122.

Gloet, M. and Terziovski, M., 2004. Exploring the relationship between knowledge management practices and innovation performance. *Journal of Manufacturing Technology Management*, 15(5), pp.402-409.

Grant, R.M., 1996. Toward a knowledge-based theory of the firm. *Strategic management journal*, *17*(S2), pp.109-122.

Green, S.G., Welsh, M.A. and Dehler, G.E., 2003. Advocacy, performance, and threshold influences on decisions to terminate new product development. *Academy of management journal*, *46*(4), pp.419-434.

Henttonen, K., 2012, January. The relation between external sources of knowledge and different types of innovation in SMEs. In *ISPIM Conference Proceedings* (p. 1). The International Society for Professional Innovation Management (ISPIM).

Jala, I., 2013. Innovation is not dead in Malaysia. *The Star Online*, [online] Available at: <http://www.thestar.com.my/business/business-news/2013/08/19/innovation-is-not-dead-in-malaysia/> [Accessed 22 August 2016].

Jones, G., George, J. and Hill, W., 2000. *Contemporary Management*. USA: Irwin McGraw-Hill.

Kang, S.C., Morris, S.S. and Snell, S.A., 2007. Relational archetypes, organizational learning, and value creation: Extending the human resource architecture. *Academy of Management Review*, 32(1), pp.236-256.

Kessler, E.H., Bierly, P.E. and Gopalakrishnan, S., 2000. Internal vs. external learning in new product development: effects on speed, costs and competitive advantage. *R&d Management*, 30(3), pp.213-224.

Kostopoulos, K.C., Spanos, Y.E. and Prastacos, G.P., 2002, May. The resource-based view of the firm and innovation: identification of critical linkages. In *The 2nd European Academy of Management Conference*.

Laine, M.O. and Laine, A.V., 2012, April. Open innovation, intellectual capital and different knowledge sources. In *Proceedings of the European Conference on Intellectual Capital* (pp. 239-245).

Lengnick-Hall, M.L., Lengnick-Hall, C.A., Andrade, L.S. and Drake, B., 2009. Strategic human resource management: The evolution of the field. *Human Resource Management Review*, 19(2), pp.64-85.

National SME Development Council, 2010. SME Annual Report 2009/2010. [online] Available at: < http://www.smecorp.gov.my/index.php/en/resources/2015-12-21-11-07-06/sme-annual-report/book/2/Array> [Accessed 1 September 2016).

Ndubisi, N.O., 2008. *Small and medium enterprises in the Pacific Rim*. Arah Pendidikan Sdn Bhd.

Nonaka, I. and Takeuchi, H., 1995. *The knowledge-creating company: How Japanese companies create the dynamics of innovation*. Oxford university press.

Robertson, M. and O'Malley Hammersley, G., 2000. Knowledge management practices within a knowledge-intensive firm: the significance of the people management dimension. *Journal of European Industrial Training*, 24(2/3/4), pp.241-253.

Romijn, H. and Albaladejo, M., 2002. Determinants of innovation capability in small electronics and software firms in southeast England. *Research policy*, 31(7), pp.1053-1067.

Rosdi, I.S., 2014. *A Human Resource Management Framework for Innovative Capability Development.*Ph.D. Multimedia University

Roxas, B.G., 2008. Social Capital for Knowledge Management: The Case of Small and Medium-Sized Enterprises in the Asia-Pacific Region, *Asian Academy of Management Journal*, 13(2), pp.57–77.

Saleh, A.S. and Ndubisi, N.O., 2006. An evaluation of SME development in Malaysia. *International Review of Business Research Papers*, 2(1), pp.1-14.

Salim, I.M. and Sulaiman, M., 2011. Organizational learning, innovation and performance: a study of Malaysian small and medium sized enterprises. *International Journal of Business and Management*, 6(12), p.118.

Scarbrough, H., 2003. Knowledge management, HRM and the innovation process. *International journal of manpower*, *24*(5), pp.501-516.

Scarbrough, H. and Carter, C., 2000. *Investigating knowledge management*. Chartered Institute of Personnel and Development.

Analyzing the geography of the innovation on a global scale, comes to light that the innovative entrepreneurship is the process which portrays the competitiveness of the regions in the knowledge-based economy as strategic process able to match human capital and market opportunities (Romano, 2013).

By exploring, the context in which the triple helix concept emerges and looking at the institutions that influence the innovative entrepreneurship culture, this study aims at exploring how those two concepts may lead to produce local development. Relying on the literature state-of-the-art and on the collection and analysis of primary data, the study puts forward a perspective of the triple helix concept as the engine of a smart and sustainable growth of a territory.

More specifically this study examines and appraises the triple helix interactions between university, industry and government to investigate how innovative entrepreneurship driven by qualified human capital affects and stimulates the triple helix and generate local development in less advantaged regions. Is the triple helix a powerful model through which achieving local development? This research aims at tackling this question.

2. Research Background

When focusing on the triple helix concept the first author you come across is Henry Etzkowitz who simply defines it as "an analytical construct that systematizes the key features of university-industry-government interactions into an 'innovation system' format defined according to systems theory as a set of components, relationships and functions". This conceptual framework organizes a broad perspective for understanding the sources and development paths of innovation, and can be an attractive paradigm for regions aiming at enhancing their knowledge base (Etzkowitz, 2013).

The discussion actually starts a bit earlier when the word first appear in the 1990s by Etzkowitz (1993) and Etzkowitz and Leydesdorff (1995), encompassing elements of precursor works by Lowe (1982) and Sábato and Mackenzi (1982), interprets the shift from a dominating industry-government dyad in the Industrial Society to a changing triadic relationship between university-industry-government in the Knowledge Society.

The Triple Helix model of knowledge-based regional development derived from MIT's role in developing a strategy for the renewal of New England during the great depression of the 1930's and was implemented during the early post-war through the institution of hybrid organizations such as venture capital firm (Etzkowitz, 2002). The strategy was transferred to northern California where it reinforced a process of knowledge-based economy originated independently. Silicon Valley's rise was supported by double helix university-industry and government-university interactions that converged into triple helix university-industry-government relationships. The Vallex has expanded from a local generator of new technologies into the key node of a global network that combine international firms, countries, regions and universities. (Etzkowitz, 2011).

To explore this concept, it is necessary to focus on the first element that makes the triple helix: university.
Universities face a tension from two urgent pressures, firstly to demonstrate that they deliver value for society in return for public investments, and secondly to demonstrate their responsibility by introducing strategic management to demonstrate to their funders that they meet their goals.

What dynamics are involved and how the three elements come together in a spiral?
As firms raise their technological level, they move closer to an academic model, engaging in higher levels of training and in sharing of knowledge. Government acts as a public entrepreneur and venture capitalist in addition to its traditional regulatory role in setting the rules of the game (Etzkowitz, 2002).

The triple helix challenge is picked up in an attempt to identify the factors that affect the ability of universities both to create new knowledge and to deploy that knowledge in economically useful ways and thereby contribute to economic success and regional development (Leysdedorf, 2006).

In an innovation-based context, the production of knowledge and the knowledge itself is the key. It is in fact largely recognized that knowledge is now playing an important role in many aspects of our society through contributing to production, human capital and economic growth. Knowledge is now recognized as the driver of productivity and economic growth, leading to a new focus on the role of information, technology and learning in economic performance. The term "knowledge-based economy" stems from this fuller recognition of the place of knowledge and technology in modern OECD economies (OECD paper, 1996). The relevance of knowledge as the key sources of competitive advantage in a knowledge economy has modified the way businesses compete (World Bank 1998). The new economic development is considered as an outcome of the new combination, for example using new knowledge, or using the same knowledge in a new way. The importance of knowledge becomes relevant when increasing the demand for industry to develop new knowledge in order to sustain its competitive advantage in the turbulent global business environment.

The Triple Helix concept is rhetorically powerful, however the theoretical base show little evidence on how the function, consequences and purpose can be achieved in a successful way outside the limited number of well-known high performance regions. Considered the increasing attention paid to the development of knowledge-based innovation in regions (Cooke, 2001), the key question that arises from the discussion is: Can knowledge-based innovation in regions be achieved through a better cooperation between university, government and industry? To make it simple, is the Triple Helix model a driving force for developing knowledge-based innovation, or simply a feature like another in the successful knowledge economy? Something to be kept in mind is that, despite the positive narratives of the framework, there is evidence for the efficiency of Triple Helix cooperation to be questioned, particularly in less developed regions (Jensen and Trgrdh, 2004).

The very fertile environment in which is possible to innovate, also taking risks, contributes to create a culture of entrepreneurship.

While focusing on the role of the university in the promotion of the entrepreneurial culture under the triple helix model, De Pablo showed that different entities involved in entrepreneurial programs with the university, despite having different goals and priorities, can establish and strengthen synergies under proper coordination, rather than overlap their functions leading to the recurrence or reduction of the results achieved. University is then considered as a catalyst of initiatives for various agents (De Pablo et al).

Is the triple helix alone a powerful model through which achieving regional development?

The triple helix of university-industry-government relations has been accepted as an important determinant of innovation. Cooperation between academia and industry plays a huge role in the development of the economy, but the cooperation needs to be healthy and fruitful. (Chen et al, 2014)

How does the geography of innovation come to the discussion?

There is a large body of literature that showed that one of the most important factors of economic growth is human capital (Riley, 2012, Lucas 1988, Mankiw et al., 1992, De La Fuente and Domenech, 2000, 2006). Bundell and others (1999) analyzing the impact of human capital on economic growth think that the growth rate of output depends on the rate of accumulation of human capital and innovation. OECD record from the 60s have highlighted rapid growth as a result of increasing the number of highly educated.

It has been demonstrated that human capital can be improved and fostered in a more efficient way when policies and institutions work at a local level (Etzkowitz, 1997; Gunasekara, 2005). At local level, the Triple Helix model made up by cooperation between University-Firms-Public institutions is the main tool for the creation of networks, social and human capital and knowledge.

The attempt to bridge education and capabilities with institutions is fruitful, but the relationship between human capital and economic growth needs to pass through education, which needs to be first produced, then disseminated, then acquired and eventually used. This process needs investment in training but also people willing to learn and share.

To address how the main factor that affects and stimulates the triple helix in the regional context we advance the following two propositions.

Proposition 1: Human capital attraction, development and training is one of the most important factors of economic growth.

Proposition 2: Human capital and capabilities are linked with institutions; institutions are needed in order to expand human capabilities and appropriate institutional policies contribute to the creation of skilled labour force.

3. Methodology

In order to illustrate the theory and the propositions made will be used the case of the Euro Mediterranean Scientific Biomedical Institute (ISBEM), which is a non-profit institute that acts as a recruiter and incubator of talents who, otherwise, would be destined to emigrate.

The case study work involved a wide range of data collection methods including desk research on a specific site, the Euro Mediterranean Scientific Biomedical Institute, is considered a good example of triple helix since it revolves around the cooperation between university-industry-government. Other specific readings and publications on the theme, reports, semi-structured interviews, direct observations of situations that developed a strong network with the university system, informal conversations with participants, field notes.
In this study, the qualitative research method is used. The empirical research for this study takes two approaches: documentation and case study.

4. The case study: ISBEM

ISBEM, the case study chosen as focus of the research is a good example of cooperation with university-industry-government.

Founded in Brindisi on May 25, 1999 by forward-looking people coming from medical, scientific and entrepreneurial fields, ISBEM is inspired by universal models of sustainable development. Therefore, it pursues a modern view according to which healthcare and quality services can stem from research (scientific work generates innovation) and from education, (training is essential to acquire skills). Therefore, today a proactive interaction among institutions, research, enterprises, active citizenship, school and the media for communications is highly needed.

ISBEM is actively engaged in social innovation as a mandatory pathway to revive the South of Italy, thus it implements focused research projects as well as interdisciplinary training (life-long learning) in topics related to health, environment, nutrition and lifestyle. Such an approach brings constantly out the relevance of science, of new technologies and of human/social capital. Thus, ISBEM interweaves research projects and training with the creation of interdisciplinary working groups, enabling them to compete on a national and international scale. The ultimate goal is to increase the number of citizens willing to change, and therefore able to act as engines of progress and as attractors of investments for their own community. In this perspective, in order to increase the rate of research and of social innovation, ISBEM invests in young people, supporting their growth both on human and scientific side in order to have them capable to become leaders and effective flywheels of development.

Isbem, in cooperation with the City of Mesagne (Brindisi Province, Italy), is making an effort to transform the former Cappuccini Convent into a Monastery of the 3rd Millennium (M3M), a place that would combine the knowledge, the people and the appropriate tools to spread the social innovation culture, helping people to be the main characters of the future of their community.

ISBEM, within the old Cappuccini Convent in Mesagne, which dates back to the 1600,'s, carries more than a symbolic aspect, as it represents a new relationship between research and education, giving back to the ancient structure its social role the one it had before the upcoming scientific methodology.

The M3M is intended as a joint strategic plan among the promoters of the progress (institutions, research world, enterprises, citizens, schools and media communication), whose cooperation is essential to pinpoint critical issues and identify problems finding appropriate and sustainable solutions that will enrich the community with economic and intangible resources.

How can this be achieved?

Let the director of the Institute answer:

> *"With powerful ideas, with properly trained and competent people, with effective planning techniques as well as the knowledge in fulfilling the procedures and rules set up for applying for local, regional, national, European and international funding. Once in the sphere of action of M3M, anyone will be certainly enriched by the well-known eight strategic competencies outlined by the European Union for the XXI century, taking active part in working groups capable of designing innovative services and solutions useful to the territory. Through virtuous pathways and counting on the contribution of its own talents, South of Italy will enter the phase of social, moral and cultural redemption. It will be able to build the future starting from today.*
>
> *With M3M, ISBEM wants to trigger and consolidate innovative research projects, training programs and services for the community, thanks to the virtuous union between the Past: "the historical Cappuccini Convent", with the Future – "A knowledgeable society" and available resources "human talents and patrimonial assets". If on one hand, donating is like bringing new life in a fallow field, on the other hand, investing in human resources represents the greatest vision for the benefit of all".*

Just to put the words into practice, ISBEM is working to implement several pilot projects in the Monastery of third millennium to achieve its goals and interconnect with the civil society. The projects are at different levels: training people consistently with proposition 1 and infrastructure consistently with proposition 2.

5. Case discussion

The ideal systems implicate connections within the three levels. The South of Italy would benefit a lot from a better definition of rules and stronger involvement between industries, government and the university, which remains the incubator of the talented people that bet with the impact of research to make a better world. The M3M system will enrich the community by bringing back essential values, as well as more quality in fields such as health, environment, food and lifestyles. The ISBEM strategy to encourage citizens to donate with long vision and foresight in order to implement M3M projects has the specific aim to activate multiple pathways to produce value and enhance the resources with a rational approach. As a matter of facts, in the vision of M3M projects, the individual gift becomes a real form of investment for the community that needs it greatly.

While ISBEM is acting as a strategic hub that produces, disseminates, acquires and uses knowledge and converts it into education for specific and highly qualified people, human capital is the most important factor that distinguishes from other similar institutions. PhD students and researchers that are willing to roll up their sleeves not to abandon the South of Italy constitute the population of ISBEM.

The result of the initiatives that rely on collaboration among business, government and academic actors, makes a self-sustaining dynamic in which the role of academia and government create a bottom up innovation policy as an outcome of collective entrepreneurship.

ISBEM, in the ecosystem of innovation, is a reference point to generate the culture of entrepreneurship, which requires a systematic cooperation between universities and enterprises.

To support innovation driven entrepreneurship in the South of Italy, ISBEM understood the need to focus, connect and collaborate. Supporting the innovations of today in isolated sectors is not enough. To compete successfully on the global stage – as envisaged by the European Commission's EU 2020 Strategy – ISBEM is an example that create ecosystems that will support innovations emerging in unconventional ways across government and business.

The TH becomes a platform for institution formation, in the sense that the interaction among university, industry and government can originate the creation of new organizational formats, e.g. the incubator, the science park or the venture capital firm (Etzkowitz, 2003a). The emergence of these new organizational formats supports the TH, underlying argument that the university is positioning itself as a leading institutional sphere, along with industry and government, in the promotion of social and economic development. This process is underpinned by the translation of research into products and into new firms (Etzkowitz, 1998).

The success of the model has been swiftly extended from the academic to policy making. In fact, it is being widely used as a reference for the design of policies and programmes aimed at improving the framework conditions supporting innovative activities (Etzkowitz and Leydesdorff, 2000).

Innovation without the entrepreneur has little value. The entrepreneur has sometimes seen as a driver with a need for appropriate instruments, a steering wheel and an inspiring vision (Karlsson, 2010).

The importance of human capital in the case of ISBEM is unique. Looking at ISBEM proposition 1, there are many activities that illustrates as ISBEM organizes to promote the attraction, development and training of human capital such as:

- Provide the researchers with specific courses (How to fill in European projects);
- Provide students with orientation courses (to help teens make an informed choice and prepare them for the transition from high school to university);
- Organize mini medical schools, i.e. lifelong learning (Events to increase awareness on new health, environment, food and lifestyles discoveries and techniques);
- Summer and winter schools on topics of science and culture (To acquire specific skills on new techniques and new professions stemming from research;
- Lessons, stages and excursions (To let young people around the world know the Italian roots (culture, history, art, music, science, literature, environment, traditions, health, industry, etc.);
- Open multimedia digital laboratory for the cultural growth (To ensure to everyone the access to webinars, e-books, journals, newspaper libraries, digital world WEB, to Skype or similar systems to interact telematically, etc. promoting events, exhibitions, concerts, conferences, working groups, reading groups (like readers fortresses), and specific courses in order to facilitate the integration of cultures, traditions as well as the cultural and experiential exchange among people of different generation);

Looking at proposition 2, there are many activities that illustrate as ISBEM organizes to connect human capital with the institutions, for example:

- A venue in the South for the European Voluntary Service (To facilitate synergies with voluntary associations of the territory and disseminate good practices of the Planet Health around Europe);
- A core of the network of the University Colleges of Salento (RECUS) (To consolidate the Cappuccini convent in its role as operational and logistical support to students, graduate students, post-docs, researchers and teachers, both Italian and foreign);
- Create a Community Foundation with a pilot project, promoted by active Citizens (To constitute in Puglia, possibly in Salento, at least one Community Foundation in which development actors strive together to train human resources, creating advanced services and promote innovative entrepreneurship programs on health, nutrition, environment and lifestyles).

To sum up, human capital and economic growth have a strong relationship. Human capital affects economic growth and can help to develop an economy through the knowledge and skills of people.

Human capital refers to the knowledge, skill sets and motivation that people have, which provide economic value. Human capital realizes that not everyone has the same skill sets or knowledge and that quality of work can be improved by investing in people's education.

In the case of ISBEM institutions cooperate and enrich human capabilities through several activities that boost the skill labour force. High qualified human capital offer better opportunities.

Seen that the technology plus the human capital, in the case of ISBEM is the means through which is possible to innovate and contribute to the boost of innovative entrepreneurship culture, the young educated people can be seen as the society changing agents.

6. Conclusion

This paper looked at the triple helix concept in connection with the innovative entrepreneurship culture. The combination of the three helices explained by the case study of ISBEM can contribute to local development in terms of qualified human capital. There is a strong connection between human capital and economic growth. The interaction between university, industry and government driven by ISBEM is an example of a system that relying on strong human capital can make a difference in a less advantaged region pushing to manage international projects that have a positive economic outcome.

The confluence of rapid technical change and globalisation in recent years has prompted governments in developed and developing countries alike to prioritise skills development as a key strategy for economic competitiveness and growth. The challenges are profound and complex. Policy makers acknowledge the critical role of a strong human resource base in complementing other investments and policies to boost productivity and economic progress. Yet while developing countries report lower average levels of educational attainment than industrialised countries, ending up with high numbers of unemployed that emigrate to other countries, it emerges the urgent of need of new strategies and approaches that focus more explicitly on the links and coherence between investments in skills development to foster local development.

The distinctiveness of this research lies in contributing to the existing theories of triple helix by highlighting the importance of redefining the strategic intentions and roles of key actors in building up knowledge-based innovation. The research findings also have significant implications for government policy makers, business practitioners and university academics when addressing the existing deficiencies in the implementation of knowledge-based innovation strategies in the regions.

References

De Pablo, I. (2010). The role of the university in the promotion of the entrepreneurship culture under the triple helix.

Cooke, P. (2007b). To Construct Regional Advantage from Innovation Systems First Build Policy Platforms, European Planning Studies, 15(2), 179-194.

Karlsson, R, Backman, M, Djupenstrom, A. (2010). Sustainability considerations and triple helix collaboration in regional innovation, chapter 2.

Hassanin, M. (2012). A dynamic open innovation framework to accelerate research and regional development in the Egyptian open university.

Chen, F, Chong, W. (2014). Research on Triple Helix of University-Industry-Government Relations: Empirical Evidence from China.

Gibbons, M., Limoges, C., Nowotny, H., Schwartzman, S., Scott, P. & Trow, M. (1994). The New Production of Knowledge: The Dynamics of Science and Research in Contemporary Societies, Sage Publications.

Charles, D. & Benneworth, P. (2001). Clustering and Economic Complexity: Regional ICT Clusters in the United Kingdom.

Inzelt, A. R. (2004). The evolution of university-industry-government relationships during transition. Research Policy, 975-995.

Shinn, T. (2002). The Triple Helix and New Production of Knowledge : Prepackaged Thinking on Science and Technology. Social Studies of Science, 32(4), 599-614.

Lambooy, J. G. (2004). The transmission of knowledge, emerging networks, and the role of universities: an evolutionary approach. European Planning Studies, 12,643- 657.

Gorddard J. (1997). Universities adn Regional Development: An Overview. for Urban and Regional Development Studies, University of Newcastle upon Tyne.

Howell. (1996). Tacit Knowledge, Innovation and Technology Transfer. Technology Analysis and Strategic Management, Vol 8, pp 91-106.

Powell W. and Kenneth W. Koput and Laurel Smith-Doerr. (1996). Interorganizational Collaboration and the Locus of Innovation: Networks of Learning in Biotechnology. Administrative Science Quarterly, 41,116 – 145.

Smith, H., Leydesdorff, L. (2012). The Triple Helix in the context of global change: dynamics and challenges.

Leydesdorff, L., & Sun, Y. (2009). National and International Dimensions of the Triple Helix in Japan: University-Industry-Government versus International Co-Authorship Relations. Journal of the American Society for Information Science and Technology 60(4), 778-788.

Leydesdorff, L. (2010). The Knowledge-Based Economy and the Triple Helix Model. Annual Review of Information Science and Technology, 44, 367-417.

The Oslo Agenda for Entrepreneurship education in Europe. Retrieved December 23, 2015, from http://ec.europa.eu/enterprise/policies/sme/files/support_measures/training_education/doc/oslo_agenda_final_en.pdf

Marshall, C. & Rossman, G. B. (1999). Designing qualitative research. Thousand Oaks. Ca: Sage.

Yin, R.K. (1994). Case study research: design and methods. Sage.

Pickard, J. A. (2007). Research methods in information. London: Cromwell Press.

Shane, S., & Venkataraman, S. (2000). The Promise of Enterpreneurship as a Field of Research. The Academy of Management Review, 25(1): 217-226

Cooke, P. (2004). The role of research in regional innovation systems: new models meeting knowledge economy demands. International Journal of Technology Management, 28,507- 533.

CHARLES, D. (2003). Universities and Territorial Development: Reshaping the Regional Role of UK Universities Local Economy 18,7-20.

OECD (1995). Technology, Productivity and Job Creation, Vol. I and II, The OECD Job Strategy, Paris, OECD.

Schumpeter, J. A. (1947). The Creative Response in Economic History. The Journal of Economic History, 7(2): 149-159.

Romano, A. (2013). Mezzogiorno 2025, Cacucci.

The Economic World Forum, retrieved 23 December, 2015 from http://www3.weforum.org/docs/WEF_EuropeCompetitiveness_FosteringInnovationDrivenEntrepreneurship_Report_2014.pdf

The World Bank Report, retrieved 23 December, 2015 from http://web.worldbank.org/WBSITE/EXTERNAL/EXTDEC/EXTRESEARCH/EXTWDRS/0,,contentMDK:22293493~pagePK:478093~piPK:477627~theSitePK:477624,00.html

Ranga, M., Etzkowitz, H. (2013). Triple Helix Systems: An Analytical Framework for Innovation Policy and Practice in the Knowledge Society.

Etzkowitz, H., Leydesdorff. L. (1995). The triple helix – university – industry – government relations: a laboratory for knowledge based economic development.

Lowe, C.U., (1982). The Triple Helix—NIH, industry, and the academic world. The Yale Journal of Biology and Medicine 55, 239-246

Sabato, Jorge, Mackenzi, M. (1982). La Produccion de Technologıa. ´ ˝ Autonoma o Transnacional. Nueva Imagen, Mexico.

Schumpeter, J. A., (1942). Capitalism, Socialism, and Democracy.

Cooke, P., Leydesdorff, L. (2006). Regional development in the knowledge-based economy: the construction of advantage.

Etzkowitz, Henry (2002). The triple helix of university-industry-government: implications for policy and evaluation, SISTER working paper 2002-11, Stockholm, Sweden.

Etzkowitz, Henry (2003). Innovation in innovation: the triple helix of universityindustry-government relations, Social Science Information, Vol. 42, no. 3, pp. 293-337.

Etzkowitz, Henry (2008). The triple helix, university-industry-government innovation in action, Routledge, New York, USA.

Etzkowitz, Henry; Klofsten, Magnus (2005). The innovating region: toward a theory of knowledge-based regional development, R&D Management, Vol. 35, no. 3, pp. 243- 255.

Etzkowitz, Henry; Leydesdorff, Loet (1999). The future location of research and technology transfer, Journal of Technology Transfer, 24, pp. 111-123.

Etzkowitz, Henry; Leydesdorff, Loet (2000). The dynamics of innovation: from national systems and 'mode 2' to a triple helix of university-industry-government relations, Research Policy, Vol. 29, pp. 109-123.

Etzkowitz, Henry; Leydesdorff, Loet (eds.) (1997). Universities and the global knowledge economy: a triple helix of university-industry-government relations, Pinter, London, UK.

Etzkowitz, Henry; Zhou, Chunyan (2006). Triple helix twins: innovation and sustainability, Science and Public Policy, Vol. 33, no. 1, pp. 77-83.

Carayannis, E. G., & Campbell, D. F. J. (2009). 'Mode 3' and 'Quadruple Helix': toward a 21st century fractal innovation ecosystem. International Journal of Technology Management, 46(3), 201-234.

Carayannis, E. G., & Campbell, D. F. J. (2010). Triple Helix, Quadruple Helix and Quintuple Helix and How Do Knowledge, Innovation, and Environment Relate to Each Other? International Journal of Social Ecology and Sustainable Development, 1(1), 41-69.

Technological Breakthroughs for Water Hyacinth: An Entrepreneurial Innovation

Margie B. Mirando, Rosalina B. Loquias and Anne Marie F. Bagadion
Ateneo de Naga University, Naga City, Philippines
margiebmirando@yahoo.com
rosalina.loquias@yahoo.com
abagadion@gbox.adnu.edu.ph

Abstract: Water hyacinth has proved to be a promising raw material for different products as shown by many entrepreneurs venturing into such kind of business. For it to continue to thrive, it is necessary to equip oneself with the appropriate technology so as to ease and increase its production thereby contributing to its profitability. This study is geared towards promoting breakthroughs and business opportunities on Water Hyacinth's contribution to small medium entrepreneurs particularly in the province of Camarines Sur, Philippines. It aims to identify the innovative opportunities in Water Hyacinth along Environmental Management, Technology, and Entrepreneurship; possible innovation to the challenges in processing Water Hyacinth and its business opportunities; determine the government programs provided for the development of Water Hyacinth and finally, formulate a strategic development plan for the Water Hyacinth Industry. The research methodology that will be used is descriptive-evaluative method. A self-constructed survey questionnaire will be formulated to be used in interviewing respondents through clustered sampling. With 37 municipalities including 2 cities in the province of Camarines Sur, only 3 municipalities and 1 city are into producing products with Water Hyacinth as a raw material. Using records from the Department of Trade and Industry in the region, researchers identified 13 active producers of water hyacinth products in 3 municipalities and 1 city in the study area who will serve as respondents. An interview will also conducted to respondents from the 4 local government units, 2 couturiers, and 2 government agencies that assist the producers. With this study, it is expected that the water hyacinth business will scale-up into a more innovative business and offer more products using upgraded technology.

Keywords: Water Hyacinth; Entrepreneurship; Breakthroughs; Innovation; Technology

1. Background of the Study

This paper aims to present challenges and technological breakthroughs brought about by Water Hyacinth in the province of Camarines Sur, Philippines.

With the cliché *"in every difficulty, there is opportunity,"* plus strong entrepreneurial spirit, it has been proven that Water Hyacinth is a promising raw material not only for novelty items but also source of energy as well. However, appropriate technology and continuing support from government and private sectors are needed to sustain, if not replicate technological breakthroughs nationwide.

1.1 Water Hyacinth

Water hyacinth is an aquatic plant native to the Amazon basin, and is often considered a highly problematic invasive species outside its native range. It is a free-floating perennial aquatic plant (or hydrophyte) native to tropical and sub-tropical South America. Each plant can produce thousands of seeds each year, and these seeds can remain viable for more than 28 years. (Sullivan, 2012).

Water hyacinth is known as an invasive species, which invades fresh water habitats and is listed along with some of the worst weeds (Center et al. 1999). Some countries have even placed this species in their quarantine list and banned their sale or movement within their sphere of influence. It cause blockage of irrigation channels affecting the flow of water to fields, get entangled with motorboat rotors, making fishing difficult, and almost makes any place inhabitable and inaccessible. They may block hydroelectric turbines causing enormous damage, which are vital for economy and green environment. They out-compete almost all other species growing in their vicinity thereby decreasing biodiversity (Crafter et al. 1992).

Due to its prolific and vigorous growth stage, it has been considered nuisance for the past decades in the Bicol River in Camarines Sur, Philippines.

1.2 Camarines Sur

Camarines sur which is approximately 400km South of Manila, is a province located in the Bicol Region in the island Luzon of the Philippines. It is the largest among the six provinces in the Bicol Region both by population and land area. Its territory has 37 municipalities which includes two cities: Naga, the lone chartered city, as the province's and the region's religious, cultural, financial, commercial, industrial and business center; and Iriga, a component city, as the center of the Rinconada area and Riŋkonāda Language. Within the province lies Lake Buhi, where the smallest commercially harvested fish, the Sinarapan (Mistichthys luzonensis), can be found. (Source: https://en.wikipedia.org/wiki/Camarines_Sur)

The economy of Camarines Sur is mostly agriculture-based. Out of the 35 towns, 29 towns are mainly agricultural, producing rice, corn, feedmeal, freshwater fish, livestock, coconut, sugar, abacá, and water-lily. (Source: https://en.wikipedia.org/wiki/Camarines_Sur)

Before 2008 the Local Government Unit (LGU) of Naga city spent funds to extract water hyacinth from the Naga city river which was already polluted from different waste matters, and one of the reasons is the fast proliferation/thriving of water hyacinth. But LGU Naga just dumped the extracted plants in one area (near Sabang, Naga city) and said plants just thrived more especially during rainy season.[1]

In 2008, with what happened, Department of Trade and Industry (DTI, CamSur Provincial Office) started using and promoting Water Hyacinth as raw material especially in Naga City and in the towns of Buhi, Bato and Milaor.[2]

- Stalks were dried and used for fuel as charcoal briquettes (Milaor); (DTI contracted Kolbi Machine to come up with mixer and molder to produce said charcoal briquettes.[3]
- Birth of TINAGO WATER HYACINTH HANDICRAFT DEVELOPMENT ASSOCIATION (TIWHADA) to use Water Hyacinth as handicrafts, as clothing material and other novelty items which generated employment for Naga city's Barangay women and Out of School Youth which helped increased household income.[4]

In 2012, DTI together with Buhi LGUs and known Cam Sur couturier feature a fashion show promoting the Water Hyacinth cloth used in dresses and blankets made from said cloth which is part of DTI's One Town One Product (OTOP) for Buhi municipality.[5] Moreover, DTI provided 40 looms and 10 sewing machines for 40 Entrepreneurs with 250 weavers. They produced Cloth yardage' table runners; bags and other novelty items.[6] However, challenges and issues arise since then, such as

1. No continuing investors;
2. Buhi women's skills are cloth loomers but not for bag making.
3. Camarines Sur entrepreneurs more on trading while provinces of Sorsogon and Albay are more on production/manufacturing (more weavers);
4. Raw material preparation not sustained due to long process (it takes 15 days just for drying);
5. Only 3 government agencies are concerned in the promotion of Water Hyacinth i.e. DTI; Department of Science and Technology (DOST), Department of Environment and Natural Resources (DENR), and Department of Agriculture (DA), with the latter not so much on development.

2. Problem/s Addressed

This research aimed to identify other technological breakthroughs and innovative opportunities for Water Hyacinth along Environmental Management, Technology, and Entrepreneurship.

This study aimed to answer specifically the following problem questions: 1). What are the other breakthroughs and innovation in Water Hyacinth along: a) Environmental Management; b) Technology; and c) Entrepreneurship; 2) What are the challenges in processing Water Hyacinth?; 3) What are the new business opportunities in Water Hyacinth?; 4) What government programs are provided for the development Water Hyacinth?; 5) What strategic development can be proposed for the Water Hyacinth?

3. Scope and Limitation of the Study

The research study focused mainly in the utilization and development of Water Hyacinth as a raw material in the province of Camarines Sur, Philippines, particularly in the city of Naga and in the municipalities of Buhi, Bato and Milaor.

4. Significance of the Study

The results of this study will serve as bases for the Researchers' University (Ateneo de Naga University) being the Center of Development for Entrepreneurship, in developing its plan to assist the Water Hyacinth industry in Bicol. The plans if implemented, can generate income for the marginalized sectors particularly the micro small entrepreneurs, Barangay women and out of school youths (OSY). This will also serve to complement and update existing technical studies on Water Hyacinth in Bicol by generating knowledge on the current socioeconomic conditions of traders and processors. The study aims to highlight best practices in the production and marketing of Water Hyacinth, the costs and benefits of developing the industry with respect to the individual entrepreneur and the region as a whole, and the various factors critical to the development of the industry. The research output will be useful to the University and public policy makers as well in designing, targeting, and evaluating development initiatives meant to advance and sustain the Water Hyacinth industry in Bicol.

5. Review of Related Literature

This section presents a review of related literature and studies culled from different journal publications, and internet.

Production and Marketing of Goods

Stevenson (2009) in his book Operations Management mentioned that the creation of goods or services begins in transforming or converting inputs into outputs. Various inputs such as capital, labor, and information or also known as 6 Ms – Money, Manpower, Machines, (raw) Materials, Management and Methodology are used to create good or services using one or more transformation process. The management of that part of an organization that is responsible for producing good and or services is known as Operations Management . It is also known that business organizations typically have three basic functional areas – finance, marketing and operations.

Considering the Marketing aspect of the business, one cannot get away with the Marketing Mix or 4Ps popularized by Philip Kotler. The Marketing Mix or also known 4 Ps which stand for Product, Price, Place (i.e. distribution) and Promotion (i.e. Advertising). According to Kotler, "the Marketing Mix is the set of controllable variables that the firm can use to influence the buyer's response." These four variables help a company develop a unique selling point as well as brand image.
(Source: http://knowledge.ckgsb.edu.cn/2013/10/08/marketing/philip-kotler-four-ps-model-marketing-still-king.)

However, in the of 21st century additional 3 Ps have been identified in the Marketing Mix – People (i.e. employees; teamwork); Physical evidence (i.e. plant facilities); Process (i.e. standardized flow of activities) (Kotler 2012). Hence, the Marketing Mix and process of production has been considered in the conceptual framework of this study.

Innovation on Water Hyacinth

In the blog article of students from Naga Central School it mentioned that Water hyacinth as an invasive pest and is responsible to many problems summarized earlier, thus, many locals, groups, organizations, local government units and the Department of Environment and Natural Resources (DENR) conducted researches and studies on the benefits that can get from this plant.

Along their journey, they have found out that the stem, leaves and flowers can be made into different materials. Below are the products made from water hyacinth.

1. Paper and Yarn. In Bangladesh, they experimented with paper production from water hyacinth for some years now. Their project proved that the water hyacinth fiber alone does not make particularly good paper but when the fiber is blended with waste paper or jute, the result is a good quality paper. The fiber from the stems of the water hyacinth plant can be used to make rope. The stalk of the plant is shredded lengthways to expose the fibers and then left to dry for several days.
2. Fiberboard. In Dhaka, Bangladesh they developed a fiberboard that has general purpose uses such as low cost roofing. The process has many steps and the labor is intensive.

3. Basket work: In the Philippines and India, water hyacinth is dried and used to make baskets and matting for homes and the local tourist trade.
4. Fertilizers. Water hyacinth can be used directly from harvesting or dried to be used to mix with the soil or as mulch.
5. Fish feed: Tilapia and silver carp consume aquatic weeds, like water hyacinth.
   (Source: http://nagacentralschool1-waterlily.blogspot.com/p/focus-study.html)

In Metro Manila, to clear the Las Piñas River of this aquatic pest, with the help of Water Hyacinth Weaving Enterprise, which provides livelihood to over 200 families, was set up by the Villar Foundation, residents harvest Water Hyacinths and dry the stalks, which become the raw material for producing baskets, trays, slippers, and other functional and ornamental items. (Source: http://www.villarsipag.org/)

There are other alternative uses for Water Hyacinth. It can be used in farming as an organic fertilizer and as a mulch crop. There has been an increase in demand for organic foods in the developed world. Besides, it helps to conserve soil moisture and nutrient reclamation. The plants can be turned into compost and used as a fertilizer. The plant tends to retain most of the nutrients (reviewed by Gunnarsson and Petersen, 2007) when dried thus decreasing our needs on chemical fertilizer. The time taken in composting is only 30 days (Polprasert et al., 1980) compared to other crop plants, which can take up to 2-3 months. They can be converted into ash (40%) [Reviewed by Gunnarson and Petersen, 2007] which is rich in micronutrients and thus can be used in soil enrichment. Thus, compost from water hyacinth tends to improve physical, chemical and biological properties of soil. They are relatively easy to transport and cost very little. They are also used in traditional medicine as their root and leaf extracts are known to cure certain diseases (swelling, burning, haemorrhage, and thyroid). They are also used to treat certain inflammatory conditions of veterinary animals. They are also used as a vegetable crop (leaves, petiole and flowers) in some parts of the world (Philippines and Java) and are known to be rich in carotene, protein and carbohydrates. In addition they can be used as a feed for livestock as a roughage component (Gunnarsson and Petersen, 2007). They can be used to grow mushroom, vegetable and floriculture plants can be grown on water hyacinth rafts. The green biomass can be used as an animal fodder and also used to make hay and silage (Lindsey and Hirt, 1999a). They are also used in furniture manufacture, which are in high demand and available through online stores (typical examples, http://www.balifurnish.com and http://www.whup.20m.com). They are also used to manufacture building board. They can be also be used in processing coffee beans and even as laundry detergents (Hassan et al., 2006). Further they can be used in paper production and also in grease- proof paper manufacture (De Groote et al., 2003). They are used as briquettes for cook stoves. Rural folks also use the plant to manufacture rope or coir.

In some South Asian countries they are used to make floating vegetable gardens. Water hyacinths can be used in reclamation of water bodies containing high levels of lead and mercury. Al Ramalli et al., (2005) have demonstrated that even dried hyacinth roots are very effective in removing arsenate from the contaminated water system. They can thus grow in highly polluted water bodies. They can be used to produce cellulase enzymes (Lindsey and Hirt, 1999b). Water hyacinths also provide food sources to aquatic fauna like snails, fish, crabs etc.

Water Hyacinth as Bio Fuel

As cited by Bhattacharya and Kumar (2010), Water hyacinth is low in lignin content (10%) and contains high amounts of cellulose (20%) and hemicellulose (33%) (Bolenz et al. 1990, Poddar et al. 1991, Gressel 2008). Detailed composition of water hyacinth is described in Table 1. A typical biomass from land plants can have 30-50% cellulose, 20-40% hemicellulose and 15-30% lignins. In plants, lignin (composed of phenylpropanoid groups) acts as a polymer around the hemicellulose microfibrils, binding the cellulose molecules together and protecting them against chemical degradation. Lignin cannot be converted into sugars. Thus, it is not practical in biofuel production. Their degradation is a high energy process. Water hyacinth has low lignin, which means the cellulose and hemicellulose are more easily converted to fermentable sugar thus resulting in enormous amount of utilizable biomass for the biofuel industry (Fig. 1a). Masami et al. (2008) suggested a new method of extracting ethanol by saccharification with diluted sulfuric acid, and hastening the process by using yeast.

Further, water hyacinth grows at a very rapid pace and contains very high nitrogen content. The mixture of cowdung and water hyacinth slurry has proven to produce more biogas than when used alone (El-Shinnawi et al. 1989). The left-over slurry or sludge can be transported as liquid fertilizer. They can practically grow in any habitat and requires little to no maintenance, but they prefer to grow in warm climate. Further, they can be used to purify water bodies containing high amounts of heavy metal contamination. The biomass can be used to produce biogas and the by products can be used as organic manure or for producing bioethanol by further decomposition of fermentable saccharides. However, there are no exact figures available for bioethanol production from water hyacinth (Nigram 2002).

In addition, aquatic plants do not compete with land resources used in arable food crop cultivation and thus are an incentive factor when it comes to biofuel production. For the past few years, there have been reports of genetic engineering of microorganisms, which can increase ethanol production from hemicellulose by fermenting it into oligosaccharides (Mishima et al. 2008). Mishima et al. (2008) also found that bioethanol generating capacity of water hyacinth can be compared to that obtained from agricultural waste, thus is a potential new crop for biofuel production and an employment generating industry.

Table 1. Average biomass composition of water hyacinth. Adapted from Poddar et al (1991); Gunnarsson and Petersen (2007).

Components	% composition
1. Lignin	10.
2. Cellulose	25
3. Hemicellulose	35
4. Ash	20
5. Nitrogen	03

Source: Bhattacharya and Kumar , Electronic Journal of Environmental and Agricultural Food Chemistry, ISSN 1579-4377

Ralph et al. (2006) found that flexible polymerization is possible in plants, whereby monolignins can be actively substituted by polyphenols. This is turn may not affect the development process of plants, but will facilitate the extraction of saccharides needed for biofuel production from the plants. This same strategy can be applied to water hyacinth, which is naturally low in lignin and thus it will be more effective to extract fermentable saccharides.

With all the innovations and alternative uses of Water Hyacinth, this research paper aims to strengthen the appropriate technology and strategic management plans that can develop Water Hyacinth into a lucrative business opportunity for the people of Camarines Sur, Philippines.

6. Theoretical Framework

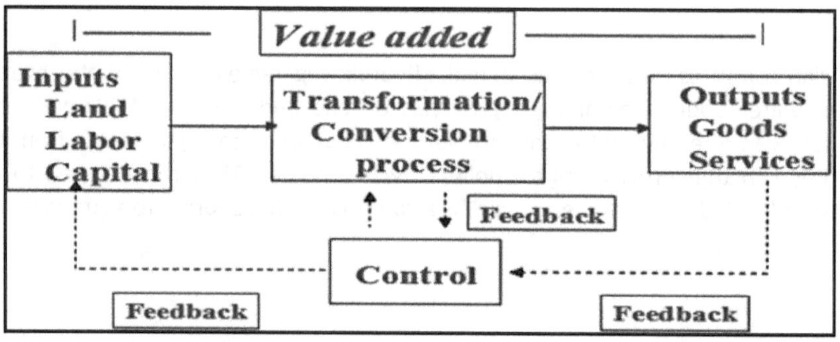

Source: W. Stevenson, 2009, Operations Management and Production 9th Ed, Mc Graw Hills publishing

Figure 1: Elements of Operations Management and Production

Stevenson (2009) gives emphasis to the three elements of production i.e. input (including raw materials), transformation (processes) and output (final product). He stresses that the essence of the operations and production functions is to add value during the transformation process. Value added is the term used to describe the difference between the cost of inputs and the value or price of outputs. For small entrepreneurs, the value of outputs is their value to society; the greater the value added, the greater the effectiveness of the operations. Moreover, feedback from customer is very crucial. Thus, this study uses Stevenson's concept on input-transformation-output with the importance of Value Added and feedback which can help Water Hyacinth producers improve and sustain its products and services in the future that can give livelihood for the marginalized member of the society.

7. Conceptual Framework

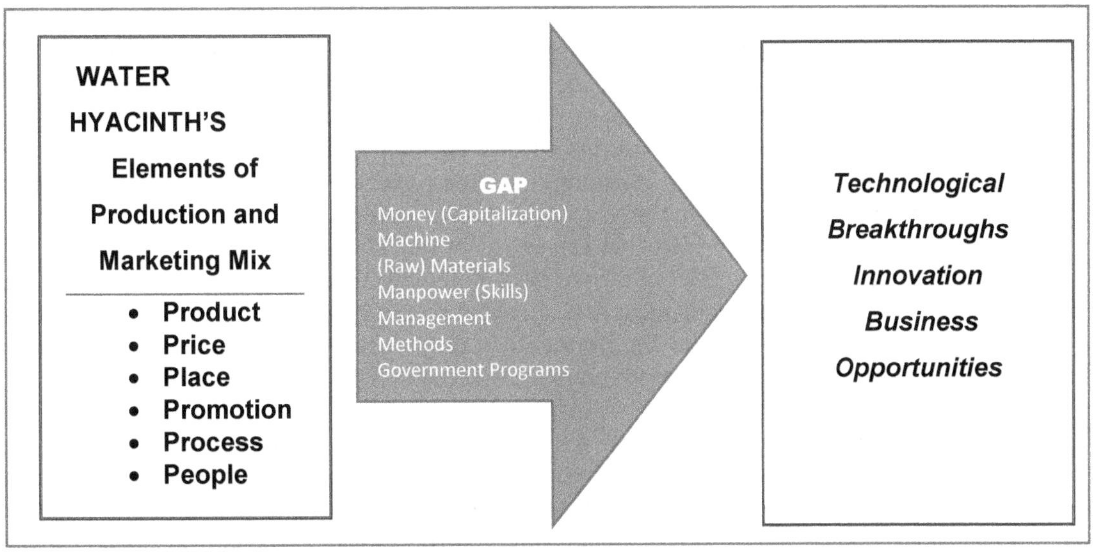

Figure 2: Technological Breakthroughs for Water Hyacinth: An Entrepreneurial Innovation

The above illustrated conceptual framework wishes to show the gap in terms of the 6Ms (Money; raw Materials; Machineries; Manpower; Management and Methodology) and government policies together with the extended Marketing Mix (Product; Price; Promotion; People; Process) needed in the production of water hyacinth. In determining the said gaps, the study can come up with proper recommendations on how to foster technological breakthroughs, innovation and business opportunities for Water Hyacinth not only in the province of Camarines Sur or within the Philippines but in other parts of the world where Water Hyacinth is abundant.

8. Research Methodology

The research design used in the study is the descriptive evaluative-method. The purpose of using this method is to evaluate or measure the entrepreneurial innovation of water hyacinth industry in the province of Camarines Sur.

The sources of data that was utilized in the study are the primary and secondary sources of data. The primary sources of data were gathered from the respondents through the use of personal interview while the secondary sources were culled from the on-line sources, journal, local and foreign studies.

The study employed the clustered sampling technique to classify the actual respondents. Through this sampling method, the researchers were able to identify the actual population of the study. With 37 municipalities including 2 cities in the province of Camarines Sur, only 3 municipalities and 1 city are into producing products with Water Hyacinth as a raw material. Using records from the Department of Trade and Industry in the region, 13 active producers of water hyacinth products in 3 municipalities and 1 city in the study area were identified. An interview was conducted to respondents from the 4 local government units, 2 couturiers, and 2 government agencies that assist the producers. The total actual respondents of the study are 21.

The list of the actual respondents is shown in table below:

The Respondents

Respondents	Actual Population
Active Producers	13
Local Government Units	4
Couturiers	2
Government Agencies	2
Total	**21**

The researchers qualitatively treated the collected data provided by the respondents.

9. Results Discussion

The challenges faced by water hyacinth producers are on the following 1) availability of supply of raw materials, 2) lack of manpower and 3) funding requirements. Respondents expressed that one of the problems they encounter is the difficulty in getting adequate supply of water hyacinth especially when they have voluminous orders. Some technology requirements such as drying equipment cannot also be afforded by producers due to its high cost which makes it difficult for them to produce more products. With regard to manpower, very few barangay constituents are interested to venture into the water hyacinth products. The industry has difficulty growing due to the reluctance of other residents to help in this barangay advocacy. This unwillingness can be traced to the fact that income is not that stable as it is only earned after a project has been accomplished. Outsourcing of labor is an immediate remedy that local government undertake to respond to the this need. Funding requirements is also a challenge since most of the respondents only have scant capital to finance their business. For big projects they would usually apply for a loan from Metro PESO, a government agency tasked to support entrepreneurs especially on finances.

Some government agencies include assistance to entrepreneurs in their mandate. These include Department of Trade and Industry (DTI), Department of Science and Technology (DOST) and Department of Labor and Employment(DOLE). The DTI takes care of organizing seminars, trainings and workshops for budding entrepreneurs. The DOST works in collaboration with the DTI through technology requirements. They provide equipment to entrepreneurs for free on the condition that the business will observe going concern. DOLE works to promote and ensure employment to people.

10. Conclusion

There are innovative opportunities along environmental management, technology and entrepreneurship. On environmental management, rivers are freed from the problem on water pollution. The Bicol river became more passable for water transportation. Moreover, with the recent study from Mishima (2008) and recent local experiment conducted, water hyacinth is a good source of charcoal briquette and biofuel. On technology, water hyacinth is a good source of animal and fish feed fertilizer. Many studies also showed that water hyacinth is a source of raw material for paper production. On Entrepreneurship, many programs have been provided to promote water hyacinth as a source of livelihood i.e. TIWHADA in Naga city, and processing of water hyacinth cloth into blankets, slippers, bags, etc.

11. Recommendation

It is recommended that continuous collaboration with different LGUs whose areas are affected by the widespread proliferation of water hyacinth be intensified. Revival of assistance programs provided by the Department of Trade and Industry and other government agencies to ensure sustainability of the water hyacinth businesses must also be made so as to encourage more people to venture in this kind of endeavour. Intensive research and development must also be conducted for biofuel production. Each local government unit must create more programs that will strengthen people's awareness on the benefits and opportunities that the water hyacinth business brings. Out-of-school youths, homemakers or housewives, solo parents' associations and other like organizations may also be brought together by the local government units to open up this business opportunity and they may be given specialized trainings and workshops particularly on business management, financial literacy and technical operations to equip them with the necessary skills and knowledge required in such kind of undertaking. DTI or one of the local government units (e.g. Naga city, Camarines Sur) should initiate partnerships with local and foreign investors to infuse funds in processing water hyacinth. Moreover, a joint venture with big corporations, MNCs and other foundations to continue and sustain the processing of water hyacinth. With the continuity of processing water hyacinth, this would provide jobs or generate income for local barangay members.

References

[1]Personal Interview with DTI Cam Sur Province Officer Ms. L. Fuentebella August 15,2016
[2] ibid
[3] ibid
[4] Ibid
[5] Ibid
[6] Ibid

Al Ramalli SW, Harrington CF, Ayub M, Haris PI (2005) A biomaterial based approach for arsenic removal from water J Environ monitoring 7: 279-282 as cited by Bhattacharya A. and Kumar P., Water Hyacinth as a Potential Biofuel Crop. Electronic Journal Environmental, Agricultural and Food Chemistry

Bhattacharya A. and Kumar P. (2010) , Water Hyacinth as a Potential Biofuel Crop. Electronic Journal Environmental, Agricultural and Food Chemistry. 9 (1), 2010. [112-122]

Bolenz S, Omran H, Gierschner K (1990) Treatment of water hyacinth tissue to obtain useful products. Bio wastes 33:263-274 as cited by Bhattacharya A. and Kumar P., Water Hyacinth as a Potential Biofuel Crop. Electronic Journal Environmental, Agricultural and Food Chemistry

Center TD, Dray Jr GA, Jubindsky GP, Drodowitz MJ (1999) Biological control of water hyacinth under conditions of maintaince management: can herbicides and insects be intregrated ? Environ man 23:241-256 as cited by Bhattacharya A. and Kumar P., Water Hyacinth as a Potential Biofuel Crop. Electronic Journal Environmental, Agricultural and Food Chemistry

Crafter SA, Njuguna SG, Howard GW (1992) Wetlands of Kenya: proceedings of the KWWG Seminar on Wetlands of Kenya, National Museums of Kenya, Nairobi, Kenya, 3-5 July 1991 as cited by Bhattacharya A. and Kumar P., Water Hyacinth as a Potential Biofuel Crop. Electronic Journal Environmental, Agricultural and Food Chemistry

De Groote H, Ajuonu O, Attignon S, Djessou R and Neuenschwander P (2003) Economic impact of biological control of water hyacinth in Southern Benin Ecol Eco 45: 105-113 as cited by Bhattacharya A. and Kumar P., Water Hyacinth as a Potential Biofuel Crop. Electronic Journal Environmental, Agricultural and Food Chemistry

El-Shinnawi MM, Alaa El-Din MN, El-Shimi SA, Badawi MA (1989) Biogas production from crop residues and aquatic weeds. Res Conser Recyc 3:33-45 as cited by Bhattacharya A. and Kumar P., Water Hyacinth as a Potential Biofuel Crop. Electronic Journal Environmental, Agricultural and Food Chemistry

Gressel J (2008) Transgenics are imperative for biofuel crops. Plant Sci 174: 246-263 as cited by Bhattacharya A. and Kumar P., Water Hyacinth as a Potential Biofuel Crop. Electronic Journal Environmental, Agricultural and Food Chemistry

Gunnarsson CC, Petersen CM (2007) Water hyacinths as a resource in agriculture and energy production: A literature review. Waste Man 27: 117-129 15 as cited by Bhattacharya A. and Kumar P., Water Hyacinth as a Potential Biofuel Crop. Electronic Journal Environmental, Agricultural and Food Chemistry

Hasan F, Shah AA, Hameed A (2006) Industrial applications of microbial lipases Enzy Microbial Tech 39:235 -251 as cited by Bhattacharya A. and Kumar P., Water Hyacinth as a Potential Biofuel Crop. Electronic Journal Environmental, Agricultural and Food Chemistry

Lindsey K, Hirt HM (1999b) Use Water Hyacinth!. Eco Books pp 816 as cited by Bhattacharya A. and Kumar P., Water Hyacinth as a Potential Biofuel Crop. Electronic Journal Environmental, Agricultural and Food Chemistry

Masami GO, Usui I, Urano N (2008) Ethanol production from the water hyacinth Eichhornia crassipes by yeast isolated from various hydrospheres. African J Microbio Res 2:110-113 as cited by Bhattacharya A. and Kumar P., Water Hyacinth as a Potential Biofuel Crop. Electronic Journal Environmental, Agricultural and Food Chemistry

Mishima D, Kuniki M, Sei K, Soda S, Ike M, Fujita M (2008) Ethanol production from candidate energy crops: Water hyacinth (Eichhornia crassipes) and water lettuce (Pistia stratiotes L.) Biores Tech 99:2495-2500 as cited by Bhattacharya A. and Kumar P., Water Hyacinth as a Potential Biofuel Crop. Electronic Journal Environmental, Agricultural and Food Chemistry

Nigam JN (2002) Bioconversion of water-hyacinth (Eichornia crassipes) hemicellulose acid hydrolysate to motor fuel ethanol by xylose-fermenting yeast. J Biotechnol 97:107–116 as cited by Bhattacharya A. and Kumar P., Water Hyacinth as a Potential Biofuel Crop. Electronic Journal Environmental, Agricultural and Food Chemistry

Poddar K, Mandal L, Banerjee GC (1991) Studies on water hyacinth (Eichhornia crassipes) – Chemical composition of the plant and water from different habitats. Ind Vet J 68:833-837 as cited by Bhattacharya A. and Kumar P., Water Hyacinth as a Potential Biofuel Crop. Electronic Journal Environmental, Agricultural and Food Chemistry

Polprasert C, Wangsuphachart S, Muttamara S (1980) Composting nightsoil and water hyacinth in the tropics. Compost Sci L and Uti 21: 220- 238 as cited by Bhattacharya A. and Kumar P., Water Hyacinth as a Potential Biofuel Crop. Electronic Journal Environmental, Agricultural and Food Chemistry

Ralph J, Akiyama T, Kim H, Lu F, Schatz PF, Marita JM et al. (2006) Effects of coumarate 3-hydroxylase down-regulation on lignin structure. J Biol Chem 281: 8843–8853 as cited by Bhattacharya A. and Kumar P., Water Hyacinth as a Potential Biofuel Crop. Electronic Journal Environmental, Agricultural and Food Chemistry

Stevenson, W. (2010) Operations Management, McGraw Publications, New York city, U.S.A

Sullivan, Paul R. and Wood, Rod. 2012. Water hyacinth, Eichhornia crassipes (Mart.) Solms, seed longevity and the implications for management. 18th Australasian Weeds Conference. Melbourne: Conference Proceedings CD retrieved from http://en.wikipedia.org/wiki/Eichhornia_crassipes on November 5, 2016

Websites:

http://en.wikipedia.org/wiki/Eichhornia_crassipes

https://en.wikipedia.org/wiki/Camarines_Sur

http://knowledge.ckgsb.edu.cn/2013/10/08/marketing/philip-kotler-four-ps-model-marketing-still-king

http://nagacentralschool1-waterlily.blogspot.com/p/focus-study.html

http://www.villarsipag.org

Can Culture Stimulate Innovation for Technopreneurship

Jamal Nassar and Zulkarnain Mohd Sori
INCEIF, Kuala Lumpur, Malaysia
tojamalnassar@gmail.com
zulkarnain@inceif.org

Abstract: Among factors that influence and shape innovation in different societies is the prevailing culture. Most forms of individualistic cultures affect innovation significantly and positively. Other key factors that influence innovation among early stage startups are government interventions, innovation policy and financing. This study has three key objectives. The first is to examine how culture influence innovation among technology startups in Malaysia. Second objective is to explore factors associated with technology innovation. The third objective is to assess how innovation influence financing for technology startups. The study employs thematic analysis as the main methodological approach to analyze primary data. Qualitative survey carried out a series of semi-structured interviews with technology entrepreneurs1, relevant government agencies, industry associations, venture capitalists and leading accelerators. The study finds culture to be an impediment to innovation. Factors such as collective culture and herd mentality behavior were identified as barriers to innovation and fear of failure was attributed to low entrepreneurial innovation. Entrepreneurial attitude on the other hand was identified as a significant quality that is positively related with innovation among technology startups. Thematic analysis reveals that technopreneurs who display positive attitude, determination, perseverance and self-efficacy are more likely to display some form of innovation in their startup. These technopreneurs were more likely to be financed by venture capital funds and private or angel investors. Other factors that influence innovation are, the capacity to commercialize, overall entrepreneurship culture, incubators facilities and capabilities and market size. Based on the findings, the study offers a proposed framework that encapsulates elements, factors and components that effect innovation.

Keywords: innovation, technology, startups, culture, entrepreneurship.

1. Technology Entrepreneurship (Technopreneurship)

Technology oriented enterprises are commonly referred to as technology startups, they are characterized by enhanced communication, faster delivery, ease of use, and interactions among various economic agents that are involved in the production cycle (Carayannis & Von Zedtwitz, 2005). A startup that does not contribute to product innovation or services and does not bear uncertainty risk is not a startup. A definition of technology entrepreneurship can be stated as recognizing, creating and exploiting opportunities, and assembling resources around a technological solution (Bailetti, 2012). Overall, startups are associated with high exponential growth, especially at the early years of its inception. Technology entrepreneurship have developed and materialized as a result of both technology and innovation in their combined influence on production and consumption on all economic factors, for both public and private sectors and for firms of different sizes (Levi Jaksic, Marinkovic, & Rakicevic, 2014).

2. Entrepreneurship Innovation Theory

Part of Schumpeter's significant contribution to the theory of innovation is his classification of the process of innovation, which he divides into four dimensions: invention, innovation, diffusion, and imitation. He further disputes that entrepreneurs seeking profit must innovate.

Entrepreneurial innovation activities feed a creative destruction process (Schumpeter, 1942), causing endless disruption to the economic system in equilibrium and creating opportunities in the economy (Wong, Ho, & Autio, 2005). In the economic adjustment process, additional opportunities are created for other entrepreneurs to venture into the new economy as more innovations are infused into the economic system. Schumpeter's theory predicts that an increasing number of entrepreneurs engaging in economic activities will lead to economic growth. According to Schumpeter (1934), entrepreneurial activities are considered instrumental for technological innovation, which is a dynamic outcome of technical knowledge. Moreover, technological output of a nation is an effective measure of its level of innovation (Coccia, 2014).

3. Anthropology Entrepreneurship Theory

Anthropology is the study of the origin, customs, beliefs and development of a community (Simpeh, 2011). In other words, it is the study of the culture of the people. Anthropological entrepreneurship, therefore, is a

[1] Technopreneurs thereafter.

study of entrepreneurs' cultural and social dimensions. Anthropological entrepreneurship theory can be explained by individual ethnicity and cultural environment, which are considered major factors in shaping the attitudes and behavioural differences among individuals (Baskerville, 2003). Anthropological entrepreneurship is a multidimensional concept that considers entrepreneurship differently across countries and time due to cultural changes (Verheul et al., 2001). Therefore, fully comprehending the influence of national culture on entrepreneurship is of high practical and theoretical importance (Hayton, George, & Zahra, 2002). The investigations of Schumpeter (1934), Weber (1930) and McClelland (1973) on entrepreneurship, sociology and psychology have led to an early assumption that countries differ in their entrepreneurial activities and national culture is relevant to entrepreneurship, as cited by North (1990) and Shane, Locke, and Collins (2003).

4. Literature Review

Entrepreneurship and innovation have a strong and direct correlation (Autio, Kenney, Mustar, Siegel, & Wright, 2014). Schumpeter (1934) was one of the early scholars to explain this relationship. In his innovation theory, he explains how entrepreneurs challenge the status quo and disrupt the economy. According to Schumpeter (1934), entrepreneurs disrupt the marketplace through the introduction of innovation in the following main streams: new products, services, processes, methods of production, new markets, acquiring new sources of supply or raw material and finally, creating new business structures. However, for innovation to take place, the entrepreneur has to transform his or her creative idea into reality (Kabukcu, 2015).

Cultures that value behaviours like risk-taking and independent thinking uphold a tendency to develop and introduce drastic innovations. On the other hand, cultures that display compliance, group interests, and control over the future are not likely to be risk-taking and entrepreneurial (Herbig, 1994; Herbig & Miller, 1992; Hofstede, 1980).

Most studies pertaining to cultural entrepreneurship have been conducted in western countries and thus may not necessarily apply to Asian countries. Herbig and Miller (1992), Herbig (1994) and Hofstede (1980) show a negative relationship between collective cultures and early stage entrepreneurship. Individuals in collective cultures are more likely to belong to a group that looks after them in exchange for loyalty (Soares et al., (2007), whereas individuals in individualistic cultures look after themselves and their immediate family independently. Some scholars suggest that cultures that adopt individualism have higher rates of technological innovation (Bagchi, 2004); however, these studies are limited and not generalized. Meanwhile, several nations that are not individualistic in nature (e.g. Finland, India, South Korea and Taiwan) have emerged in the past two decades with significant technological innovations and have built global and competitive high tech industries (Taylor & Wilson 2010).

Studies examining cultural variance among ethnic entrepreneurs in Malaysia are limited and a literature gap does exist in ethnic entrepreneurial development in Malaysia. Despite government efforts, Malay entrepreneurship is lagging behind that of their Chinese counterparts and the impact of government programs towards ethnic groups is limited. Studies (Ariff and Abubakar 2002; Hamidon 2008; Hariri and Osman 2011; Hussain 2006; Juri 1999; Menon 2009; Nawi 2015; Zainol and Daud 2011) suggest that ethnic culture is central to explaining entrepreneurship behaviour in Malaysia. An example may be the Chinese Malaysian group's dominance in the business economy and their deterministic approach in building ventures. Moreover, the same studies indicate that Malay (Bumiputra) entrepreneurs have a relaxed attitude toward entrepreneurship and are more likely to rely on government facilities to grow their business. This cultural gap in attitudes toward entrepreneurship may be explained by historical events of immigration and colonization (Booth, 1999; Chakraborty, Thompson, & Yehoue, 2016; Noor & Leong, 2013).

Turró et al., (2014) strongly argue that innovation is a key determinant not only for firms' performance, but also for national economic performance. Recent studies have tried to explain innovation in startup firms in relation to culture, ethnicity and government role in formulating effective policies (Aggarwal & Goodell, 2014; Barakat, Boddington, & Vyakarnam, 2014; Braunerhjelm, 2010; Chakraborty et al., 2016; Coccia, 2014; Herbig, 1994; Kabukcu, 2015; Paradkar, Knight, & Hansen, 2015; S.Gans, Hsu, & Stern, 2000; Schumpeter, 1934; Taylor & Wilson, 2012; Turro et al., 2014; Yoon, Yun, Lee, & Phillips, 2015; Zhao, Li, & Rauch, 2012).

The relationship between innovation, culture and financing entrepreneurship among Malaysian tech startups is not well established in academic research and a significant knowledge gap exists. Current studies indicate that investors are less likely to finance innovative startups at the early stage (Ajagbe, Long, Aslan, & Ismail, 2012; Ismail, Aslan, & Ajagbe, 2011; Wahab & Buyong, 2008). Evidence in other countries indicate that venture capital display ethnic bias in financing ethnic enterprises (Bengtsson & Hsu, 2015; Chand & Ghorbani, 2011).

5. Methodology

The study qualitative in nature, qualitative studies often use grounded theory or thematic analysis as the choice of method (Braun & Clarke, 2006; Corbin & Strauss, 1990). Thematic analysis method approach include face to face interviews with various groups in the Technopreneurship field in Malaysia. Semi structured interviews were most suited since they allow some degree of flexibility for respondents to share their insights and provide valuable feedback, unlike structured interviews (Rubin & Rubin, 2011). Interview took place with technopreneurs, government organization executives, selected incubators and accelerators, non-government organizations (NGOs) and venture capitalist (VCs).

5.1 The Interview Approach

The study approached 22 participants for the purpose of face to face interview, however interviews conducted were 17.

Data collected through interviews with technopreneurs, government agencies, associations and venture capitalists were analyzed in a similar way based on a three-stage procedure as suggested in the literature (Creswell, 2007; Miles and Huberman, 1994). Main analysis method was thematic analysis which is generally is a three-step process:

1. Obtaining open codes from the interview transcript
2. Developing axial codes as certain themes and pattern start to appear
3. Define final factors that emerge out of themes and pattern

Table 1.1 below include participants category, their Participant Identification number (PID) and nature of their organization.

Table 1.1: Main Interview Survey Participants

Main Interview Survey Summary

Category	Participants	Type
Public Organizations (7)	R11 – R17	Public
Associations (2)	R9, R10	Ngo
Entrepreneurs (6)	R1 – R6	Tech Startups
Venture Capitalist (2)	R7, R8	Investment
Total Interviewed	17	

6. Thematic Analysis

Respondents elaborate on their general views on innovation within a local and international context, they also shared their views on what they thought was most critical about innovation at this stage of development of entrepreneurship ecosystem. On the subject matter, some respondents were more engaged and elaborative than others and those who were more engaged provided suggestions and insights on the development of innovation from a localized perspective. Table 1.2 include list seven factors the study present as a results of analysis on this category, factors are listed alphabetically.

Table 1.2: Innovation Factors, PID* Participant Identification Number.

	Respondents PID*																
Innovation Factors	ENTREPRENEURS						VC		ASSOC.		GOV. AGENCIES						
	R1	R2	R3	R4	R5	R6	R7	R8	R9	R10	R11	R12	R13	R14	R15	R16	R17
Commercialization									⍰	⍰	⍰		⍰				⍰
Entrepreneurship										⍰		⍰					
Incubation	⍰	⍰	⍰				⍰					⍰	⍰	⍰			⍰

Innovation Factors	Respondents PID*																
	ENTREPRENEURS						VC			ASSOC.			GOV. AGENCIES				
	R1	R2	R3	R4	R5	R6	R7	R8	R9	R10	R11	R12	R13	R14	R15	R16	R17
Innovation Strategy	?					?	?	?	?		?	?	?			?	
Innovation Culture	?					?	?	?	?			?					
Market Size							?		?	?	?	?					?

6.1 Commercialization

Respondents (R9, R11, R13) emphasis on commercialization as an end goal to innovative ideas and new ventures, whereby new entrepreneurs focus tend to be on the current stage of development. Respondents who stress on commercialization are those with business and cultural exposure and more experienced. Respondents (R9, R11, R13) are from association and government agencies. Excerpts from the interviews stated below:

> *Innovation here in this country overall we hold up high... it's not many people take IP (Intellectual Property) into consideration, many think about commercialization verses innovation, which in this market makes sense. (R9)*

Respondent (R9) and respondent (R4) highlight the issue of intellectual property rights, insinuating that challenges exist in the local market where ideas are not valued for their worth and they can be replicated without any copy rights. Such sensitive issue represents a serious threat for first time entrepreneurs, especially those who lack both the depth of business experience and skills.

6.2 Entrepreneurship Spirit

Vision, belief and desire to succeed are some of the essential ingredients of entrepreneurship, respondents (R1, R6, R10 and R12) agree that failure is a corner stone for most entrepreneurs, it's part of the journey that many will have to go through.

Entrepreneurs who are discouraged by failure, are less likely to achieve their goals and dream say respondent (R1). He further states that entrepreneurs need to overcome any obstacles to progress.
Local culture still view failure as a taboo and this may lead entrepreneurs to avoid innovation all together to avoid failure. Innovation is a process of high risk and high return scenario and innovations may be commercialized.

As an experienced angel investor and mentor, respondent (R10) provide a personal view on failure and his investment preference.

> *I am not in disagreement with failure, its fine, we see more entrepreneurs who have failed, and I personally invest in entrepreneurs who have failed before and they are over 30. (R10)*

Furthermore,

> *"The faster you fail the faster you move on." (R13)*
>
> *"You must be not afraid of failure, in Malay society failure is a taboo, but for innovation failure is a must, like Thomas Edison..." (R11)*

6.3 Incubation

Incubators provide services to support startups at the early stage of their existence, they provide training, coaching, mentoring, working space and other resources as per the incubator mandate. Some incubators provide regional support, says respondent (R10), the objective is to link startups with their regional counterparts or with government agencies to facilitate market penetration. Incubators partner with one another, share best practices and some evolve to become venture capitalist of some kind and end up investing in startups they accept into the program.

Respondents (R1, R2, R3, R7, R11, R12 and R13) all highlight the role incubators and accelerator play in sponsoring innovative ideas. Local government is par-taking efforts on different fronts to establish a well connected entrepreneurship ecosystem, innovation remains limited.

Incubators play a fundamental role with startups in building their first Minimum Viable Product (MVP) or what is commonly referred as prototype. Incubators offer a host of other services such as, validation of the prototype or MVP, assisting teams in business planning, AB testing and finally, present and pitch to investors and venture capitalists.

6.4 Innovation Culture

Innovation factor is influenced by various elements, most important and critical for innovation to thrive is a supportive culture, according to respondents (R1, R6, R7, R9, R11 and R12). A venture capital respondent (R7) address a highly sensitive and important element of innovation culture, the mindset!

> *"There are many ASEAN entrepreneurs who are focused, but say the real innovation comes from Silicon Valley and that is a mindset issue, and I think I see that apply to Muslim entrepreneurs as well." (R7)*

Other respondents claim that most innovation are exported from Silicon Valley, and local participants are not being genuinely disruptive in their innovation. Out of his frustration with the lack of innovation among local entrepreneurs, participant (R10) provide an advice to entrepreneurs in this area.

> *"Be contrarian, it's hard, but you have higher chances of success. Copycat ideas have 80% failure risk, look at what market needs." (R10)*

Although he addresses market needs, (R10) call for entrepreneurs to be genuine in their ideas and not just apply what has worked in Silicon Valley or elsewhere, he believes Malaysian entrepreneurs are more likely to start a business that is tested and tried, and not take big risk with their own ideas. Culture role in supporting innovation, tolerating and embracing failure maybe a starting point for innovation to lead the way for future entrepreneurs.

6.5 Innovation Strategy

Respondents provided feedback of high value throughout this study, most notable their articulated thoughts that addressed the challenge and the remedy at often times. In this section, respondents (R1, R6, R7, R8, R9, R12, R16) raised technical points with some suggestions that perhaps could be considered as strategies in improving the local approach to innovation imperfections. (R9) proposes scale innovation, whereby Malaysia can be a suitable test market for innovative entrepreneurs and a base for them to expand and scale their tested innovations in larger markets like Indonesia and China.
He further declares:

> *"Necessity is what breads innovation, not the need for innovation." (R9)*

Respondents (R12 and R16) cite innovation with certain ethnic clusters, where in certain industry clusters the likelihood increases of certain ethnic group verses the others. Example where given to R&D, biomedicine, graphic design and fashion are more Malay concentrated whereas IT is more likely to be an Indian and so on.

6.6 Market Size

Few respondents claim market size to be a determinant factor to innovation, whereby small markets do not absorb as much innovation as larger markets, comparison were made frequently between Malaysia and Indonesia, and at times with China. Therefore, smaller markets were a limiting factor to innovation.

> *"In China for example they have 3D printed a house!*
>
> *Now why doesn't something like this happen in Malaysia? It's because in China there are lots of people, and people do need housing, and they would probably sell fast, there is a lot of room for innovation." (R9)*

7. Conclusion

Building and developing innovation culture seems to be a significant contributor to building a supportive entrepreneurship ecosystem (Bennett & Parks, 2015; Coccia, 2014; Taylor & Wilson, 2012). One could conclude that innovation culture is one of the essential pillars in building conducive entrepreneurial environment that encourages innovation and tolerate failure.

Commercialization seems to be overriding factor among successful technology startups. Startups that are able to commercialize their ideas and demonstrate market traction are able to secure financing from private investors and venture capital. Fear of failure seems to be a dominant factor that derails many individuals from engaging in entrepreneurial activities according to our study. The study recommends government agencies to focus on supporting innovative ideas and entrepreneurial spirit regardless of ethnicity and background.

Respondents emphasize on the role incubation play in increasing the viability of commercial ideas among startups at the very early stage. Developing an MPV is a challenge to many entrepreneurs venturing into technology and online business. Incubators provide technical assistance, coaching, and mentoring services to entrepreneurs helping them in translating their ideas into commercial concepts (Mian, Lamine, & Fayolle, 2016). We anticipate incubators role to become even more important, especially in their capacity to decrease failure rate at the early stage while increasing the startup likelihood of securing first round of pre-seed funding.

Coaching and mentoring help entrepreneurs align their short terms goals with their long-term strategy and objectives. One of the reasons entrepreneurs prefer to raise funds from venture capital is the advisory benefits offered by experienced venture capitalists (Da Rin, 2016).

Recent studies indicate strategic partnerships between corporate accelerators and startups could be an effective method for paving the way for innovation (Berger & Udell, 1998; Kohler, 2016). This partnership is based on two principles, first, startups are a source of innovation and they are continuously reinventing business models. The second is the capacity and resources corporates at their disposal. Startups may collaborate with corporates to become part of an existing corporate accelerator, or both parties can establish an independent accelerator. The level of freedom, innovation and control will dictate the nature of the accelerator. Overall, this partnership-based collaboration could be an effective technique for the private sector to support the existing entrepreneurship ecosystem in Malaysia. Whereby corporates may benefit by raising their level of innovation and test new inventions, products or services without a considerable upfront investment. This collaboration may lead the path for significant development in the private sector and extend support to build a strong and sustainable startup ecosystem.

In conclusion, the study presents a proposed innovation framework illustrated in figure 1.1. The framework attempts to link factors, programs and initiatives needed to drive innovation culture forward for technology startups.

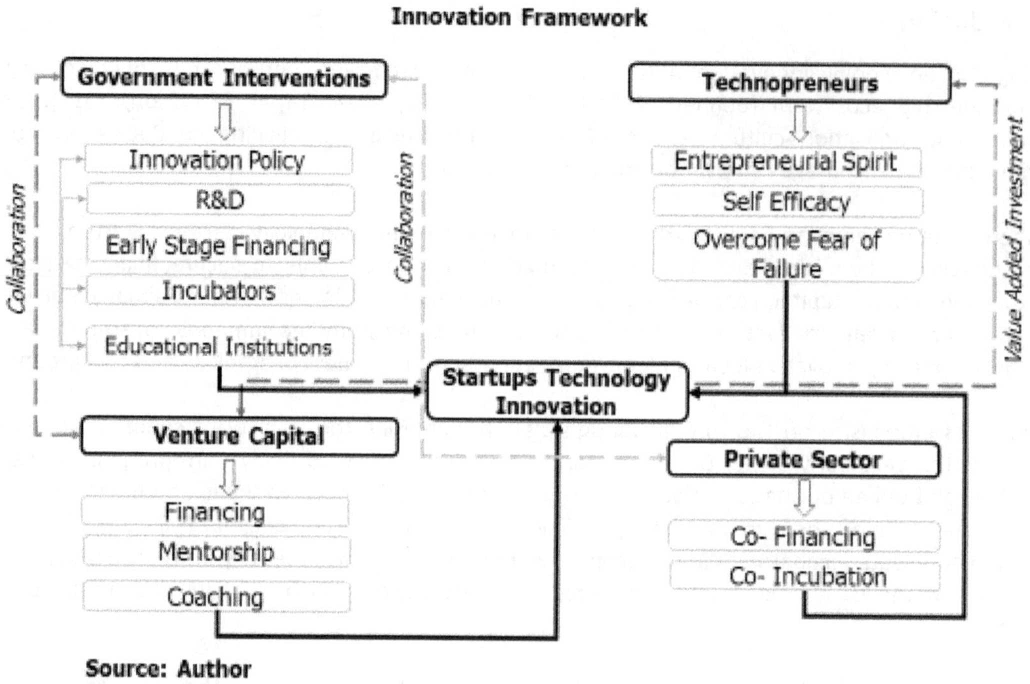

Figure 1.1: Innovation Framework

Current government innovation policies, seem to be strategic and supportive of both technology and innovation as key measures in the national transformation program for the country (Economic Planning Unit, 2015). The emphasis on private sector participation is crucial to the development of sustainable innovation model as proposed in figure 1.1. Private sector jointly with government funding agencies can co-fund risky venture at their early stages. Co-financing and private public partnership increases the level of support, collaboration and minimized risk involved. Efforts should be directed to building a supportive culture that is resilient and adaptive. In such cultures, entrepreneurs are inspired and encouraged to passionately engage in creating ventures that make a difference for their societies and ultimately for the world.

However, innovation culture comes at a cost, failure cost should be absorbed and welcomed, not feared. Moreover, perception of failure should be perceived as partial success not ultimate failure.

References

Aggarwal, R., & Goodell, J. W. (2014). Cross-national differences in access to finance: Influence of culture and institutional environments. *Research in International Business and Finance*, *31*, 193–211. http://doi.org/10.1016/j.ribaf.2013.09.004

Ajagbe, M. A., Long, C. S., Aslan, S. A., & Ismail, K. (2012). Investment in Technology Based Small and Medium Sized Firms in Malaysia : Roles for Commercial. *International Journal of Research in Management & Technology*, *2*(2), 147–153.

Ariff, M., & Abubakar, S. Y. (2002). Strengthening entrepreneurship in Malaysia. *Research Paper*, 1–22. http://doi.org/10.5539/ass.v10n6p122

Autio, E., Kenney, M., Mustar, P., Siegel, D., & Wright, M. (2014). Entrepreneurial innovation: The importance of context. *Research Policy*, *43*(7), 1097–1108. http://doi.org/10.1016/j.respol.2014.01.015

Bailetti, T. (2012). Technology Entrepreneurship:\nOverview, Definition, and Distinctive Aspects. *Technology Innovation Management Review*, (February), 5–12.

Barakat, S., Boddington, M., & Vyakarnam, S. (2014). Measuring entrepreneurial self-efficacy to understand the impact of creative activities for learning innovation. *International Journal of Management Education*, *12*(3), 456–468. http://doi.org/10.1016/j.ijme.2014.05.007

Baskerville, R. F. (2003). Hofstede never studied culture. *Accounting, Organizations and Society*, *28*(1), 1–14. http://doi.org/10.1016/S0361-3682(01)00048-4

Bengtsson, O., & Hsu, D. H. (2015). Ethnic matching in the U.S. venture capital market. *Journal of Business Venturing*, *30*(2), 338–354. http://doi.org/10.1016/j.jbusvent.2014.09.001

Bennett, N., & Parks, J. M. (2015). Struggling to innovate? Examine your structure, systems, and culture. *Business Horizons*, *58*(5), 563–569. http://doi.org/10.1016/j.bushor.2015.05.009

Berger, A. N., & Udell, G. F. (1998). The economics of small business finance: The roles of private equity and debt markets in the financial growth cycle. *Journal of Banking & Finance*, *22*(6–8), 613–673. http://doi.org/10.1016/S0378-4266(98)00038-7

Booth, A. (1999). Initial conditions and miraculous growth: Why is South East Asia different from Taiwan and South Korea? *World Development*, *27*(2), 301–321. http://doi.org/10.1016/S0305-750X(98)00126-0

Braun, V. and, & Clarke, V. (2006). "Using thematic analysis in psychology." Qualitative research in psychology, *3*(2), 77–101.

Braunerhjelm, P. (2010). Entrepreneurship , Innovation and Economic Growth Working Papers Series from Swedish Entrepreneurship Forum. *Swedish Entreprenourship Forum*, 1–75.

Carayannis, E. G., & Von Zedtwitz, M. (2005). Architecting gloCal (global-local), real-virtual incubator networks (G-RVINs) as catalysts and accelerators of entrepreneurship in transitioning and developing economies: Lessons learned and best practices from current development and business incubation . *Technovation*, *25*(2), 95–110. http://doi.org/10.1016/S0166-4972(03)00072-5

Chakraborty, S., Thompson, J. C., & Yehoue, E. B. (2016). The culture of entrepreneurship. *Journal of Economic Theory*, *163*, 288–317. http://doi.org/10.1016/j.jet.2015.12.007

Chand, M., & Ghorbani, M. (2011). National culture, networks and ethnic entrepreneurship: A comparison of the Indian and Chinese immigrants in the US. *International Business Review*, *20*(6), 593–606. http://doi.org/10.1016/j.ibusrev.2011.02.009

Coccia, M. (2014). Socio-cultural origins of the patterns of technological innovation: What is the likely interaction among religious culture, religious plurality and innovation?? Towards a theory ofsocio-cultural drivers of the patterns of technological innovation. *Technology in Society*, *36*(1), 13–25. http://doi.org/10.1016/j.techsoc.2013.11.002

Corbin, J. M., & Strauss, A. (1990). Grounded theory research: Procedures, canons, and evaluative criteria. *Qualitative Sociology*, *13*(1), 3–21. http://doi.org/10.1007/BF00988593

Creswell, J. W. (2007). Qualitative inquiry and research design: choosing among five approaches. *Thousand Oaks, London: Sage.*

Da Rin, M. (2016). *FINANCING GROWTH THROUGH VENTURE CAPITAL IN ASIA AND THE PACIFIC. United Nations, Economic and Social Commission for Asia and the Pacific.*

Economic Planning Unit. (2015). *Strengthening Infrastructure to Support Economic Expansion. Rancangan Malaysia Kesebelas (Eleventh Malaysia Plan) : 2016-2020.*

Hamidon, S. (2008). The Development of Malay Entrepreneurship in Malaysia. *Asian Journal of Technology Innovation*, *16*, 101–116. http://doi.org/10.1080/19761597.2008.9668649

Hariri, K., & Osman, J. (2011). The Stages Of Entrepreneurship Personality Criteria Among Malaysian High School Students.

Hayton, J. C., George, G., & Zahra, S. A. (2002). National Culture and Entrepreneurship: A Review of Behavioral Research. *Entrepreneurship Theory and Practice*, *26*(4), 33–52. http://doi.org/Article

Herbig, P. A. (1994). The innovation matrix: Culture and structure prerequisites to innovation. *Praeger Pub Text.*

Herbig, P. A., & Miller, J. C. (1992). "The United States versus the United Kingdom, Canada, and Australia: The case for structural influences on innovation." *Technological Forecasting and Social Change*, *41*(4), 423–434.

Hofstede, G. (1980). "Culture's consequences: National differences in thinking and organizing." *Beverly Hills, Calif.: Sage.*

Hussain, S. M. (2006). Cultural Constraints In Leading Malaysian SMEs To Global Markets, (35423). http://doi.org/10.5897/JAERD12.088

Ismail, K., Aslan, A., & Ajagbe, A. (2011). An investment framework to help equity financiers select tech SMEs in Malaysia. *Interdisciplinary Journal of Contemporary Research in Business.*, *3*(5), 967–985.

Juri, K. A. B. M. (1999). The relationship between cultural values and innovativeness: a study of Malay and Chinese entrepreneurs in Malaysia. *University of Malaya*.

Kabukcu, E. (2015). Creativity Process in Innovation Oriented Entrepreneurship: The case of Vakko. *Procedia - Social and Behavioral Sciences*, *195*, 1321–1329. http://doi.org/10.1016/j.sbspro.2015.06.307

Kohler, T. (2016). Corporate accelerators: Building bridges between corporations and startups. *Business Horizons*, *59*(3), 347–357. http://doi.org/10.1016/j.bushor.2016.01.008

Levi Jaksic, M., Marinkovic, S., & Rakicevic, J. (2014). Sustainable Technology Entrepreneurship and Development – the Case of Serbia. *Management - Journal for Theory and Practice of Management*, *19*(70), 65–73. http://doi.org/10.7595/management.fon.2014.0004

McClelland, D. C. (1973). Testing for competence rather than for "intelligence". *The American Psychologist*, *28*(1), 1–14. http://doi.org/10.1037/h0038240

Menon, J. (2009). Macroeconomic management amid ethnic diversity: Fifty years of Malaysian experience. *Journal of Asian Economics*, *20*(1), 25–33. http://doi.org/10.1016/j.asieco.2008.05.005

Mian, S., Lamine, W., & Fayolle, A. (2016). Technology Business Incubation: An overview of the state of knowledge. *Technovation*, *50–51*, 1–12. http://doi.org/10.1016/j.technovation.2016.02.005

Miles, M.B. and Huberman, A. M. (1994). Qualitative data analysis: a sourcebook of new methods. *Thousand Oaks, CA: Sage Publications.*

Nawi, H. (2015). Determinants of capital structure in small and medium sized enterprises in Malaysia, (May).

Noor, N. M., & Leong, C. H. (2013). Multiculturalism in Malaysia and Singapore: Contesting models. *International Journal of Intercultural Relations*, *37*(6), 714–726. http://doi.org/10.1016/j.ijintrel.2013.09.009

North, D. C. (1990). Institutions, institutional change and economic performance. *Cambridge University Press*.

Paradkar, A., Knight, J., & Hansen, P. (2015). Innovation in start-ups: Ideas filling the void or ideas devoid of resources and capabilities? *Technovation*, *41*, 1–10. http://doi.org/10.1016/j.technovation.2015.03.004

Rubin, H. J., & Rubin, I. S. (2011). Qualitative interviewing: The art of hearing data. *Sage Publications*.

S.Gans, J., Hsu, D. H., & Stern, S. (2000). When Does Start-Up Innovation Spur The Gate of Creative Destruction? *National Bureau of Economic Research*.

Schumpeter. (1934). Entrepreneurship as innovation. *Entrepreneurship: The Social Science View*.

Schumpeter, J. A. (1943). Capitalism, Socialism and Democracy, 3rd edition 1976. *London: George Allen and Unwin*.

Shane, S., Locke, E. A., & Collins, C. J. (2003). Entrepreneurial motivation. *Human Resource Management Review*, *13*(2), 257–279. http://doi.org/10.1016/S1053-4822(03)00017-2

Simpeh, K. N. (2011). Entrepreneurship theories and Empirical research : A Summary Review of the Literature. *European Journal Of Business and Management*, *3*(6), 1–9.

Soares, A. M., Farhangmehr, M., & Shoham, A. (2007). Hofstede's dimensions of culture in international marketing studies. *Journal of Business Research*, *60*(3), 277–284. http://doi.org/10.1016/j.jbusres.2006.10.018

Sumaco, F. T., Imrie, B. C., & Hussain, K. (2014). The Consequence of Malaysian National Culture Values on Hotel Branding. *Procedia - Social and Behavioral Sciences*, *144*, 91–101. http://doi.org/10.1016/j.sbspro.2014.07.277

Taylor, M. Z., & Wilson, S. (2012). Does culture still matter?: The effects of individualism on national innovation rates. *Journal of Business Venturing*, *27*(2), 234–247. http://doi.org/10.1016/j.jbusvent.2010.10.001

Turro, A., Urbano, D., & Peris-Ortiz, M. (2014). Culture and innovation: The moderating effect of cultural values on corporate entrepreneurship. *Technological Forecasting and Social Change*, *88*, 360–369. http://doi.org/10.1016/j.techfore.2013.10.004

Verheul, I., Wennekers, S., Audretsch, D., & Thurik, R. (2001). *An Eclectic Theory of Entrepreneurship: Policies, Institutions and Culture*.

Wahab, I., & Buyong, S. Z. (2008). *"Financing technology-based SMEs in Malaysia: practices and problems." SMEs in global economy series: SMEs and industrial development in Asian countries 2008*.

Weber, M. (1930). . The Protestant Ethic and the Spirit of Capitalism: and other writings. Translated by Talcott Parsons... With a Foreword by RH Tawney. G. Allen & Unwin.

Wong, P. K., Ho, Y. P., & Autio, E. (2005). Entrepreneurship, innovation and economic growth: Evidence from GEM data. *Small Business Economics*, *24*(3), 335–350. http://doi.org/10.1007/s11187-005-2000-1

Yoon, H., Yun, S., Lee, J., & Phillips, F. (2015). Entrepreneurship in East Asian Regional Innovation Systems: Role of social capital. *Technological Forecasting and Social Change*, *100*, 83–95. http://doi.org/10.1016/j.techfore.2015.06.028

Zainol, F., & Daud, W. W. (2011). Indigenous ("Bumiputera") Malay Entrepreneurs in Malaysia: Government Supports, Entrepreneurial Orientation and Firms Performances. *International Business and Management*, *2*(1), 86–99.

Zhao, X., Li, H., & Rauch, A. (2012). Cross-Country Differences in Entrepreneurial Activity: The Role of Cultural Practice and National Wealth. *Frontiers of Business Research in China*, 1–25. http://doi.org/10.3868/s070-001-012-0021-0

Intrapreneurship Approach to Innovation among Saudi Arabian Firms

Florabel O. Nieva
Asst. Professor, Department of Entrepreneurship, Effat University, Jeddah, Kingdom of Saudi Arabia
fnieva@effatuniversity.edu.sa

Abstract: Industrial firms today are actively promoting intrapreneurship within the systems, and permitting employees to spend some time on innovative ideas unrelated to their normal jobs. This paper provides an overview of the intrapreneurship approach to innovation among Saudi Arabian firms. It focuses on the organisational characteristics of Saudi Arabian firms, the internal organisational factors influencing intrapreneurship behaviour and innovation in terms of management support, work discretion, rewards/reinforcement, time availability, and organisational boundaries; and the relationship between organisational characteristics and the factors influencing intrapreneurship behaviour and innovation along the aforementioned five areas. The study utilised descriptive-correlational method using a questionnaire as the main instrument in gathering the data. The respondents composed of fifty employees holding managerial position from all levels and one hundred non-managers of different industries of Saudi Arabian firms. The findings revealed that there are organisational characteristics conducive to entrepreneurship such as removing the formal structure and sidestepping organisational bureaucracy and start-up style of management. The relationship between two variables was statistically significant. In other words, the employees in Saudi Arabian firms were positive in becoming entrepreneurs within the existing organisation.

Keywords: innovation, intrapreneurship, organisational characteristics, organisational factors, Saudi Arabian firms

1. Introduction

Today's business environment is defined by a change in the organisation (Alsaif, 2015). However, Abrahamson (2000) said that change can be very disruptive to any organisation. By introducing technological change will increase sociotechnical in the implementation associated with people. This technological change will influences management activities in an organisation (Palmer et al., 2006). The relentless pressures of competition stemming from globalisation, technological changes today are increasingly buffeting organisations. One of the pathways for companies to weather these storms is through unleashing the entrepreneurial spirit latent in its employees, enabling them to carve out new paths, initiate new ventures, defy the status quo in their organisations, and break fresh ground. On the other hand, intrapreneurship is a major driver for organisational renewal or 'reinvention' (Seshadri and Tripathy, 2006). Similarly, Eesley and Longenecker (2006) pointed out that intrapreneurship is a key component of a firm success, especially in organisations operating in rapidly changing industries.

The Kingdom of Saudi Arabia which has launched the ambitious Vision 2030 plan to reduce its dependence on oil, has scored highest among the most innovative countries of the world. Moreover, the Kingdom has launched a National Science, Technology and Innovation Strategic Plan (NSTIP), which is among many other national plans followed in Saudi Arabia to shift its economy from oil based to knowledge based (Khan 2016). The Saudi Fast Growth 100 is a new national program designed to promote entrepreneurship and innovation, ranking the fastest-growing companies in the Kingdom based on their revenues. It is estimated over 70 percent of the Saudi Fast Growth CEOs are serial entrepreneurs who have founded other companies, however, the majority of which are still in business. These "high-intensity entrepreneurs" exceed the U.S. Inc. 500 for their rate of new business formation. Highly competitive, their revenues grow at an average of 43 percent annually, more than ten times the rate of the Kingdom's private sector growth of four percent per year. Saudi Arabia is committed becoming "one of the most competitive nations in the world, and in order to achieve this ambitious goal, the Kingdom must nurture emerging growth companies since they are the oxygen of the economy," according to H.E. Amr Al-Dabbagh, Governor of the Saudi Arabian General Investment Authority (SAGIA). The process of entrepreneurship must, therefore, start at the very top of the organization (Quinn, 1979). Innovation is the specific instrument of entrepreneurship; and the act that endows resources with a new capacity to create wealth. Drucker (2006). Innovation contributes to the growth of the economy because intrapreneurs produce innovations. As such, this research tries to integrate the intrapreneurship approach to innovation and creating a climate that stimulates the creativity, spirit of innovation, and entrepreneurial mindset of employees in the organization. Thus, the researcher embarked on this kind of study.

2. Literature Review

2.1 Intrapreneurship

The intrapreneurship phenomenon has been explained in various terms such as intrapreneuring; corporate entrepreneurship; internal corporate entrepreneurship; corporate venturing; internal corporate entrepreneurship; strategic renewal; internal entrepreneurship and venturing (Antoncic, 2007; Sharma and Chrisman, 1999). Intrapreneurship is a word shortened from the term intra-corporate entrepreneurship, refers to the entrepreneurial activities of employees within the boundaries and auspices of a larger organisation (DeSai, 2013). The term has been described as entrepreneurship within an existing organisation. It is a process by which individuals in organisations pursue opportunities without regard to the resources they currently control. Intrapreneurship can also be conceptualised in terms of its content, its underlying dimensions based on the Schumpeterian innovation concept. It involves the pursuit of creative or new solutions to the challenges confronting the firm, including the development or enhancement of old and new products and services, markets, and administrative techniques and technologies for performing organisational functions (Stevenson and Jarillo, 1990).

According to Branson (2015), intrapreneurship is a corporate entrepreneurship comes from the idea of using entrepreneurial ideas, innovation, and start-up business techniques within a large (or medium size) organisation. Khang (2014) stated that intrapreneurship is a strategy for stimulating innovation by making better use of entrepreneurial talent. When effectively promoted, it not only fosters innovation but also helps employees with good ideas to better channel the resources of a corporation to develop more successful products and services. On the other hand, Nies (2006) stated that intrapreneurship is the ability of a company to support, with economic and technical resources, expedited decision-making processes. Emmanuel (2009) defined that intrapreneurship as an innovation that occurs inside established companies through the efforts of creative employees. Pinchot and Pellman (1999) asserted that intrapreneurship gives the managers of a corporation the freedom to take initiative and try new ideas. The intrapreneurs develop their innovative ideas within the organisation to which they belong and are committed to implementing them within the confines of their organisation, even when confronted with organisational change and possible organisational conflicts.

2.2 Innovation

Innovation is one of the most fundamental practises underpinning economic growth, and it has great potential to develop solutions to economic and social challenges. Innovation is the key to the survival of commercial firms in today's business and market environments. It enables different firms to survive and prosper by creating market value and competitive advantage (Al-Ansari, 2014). The innovation is the explicit instrument of entrepreneurship (Drucker, 1985) and the act that endows resources with a new capacity to create wealth. Trewin (2004) explained that innovation is the introduction of new or significantly improved goods, services or operational, organisational or managerial processes. Bolton and Thompson (2013) stressed that innovation and intrapreneurship have a number of constituent elements, such as: ideas (spin-off points), infrastructure (premises, incubators, suppliers, venture capital, and corporate resources), networks (support structures and effective enablers, educated and capable people (to help with the maturation of the initiative or business) and entrepreneurs themselves.

2.3 Organisational Characteristics

The organisational characteristics affect employees' intrapreneurial behaviour with the organisation (Axtell et al., 2000; Zampetakis et al., 2009). As explained by Mokaya (2012), the single most important factor in establishing an "intrapreneur-friendly" organisation is making sure that the employees are placed in an innovative working environment. Rigid and conservative organisational structure often has a stifling effect on intrapreneurial efforts. Reightering and Weitzel (2013) affirmed the employee behaviour as antecedents for intrapreneurship, such as (1) Intrapreneurship within organisations is not affected directly by the work context, but indirectly through innovative workplace behaviour and personal initiative by employees; (2) Formal organisational work context characteristics such as horizontal participation and the number of resources affect the level of innovative behaviours and personal initiative within an organisation, but not risk taking; (3) Trust in the direct manager plays an important role in the stimulation of innovative behaviours and personal initiative amongst employees, and (4) Risk taking behaviour by employees are not related to the involvement in an intrapreneurial project.

Lassen et al. (2006) discussed the structural equation model estimations indicate that formal organisational factors (horizontal participation, resource availability) affect employees' intrapreneurial behaviour, but also highlight informal factors such as trust in the direct manager. Entrepreneurial oriented firms had proactive and risk-taking behaviour, that is needed for radical innovation development. Eesley and Longenecker (2006) explained that the organisational intrapreneurship in this context does not only cover the barriers to intrapreneurship, such as 1) punishing risk- taking, new ideas, and mistakes; 2) ideas with nowhere to go for follow-up or action; 3) falling to sanction, promote, and encourage intrapeneurship; 4) unhealthy politics: infighting and lack cooperation; 5) poor communications and organisational silos; 6) people not encouraged to think about opportunities; 7) unclear organisational mission, priorities, and objectives; 8) lack of real management support; 9) improvement and risk taking activity not rewarded; and 10) inadequate time or resources. Nørgaard (2012) explained that the top management needs to encourage intrapreneurial activities through failure acceptance. Also, the majority of the firms does not support innovation, are low on failure acceptance and do not reward entrepreneurial behaviour.

3. Methodology

The descriptive-correlational method of research was used in the study using a questionnaire as the main instrument in gathering the data. It involves the description, recording, analysis, and interpretation of the present nature, composition or the processes of phenomena. The correlational study employing the relationship of two variables under study. It is designed to estimate the extent to which the two variables are related to each other. A total of fifty employees holding managerial position from all level and one hundred non-managers from various industries in Saudi Arabia participated in the survey. An interview was conducted several times by the researcher to identify the perceptions and opinions expressed by the individual, which are revealed through careful and systematic analysis. These informal interviews were aimed at bridging the gap which is not answered by the quantitative data and clarified some missing links from the survey. It became the sources of primary data of the study. The data were given a deeper analysis in order to arrive at a more concrete, reliable and viable result. The key internal organisational factors were assessed using five factors, such as management support, work discretion, rewards/reinforcement, time availability, and organisational boundaries.

The data were gathered and statistically analysed using the IBM Statistical Package for the Social Sciences (SPSS Version 24, 2016). The significant relationship was validated using p-value approach. The numerical findings of the study were statistically analysed and interpreted using the frequency count ranking, weighted mean and Kendall's tau correlation coefficients. Since most of the options are of the Likert-scale type, weights and corresponding adjectival descriptions. The correlation coefficient (r) measures the strength and direction of a relationship between organisational characteristics and internal organisational factors influencing intrapreneurship behaviour along the aforementioned five areas.

4. Results and Discussion

4.1 Organisational characteristics

Organisation is a process which integrates the different type of activities to achieve organisational goals. A competent management responsible for managing an organisation and creating an intrapreneur-friendly environment is important in order to reach the goals. In Saudi Arabian firms, there are some noticeable organisational characteristics conducive for fostering intrapreneurship and innovation. One of the major characteristics highly practised by the firms was "removing the formal structure and sidestepping organisational bureaucracy". This implicates a set of culture encouraging creativity and innovation evident among Saudi Arabian firms. They endeavour in establishing an environment wherein creative employees can pursue new ways of doing things and new product ideas within organisation context. Employees are given enough time away from their jobs to work on creative ideas while setting up a formal process for encouraging intrapreneurship through its innovation. When these efforts are supported and coordinated by managers, these endeavours will result in sustainable competitive advantages through innovation in the form of new products, services, and processes.

The Saudi Arabian firms are characterised by "start-up style of management". Flexibility, innovation, and risk-taking describes this type of management. The objective is circumvented bureaucracy by taking advantage of new opportunities and new processes or designs. Ideally, entrepreneurial organisations should be decentralised, flexible, and experiential- providing opportunities to experiment and learn by doing.

Entrepreneurial organisations have fewer layers of management known as the flat structure. The fewer obstacles employees face, the more innovative they can able to be (Bygrave and Zacharakis 2010). Empowerment, freedom, and openness to innovation are the hallmarks of intrapreneurship success. Other characteristics practised by the Saudi Arabian firms were; reward systems reflect the organisation's interest and commitment to innovation, a culture of workforce empowerment and action, failure is an option and unique and relevant strategy.

4.2 Internal Organisational Factors

The key internal organisational factors were evaluated using five factors: management support, work discretion, rewards/reinforcement, time availability, and organizational boundaries. These were measured using the Corporate Entrepreneurship Assessment Instrument (CEAI) by Kuratko, Holt, Wales, Ireland, Covin, Hornsby, and Davis.

4.2.1 Management support

Organisational support from senior leaders plays an important role in developing intrapreneurs. The respondents agree with the statement that there was a management support for "a worker with a potential idea and a free time to build up that idea is given to them". This implies autonomy and freedom in a quest for creativity and innovation starting from idea generation. The management support employees' creative free spirits seeking to pursue better opportunities, in the process build new businesses within the company. It is important because it indicates the managers' willingness to facilitate, promote and institutionalise the entrepreneurial spirit and activity within the organisation's systems and processes (Hornsby et al., 2002) which would encourage the intrapreneurs to engage in innovative efforts. These institutionalised support mechanisms contribute to the formalisation and efficiency of the organisations innovative efforts and projects. Management support for problem solving and conflict resolution in the intrapreneurship process is required in the idea generation, development, and particularly implementation stages of the ideas. Moreover, the respondents agree with the statement "there is an intelligent allocation of resources to stimulate innovative behaviour among employees". Intrapreneurial firms provide employees easy access to all the resources not only technical, physical as well as financial needed to develop and implement ideas. Time, physical and financial resources required to facilitate individuals within the organisation involving innovative activities.

4.2.2 Work discretion

Sometimes termed as autonomy reflects the top managers' commitment to tolerate failure, provide decision-making latitude and freedom from excessive oversight, and to delegate responsibility and authority to middle managers (Kuratko, Ireland et al., 2005). The respondents agree that the convenience of the organisational structure, concerning especially decentralisation on decision-making for lower level managers and employees provides them autonomy and freedom to make their own judgement. Such structure promotes risk-taking, allowing employees in making decision, fully prepared, accountable, and not fear persecution or ridicule if they fail. Risk-taking and failure are an important part of the innovation process that every organisation needs to understand and embraced. This is an important element to trigger intrapreneurial spirit among employees in an organisation. Employee empowerment is another element as a result of giving them autonomy. The management allows them to be accountable and make their own decisions. Hence, the management role is to encourage and support the decision-making environment and to give employees the tools and knowledge they need to make and act on their own. Leadership gurus always encourage managers to empower employees and giving them the freedom and support to succeed.

4.2.3 Rewards/Reinforcement

Refers to the extent to which managers reinforce the entrepreneurial and innovative behaviour by explicitly linking performance and achievement to rewards (Kuratko et.al.1990). Employees' motivation is important in achieving organisational goals. Management needs to build a reward structure that encourages all employees to contribute to the success of the organisation. Giving rewards based on entrepreneurial performance both intrinsically and extrinsically are integral factors for motivation. Management has to acknowledge and cherish ideas while tolerating mistakes or failure in order to encourage employee in committing towards their entrepreneurial endeavours. The findings revealed that there are motivational factors like rewards presents to support intrapreneurial behaviour among employees. The respondents agree with the statement that their company reinforces "individuals with successful innovative projects receive additional compensation for ideas and efforts beyond the standard reward system". Employees enjoyed both formal rewards and organizational freedom. In an intrapreneurial firm, formal rewards could include pay-for-performance, significant financial rewards for cost-saving ideas, and promotion as a result of successful project implementation. Organizational freedom describes the autonomy and discretion employees enjoy when making decisions about performing their work in the way they believe is most effective. In intrapreneurial work environments, employees are allowed to make decisions about their work process and failure is tolerated during the innovation process (Hornsby et al, 2002) and this creates a positive and motivating work environment. The willingness and ability of employees to engage in intrapreneurship are influenced by the type of rewards and reinforcement offered. For this reason the human resource system, and especially the reward and compensation arrangements, plays a vital role in creating a climate conducive to intrapreneurship which requires a high degree of commitment from the management. Given the employees high needs for achievement, status, and affiliation, an organisation structure that will motivate them to pursue creative and effective ideas is essential. Supporting a creative environment requires innovation to be recognised, nurtured, and rewarded.

4.2.4 Time Availability

Time is an important resources in generating an intrapreneurial outcome. The management gives the employees' ample time to develop new ideas. In general, the respondents agree that internal organisational factors along time availability influencing intrapreneurship behaviour were highly observed. Saudi Arabian firms highly encouraged intrapreneurship initiatives. Employees are encourage to set aside work hours to develop new ideas and deviate from regular patterns of behaviour. Time and resources needed are available to allow for exploration, investigation, and experimentation among employees. In turn, fresh ideas develop that lead to a better competitive position in the marketplace. Although it is crucial and often difficult to implement, but it is an effective way to encourage intrapreneurship to individuals looking to develop new ideas and come up with innovations. Similarly, the respondents agree with the statement that "during the past three months, my workload was too heavy to spend time on developing new ideas", and "I always seem to have plenty of time to complete everything done". The findings mean that Saudi Arabian firms recognise the vital role of intrapreneurship in their organisation. They provide employees time to try new things, to create new ideas, work on extraneous projects and pursue innovative efforts within and outside their work schedule. Ensuring they have sufficient time and space for creativity and letting their imagination flow.

4.2.5 Organisational Boundaries

Refer to the extent in which one feels that precise explanations of the outcomes expected from organisational work and the development of mechanisms for evaluating, selecting, and using innovations exist within the organisation (Kuratko et.al.1990). In order to support the ideas, they do not stop with the organisational boundaries but bend the rules that hinder them in achieving their goals. In fostering intrapreneurship encouraged employees to look at the organisation from a broad perspective. As such, top-level managers should avoid having standard operating procedures for all major parts of jobs and reduce dependence on narrow descriptions and rigid performance. The findings revealed that the respondents agree with the statement "my job description clearly specifies the standards of performance on which my job is evaluated." This denotes the existence of well-define company policy and employees know that management expects them to exhibit intrapreneurship behaviour as part of measuring their work performance. Through performance evaluation feedback the organisation can identify the suitable training and development needs and at the same time determine the appropriate rewards to reinforce the employees' behaviour towards entrepreneurship within the existing firm. Intrapreneurship behaviour involves the proactive pursuit of creative or new solutions to challenges confronting them. Giving employees work discretion, rewards, time availability, training, trust, loose intra-organisational boundaries, and management support, commitment and involvement are conducive for creating an intrapreneurship friendly environment.

4.3 Correlation Coefficient (r)

These analyses were in accord with the previous findings: organisational characteristics ($\bar{x}$ =4.08) and management support ($\bar{x}$ =3.65; r = .327; p < .01) were significantly correlated; followed by work discretion ($\bar{x}$ =3.51; r = .573; p < .01) were significantly correlated; and rewards/reinforcement ($\bar{x}$ =3.55; r = 1.000; p < .01) were significantly correlated. The results revealed that the correlation coefficients (r) between organisational characteristics and availability ($\bar{x}$ =3.53; r = .348; p < .01) were significantly correlated; and organisational boundaries ($\bar{x}$ =3.67; r = .327; p < .01) were significantly correlated. The findings further revealed that all pair's variables recorded a positive and significant correlation. Therefore, the hypothesis is that, there is a significant relationship between the organisational characteristics and the factors influencing intrapreneurship behaviour and innovation along the aforementioned five areas of research. In other words, the employees in Saudi Arabian firms were positive in becoming entrepreneurs within the existing established organisations.

5. Conclusions

Based on the foregoing findings, the following conclusions are drawn: There exist certain organisational characteristics among Saudi Arabian firms conducive for creating intrapreneurship friendly environment. The organisational internal factors influencing intrapreneurship behaviour and innovation varied from one firm to the other. The degree of actual practises and influence is an ingredient of management support, work discretion, rewards/reinforcement, and time availability. In this age of corporate austerity and intensified environmental threat, entrepreneurial firms need to create and foster intrapreneurial values and behaviour across the whole organisation, in order to encourage and nurture innovation and the entrepreneurial spirit, increase efficiencies and remain competitive. Successfully implementing intrapreneurship in organisation stimulates innovation by tapping into each employee's entrepreneurial talent. By embracing intrapreneurship, an organisation builds a culture for employees with potential ideas to better channel the resources to develop unique products or services, processes or system. Culture is the crucial intrapreneurial ingredient. Without an organisational culture supportive of internal innovation there can be no entrepreneurial initiatives within existing firm. Intrapreneurship empowers and enables employees to become change agents in the organisation; bringing novel ideas and advocating their implementation. Intrapreneur roles can certainly act as catalysts, however, intrapreneurship should be embedded in the overall culture of the organisation: adopted, accepted and celebrated as a core practise and directed towards the organisational goals, in order to maintain their competitiveness and excellence in innovation. This remains a challenge and subject of inquiry among different organisations not only in Saudi Arabian firms. Hence, organisations must therefore, become, versed in the methods and practises for activating and developing intrapreneurship as an approach to innovation to meet the demands of today's brave new world. Further research on this area is highly recommended in advancing this study.

References

Abrahamson, E. (2000) "Change Without Pain," Harvard Business Review, July–August, 78, 75–79.

Al Ansari, Y.D. (2014) Innovation Practices as a Path To Business Growth Performance: A Study of Small and Medium Sized Firms in the Emerging UAE Market. Doctoral Thesis, Southern Cross University, Queensland, Australia.

Alsaif, T. (2015) Today business environment implements relevant change in organisation. Retrieved from https://www.linkedin.com/pulse/today-business-environment-implements-relevant-change-tareq-alsaif

Antoncic, B. (2007) "Intrapreneurship: a comparative structural equation modeling study", Industrial Management & Data Systems, 107(3), 309-25.

Antoncic, B. and Hisrich, R.D. (2001) "Intrapreneurship: construct refinement and cross-cultural validation", Journal of Business Venturing, 16(5), 495-527.

Axtell, C. M., Holman, D. J., Unsworth, K. L., Wall, T. D., Waterson, P. E., & Harrington, E. (2000) Shop floor innovation: Facilitating the suggestion and implementation of ideas. *Journal of Occupational and Organisational Psychology*, 73(3), 265-285.

Bolinao, E. N. (2009) Innovation Process and Performance in Small- to Medium-Sized Firms: A Conceptual Framework . *DLSU Business & Economics Review, 19(1)*. Retrieved from http://www.ejournals.ph/form/cite.php?id=6399

Bolton, B., & Thompson, J. (2013) *Entrepreneurs: Talent, temperament, opportunity* (3rd ed.). London: Routledge.

Branson, R. (2015) Case Studies: Intrapreneurship. Intrapreneurship Institute. Retrieved from http://www.intrapreneurshipinstitute.com/intrapreneurship-case-studies/sir-richard-branson-successful-multi-billionaire-entrepreneur-supports-and-uses-intrapreneurship/

Bygrave, W and Zacharakis, A. (2010) *Entrepreneurship*. John Wiley & Sons.

DeSai, J. (2013) Innovation Engine: Driving Execution for Breakthrough Results. John Wiley & Sons.

Drucker, P. F. (1985) *Innovation and Entrepreneurship*, New York, Harper Trade.

Eesley, D.T. and Longenecker, C.O. (2006) "*Gateways to Intrapreneurship*" Industrial Management, p.19. Retrieve from http://cba2.unomaha.edu/defa/entrepreneurpubs/BarriersandGateways.pdf

Emmanuel, M. (2009) Methodology of Business Studies. Pearson India. http://academic.safaribooksonline.com/book/business/9788131730690

Hornsby, J. S., Kuratko, D. F. & Zahra, S. A. (2002) Middle managers' perception of the internal environment for corporate entrepreneurship: Assessing a measurement scale. *Journal of Business Venturing, 17*, 253-273.

Khan, G.A. (2016) Kingdom among top innovative countries. Arab News. http://www.arabnews.com/node/972946/saudi-arabia

Khang, C. (2014) Intrapreneurship: new growth engine. *The Korea Times*. 11 May, Retrieved from http://www.koreatimes.co.kr/www/news/biz/2016/08/333_156922.html

Kuratko, D.F., Hornsby, J.S. and Bishop, J.W. (2005) "Managers' corporate entrepreneurial actions and job satisfaction", International Entrepreneurship and Management Journal, 1(3), 275-91.

Kuratko, D. F., Montagno, R. V. & Hornsby, J. S. (1990) Developing an intrapreneurial assessment instrument for an effective corporate entrepreneurial environment. *Strategic Management Journal, 11*, 49-58.

Kuratko, D. F., Ireland, R. D., Covin, J. G., & Hornsby, J. S. (2005) A model of middle level managers' entrepreneurial behavior. Entrepreneurship Theory and Practice,29(6), 699-716.

Lassen, A.H., Gertsen, F. & Riis, J.O. (2006) The Nexus of Corporate Entrepreneurship and Radical Innovation. Corporate entrepreneurship and radical innovation- creativity and innovation management. Journal compilation, Blackwell Publishing.

Mokaya S.O, (2012) Corporate Entrepreneurship and Organisational Performance Theoretical Perspectives, Approaches and Outcomes. *International Journal of Arts and Commerce, 1(4).*

Nies, T. (2006) Intrapreneurship. *Chief Executive Officer (CEO)*, 17 May. Retrieved from http://www.the-chiefexecutive.com/features/feature254/

Nørgaard, J.H. (2012) Managing Intrapreneurship in the Recession: Understanding How Organisational Conditions Affect Intrapreneurial Efforts. Master's Thesis In Mssoc In Organisational Innovation & Entrepreneurship. Copenhagen Business School, Denmark. Retrieved from http://studenttheses.cbs.dk/bitstream/handle/10417/3045/julie_hovald_noergaard.pdf?sequence=1

Palmer, I., Dunford, R., & Akin, G. (2006) *"Managing Organisational Change": A Multiple Perspectives Approach*, McGraw-Hill Irwin, New York, NY.

Pinchot, G., & Pellman, R. (1999) Intrapreneuring in action: A handbook for business innovation. San Francisco, CA: Berrett-Koehler. Web of Science® Saudi Digital Library.

Quinn, J.B. (1979) Technological innovation, entrepreneurship and strategy. Sloan Management Review, 19-30.

Reightering, J.P.C. and Weitzel, U. (2013) *Work Context and Employee Behaviour as Antecedents for Intrapreneurship*.

Rule, E.G & Irwin, D.W. (1988) "Fostering Intrapreneurship: The New Competitive Edge", *Journal of Business Strategy*, 9(3), 44 – 47.

Seshadri, D.V.R. and Tripathy, A. (2006) Innovation through Intrapreneurship: The Road Less Travelled. *VICALPA 31(1),* p. 17. Retrieved from http://www.vikalpa.com/pdf/articles/2006/2006_jan_mar_17_29.pdf

Sharma, P. and S. J. J. Chrisman (1999) "Toward a Reconciliation of the Definitional Issues in the Field of Corporate Entrepreneurship", *Entrepreneurship Theory and Practice, 23(3),* 11-27.

Stevenson, H.H. and C.J. Jarillo (1990) *"A Paradigm of Entrepreneurship: Entrepreneurial Management", Strategic Management Journal, 11,* 17-27

Trewin, D. (2002) Counts of Australian Business Numbers. Cabrera, A Report Published by the Australian Bureau of Statistics.

Zampetakis, L. A., Beldekos, P., & Moustakis, V. S. (2009) "Day-to-day" entrepreneurship within organisations: The role of trait Emotional Intelligence and Perceived Organisational Support. European Management Journal, 27(3), 165- 175.

Understanding the Drivers for Innovative Work Behavior in Malaysian SMEs

Rojan Noori, Mazni Alias and Intan Soraya Rosdi
Multimedia University, Cyberjaya, Malaysia
rojan.noori@gmail.com
mazni.alias@mmu.edu.my
soraya.rosdi@mmu.edu.my

Abstract: In Malaysia, small and medium enterprises (SMEs) represent 97.3% of the total business establishment and contribute around 31% to the country's gross domestic product (GDP), but this GDP contribution is relatively low compared to SMEs in other countries i.e. 51% in advanced economies and 39% in high middle income countries. Researchers argue that the low SME contribution to Malaysia's GDP is caused by poor organizational innovation performance. The government's economic transformation programme (ETP) features various initiatives designed to harness SME innovation potential, but there exist internal barriers such as lack of knowledge, funds, or even leadership support for innovation. As good leadership is a vital element in successful SMEs, this paper describes a research project focusing on leadership impacts on innovative work behaviour in Malaysian SMEs. It tests a model capturing how transformational leadership positively influences employees' affective commitment levels, which in turn positively impact innovative work behaviour. Transformational leadership is a leadership style that creates a vision for the organization, and inspires followers to voluntarily expend extraordinary effort to achieve organizational goals. Affective commitment is commitment resulting from employee loyalty and emotional attachment to the organization. The target respondents to be surveyed in the study are 4019 middle managers in medium-sized manufacturing firms in a prime urban area in Malaysia. Middle managers were chosen because their closeness to staff provides a safe psychological environment for employees' trying out new methods and solutions for existing problems. Much of the research on leadership and innovation are on organizations in the West, so findings from the study would shed more light onto the situation in a developing country like Malaysia. It would be important reference for SMEs and any institutions tasked to improve SME innovation performance.

Keywords: Malaysia, small and medium enterprises, innovative work behavior, organizational commitment, transformational leadership.

1. Introduction

Globally, Small and Medium Enterprises (SMEs) are considered the most common type of business and they play a crucial role in job creation, motivating engine of economic development, and competitiveness in both local and international markets (Hashim & Ismail, 2011). Despite the important role of SMEs in the country's development, Malaysian SMEs' performance still has not reached the point of full potential (Zakaria, 2013). In addition, even though SME contribution to the national GDP has increased consistently from 29.6% in 2005 to 35.9% in 2014, the contribution of Malaysian SMEs to the overall economy remain relatively small compared to their counterparts in advanced countries (51%) and other high middle income countries (39%). According to Rasiah and Yap (2015), this slow pace of GDP growth is largely a consequence of poor performance of innovation. Lee and Zheng (2014) stated that in order to get and sustain a competitive advantage, and keep on surviving, SMEs must innovate continuously.

Thus, the concept of innovation becomes relevant and the Malaysian government has embarked on various methods to support innovation development. One of them to promote innovation culture in organizations, especially the small and medium enterprises (SMEs). The government had launched the Eleventh Malaysia Plan (2016-2020) with the aim to chart the development of SMEs in line with Malaysia's aspirations to become a high-income country by 2020 (SMEcorp, 2016). Unfortunately, despite the intensive efforts by the Malaysian government, the level of innovation in SMEs is still low (Lee & Ging, 2007; Abdul Halim, Ahmad, Ramayah & Hanifa, 2014).

There is a growing interest to study numerous predictors of innovation including leadership (Halvorsen, 2011), human resource practices (Li et al, 2005; Abdullah et al, 2012), and commitment (Schimansky, 2014). Leaders encourage employees to enhance their innovative work behavior (Duanxu et al., 2010). In the same line, transformational leaders can stimulate employee innovative work behavior within the organization (Reuvers, Van Engen, Vinkeburg, & Wilson-Evered, 2008). On the other hand, specific attention should be paid to employees' commitment levels which may enhance employee innovative work behavior (Agarwal, 2014; De

Jong & Den Hartog, 2007; Kehoe & Wright, 2013). Furthermore, transformational leaders motivate employees to be committed (Bushra, Usman, & Naveed, 2011). Hence, the aim of the present study is to develop a theoretical model of drivers of innovative work behavior in Malaysian Small and Medium-sized Enterprises (SMEs).

2. Literature Review

This section discusses literature on the various constructs and underlying theories relevant to constructing the proposed conceptual framework.

2.1 Innovative Work Behavior

Employees are the essential ingredients to initiate innovation and imperative for any organization aiming at increasing its innovativeness (De Jong & Den Hartog, 2007). Organizations that intend to enhance their competitive advantage through innovation need to pay attention to employees' ideas to identify areas of improvement based on employees' knowledge (Scott & Bruce, 1994). Yuan and Woodman (2010) suggest innovative work behavior (IWB) as involving both the generation and introduction of new ideas and the realization or implementation of new ideas. Innovative work behavior generates, promotes and implements innovative thinking in the organization, which assists individuals to use innovative thinking to quickly and effectively cater to changes in the demands of customers (Robert, 2001; Scott & Bruce, 1994). IWB has been defined by Carmeli et al., (2006) as a multi-staged process, including recognizing a problem, exploring new ideas, solving the problem, and supporting the use of new ideas in the organization. For the purpose of this study, innovative work behavior refers to a multi-stage process which includes identifying a problem, generating new ideas, promoting employees to support these ideas, and implementing them in the organization.

Most of the work on innovative work behavior (IWB) academically discriminates between some components that are regularly related to diverse phases of the process of innovation. For instance, Scott and Bruce (1994) considered IWB as a multi-dimensional model comprises of three stages: (a) idea generation, (b) idea promotion, and (c) idea realization. De Jong and Den Hartog (2010) notice that the first stage of innovative work behavior, which is idea generation, is divided to idea exploration and generation. Accordingly, they separate the four components of IWB: a) idea exploration, b) idea generation, c) idea championing, d) and idea implementation.

2.2 Attribution Theory

Attribution theory suggests that individuals observe behavior and then attribute causes to it. Heider (1958) was among the first who analyze the process of attribution. He argued that people are "simple psychologists" who have a natural desire to recognize behaviors and outcomes causes. Attribution theory holds that attribution for these behaviors and outcomes eventually assists to form behavioral and emotional responses (Weiner, 1985). This theory distinguishes between two general categories of explanation to describe employee behavior, i.e. dispositional and situational attribution. Dispositional attribution relates to the internal factors of employee behavior such as ability, personality, moods, attitudes, and effort. Whereas, situational attribution relates to external factors of employee behavior such as the task, other people or luck. Leadership in organizations is an example of an external factor. Leaders influence employees' interpretations, responses, and behaviors. Among the various leadership styles, transformational leadership style influences employee behavior effectively. By intellectual stimulation, transformational leaders enhance employee innovative work behavior by generating new ideas and explanations, and identifying current work processes (Ferris, Bhawuk, Fedor & Judge, 1995; De Jong & Den Hartog, 2007).

2.3 Transformational Leadership Theory

The theory of transformational leadership was first identified by Burns (1978), and then later developed by many other scholars (Bass & Riggio, 2012). According to Bass and Reggio (2012), transformational leadership theory emphasizes on change, motivating employees to commit to a common organizational vision and goals, and challenging them to be innovative. Transformational leadership style positively affects attitudes and commitment of followers (Bass & Riggio, 2012).

Many studies have examined the relationship between transformational leadership style and employees' innovative work behavior (Reuvers et al., 2008; Abbas et al., 2012; Halvorsen, 2011; Kroes, 2015).

Furthermore, many studies (Bushra et al., 2011; Riaz et al., 2011; Seyyed et al., 2012) have found a positive relationship between transformational leadership style and organizational commitment.

In addition, several studies (Jafri, 2010; Zannad & Rouet, 2003; Tao & Kang, 2012; Xerri & Brunetto , 2013; Xerri, 2013; Pukiene, 2016) state that organizational commitment influences employees innovative work behavior. Besides the direct relationship between transformational leadership style, innovative work behavior, and organizational commitment mentioned above, few studies indicate that affective commitment mediates the relationship between transformational leadership and employees' innovative work behavior (Abdullah et al., 2011; Kroes, 2015).

2.4 Transformational Leadership

Transformational leadership theory was first identified by James McGregor Burns (1978) and later developed by many other researchers (Bass & Riggio, 2012). During the past few decades, transformational leadership style has become the most regularly studied theory (Avolio, Walumbwa, & weber, 2009). Burns (1978) stated that transformational leadership occurs when organizational leaders involve their followers in such a way that raises both of them to superior levels of morality and motivation resulting in a correlation of shared stimulation and altitude. In addition, Burns (1978) proposed that transformational leaders inspire their followers to achieve more by focusing on the followers' values and helping them associate their values with the organization's values. Burns also explained that these type of leaders are more interested in the shared concerns of followers and the organization compared to their own self-interests. Furthermore, according to Pounder (2008), transformational leaders exercise two main behaviors, which are deep thinking and empathy.

In the modern leadership literature, transformational leadership style is considered one of the most dominant patterns because of its extensive motivational strength for realizing many of the outcomes of employees such as commitment, self efficacy (Rafferty & Griffin, 2004), wellbeing (Nielsen, Yarker, Barnner, Randoll & Brog, 2008) and job satisfaction (Nemanich & Keller 2007. The transformational leadership style is identified as a factor that guides and influences good governance practices in the organization (Indrianawati, 2010). Effective transformational leaders get the respect, trust, and commitment of followers to move forward. Consequently, transformational leaders are more likely to accomplish a collective "buy-in" to their vision. At the same time, followers voluntarily expend extraordinary efforts to achieve organizational goals (Lussier and Achua, 2013). Many researchers have established that transformational leadership predicts innovative work behavior (Afsar, Badir & Saeed, 2014; Jamshed Khan, Aslam & Riaz, 2012; Reuvers et al., 2008).

There are four dimensions of transformational leadership that were identified by Bass and Avolio (1994) in their research (also known as the "four I's"). These dimensions are idealized influences, inspirational motivation, intellectual stimulation and individualized consideration. Idealized influence behavior refers to the degree in which a leader is observed as an encouraging role model (Mass & Ritossa, 2007). This dimension is also defined "as a behavior that enhances follower's association with the leaders, for example setting an example of dedication and courage and making self-sacrifices to benefit their followers" (Yukl, 2013). According to Piccolo and Colquitt (2006), Inspirational motivation refers to leaders' capability to produce a vision in a way that motivates followers and makes them a valuable asset in the organization. Furthermore, an inspirational leader expresses mutual understanding and shared goals to their employees in simple ways (Bass & Riggio, 2012). Intellectual stimulation is a behavior that influences followers to view problems from a new perspective and look for more creative solutions (Yukl, 2013). In other words, Intellectual stimulation also explains the level in which leaders in the organizations motivate their subordinates' efforts to be analytic, creative, and innovative by solving old problems in new ways (Voon et al., 2011; Limsila & Ogunlana, 2008). The fourth dimension of transformational leadership style is individualized consideration, which means that leaders provide special consideration to followers and deal with them separately (Bass & Riggio, 2012). Furthermore, Yukl (2013) states that individualized consideration is the degree in which leaders provide encouragement, support, coaching to followers. In other words, the individualized consideration component is the extent to which an organizational leader acts as a coach or mentor and pays specific attention to followers' distinctions (Muenjohn & Armstrong, 2008).

2.5 Transformational Leadership and Innovative Work Behavior

Many studies show that innovative work behavior is positively affected by transformational leadership (Afsar, et al., 2014; Jamshed Khan et al., 2012; Reuvers et al., 2008). The relationship between transformational leadership style dimensions and employees' innovative work behavior in educational institutions is examined by Abbas et al., (2012). Data was collected from 200 employees in educational institutions and findings of the study indicate that the 5 dimensions of transformational leadership style are positively related with 4 components of innovative work behavior. Hence the following propositions:

P1a: Idealized influence has a significant positive relationship with innovative work behavior in Malaysian SMEs.

P1b: Intellectual stimulation has a significant positive relationship with innovative work behavior in Malaysian SMEs.

P1c: Inspirational motivation has a significant positive relationship with innovative work behavior in Malaysian SMEs.

P1d: Individualized consideration has a significant positive relationship with innovative work behavior in Malaysian SMEs.

2.6 Affective Commitment

Employee commitment has continued to be an issue of high interest among researchers and managers for more than three decades (Hussin, 2000). Meyer and Allen (1991) were the first to establish the three component-model to measure organizational commitment. The three dimensions of organizational commitment are affective commitment (desire), continuance commitment (need), and normative commitment (obligation).

Mowday et al (1979, p.226) defines affective commitment as "the relative strength of an individual's identification with and involvement in a particular organization". This type of commitment refers to an employee's orientation regarding organizational association, loyalty, and participation (Robbins, Judge, Odendaal & Roodt, 2010). Employees with high levels of emotional attachment normally stay in the organization since they believe that their employment is linked with the organizational values and goals (Ferreira, Basson & Coetzee, 2010).

2.7 Transformational Leadership and Affective Commitment

Numerous studies suggest that the transformational leadership style is significantly associated to organizational commitment in various organizational cultures and settings (Khasawneh, Omari, Abu-Tineh, 2012). A study by McLaggon, Bezuidenhout, and Botha (2013) show that transformational leadership components (idealized influence, intellectual stimulation, inspirational motivation, and individualized consideration) significantly and positively relate with affective commitment. Thus, the following propositions:

P2a: Idealized influence has a significant positive relationship with affective commitment in Malaysian SMEs.

P2b: Intellectual stimulation has a significant positive relationship with affective commitment in Malaysian SMEs.

P2c: Inspirational motivation has a significant positive relationship with affective commitment in Malaysian SMEs.

P2d: Individualized consideration has a significant positive relationship with affective commitment in Malaysian SMEs.

2.8 Affective Commitment and Innovative Work Behavior

There is a plethora of studies examining the antecedents and correlates of organizational commitment, but few studies have tested the relationship between organizational commitment and employees' innovative work behavior. A study by Li and Zheng (2014) shows that organizational commitment is one of the main factors that affect employee innovative work behavior. Many researchers in different settings (Jafri, 2010; Zannad and Rouet; 2003; Tao and Kang, 2012; Xerri and Brunetto, 2013; Pukiene, 2016; Xerri, 2013) have supported these findings. Hence, the following proposition:

P3: Affective commitment has a significant positive relationship with innovative work behavior in Malaysian (SMEs).

2.9 Affective Commitment as a Mediating Variable Between Transformational Leadership and Innovative Work Behavior

Based on the association between transformational leadership and affective commitment (Avolio, Zhu, Koh & Bhotia, 2004), and the link between affective commitment and employees' innovative work behavior (Mathieu & Zajac, 1999), it can be supposed that the influence of transformational leadership behavior on employees' innovative work behavior (IWB) would depend on employees' affective commitment levels. It is therefore postulated that affective commitment mediates the relationship between transformational leadership and innovative work behavior. Hence the following propositions:

P4a: Affective commitment mediates the relationship between idealized influence and innovative work behavior in Malaysian (SMEs).

P4b: Affective commitment mediates the relationship between intellectual stimulation and innovative work behavior in Malaysian (SMEs).

P4c: Affective commitment mediates the relationship between inspirational motivation and innovative work behavior in Malaysian (SMEs).

P4d: Affective commitment mediates the relationship between individualized consideration and innovative work behavior in Malaysian (SMEs).

The previous discussion leads to the derivation of a theoretical framework for measuring innovative work behavior among Small and Medium Enterprises (SMEs) in Malaysia. See Figure 1.

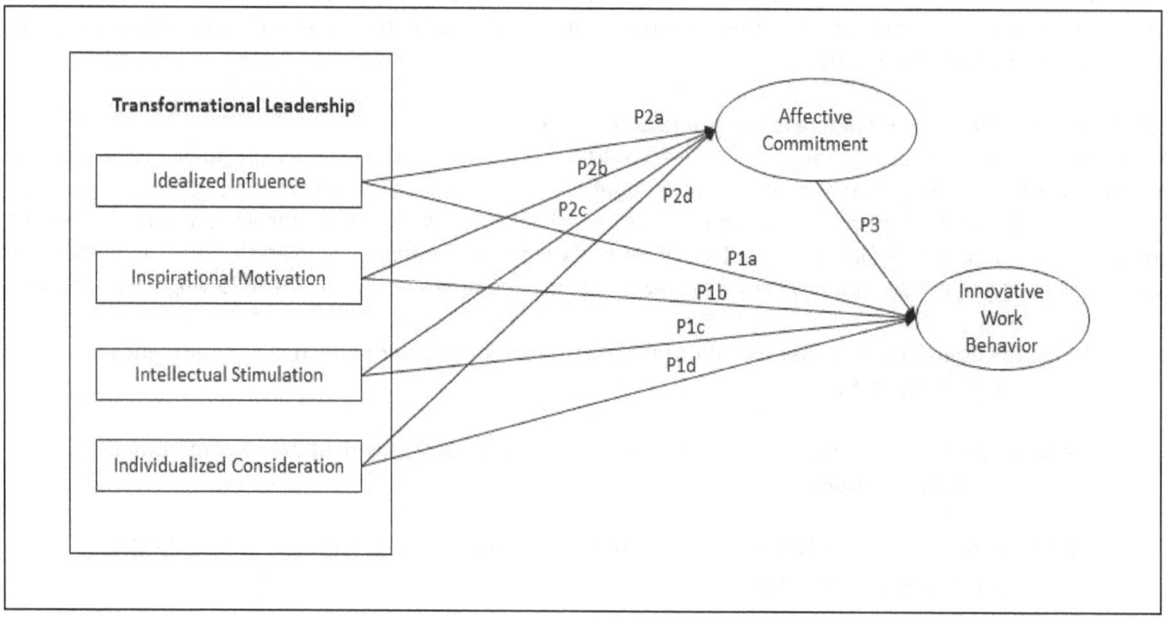

Figure 1: Proposed Theoretical Framework

3. Contributions to Theory

There are research gaps that are able to be addressed from this study. First, the study is able to clarify how transformational leadership can lead to motivating innovative behavior in the workplace. Although many previous studies had found that transformational leadership positively affects innovative work behavior, most research focuses on transformational leadership as a one-dimensional construct (Afsar, Badir & Saeed, 2014; Jamshed Khan, Aslam & Riaz, 2012; Reuvers et al., 2008; Abbas, Iqbal, Waheed, & Riaz, 2012; Halvorsen, 2011). Little is known about which specific dimension of transformational leadership is able to influence innovative work behavior. Second, many studies have examined the antecedents and correlates of organizational commitment, but only minimal studies look into the relationship between organizational commitment and employees' innovative work behavior. Third, few studies have examined the mediating role of organizational commitment on the relationship between transformational leadership and innovative work behavior. This study therefore provides the needed details on how specific transformational leadership dimensions and organizational commitment come together to influence innovative work behavior in SMEs

4. Implications for Practice

The main objective of the study is to propose a framework capturing the drivers of innovative work behavior in SMEs. The study has met its main objective, and the proposed framework is significant for organizations to understand the critical importance of leadership and employee commitment to producing innovative work behaviour in organizations. The proposed framework can be used by SMEs to devise strategies in enhancing innovative work behavior in their firms and consequently improve their innovation performance. It will be useful to the top management of SMEs when implementing policies relating to innovation. The findings of the present research will also help SME Corp in their efforts to improve innovation in Malaysian SMEs, e.g. training programs for SME leaders. Enhancement of leadership capabilities and the innovative capacity of SMEs would help them improve their competitive advantage and their chances for survival in the present highly competitive and complex business environment.

5. Conclusion

SMEs need to gain competitive advantage by enhancing their innovative capability. This study argues that particular leadership styles and employee commitment can influence tendencies towards innovative work behaviour in SMEs, which can be perceived as subsequently affecting the SMEs' innovative capability. Hence, this study provides a predictive framework and hypotheses which could be tested to further explain the drivers of innovative work behavior in Malaysian SMEs. The ultimate goal would be to motivate innovative work behaviour in Malaysian SMEs so as to increase their innovative capability, making them better able to compete and conquer challenges of the knowledge economy.

References

Abbas, G., Iqbal, J., Waheed, A., & Riaz, M. N. (2012). Relationship Between Transformational Leadership Style and Innovative Work Behavior in Educational Institution. Journal of behavioral Science, 22 (3), 18-32.

Abdullah, N. H., Shamsuddin, A., Wahab, E., & Abdul Hamid, N. (2012). Preliminary Qualitative Findings on Technology adoption of Malaysian SME. Kota Kinabalu, Sabah, Malaysia: Colloquium on Humanities Science & Engineering Research (CHUSER 2012).

Afsar B., Badir Y., & Saeed B. (2014). Transformational leadership and innovative work behavior. Industrial Management & Data Systems, 114(8), 1270–1300. http://doi.org/10.1108/IMDS-05-2014-0152

Agarwal, U. A. (2014). Linking justice, trust and innovative work behavior to work engagement. Personnel Review, 43(1), 41-73.

Avolio, B. J., Walunbwa, F. O., & Weber, T. J. (2009). Leadership: Current Theories, Research, and Future Directions. Annual Review of Psychology, 60, 421-449.

Avolio, B. J., Zhu, W., Koh, W., & Bhatia, P. (2004). Transformational leadership and organizational commitment: Mediating role of psychological empowerment and moderating role of structural distance. Journal of Organizational Behavior, 25, 951-968.

Bass, B. M., & Avolio, B. J. (2004). Multifactor Leadership Questionnaire: Manual and Sampler set (3 ed.). Redwood City: CA: Mind Garden.

Bass, B. M., & Reggio, R. E. (2012). Transformational Leadership. Psychology Press.

Burns, J. M. (1978). Leadership and Followership. Leadership, 18-23.

Bushra, F, Usman, A & Naveed, A 2011, 'Effect of transformational leadership on employees' job satisfaction and organizational commitment in banking sector of Lahore (Pakistan)', International Journal of Business and Social Science, vol. 2, no. 18, pp. 261-7.

Carmeli, A., Meitar, R., & Weisberg, J. (2006). Self-leadership skills and innovative behavior at work. International Journal of Manpower, 27(1), 75-90.

De Jong, J. P. J., & Den Hartog, D. (2010). Measuring innovative work behavior. Creativity and Innovation Management, 19(1), 23–36.

De Jong, J. P., & Den Hartog, N. (2007). How leaders influence employees' innovative behavior. European Journal of Innovation Management, 10(1), 41-64.

Ferreira, N., Basson, J., & Coetzee, M. (2010). Psychological Career Resources in relation to Organizational commitment: An Exploratory Study. South African journal of Human Resource Management, 8 (1), 1-10.

Ferris, G. R., Bhawuk, D. P. S., Fedor, D. F., & Judge, T. A. (1995). Organizational politics and citizenship: Attributions of intentionality and construct definition. In Martinko, M.J. (Ed.).

Halvorsen, L. E. (2011). Promoting Innovation Implementation Behavior by Transformational Leadership: A Multiple Mediation Analysis. University of Oslo, Master of Philosophy in Psychology.

Halim, H. A., Ahmad, N. H., Ramayah, T., & Hanifah, H. (2014). The Growth of Innovative Performance among SMEs: Leveraging on Organizational Culture and Innovative Human Capital, 2(1), 107–125.

Heider, F. (1958). The Psychology of Interpersonal Relations. New York: Wiley.

Hussin, A. R. (2000). A study of employees' commitment in customer network operation division in Telekom Malaysia.

Hashim, J., & Ismail, Y. (2011). HRM Practices in Micro Enterprises Focusing on Employees' Satisfaction and Commitment. 10th International Conference of the Academy of HRD (Asia Chapter), (pp. 3-6). Kuala Lumpur, Malaysia.

Indrianawati, U. (2010). The effect of leadership on performance management, good governance, internal and external satisfaction in study programs. China-USA Business Review, 9(5), 8-28.

Jafri, M. H. (2010). Organizational commitment and employee's innovative behavior: A study in retail sector. Journal of Management Research, 10(1), 62-68.

Jamshed-Khan, M., Aslam, N., & Riaz, M. N. (2012). Leadership Style as Predictors of Innovative Work Behaviour. Pakistan Journal of Social and Clinical Psychology, 10 (1), 17-22.

Kehoe, R. R., & Wright, P. M. (2010). The Impact of High-Performance Human Resource Practices on Employees' Attitudes and Behaviors. Journal of Management, 39 (2), 366-391.

Khasawneh, S. Alomari, A. and Abu-Tineh, A. (2012). The relationship between transformational leadership and organizational commitment: The case for vocational teachers in Jordan. Educational Management Administration & Leadership, 40(4), 494-508.

Kroes, B. (2015). The Relationship between Transformational Leadership and Innovative Work Behavior: The Role of Self-Effecacy and the Effect of Perceived Organizational Support on Innovative Work Behavior. TILBURG UNIVERSITY.

Lee, C., & Ging, L. C. (2007). SME Innovation in the Malaysian Manufacturing Sector. 12, 1-12.

Li, X., & Zheng, Y. (2014). The Influential Factors of Employees' Innovative Behavior and the Management Advices, (December), 446–450.

Limsila, K., & Ogunlana, S. O. (2008). Performance and Leadership Outcome Correlates of Leadership Styles and Subordinate Commitment. Engineering, Construction and Architectural Management, 15 (2), 164-184.

Lussier, R. N., & Achua, C. F. (2013). Leadership, Theory, Application, and Scale Development (5 ed.). South-western: GENGAGE Learning.

Mathieu, J. and Zajac, D. (1990), "A review of meta-analysis of the antecedents, correlates and consequences of organizational commitment", Psychological Bulletin, Vol. 108 No. 2, pp. 171-94.

McLaggan, E., Bezuidenhout, A., and Botha, C. T. (2013), Leadership style and organizational commitment in the mining industry in Mpumalanga, SA Journal of Human Resource Management; Vol 11, No 1, 9 pages. doi: 10.4102/sajhrm. v11i1.483.

Meyer, J. P., & Allen, N. J. (1991). A three-component Conceptualization of Organizational Commitment. Human Resource Management Review, 1 (1), 61-89.

Moss, S. A., & Ritossa, D. A. (2007). The Impact of Goal Orientation on The Association between Leadership Style and Follower Performance, Creativity and Work Attitudes. Leadership and Organization Development Journal, 3 (4), 433-456.

Mowday, R. T., Richard, R. T., Steers, R. M., & Porter, L. W. (1979). The Measurement of Organizational.

Muenjohn, N., & Armstrong, A. (2008). Evaluating the Structural Validity of Multifactor Leadership Questionnaire (MLQ), Capturing the Leadership Factors of Transformational, Transactional Leadership. Contemporary Management Research, 4 (1), 3-14.

Nemanich, L., & Keller, R. T. (2007). Transformational Leadership in an Acquisition: A Field Study of Employees. The Leadership Quarterly, 18, 49-68.

Nielsen, K., Yarker, J., Brenner, S., & Randall, R. (2008). The Importance of Leadership Style for the well-being of Employees Working with Older People. Journal of Advanced Nursing, 63, 165-175.

Piccolo, R. F., & Colquitt, J. A. (2006). Transformational Leadership and Job Behaviors: The Mediating Role of Core Job Characteristics. Academy of Management Journal, 49, 327-340.

Powell, D. M., & Meyer, J. P. (2004). Side-Bet Theory and Three-Component Model of Organizational Commitment. Journal of Vocational Behavior, 65, 157-177.

Rafferty, A. E., & Griffin, M. A. (2004). Dimensions of transformational leadership: Conceptual and empirical extensions. The Leadership Quarterly, 15, 329–354

Rasiah, R., X.S. Yap, and S.F. Yap (2015). 'Sticky spots on slippery spaces: The development of the integrated circuits industry in emerging East Asia'. Institutions and Economies, 7(1): 52-79.

Reuvers, M., Engen, M. L. Van, Vinkenburg, C. J., & Wilson-Evered, E. (2008). Transformational Leadership and Innovative Work Behavior: Exploring the Relevance of Gender Differences, 17(3), 227–244. http://doi.org/10.1111/j.1467-8691.2008.00487.x

Riaz, T., Akram, M. U., & Ijaz, H. (2011). Impact of Transformational Leadership Style on Affective Employees' Commitment: An Empirical Study of Banking Sector in Islamabad(Pakistan). Journal of Commerce, 3 (1), 43-51.

Robbins, S. P., Judge, T. A., Odendaal, A., & Roodt, G. (2010). Organizational Behavior: Global and South African Perspective (2 ed.). Cape Town: Pearson Education.

Robert F. Kleysen, Christopher T. Street, (2001) "Toward a multi-dimensional measure of individual innovative behavior", Journal of Intellectual Capital, Vol. 2 Iss: 3, 284-296.

Scott, S. G., & Bruce, R. A. (1994). Determinants of innovative behavior a path model of individual innovation in the workplace. Academy of Management Journal, 580-607.
Schimansky, S. (2014). The Effect of a High-Commitment Work System on Innovation Behavior of Employees. Netherlands: University of Twente.
Seyyed, A.A.A, Freyedon, A. & Mina, Z. (2012). Effect of leadership styles on the organizational commitment given the staff personality traits (The case study: Iran's State Retirement Organization). Interdisciplinary Journal of Contemporary Research Business, 4(1), 247-264.
Tao, Y.M. and Kang, Y. (2012) The Relationship Study Based on the Organizational Commitment between Organizational Innovation Climate and Individual Innovation Behavior. Industrial Technology and Economy, 6, 145-150.
Voon, M. L., Lo, M. O., Ngui, K. S., & Ayob, N. B. (2011). The Influence of Leadership Styles on Employees' Job Satisfaction in Public Sector Organizations in Malaysia. International Journal of Business, Management and Social Science, 2 (1), 24-32.
Wang, D.X. and Hong, Y. (2010) The Mechanism Study of Leaders' Support Promotes Employees' Creativity. Nan Kai Business Review, 4, 109-114.
Wiener, Y. (1982). Commitment in Organization: A normative View. Academy of Management Review, 7 (3), 419-428.
www.smecorp.gov.my/
Xerri, M. J. (2013). Are committed employees more likely to exhibit innovative behavior: a social exchange perspective.
Xerri, M. J., & Brunetto, Y. (2013). Fostering innovative behavior: the importance of employee commitment and organizational citizenship behavior. The International Journal of Human Resource Management, 24(16), 3163-3177.
Yuan, F & Woodman, RW, 2010 ‗Innovative Behavior in the Workplace: The role of Performance and Image Outcome Expectations, Academy of Management, vol. 53, no. 2, pp 323-342.
Yukl, J. (2013). Leadership in Organizations (8 ed.). Upper Saddle River, New Jersey: Pearson.
Zakaria, N. (2013). Enhancing Organizational Performance of Malaysia SMEs Through Human Resource Management(HRM) Practices and Organizational Innovative Capability: A Proposed Framework. International Conference on Management. Penang, Malaysia.
Zannad, H., & Rouet, V. (2003). Organizational commitment in innovative companies. Proceedings of the XIIème Conférence de l'Association Internationale de Management Stratégique, held at Les Côtes de Carthage from 3–6, June 2003.

Embedding Human Capital, Social Capital and Cultural Capital in Entrepreneurial Networking Practices: Cases of Small Manufacturing Firms in the Southern Part of Malaysia

Siti Sarah Omar[1], Muhamad Saufi Che Rusuli[2] and Lee Hui Yee[3]
[1,3]Faculty of Technology Management and Business, Universiti Tun Hussein Onn Malaysia, 86400 Batu pahat Johor Malaysia
[2]Malaysian Graduate School of Entrepreneurship & Business, Universiti Malaysia Kelantan, Kampus Kota Pengkalan Chepa 16100 Kota Bharu, Kelantan Malaysia
sarah@uthm.edu.my

Abstract: Networking relationship is considered a significant component of successful entrepreneurship. The purpose of social networking in business practices is to build social interaction and to maintain professional relationships with relevant stakeholders. No previous study has examined the impact of entrepreneurial capital on networking practices in Johor. The current study attempts to investigate effects of entrepreneurial capital elements on networking practices in manufacturing firms in Johor. In this exploratory study, qualitative approach was used to explore the subjective nature of entrepreneurial capital. In-depth face to face interview with six owners of small and medium enterprises (SMEs) manufacturing companies was conducted and analyzed with method of Miles and Huberman (1994).The findings show that three capital elements namely, human capital, social capital and cultural capital are important in entrepreneurial networking. Since majority of the entrepreneurs were second generation of their parent's business, it was observed that family business background is a critical factor in establishing new business. This study provides substantial insights about the importance of three capital elements in entrepreneurial networking and their practical implications.

Keywords: human capital, social capital, cultural capital, entrepreneurial networking

1. Introduction

Entrepreneurial networking is becoming more indispensable in the entrepreneurship, especially in the start-up stage (Engel, Kaandorp & Elfring, 2017; Firkin, 2003). Entrepreneurial networking connects all the relevant stakeholders, such as partners, suppliers, customers, employee, bankers, family members and others (Omar, 2015). Long-term entrepreneurial networking relationship can strength business ties and increase the possibility of further interaction (Martinez and Aldrich, 2011). It is also regarded one of the key success factors (Jean and Linan, 2013). There are several different forms of capital, such as cultural capital, human capital, social capital, financial capital and symbolic capital (Stringfellow and Shaw, 2009).

Small and medium enterprises (SMEs) are crucial for the growth of Malaysia economy (Omar, 2015). They are facing stiff competition and survival challenges. Rose, Kumar and Lim (2006) found that entrepreneurs who are equipped with required skills and competencies in managing business, such as operations, finance, marketing and human resources are more likely to be successful at the starting-up stage. The main failure factor of business venture is mismanagement and ineffective human resource development(Omar et al., 2015; Rose, Kumar and Lim, 2006). Existing literature highlighted several challenges faced by SMEs in the global environment, such as coping with downturn, lack of human and financial capital, adopting of advanced technology (Omar et.al, 2015; Muhammad et al., 2010) and lack of access to formal business and social network (Teoh & Chong, 2008). Most of the previous researches discussed theory of entrepreneur capital and networking in European countries, such as (Battisti, 2016); Vershinina, Barrett and Meyer, 2009), Ram, Theodorakopoulos and Jones (2008). Therefore, the objective of this study is to identify the impacts of human capital, social capital and cultural capital on entrepreneurial networking Johor.

2. Literature Review

2.1 Human Capital

Human capital is the study of intellectual factors that measure knowledge and skill of a person to start-up a new business (Huggins, Prokop & Thompson, 2017). The theory asserts that knowledge can produce greater reasoning capacity dynamic efficiency (Alvarez and Rodriguez, 2011). It also enables to determine entrepreneurial opportunities (Davidsson and Honig, 2003). Human capital also refers to individual's asset, such as formal education (Davidsson and Honig, 2003), entrepreneurial experience (DeTienne and Chandler,

2007; Ucbasaran et al., 2003), working experience (DeTienne and Chandler, 2007; Shane, 2000), prior general knowledge (Shane, 2000) and prior knowledge of customers' problems (Sheperd and DeTienne, 2004). These assets can build-up human capital that identifies new opportunities and assembles resources for new ventures (Ruzzier et al., 2007; Alvarez and Busebitz, 2001). However, some researchers argue that it is hard to determine entrepreneurial opportunities based on individual's knowledge. They consider it as source of confidence and potential growth (Alvarez and Rodriguez, 2011).

On the other hand, Solesvik et al., (2013) and Becker (1975) define human capital as a set of capabilities, idiosyncratic skills, ability to increase capital and motivations to increase firm's productivity. Furthermore, enthusiasm, proactivity and commitment are also component of human capital (Firkin, 2003). There is a link between entrepreneur's demographic characteristics, attributes, experience and productivity. Human capital is classified into specific and general human capital. Specific human capital concerns about managerial s, technical and entrepreneurial capabilities. While the latter refers to gender, age, ethnicity, education and social class (Solesvik et al., 2013, Firkin, 2003). Furthermore, firms with greater human capital would become more efficient and grow faster (Sun & Wang, 2017).

2.2 Social Capital

Social capital refers to social relationships that generate productive result (Ramirez et al., 2010; Szreter, 2000). Social capital creates network, which is a valuable resource as it facilitates economic activity generates efficiency, business opportunities and innovation (Nahapiet and Ghoshal, 1998; Burt, 1992). Social capital enriches success by supporting an entrepreneur's status and image of power. It focuses on an entrepreneur's formal or informal relations with agents and resources (Burt, 1992). Some researches show that formation of network with other companies can enhance performance (Lee et al., 2001) that decreases redundancy and conflict (Chao, 2011; Sebora and Theerapatvong, 2010; Baum et al., 2000). It impacts entrepreneurial activity and improves venture. Entrepreneurs involved in social network are expected having higher success rate after launching their business (Baron and Markman, 2000). Mutual trust among members in social network reduces entrepreneurial risks, particularly in risky environment (Moran, 2005).

Social capital creates means that enable entrepreneurs to optimize their efforts in gaining resources (Lindblom and Tikkanen, 2010; Oh et al., 2006), mutual support (Semrau, Ambos & Kraus, 2016) and maximizing the value of resources (Arendt and Brettel, 2010; Boran and Markman, 2000). Newly established ventures cannot neglect social capital as they need resources for survival and growth. Concept of social capital is embodied in human relations (Coleman, 1990), which can be identified with in social activities (Ruzzier and Antoncic, 2007; Putnam et al., 2000). The term social capital has become generalized (Casson and Della Giusta, 2007) and used to explain a unified approach, which facilitates social relationship and economic exchanges (Grootaert and van Bastelaer, 2002).

2.3 Cultural Capital

According to Schwartz (2004) theories, there are seven cultural dimensions, namely embeddedness, intellectual, autonomy, affective autonomy, hierarchy, egalitarianism, mastery and harmony. Previous researches suggested that societies holding different cultural valueless and experience, can generate different levels of entrepreneurial activities (Begley, 2001). They assume that dominant societal culture impacts entrepreneurial practices. These behaviors lead to formation of different cultural values in different societies that will influence business (Shane, 1993). Anthropologists recommend that culture is related to the ways in which societies form social behavior and knowledge. Cultural values are described as the collective programming of the mind, which differentiates group members and recognizes their respective responses to environments (Hofstede, 1980).

2.4 Entrepreneurial Networking

In start-up business, networking is crucial due to its significance in dealing with various parties. The concept of networking has been commonly used in recent years. Network theory shows the social links that facilitate and constraint entrepreneurs (Amit, Glosten and Muller, 1993). In the past fifteen years, entrepreneurs viewed networking as a part of a wider context, which consist of crucial social activity among actors (Antonic and Hoang, 2003). Furthermore, Omar (2015) asserts that many entrepreneurs joined social networking due to its vital role in the entrepreneurial process.

3. Methodology

This is a qualitative study by nature, which adopted semi-structure and unstructured interview technique. Six cases were studied in this research, which are sufficient to illuminate the rich data in qualitative study (Omar, 2015). A purposive sampling was conducted, which includes SMEs, manufacturing companies, and food industry in Johor. The interviews were analyzed through the method introduced by Miles & Huberman (1994). Thematic analysis was employed for identifying, analyzing and reporting themes within data. This method organizes themes in data with detailed description. Reflexivity has also been carried out to ensure that the analytical process is performed correctly (Braun and Clarke, 2006).

4. Findings and Analysis

The major findings of this study show that human, social and cultural capital are equally important for entrepreneurial networking in Johor, Malaysia.

Table 2: Summary of the Entrepreneurial Capital Element Involvement of the Cases

Themes	Sub-themes	Cases					
Human capital		1	2	3	4	5	6
Knowledge	Academic level		/	/	/	/	
	Training		/		/		
Experience	Previous experience			/		/	/
General Human Capital	Gender , Age, Ethnic						
Specific Human Capital	Attitude	/	/	/	/	/	/
Social Capital							
Family support	Family linking	/	/	/	/	/	
	Association	/	/	/	/		
Complicity	Interpersonal confidence	/	/	/	/	/	/
Cultural Capital							
Environment	Company environment/ location	/	/	/	/	/	/
	Traditional method	/				/	
Hierarchy	Power and authority	/		/		/	
	Responsibility and honestly	/	/	/	/	/	/

Respondents stressed that social capital is an important factor in building a business networking. Five out of six respondents have family business background. Family businesses offered them an opportunity to acquire human capital for operating a business. Five of them confirmed that the family support played an important role at the initial stage of their business. For association involvement, respondent 5 and 6 regarded it irrelevant. While respondent 1,2,3 and 4 believed it is supportive for personal interconnection customers attraction. For interpersonal confidence, all respondents agreed that it is a necessary criterion for creating networking and earning customers' trust. In the case of cultural capital, all of the respondents affirmed that company location is a main factor in building business networking. Furthermore, respondent 2, 3, 4 and 6 were not in the favor of traditional method of "GuanXi", "RenQing" and "MianZi" in their networking. For gaining power and authority as an entrepreneur, three respondents considered it irrelevant, while another three emphasized on its importance. It should be taken into consideration that power and authority may support business at early stage, but good quality of product is a significant factor contributing to networking relationship in long term. For the criteria of responsibility and honesty, all respondents showed their confirmation. Respondent 2, 3, 4 and 5 realized that academic knowledge is not important human capital, but respondent 1 and 6 regard it essential. However, for training, most of them disagreed with it, except respondent 2 and 4. For previous experience, respondent 2, 3, 4, 5 and 6 noted that it is necessary for future business. Moreover, all respondents agreed that proficiency is important, while general human capital such as gender, age and ethnicity will not bring any effect in build networking relationship.

5. Discussion

This study produced a model of intersection of entrepreneurial capital elements in entrepreneurial networking practices. The model shows that three capital elements namely human capital, social capital and cultural capital are equally significant for an entrepreneur to build business networking relationship. These three capital elements should be applied equally to form a strong and long lasting entrepreneurial networking.

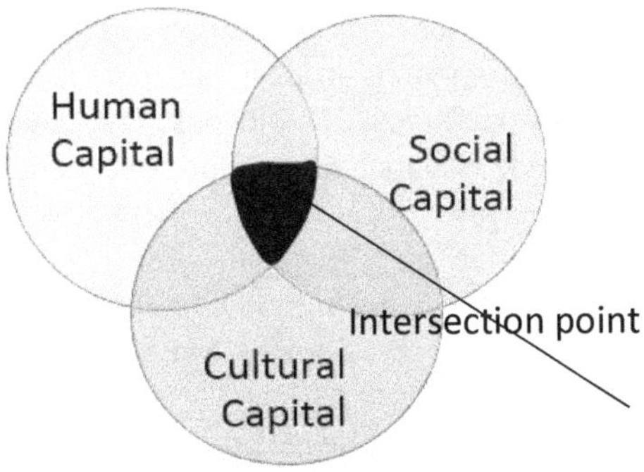

Figure 1: Model of Intersection

5.1 Human Capital

In the current business environment, respondents decided that human capital is important, but some of the sub-themes are irrelevant. Gender, age and ethnic do not influence directly entrepreneurial networking. However, certain entrepreneurships require specific gender. For example, female is favored for administrative work, as they are more circumspect in paper work. Conversely, male is preferred in production line, due to his strength. In the case of ethnicity, it has minor effects on building networking. Ethnicity is considered in customer field according to type of food industry. For instance, according to respondent 3, Chinese ethnicity could be better for entrepreneurship of Chinese medicine. This is because most of the consumer are Chinese.

Researchers indicated that higher level of education is positively related to performance (Felicio, 2014). This is in contrast with the finding of this study which found that academic education acts as a foundation to start a business. Academic knowledge might be essential for communication, general knowledge and business theory, but not a priority in building entrepreneurial networking. In a business, the most important criterion is the quality of product. A good reputation can lead to success of business. Previous studies proved that prior knowledge of human capital can increase owner's entrepreneurial expertise and competency (Westhead, Ucbasaran & Wright, 2005).

Moreover, previous experience is much more precious than join in training class before becoming a manager, these are related to firm activity (Shepherd, 2005). Previous managerial and entrepreneurial experience influence positively the economic performance of new firms (Gimeno et al., 1997). Experience in same industry gives more confidence in building networking. The previous experience also prevents errors in managerial work. It is a useful tool to find suppliers and other associates. Professional proficiency is one of the attitudes that contribute to the success of business. As an entrepreneur, language efficiency plays crucial role in attracting customers and extending social network.
In sum, this research confirms the findings of previous studies that human capital is a determinantal factor in entrepreneurship (Davidsson and Honig, 2003).

5.2 Social Capital

The respondents opined that social capital is important for the business growth. A good social relationship has some benefits, such as retaining customers, keeping staff and discovering new business networking. Social capital affects an entrepreneurial task from its early stage to the end. This finding is consistent with Baron and Markman (2000) that entrepreneur who enjoys vigorous social network, has higher rate of success. Five out of six respondents have business family background. They accepted that family background made it easier for them to succeed. Family firms are one of the sources of intangible assets, which serve as a basic for achieving competitive advantages (Habbershon and Williams, 2000). Some of entrepreneurs get their first batch of financial capital, employees, customers and suppliers from their parents.

Social network serves as a platform for entrepreneurs to share experience, contacts and to join exhibition. It is commonly accepted that social network has a deep influence on business relationship. Social networking also impacts decision making process in business (Davidsson and Honig, 2003).

5.3 Cultural Capital

The selected entrepreneurs believed that cultural capital is crucial for sustainability of the business in the market. Company location is deemed a critical factor. A preferable location would be more convenient for customers and suppliers. Furthermore, if the entrepreneur is a local resident, it could be a competitive advantage to build networking relationship with customer. Employees favor a safe and convenient environment where they can find basic facilities, such as parking and food. Good environment increase the productivity of employees.

On the other hand, traditional method is not encouraged by entrepreneurs to apply in building entrepreneurial networking. Cultural capital also refers to higher status, such as power and authority. Responsible behavior and honesty can produce strong and stable business networking (Schwartz, 2004). Societies are given by nature with dissimilar physical environment, environmentally relevant pattern of behavior can be adapt by member of society to achieve success. These behavior lead to formation of different cultural values in societies that influence the establishment of new businesses (Shane, 1993).

6. Conclusion

The findings of this research show that three capital elements i.e. human capital, social capital and cultural capital are important for entrepreneurial networking. Since majority of the entrepreneurs were second generation of their parent's business, it was observed that family business background is a critical factor in establishing new business. Furthermore, social capital not only supports entrepreneurs to maintain a good networking relationship, but it also increases the possibility of success. By doing so, entrepreneur can count on these people when they are in need. Hence, social networking is crucial because successful networking is all about building and maintaining solid, professional relationships with people. In the case of cultural capital, it is noticed that the environment impacts significantly the business. In a nutshell, SMEs are a major part of industrial economies, as they contribute to the growth of Malaysian economy. Indeed, the above mentioned entrepreneurial capital elements are playing role in building business networking developing successful business.

Acknowledgement

This research is funded by the Contract Research Grant Universiti Tun Hussein Onn, Malaysia, Number U430.

References

Alvarez, S. and Busenitz, L. (2001), "The entrepreneurship of resource-based theory", Journal of Management, Vol. 27, pp. 755-75.

Alvarez, N. G., & Rodriguez, V. (2011). Discovery of entrepreneurial opportunity: A gender perspective. Emeraldinsight, 755-775.

Amit, R., Glosten, L., Muller, E. (1993). Challenges to theory development in Entrepreneurship research. Journal of Management Studies, 30, pp. 815-834.

Battisti, D. D. (2016). Entrepreneurial Skill and regulation: Evidence from primary sector rural entrepreneurs. Emeraldinsight, 1-22.

Baum, J., Calabrese, T. and Silverman, B. (2000), "Don't go it alone. Alliance formation and start-up in Canadian biotechnology", Strategic Management Journal, Vol. 21, pp. 267-94.

Becker, G.S. (1975), Human Capital, National Bureau of Economic Research, New York, NY.

Begley, T.M. and Tan, W-L. (2001), "The socio-cultural environment for entrepreneurship: a comparison between East Asian and Anglo-Saxon countries", Journal of International Business Studies, Vol. 32 No. 3, pp. 537-53.

Braun, V., & Clarke, V. (2006). Using thematic analysis in psychology. Qualitative Research in Psychology, 77-101.

Burt, R. (1992), Structural Holes: The Social Structure of Competition, Harvard University Press, Cambridge, MA.

Casson, M. and Della Giusta, M. (2007), "Entrepreneurship and social capital: analyzing the impact of social networks on entrepreneurial activity from a rational action perspective", International Small Business Journal, Vol. 25, pp. 220-44.

Chao, Y.C. (2011), "Decision-making biases in the alliance life cycle: implications for alliance failure", Management Decision, Vol. 49 No. 3, pp. 350-64.

Coleman, J.S. (1990), Foundations of Social Theory, Harvard University Press, Cambridge, MA.

Cook, P. (2007), "Social capital, embeddedness and market interactions: an analysis of firm performance in UK regions", Review of Social Economy, Vol. 65 No. 1, pp. 79-106.

Davidsson, P. and Honig, B. (2003), "The role of social and human capital among nascent entrepreneurs", Journal of Business Venturing, Vol. 18 No. 3, pp. 301-332.
Firkin, P. (2003). A Resource-Based Conceptualisation of The Entrepreneurial Process. Labour Market Dynamic Research Programme, 1-27.
DeTienne, D. and Chandler, G. (2007), "The role of gender in opportunity identification", Entrepreneurship Theory & Practice, Vol. 31, pp. 365-86.
Firkin, P. (2001). A Resource-Based Conceptualisation of The Entrepreneurial Process. Labour Market Dynamic Research Programme, 1-27.
Felicio, J. A., Couto, E., & Caiado, J. (2014). Human capital, social capital and organizational Performance. Emeraldinsight, 350-364.
Gimeno, J., Folta, T., Cooper, A. and Woo, C. (1997), "Survival of the fittest? Entrepreneurial human capital and the persistence of underperforming firms", Administrative Science Quarterly, Vol. 42, pp. 750-783.
Grootaert, C. and van Bastelaer, T. (2002), Understanding and Measuring Social Capital: A Synthesis of Findings and Recommendation from the Social Capital Initiative, The World Bank, Washington, DC.
Habbershon, T.G. and Williams, M.L. (2000), "A model for understanding the competitiveness of family-controlled companies", in Poutziouris, P.Z. (Ed.), Tradition or Entrepreneurship in the New Economy, Manchester Business School, Manchester, pp. 94-115.
Hall ET (1973) The Silent Language. New York: Anchor.
Hoang, H., Antonic, A. (2003). Network-based research in entrepreneurship. A critical review. Journal of Business Venturing, 18, pp. 165–187.
Hofstede G (1980) Culture's Consequences: International Differences in Work-related Values. Beverly Hills, CA: SAGE.
Kroeber AL and Parsons T (1958) The concepts of culture and social system. American Sociological Review 23: 582–83.
Lee, C., Lee, K. and Pennings, J. (2001), "Internal capabilities, external networks, and performance: a study on technology based ventures", Strategic Management Journal, Vol. 22 Nos 6-7, pp. 615-40.
Lindblom, A. and Tikkanen, H. (2010), "Knowledge creation and business format franchising", Management Decision, Vol. 48 No. 2, pp. 179-88.
Martinez A. M, Aldrich. H .E (2011). Networking Strategies for entrepreneurs: balancing cohesion and diversity. International Journal of Entrepreneurial behavior & Research, 7-38.
Miles, M., & Huberman, A. (1994). Qualitative Data Analysis: An Expanded Sourbook. 2nd ed. United State of America: SAGE.
Moran, P. (2005), "Structural vs relational embeddedness: social capital, and managerial.
Muhammad M. Z, Char. A. K, Yasoa. M. R, Hassan Z. (2010). Small and Medium Enterprises (SMEs) Competing in the Global Business Environment: A Case of Malaysia. International Business Research, 66-75.
Nahapiet, J. and Ghoshal, S. (1998), "Social capital, intellectual capital and the organizational advantage", Academy of Management Review, Vol. 23 No. 2, pp. 242-66.
Oh, H., Labianca, G. and Cheng, M. (2006), "A multilevel model of group social capital", Academy of Management Review, Vol. 31 No. 3, pp. 569-82.
Omar, S. S. (2015). The Entrepreneurial Network of Muslim Women Entrepreneurs: The Study of Multiple-Cases of Small Businesses in the Southern Region of Malaysia. International Journal of Economics and Financial Issues, 106-115.
Omar, S.S, Arokiasamy. L (2009). The Background and Challenges faced by the Small Medium Enterprises: A Human Resources development Perspective. International Conference on Human Capital Development, 1-8.
Putnam, R. (2000), Bowling Alone: The Collapse and Revival of American Community, Simon & Schuster, New York, NY.
Ram, M., Theodorakopoulos, N., & Jones, T. (2008). Form of Capital, mixed embeddedness and Somali enterprise. work, employment and society, 428-446.
Ramıirez, A.R., Orejuela, A.R. and Vargas, G.M. (2010), "New perspectives for the managerial entrepreneurship", International Entrepreneurship and Management Journal, Vol. 6 No. 2, pp. 203-19.
Rose, R. C., Kumar, N., & Lim , L. (2006). Entrepreneurs Success Factors and Escalation of Small and and Mediun Size Enterprise In Malaysia. Journal of Social Sciences,74-80.
Ruzzier, M. and Antoncic, B. (2007), "Social capital and SME internalization: an empirical examination", Transformations in Business & Economics, Vol. 6, pp. 122-38.
Schwartz, S.H. (2004), "Mapping and interpreting cultural differences around the world", in Vinken, H., Soeters, J. and Ester, P. (Eds), Comparing Cultures, Dimensions of Culture in a Comparative Perspective, Brill, Leiden.
Sebora, T.C. and Theerapatvong, T. (2010), "Corporate entrepreneurship: a test of external and internal influences on managers' idea generation, risk taking, and proactiveness", International Entrepreneurship and Management Journal, Vol. 6 No. 3, pp. 331-50.
Segal, G., Borgia, D. and Schoenfeld, J. (2002), "Using social cognitive career theory to predict self-employment goals", New England Journal of Entrepreneurship, Vol. 5, pp. 47-56.
Shane, S. (2000), "Prior knowledge and the discovery of entrepreneurial opportunities", Organization Science, Vol. 11 No. 4, pp. 448-469.
Shane S (1993) Cultural influences on national rates of innovation. Journal of Business Venturing 8: 59–73.
Shapero A and Sokol L (1982) The social dimensions of entrepreneurship. In: Kent C, Sexton L and Vesper K (eds) Encylopedia of Entrepreneurship. Englewood Cliffs, NJ: Prentice Hall, 72–90.

Sheperd, D. and DeTienne, D. (2004), “Prior knowledge, potential financial reward and opportunity identification”, Entrepreneurship Theory & Practice, Vol.
29, pp. 91-112.
Solesvik, M. Z., Westhead, P., Matlay, H., & Parsyak, V. (December 2013). Entrepreneurial assets and mindset. ResearchGate, 748-762.
Stringfellow, L., & Shaw, E. (2009). Conceptualising entrepreneurial capital for a study of performance in small professional service firms. Emeraldinsight, 137-161.
Szreter, S. (2000), “Social capital, the economy, and education in historical perspective”, in Schuller, T. (Ed.), Social Capital: Critical Perspectives, Oxford University Press, Oxford, pp. 56-77.
Teoh, W. M. Y. & Chong, S. C. (2008). Improving women entrepreneurs in small and medium enterprises in Malaysia: policy recommendations. Communication of the IBIMA, 2, 31-38.
Thompson, J. L. (2004). The facet of the entrepreneur : Identifying entrepreneurial potential. Emeraldinsight, 243 – 258.
Ucbasaran, D., Westhead, P., Wright, M. and Binks, M. (2003), “Does entrepreneurial experience influence opportunity identification?”, Journal of Private Equity, Vol. 7, pp. 7-14.
Vershinina, N., Barrett, R., Meyer, M. (2009). Polish Immigrant In Leicester : Forms of Capital Underpinning Entrepreneurial Activity. Leicester Business School Occasional Paper 86, 1-18.
Westhead, P., Wright, M. and McElwee, G. (2011), Entrepreneurship: Perspectives and Cases, Pearson Education Limited, Harlow.

Human Capital of the Entrepreneur – Impact on the Microenterprise's Survival

Aneta Ptak-Chmielewska
Warsaw School of Economics, Poland
aptak@sgh.waw.pl

Abstract: The human capital is one of the most important factors supporting the survival of microenterprises. The success of the enterprise depends on the relevant preparation, knowledge and education of the owner. In the analysis the sample of 711 enterprises from one of the regions based on retrospective survey was used. Only microenterprises without employed workers at start of their activities were selected. In such a situation the human capital of the enterprise can be directly linked to the human capital of the entrepreneur (the owner). The logistic regression model was used to analyse the enterprises' survival chances with variables describing the human capital of the entrepreneur. The older the owner is and the higher educational level he represents, the higher survival chances of the enterprise. The goal of this paper was the verification of the hypothesis: High level of the human capital of the entrepreneur increases the chances of the microenterprise's survival on the market.

Keywords: enterprises' survival, human capital in the enterprise, logistic regression model.

1. Background

Determinants influencing the enterprises are not only internal but also external. Among determinants influencing survival of enterprises three groups are considered. Those groups of determinants may be sorted in following order:

1. Determinants on the market level: all macroeconomic characteristics of the market, demand increase, concentration of the capital. Those are factors describing the economic situation of the country.
2. Determinants on the sector level: those are social factors, concerning sector of activity. Those determinants describe barriers of entry, concentration of the capital on the sector level, innovation, cost of the scale, monopoly and oligopoly, sector attractiveness and growth.
3. Determinants on the enterprise level: all characteristics of the enterprise that influence (positively or negatively) the survival of the enterprise since entry to liquidation.

To the latest category (group) of determinants we can include capital at the start, real estate, properties and non-material properties: size, age of the enterprise, human capital. Some of those characteristics describe enterprise, some describes entrepreneur (the owner). Among entrepreneur's characteristics the age, sex, race, social status, education, previous experience of the owner was researched. Those characteristics describe the human capital of the enterprise which is sometimes categorized as enterprise characteristic. In human capital we can distinguish two groups of categories: general (education, demographic characteristics, motivation) and specific (previous experience).

Arribas and Vila (2007) introduced also the definition of accumulated human capital, which is used for sum of human capital of the owners (more than one person). They proved that enterprises owing such accumulated human capital live longer and have higher chances for success, which is also determined the better financial condition of the enterprise. Initial capital is distributed on more people so is better secured form individual failures of one of the owners.

Accoring to Bastie and others. (2011) the situation of the entrepreneur just before starting the business is also important. Being employed before starting the business increases chances for bank loan comparing to unemployed person. Long term employment also increases chances of survival comparing to short term employment. Authors of this publication also state that the situation of the enterprise on the market is also determined by previous preparation process like business plan or consultancy with accounting services. Among factors increasing capital of the enterprise they list four: participating in trainings, market research and prognoses, setting banking account, consulting with experts. Market research and prognoses increase enterprises survival and access to banking loans. Banks assess the chances of enterprises survival, human capital, project specification, collaterals.

From literature review the very important factor in microenterprises' survival is human capital of the entrepreneur. In 1962 Becker defined human capital as: studies concerning actions influencing future income material and non-material by increase of human resources, those actions are defined as investment in human capital. Those actions are: education, professional training, medical care, seeking information about prices and income. Those actions are dedicated to increasing the abilities, knowledge, health in the goal of increasing income. [Becker 1993, p. 11].

Human capital is a part of the enterprise but is connected with a worker and is worker's property. Investment in human capital increases the potential of return ratio. The most important in investment in human capital is education and professional training. People with higher education level have more possibilities and chances on the labour market. It is important to compare the costs and income from education. It is visible in case of women education. Education and training increases the worker's abilities and efficiency also in managerial abilities.

First methods of measurement like simple ratios income on a worker did not differentiated the single worker input. The weakness of such approach imposed more advanced techniques and methods. The most frequently used models of human capital measurement are models so called cost models based on factors like [Wyrzykowska, 2008]:

- historical cost – cost of acquiring and training of the worker,
- the regeneration cost of human resources – cost of worker's leaving the enterprise, acquiring the new worker and his training,
- alternative cost of potentially lost possibilities.

Scoring models are also applied. Some nonfinancial ratios are scored according to the level in which this characteristic is specific for particular organization [Stańczyk, Kryński 2007] (like, innovativeness, informatics knowledge etc.). Models using financial statements and enterprise's pricing are also used.

Research hypothesis
Human capital of the entrepreneur increases the chances of the microenterprises survival on the market.

Human capital is important factor supporting the survival of the microenterprises on the market. The success of the microenterprise is determined with proper preparation, knowledge and education of the entrepreneur (the owner).

2. Data and Methods

Data on the sample of micro-enterprises (self-employed entrepreneurs) from retrospective survey was used (n=711). The survey was conducted in 2011 and was based on the sample of micro enterprises in one of the regions in Poland. The sample consisted of enterprises registered in one year (2006) and followed till 2011. Self-employment caused the direct connection of human capital with the worker (entrepreneur) and assess the inequalities in gender and human capital.

Logistic regression model was proposed with variables *sex of the main owner* (male, female), *age of the main owner* (below 25, above and 25 years), human capital (*education* (higher, low), *managerial experience* (yes, no)). Controlling variables were included: *sector of activity* (Industry, Construction, Services, Trade), *region of activity* (local, regional, national, international), *exporting* (yes, no), *percent of sources from bank loan at start* (interval). Empirical analysis were used to verify the research hypotheses.

Logistic regression function is S-shaped and described by following formulae:

$$P(Y=1)=\frac{1}{1+\exp^{-(\beta_0+\beta_1x_1+...+\beta_kx_k)}}$$

where:

P(Y=1) – dependent variable,

β0 – intercept,

βi, i = 1, 2, ..., k – coefficients,

xi, i = 1, 2, ..., k – explanatory variables.

The P(Y=1) takes the values from interval [0;1]. Important in logistic regression model is a cut-off point. Estimation based on balanced sample usually takes the 0.5 as a cut-off value. The structure of the sample (percent of liquidated enterprises) determines the cut-off value.

Interpretation of results is usually based on odds ratios (ratio of odds in two groups or in change of one unit in explanatory variable). Logistic regression requires a lot of different assumptions to be fulfilled. The most important assumptions are: randomness of the sample, big sample, no collinearities in explanatory variables, and independence of observations.

3. Empirical results

First step was application of univariate method to select only variables which show significant differences between groups. Variables with nonsignificant differences between groups (categories) were not included. Nonparametric chi-square test was used.

3.1 Univariate analysis

Univariate analysis was based on nonparametric chi-square tests for difference between groups. In nonparametric univariate analysis only variables describing human capital were included: *sex of the main owner* (female, male), *educational level of the main owner* (higher, lower), *age of the main owner* (below 25 years, 25 years and older). For those variables the differences between groups in liquidated enterprises' percentage were significant. For two other variables: *managerial experience of the owner* (yes, no) and *enterprise as the main source of maintenance* (yes, no) the difference between groups were not significant at 0.05 level.

In total sample of 711 microenterprises registered in 2006 there were 391 enterprises (54,99%) still active in December 2011.

Microenterprises which owner is a male have higher chances of survival on the market. Among all enterprises 64% were managed by male owner. The percentage of enterprises that survived at least 5 years on the market among enterprises manager by male owner amounted to 58%, in contrary this percentage for female owned enterprises amounted to 49,6%. The difference between groups was significant at the 0.05 significance level (p-value in chi-square test amounted to 0.032).

The entrepreneurs that started business before the age of 25 years were about 20% in this sample. In this group the percentage of liquidated enterprises amounted to 56%. The percentage of liquidated enterprises in the group of enterprises with owner older than 25 years at the start of activity was much lower and amounted to 44%. The difference between those groups was statistically significant at 0.05 significance level (p-value amounted to 0.0085).

Enterprises were divided into two groups according to the educational level of the main owner: enterprises owned by the entrepreneur with higher educational level (35%) and enterprises owned by the entrepreneur with lowed educational level (65%). Difference between groups in percentage of liquidated enterprises was statistically significant at the 0.05 significance level (p-value for chi-square test amounted to 0.0225). Microenterprises owned by the highly educated owner stayed on the market longer. The percentage of liquidated enterprises in this group amounted to 40%. In the group of enterprises owned by the entrepreneur with lower level of education this percentage amounted to almost 50%.

In case of following variables:

- managerial experience of the owner (yes/no) (p-value 0.5057),
- enterprise as the main source of the maintenance (yes/no) (p-value 0.6009),
- the differences between categories in the proportion of liquidated enterprises were not significant at the 0.05 significance level.

3.2 Multivariate analysis

For multivariate analysis the logistic regression model was applied. Only variables with significant differences between groups were included: *sex of the main owner, educational level of the main owner, age of the main owner.* Variables with nonsignificant differences between groups were not included. Additionally the controlling variables were included: *sector of activity, region of activity, exporting, percent of sources from bank loan at start.*

For variable *sex of the main owner* the category „male" is reference category, for variable *age of the main owner* the group „below 25 years" was set up as reference category, for *educational level of the main owner* the category „higher" was a reference. For controlling variables the reference category was set up following: *sector* – „trade", *region* – „regional", *exporting* – „yes".

Results of estimation of the model with variables describing human capital and *sex of the owner* were presented in Table 1.

Women have higher risk of liquidation (about 58%) comparing to male entrepreneurs. Younger entrepreneurs have higher risk (about 92%) of liquidation comparing to older. Lower level of education of the owner increases the risk of enterprise liquidation (about 42%) comparing to higher educational level of the owner.

Table 1: Results of estimation of logistic regression model for human capital

Variable	Parameter (std error.)	*p-value*	Odds ratio (95% CL)
Intercept	-0.7064 (0.1917)	0.0002	
Sex of the owner (female)	0.4612 (0.1641)	0.0049	1.586 (1.150-2.188)
Age of the owner (<25 years)	0.6528 (0.1990)	0.0010	1.921 (1.300-2.837)
Educational level of the owner (lower)	0.3539 (0.1639)	0.0309	1.425 (1.033-1.964)

Source: own elaboration using SAS.

In this model ROC amounted to 0.5955 which is very low level. There was 59.4% of correctly classified cases (at 0.5 cut-off), with sensitivity at 41.4% and specificity at 74.2%.

Hosmer-Lemeshow test revealed the very high goodness of fit (p-value 0.8750) for this model.

Next the full model with all variables: describing human capital and controlling variables was estimated (see Table 2). Among human capital and demographic characteristics only education level was not significant on 0.05 significance level in multivariate model with controlling variables.
Among controlling variables only *sources from bank loan*, *region of activity* and *section* were significant.

Table 2: Results of estimation of logistic regression model

Variable	**Parameter (std error.)**	***p-value***	**Odds ratio (95% CL)**
Intercept	-1.6027 (0.6015)	0.0077	
Sex of the owner (female)	0.4134 (0.1761)	0.0189	1.512 (1.071-2.135)
Age of the owner (<25 years)	0.6565 (0.2051)	0.0014	1.928 (1.290-2.882)
Education (lower)	0.2301 (0.1820)	0.2061	1.259 (0.881-1.798)
Sector of activity:			
(construction)	0.7316 (0.2682)	0.0064	2.078 (1.229-3.516)
(industry)	0.0014 (0.3029)	0.9964	1.001 (0.553-1.813)
(services)	0.2992 (0.2003)	0.1352	1.349 (0.911-1.997)
Region of activity:			
(national)	-0.5756 (0.2433)	0.0180	0.562 (0.349-0.906)
(local)	0.2954 (0.2049)	0.1493	1.344 (0.899-2.008)
(international)	0.1959 (0.4635)	0.6725	1.216 (0.490-3.017)
Exporting (no)	0.8655 (0.5555)	0.1192	2.376 (0.800-7.058)
Percent of sources from bank loan at start (interval)	-0.0161 (0.00817)	0.0482	0.984 (0.968-1.000)

Source: own elaboration using SAS.

In this model ROC amounted to 0.6534 which is low level. There was 57% of correctly classified cases (at 0.5 cut-off) with sensitivity at 45.3% and specificity at 66.6%.
Hosmer-Lemeshow test revealed the high goodness of fit (p-value 0.3238) for this model.

Finally the selection of variables was proposed using stepwise selection method. Stepwise selection method selected only variables significant at 0.05 level, leading to the model presented in Table 3.

Table 3: Results of estimation of stepwise logistic regression model

Variable	Parameter (std error.)	*p-value*	Odds ratio (95% CL)
Intercept	-0.6980 (0.2351)	0.0030	
Sex of the owner (female)	0.4196 (0.1725)	0.0150	1.521 (1.085-2.134)
Age of the owner (<25 years)	0.6077 (0.2013)	0.0025	1.836 (1.238-2.724)
Sector of activity:			
(construction)	0.7685 (0.2561)	0.0027	2.157 (1.305-3.563)
(industry)	-0.0108 (0.2992)	0.9712	0.989 (0.550-1.778)
(services)	0.2216 (0.1904)	0.2445	1.248 (0.859-1.813)
Region of activity:			
(national)	-0.5772 (0.2422)	0.0172	0.561 (0.349-0.903)
(local)	0.3105 (0.2031)	0.1263	1.364 (0.916-2.031)
(international)	-0.2630 (0.3612)	0.4665	0.769 (0.379-1.560)

Source: own elaboration using SAS.

In this model ROC amounted to 0.6433, which is low level. There was 58% of correctly classified cases (at 0.5 cut-off) with sensitivity at 47.2% and specificity at 67.4%.
Hosmer-Lemeshow test revealed the lower goodness of fit (p-value 0.0572) for this model.

Research hypothesis assumed that: *Human capital of the entrepreneur increases the chances of the microenterprises survival on the market.* Empirical results confirmed this hypothesis. Older, more experienced and highly educated entrepreneurs are more successful and increase the survival of owned microenterprises.

4. Conclusions and discussion

As was stated in the introduction as human capital we consider the knowledge accumulated by all members of the institution, their abilities, ambitions and innovations. The difference between traditional meaning of the capital and human capital is that in contrary to traditional capital human capital cannot be separated with person (human) being it's owner. Human capital is a part of enterprises capital but cannot be separated from the worker and is worker's property not enterprise's property. In the moment of worker's leaving the enterprise the human capital is lost for the enterprise. In case of micro-enterprise the connection between human capital and the entrepreneur is visible. The abilities (human capital) of the entrepreneur influences the enterprises success (survival).

Investment in human capital has high potential return rate. The most important in investment in human capital are education and professional training. People with high educational level have higher chances as entrepreneurs on the labour market. Everything depends on the rational choice between costs and profits of higher education.

Results of estimation confirmed the research hypothesis about positive influence of human capital of the entrepreneur on microenterprises survival on the market. As higher level of human capital as higher chances of survival of the enterprise on the market. Measuring the human capital is very complicated issue. Applying the simple measures like: age, educational level, managerial experience of the owner is one of the proposals of measuring the influence of human capital on enterprises survival.

However, this paper is by no means exhaustive. The measurement of human capital of the entrepreneur and its influence on enterprise survival still needs more research.

References

Becker, G.S. (1993) Human Capital. A Theoretical and Empirical Analysis with Special Reference to Education, University of Chicago Press.

Geroski, P.A., Mata, J. and Portugal P. (2007) Founding Conditions and the Survival of New Firms, DRUID Working Papers 07-11, DRUID, Copenhagen Business School, Department of Industrial Economics and Strategy/Aalborg University, Department of Business Studies.

Stańczyk, J. and Kryński, Z. (2007) Metody pomiaru wartości kapitału intelektualnego przedsiębiorstwa, in: M.G. Woźniak (ed) Nierówności społeczne a wzrost gospodarczy. Z. 10, Gospodarka oparta na wiedzy. Uniwersytet Rzeszowski. Katedra Teorii Ekonomii, pp. 225-254.

Wyrzykowska, B. (2008) Pomiar kapitału ludzkiego w organizacji. Zeszyty Naukowe SGGW - Ekonomika i Org. Gosp. Żywnościowej, no 66, pp. 159-170.

Agarwal, R. and Gort, M. (1996) "The Evolution of Markets and Entry, Exit and Survival of Firms", The Review of Economics and Statistics, vol. 78, no. 3, pp. 489–498.

Bastie, F., Cieply, S. and Cussy, P. (2011) The Survival of New Firms: Do Bank Loans at Birth Matter?, Economics Working Paper Archive (University of Rennes 1 & University of Caen), no. 201110.

Arribas, I. and Vila, J. (2007) "Human Capital Determinants of the Survival of Entrepreneurial Service Firms in Spain", International Entrepreneurship and Management Journal, no. 3(3).

Learning Organization and Knowledge Management to Innovation and Entrepreneurship in Private Higher Learning Institutions

Kalsom Salleh and Norhayati Wahib
College University Poly-Tech Mara Kuala Lumpur, Malaysia
kalsom@gapps.kptm.edu.my
hayati_w@gapps.kptm.edu.my

Abstract: This paper attempts to investigate the role of knowledge management in enhancing innovation and knowledge entrepreneur with the support of the learning organization concept. Hence, the research objective of this paper is to empirically investigate the conceptual relationship between learning organization and knowledge management process of tacit knowledge which can contribute to innovation and entrepreneurship activities of the higher learning institutions. A survey questionnaire was employed as the main instrument to collect data for statistical analysis from the academicians in the selected private higher learning institutions in Malaysia. The empirical findings of this study may provide an initial step forward in recognizing the role of Knowledge Management as an enabler of innovation and in transforming higher learning institutions in Malaysia into a learning organization and knowledge entrepreneurship. This research paper adapts the studies of Watkins and Marsick (1993:1996), Hernandez (2000) and Salleh, K. (2014) to identify the ways in which the seven dimensions of Learning Organization concept and the transfer process of tacit knowledge through knowledge management approach could enhance innovation and knowledge entrepreneur of the selected private higher learning institutions in Malaysia.

Keywords: Learning Organization, Knowledge Management, Tacit Knowledge, Innovation, Entrepreneurship

1. Introduction

The need for organizations to survive in a changing environment has led to the development of the concept of the learning organization (LO) and knowledge management (KM). To strive for academic and research excellence, it is imperative for a public or private university in Malaysia to become a LO (Hussein et al., 2016). The university needs to undergo the transformation process of LO by adopting the knowledge management process (KMP) of transferring tacit knowledge for its future value driven of academic and research excellence (Salleh, 2014 & Hernandez, 2000).

When knowledge becomes core competency of the organization, a successful organization is one that pays greater attention to the development and preservation of internal skills and capabilities through the process of learning and sharing knowledge among individuals and organization units (Misha & Bhaskar, 2010; Salleh, 2014; Salleh, Chong,Syed Ahmad & Syed-Ikhsan, 2012; Salleh, Syed Ahmad, Syed-Ikhsan & Lin, 2011). The Higher Learning Institutions (HLIs) should invest in intangibles such as human capital and research and development capacity through the integrative concept of LO and KM in order to create and increase its knowledge assets and intellectual capital for the future value driven of innovation and entrepreneurship.

This research paper adapts the studies of Watkins and Marsick (1993:1996), Hernandez (2000) and Salleh, K. (2014) to identify the ways in which the seven dimensions of the learning organization and the transfer process of tacit knowledge via knowledge management approach for the learning strategy, process improvement and knowledge capital of the selected private HLIs. Hence, the objective of this research paper is to empirically investigate the conceptual relationship between the seven dimensions of the LO and the transfer of tacit knowledge through KMP for innovation and entrepreneurship of the selected private university in Malaysia whose vision is to become the leading entrepreneurial technical university and the private institution or college in Malaysia whose vision is to become a competitive college in delivering high quality technical education, training and services.

A survey questionnaire was employed as the main instrument to collect data for statistical analysis from the academicians in the selected private HLIs in Malaysia and the standard regression model is proposed for each of the selected private HLIs to demonstrate the conceptual relationship between the relevant dimensions of LO together with the KM process of tacit knowledge transfer which can have a direct impact on the organizational performance improvement of the selected private HLIs.

The motivation of this study and its expected contribution is to develop an integrated conceptual model of LO and KM in the context of a private HLIs in Malaysia which can be used as replication studies for other public and private universities in Malaysia and in other countries.

2. Literature Review and Research Model

LO is defined by Watkins, 1996 (p.32) as one in which learning and work are integrated in an ongoing and systematic fashion to support continuous improvement at the individual, group and organizational levels. In other words, learning takes place in the individuals, teams and organization and even the communities with which the organization interacts. LO is said to be about increasing an organization's problem solving capability and about changing behaviour in ways leading to improved performance at the individual, team and organizational level (Buckler, 1998). The goals of LO based on team building and technological concept can enhance knowledge performance and process innovation (Watkins, 1996 and Marquardt & Kearsley, 1999).

According to Watkins & Marsick (1993; 1996), characteristics of an LO are the seven complementary action imperatives which are important in LO:

1. create continuous learning opportunities,
2. promote inquiry and dialogue,
3. encourage collaboration and team learning,
4. establish systems to capture and share learning,
5. empower people toward a collective vision,
6. connect the organization to its environment and
7. provide strategic leadership for learning

KM is defined as the process of capturing the collective expertise and intelligence in a LO and using them to foster knowledge performance and innovation through continued organizational learning (Davenport, DeLong & Beers, 1998; Meso & Smith,2000; Nonaka & Takeuchi, 1995; Quinn, Anderson & Finkelstein,1996, Salleh, 2013a & Salleh,Chong, Syed Ahmad & Syed-Ikhsan, 2013b). The ultimate goal of KM is to convert tacit knowledge (personal ideas and experiences) from individual knowledge to explicit organizational knowledge (documents, products and procedures) and utilized shared knowledge across organization effectively (Bennet & Bennet, 2003; Davenport, et al. 1998; Gupta, Iyer & Aronson, 2000, Nonaka & Takeuchi, 1995; Quinn, et al. 1996).

KMP of tacit knowledge transfer is the process by which tacit knowledge is moved and shared throughout organization through individuals and groups across various functions by personal, mechanical and electronic means (Hernandez, 2000; 2003). Hernandez (2000; 2003) had carried out an empirical study to identify the ways the LO dimensions impact the transfer process of tacit knowledge which can improve the knowledge and financial performance within the private manufacturing companies in Colombia. The findings showed the positive structural relationship between the seven LO dimensions and the transfer of tacit knowledge process for a positive influence on knowledge performance.

According to Rowley (2000), a number of characteristics of knowledge need to be recognized and accommodated in learning processes and knowledge management. The concept of Knowledge Entrepreneur is proposed by Rowley (2000) which recognizes the multi-faceted nature of knowledge and defines cultures, values and systems that encourage appropriate organizational learning. Knowledge entrepreneurship cannot be achieved without an understanding of the knowledge which an organization and its learners need to achieve its vision. Therefore, the key competence for the knowledge entrepreneur and intellectual entrepreneurship of HLI is the ability to learn how to manage systems evolution to support individual and organizational learning for the articulation of tacit knowledge.

The following research model (see Figure 1) is proposed for the hypothesis development and testing the conceptual relationship between LO and KM in terms of the impact between the seven dimensions of LO and the KM process of tacit knowledge transfer on the organizational performance of the selected private HLIs in Malaysia.

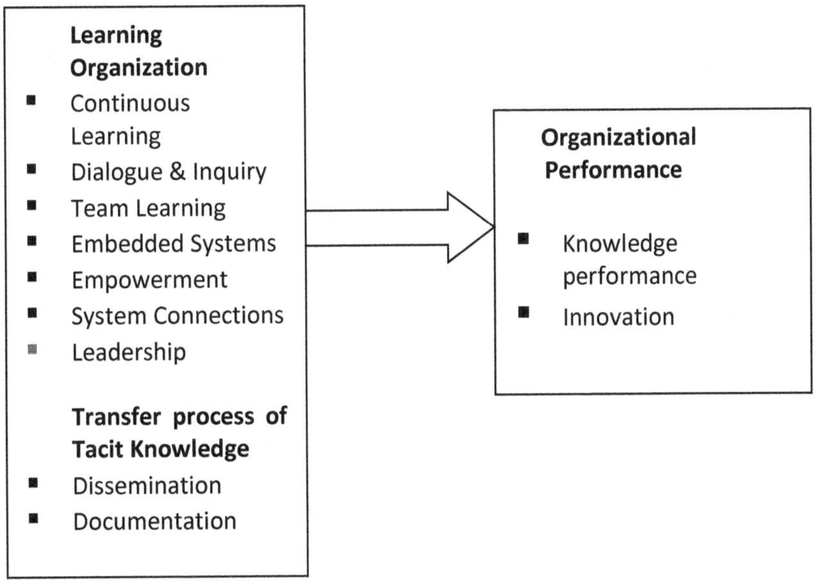

Figure 1: Research Model

3. Research Methodology

In this study, a survey questionnaire was used as the main instrument to collect data from all academicians employed by the selected private university and college in Malaysia. The selected case evidence for a private university is a Malaysia's leading university in engineering technology established in 2002. Its vision is to become the leading entrepreneurial technical university in the country by 2020 through excellence in research, education, training, entrepreneurship, consultancy and community services. On the other hand, the private institution or college established in 1991 offers a broad-based engineering education with opportunities for specialization and self-directed learning and development. The vision of this private institution is to become an internationally competitive learning organization in delivering high quality technical education, training and services; responsive to global industry demands.

Survey questionnaires were posted to a total of 800 academicians from the two selected private HLIs in Malaysia. Only 318 out of 800 questionnaires (39.75%) were received and usable for analysis purposes. The breakdown details of survey questionnaires distributed and returned for data analysis are shown in Table 1

Table 1: Distribution and Collection of Survey Questionnaires

PRIVATE HIGHER LEARNING INSTITUTIONS	DISTRIBUTION	COLLECTION	
	Number	Number	Percentage
Private Institution	300	174	58%
Private University	500	144	28.8%
Total	800	318	39.75%

In this study, the multiple question items in the questionnaire were adapted from literature and past studies on LO, transfer process of tacit knowledge and knowledge performance improvement. Besides demographic profile data, three (3) main questions for the measurement of study variables were developed in the questionnaire. The first question concerns the perception of respondents on the seven complementary action imperatives in the LO. The second question is regarding the perception on the level of the tacit knowledge (expertise, ideas, experiences, etc.) being disseminated and documented for information accessibility and usability. The third question asks about the relative performance of the LO and the effect of tacit knowledge on the organizational performance in terms of the knowledge performance and innovation of the selected private HLIs. A seven-point scale from '1' to '7' was used for respondents to indicate the level of importance of the multiple question items of the identified three study variables. The Likert - point scale is used ranging from "1" is for almost never , "2" is for seldom, "3 " is for occasionally, "4" is for not sure, "5" is for frequently, "6" is for usually and "7" is for "almost always".

These multiple question items used for study variables were adapted from those developed by Watkins and Marsick (1993; 1996) and Hernandez (2000). Thus, the final list comprising 42 items for LO dimensions, 12 KM items on the transfer process of tacit knowledge and 7 items of knowledge performance and innovation which were deemed relevant and valid to the private university and institution were included in the survey questionnaire. Statistical Package for Social Sciences (SPSS) version 23 was employed to analyse the data collected.

4. Data Analysis and Discussion of Results

4.1 Survey Questionnaires and Respondents' Demographic Profile

The demographic questions for this study consist of the gender of the respondents, the levels of academic qualification and the number of working years. As for the gender of the respondents, 51% of the respondents are females and 49% are males in the private university and 52.3% of the respondents in the private institution or college are male, 42% are female and 5.7% are from non-stated answers.

Table 2 reveals the academic qualification of the respondents. The majority (44%) of the respondents in a private university holds a Masters degree and 30% have a Doctoral degree. Likewise, the majority (51%) of respondents in a private institution or college holds a Masters degree and 1% have a Doctoral degree. Most of the respondents of both selected private HLIs in Malaysia are highly educated and thus, their responses are useful and relevant to this study.

Table 2: Academic Qualification of Survey Respondents

Current Position	Private University		Private Institution	
	No	%	No	%
Doctorate Degree (PhD)	43	30	1	1
Master Degree	64	44	89	51
Professional Degree	19	13	-	-
Degree	15	11	65	37
Diploma	2	1.30	4	2.3
Not Stated	1	0.70	15	8.6
Total	**144**	**100**	**174**	**100**

In terms of working experience, most of the respondents (57%) in the selected private university have worked for 10 years or less. Only 33% have worked between 11 to 20 years and 9% have worked between 21-30 years. However, 1% of respondents did not state his/her working experience. In terms of working experience of private institute's academic staff, most of the respondents (45%) have worked for 5 years or less. Only 33% have worked between 6 to 15 years and 9% have worked between 16 - 25 years. However, 14% of respondents in the private institution or college did not state his/her working experience.

The Cronbach's Alpha is computed to verify the reliability of the data collected and the study variables of this empirical research. According to Sekaran (2000), the closer the Cronbach's Alpha to 1, the higher is the internal consistency reliability. The Cronbach's Alpha coefficient for each study variable of this empirical study for the selected private HLIs is presented in Table 3.

Table 3: Coefficient of Cronbach's Alpha

Variables	Number of Items	Cronbach's Alpha Coefficients	Cronbach's Alpha Coefficients
		Private University (n = 144)	Private Institution (n = 174)
Learning Organization Dimensions	**42**	0.983	0.982
1. Create continuous learning	5	0.838	0.763
2. Promote inquiry and dialogue	7	0.909	0.905
3. Team learning	6	0.911	0.914
4. Embedded Systems	6	0.922	0.946
5. Empowerment	6	0.938	0.946
6. System connection	6	0.923	0.940
7. Leadership	6	0.949	0.964
KM Process of Tacit Knowledge	**12**	0.942	0.953
Organizational Performance	**7**	0.920	0.949

The main objective of this paper is to investigate the effect of seven dimensions of the LO and the KMP of tacit knowledge which are deemed important in improving the knowledge performance and innovation in the selected private HLIs in Malaysia. Thus, the following statistical analysis such as factor analysis and standard multiple regression analysis (Tabachnick and Fidell, 2001) are used to extract the valid factors and to investigate the relationships between LO components and KMP of tacit knowledge (independent variables) and the organizational performance (dependent variable) in terms of knowledge performance and innovation of the selected two private HLIs in Malaysia.

4.2 Factor Analysis and Multiple Regression Analysis for the Private University's Research Model

Factor Analysis was used to confirm that only five (5) out of seven (7) LO components are in conformity to the literature review and are valid for this empirical study. This is due to fact that factor analysis for this study has combined or grouped the two (2) components of LO i.e. empowerment and system connections as one (1) appropriate LO component.

Table 4 shows the summary of factor analysis results, factors and Cronbach's alpha scores to justify the study variables used in the study of a private university which were reliable for hypotheses testing via the standard multiple regression analysis. Factor Analysis was used to confirm that only five (5) out of seven (7) LO components are in conformity to the literature review and are valid for this study of a selected private university. The factor analysis for this study has combined or grouped the three (3) components of LO i.e. leadership, empowerment and system connections as one (1) appropriate LO component. The next three (3) components of LO i.e. Promoting Dialogue and Inquiry, Team Learning and Creating Continuous Learning are combined or grouped as another two (2) appropriate LO components i.e. 1) Promote Dialogue and Team Learning and 2) Continuous Learning & Inquiry/Feedback. In addition, factor analysis has also created the new study variable with a new title known as Recognition and Rewards based on the literature evidence.

Table 4: Summary of Factor Analysis Results, Factors and Cronbach's Alpha Scores for the Private University

Factors	Items	Factor Loadings	Eigenvalue (%)	Cronbach's alpha
LO Components	**KMO = 0.950, Sig. = 0.000, Eigenvalue= 73.5%**			
Leadership & Empowerment & System Connections	21	0.459 – 0.767	60.025	0.976
Promote Dialogue and Team Learning	9	0.480 – 0.777	4.852	0.945
Continuous Learning & Inquiry/Feedback	5	0.562 – 0.700	3.272	0.894
Embedded System	4	0.635 – 0.715	2.808	0.924
Recognition & Rewards	3	0.644 – 0.747	2.589	0.809
KM Process of Tacit Knowledge	**KMO = 0.925 Sig. = 0.000, Eigenvalue= 73.80%**			
Knowledge Disemination	9	0.564 - 0.863	61.688	0.944
Knowledge documentation	3	0.859 - 0.889	12.116	0.905
Organizational Performance	**KMO = 0.888 Sig. = 0.000, Eigenvalue= 67.915%**			
Knowledge Performance and Innovation	7	0.763 – 0.879	67.915	0.920

Standard Multiple Regression Analysis was used for finding the relationship model between LO components and KMP of tacit knowledge being identified as independent variables and the organizational performance as dependent variable. This statistcial technique also helps to identify the significant predictors between LO components and the KMP of tacit knowledge that could contribute to the knowledge performance and innovation of the selected private university.

The regression model in Table 5 had presented the integrated model of LO, KMP of tacit knowledge and organizational performance in the selected private university. This regression model shows the value of R-Square is 0.663 or 66.3% which indicates that 66.3% of the variances in the organizational performance in terms of knowledge performance and innovation had been explained by the regression model for LO components and KMP of tacit knowledge. When both the LO components and KMP of tacit knowledge are regarded as antecedents of organizational performance, KMP of tacit knowledge disemination is found as the highly significant predictor with p-value = 0.001. The co-existence of leadership, empowerment and system connections with p-values of less than 10% are found to be the more moderately significant LO component that has a positive and significant relationship to the organizational performance of the selected private university.

Table 5: Summary of Regression Results of Relationship Model for the Private University

An Integrtated Model of LO Components, KMP of Tacit Knowledge and Organizational Performance for the Private University	
Standard Multiple Regression Result	**R^2 = 0.663** F = 38.221 Sig. = 0.000***
LO Components	**B = Beta Coefficients** **P = P-Value**
Leadership & Empowerment & System Connections	B = 0.239 **p = 0.096***
Promote Dialogue and Team Learning	B = 0.022 p = 0.833
Continuous Learning and Inquiry/Feedback	B = 0.062 p = 0.552
Embedded System	B = 0.140 p = 0.129
Recognition and Rewards	B = 0.017 p = 0.816
KMP of Tacit Knowledge	**B = Beta Coefficients** **P = P-Value**
Knowledge Disemination	B = 0.423 **p = 0.001*****
Knowledge Documentation	B = - 0.051 p = 0.450
Dependent Variable	Organizational Performance
Note: Supported Hypotheses in boldface type:*p<0.01, **p<0.05, * p< 0.1**	

The following are the top ranked information of tacit knowledge dissemination through KMP which can contribute to the concept of knowledge entrepreneur of the selected private university:

1. When encountering operational problems, attempts were made to look at other departments' experience for critical information and knowledge
2. New ideas or methods are disseminated and spread to other colleagues in helping to articulate the problem
3. Organization shares with other members what works and what does not work when developing new ideas
4. Cross-functional teams are used to transfer important learning across groups, divisions and departments
5. Insights from colleagues across departments were obtained when dealing with complex problems
6. Recognition given to the value of the ideas and methods which have been made available to employees and organization

The co-existence of leadership, empowerment and system connections are among the moderately significant LO components that are regarded as paramount importance to the integration concept of LO and the KMP of tacit knowledge dissemination for the knowledge entrepreneurship of the selected private university. The following components for creating the environment of co-existence of leadership, empowerment and system connections approach is considered to be critically important by the respondents of the private university for the integration concept of LO and KM and for the way forward concept of knowledge entrepreneur:

1. Leaders continually look for opportunities to learn
2. Leaders mentor and coach those they lead
3. Leaders ensure that the organization's action are consistent with its values
4. Organization invites employees to contribute to the organization's vision
5. Organization works together with the outside community to meet mutual needs
6. Organization encourages employees to think from a global perspective
7. Organization helps employees balance work and family
8. Organization builds alignment of visions across different levels and work groups
9. Leaders generally support requests for learning opportunities and training
10. Organization gives employees choices in their work assignment
11. Leaders share up-to-date information with employees about competitors, industry trends, and organizational directions
12. Organization supports employees who take calculated risks

4.3 Factor Analysis and Multiple Regression Analysis for the Private Institution's Research Model

Factor Analysis was used to confirm that only five (5) out of seven (7) LO components are in conformity to the literature review and are valid for this study of this selected privateinstitutionor college. This is due to fact that factor analysis for this study has combined or grouped the two (2) components of LO i.e. leadership and System Connections as one (1) appropriate LO component and also has combined promote inquiry/dialogue and team learning as another one of the approparaite LO component. Table 7 shows the summary of factor analysis results, factors and Cronbach's Alpha scores to justify that the study variables in this study of private institution were reliable for hypotheses testing via the multiple regression analysis.

Table 7: Summary of Factor Analysis Results, Factors and Cronbach's Alpha Scores for the Private Institution

Factors	Items	Factor Loadings	Eigenvalue (%)	Cronbach's alpha
LO Components	**KMO = 0.968, Sig. = 0.000, Eigenvalue= 74.286%**			
Promote Inquiry and Dialogue & Team Learning	13	0.507 – 0.822	25.093	0.956
Embedded Syatem	11	0.478 – 0.752	2.550	0.959
Leadership and System Connections	10	0.526 – 0.783	1.489	0.969
Empowerment	7	0.521 – 0.641	1.055	0.930
Create Continous Learning	1	0.679	1.014	0.679
KM Process of Tacit Knowledge	**KMO = 0.928 Sig. = 0.000, Eigenvalue= 76%**			
Knowledge Dissemination	9	0.698 – 0.840	7.949	0.954
Knowledge Documentation	3	0.802 -0.883	1.187	0.886
Organizational Performance	**KMO = 0.924 Sig. = 0.000, Eigenvalue= 77%**			
Knowledge Performance and Innovation	7	0.814 – 0.928	5.369	0.948

Multiple Regression Analysis was used for finding the relationship model betweem LO components and KMP of tacit knowledge transfer and the organizational performance of this empirical study of a private institution. This statistcial technique also helps to identify the significant predictors between LO components and the KMP of tacit knowledge that could contribute to the knowledge performance and innovation of the selected private institution. Table 8 shows the summary of regression results for the research model on the conceptual relationship between LO Components (independent variable) and KMP of tacit knowledge (independent variable) on the organizational performance (dependent variable) in the private institution.

Table 8: Summary of Regression Results of the Relationship Model for the Private Institution

An Integrtated Model of LO Components, KMP of Tacit Knowledge and Organizational Performance for the Private Institution	
Standard Multiple Regression Result	**R^2 = 0.704** F = 56.418 Sig. = 0.000***
LO Components	**B = Beta Coefficients** **P = P-Value**
Promote Inquiry and Dialogue and Team Learning	B = 0.079 **p = 0.000*** **
Embedded System	B = 0.009 p = 0.936
Leadership & System Connections	B = 0.027 p = 0.785
Empowerment	B = 0.049 p = 0.623
Create Continous Learning	B = - 0.002 p = 0.971
KMP of Tacit Knowledge	**B = Beta Coefficients** **P = P-Value**
Knowledge Disemination	B = 0.358 **p = 0.001*** **
Knowledge Documentation	B = 0.269 **p = 0.000*** **
Dependent Variable	Organizational Performance
Note: Supported Hypotheses in boldface type:*p<0.01, **p<0.05, * p< 0.1**	

When both the LO components and KMP of tacit knowledge are regarded as antecedents of organizational performance, KMP of tacit knowledge for both knowledge disemination and knowledge documentation are found as the highly significant predictor with p-value = 0.001 for the prediction indicator of organizational performance of the selected private institution. The co-existence of Prmoting Inquiry/Dialogue and Team Learning with p-values of less than 1% ia also found to be a highly significant of LO component that equally has a positive and significant relationship to the organizational performance of the selected private institution.

The following are the top ranked information of tacit knowledge dissemination and documentation through KMP which can contribute to the concept of knowledge entrepreneur of the selected private institution or college:

a) Knowledge Dissemination Process
 1. New ideas or methods are disseminated and spread to other colleagues in helping to articulate the problem
 2. Insights from colleagues across departments were obtained when dealing with complex problems
 3. Organization share with other members what works and what does not work when developing new ideas
 4. Pointer systems' are used in faculty/unit/institute to find in-house expert in different areas such as yellow pages, help desks, centre of excellence, etc.
 5. Cross-functional teams are used to transfer important learning across groups, divisions and departments

b) Knowledge Documentation Process
 1. There are written manuals describing work processes
 2. Existence of documentation describing administrative procedures
 3. Parts of the work processes are embodied in software that have been modified/customized

The following components of promoting inquiry and dialogue together with team learning are considered to be critically important by the respondents of the selected private institution or college for the integration concept of LO and KM and for the way forward concept of knowledge entrepreneur:

a) Promote Inquiry/Dialogue and Team Learning
 1. Employees treat each other with respect
 2. Teams/groups focus on both the group's task and on how well the group is working
 3. Teams/groups revise their thinking as a result of group discussions or information collected
 4. Team /groups treat members as equals, regardless of rank , culture or other differences
 5. Employees spend time building trust with each other
 6. Employees help each other to learn

5. Conclusion

This survey research has found that the integration of LO and KMP of tacit knowledge as antecedents to organizational performance for the two (2) selected HLIs in Malaysia that can improve the percentage of their skilled workers /expertise, improve individual's learning new skills, greater levels of innovation and improved processes and entrepreneurship in terms of the increase in research products and patents.

KMP of tacit knowledge dissemination and documentation process is found to be highly significance in the integrated model of the selected private institution as well as the moderately significant role of KMP of tacit knowledge dissemination process of the selected private university. Knowledge sharing when developing new ideas, dissemination of new ideas/methods for solving complex problem, cross-functional teams, database technology and recognition given to the value of new ideas are found to have significant values for the new integrated concept of learning organization and knowledge management towards innovation and knowledge entrepreneurship of the selected private HLIs in Malaysia.

The spirit of promoting inquiry/dialogue, and team learning in the selected private institution and the co-existence of leadership, empowerment and system connections in the selected private university are among the highly significant component and moderately significant LO components in this integrated conceptual model for the knowledge performance and innovation of the selected private HLIs in Malaysia.

The empirical findings from this comparative study of LO and KM for innovation and entrepreneurship of the selected private university and private institution in Malaysia appear to be slightly consistent with the integration study of LO dimensions and KM process of tacit knowledge carried out by Hernandez (2000; 2003) on the organizational performance of the manufacturing companies. Hernandez (2000; 2003) had discovered that the structural relationship between the seven LO dimensions and the transfer process of tacit knowledge consecutively showed a positive influence on knowledge performance of the manufacturing organizations in Colombia.

The empirical findings from this comparative study of LO and KM for innovation and knowledge entrepreneurship of the selected private university and private institution in Malaysia can also be compared with the similar empirical study conducted by Salleh (2014) for a selected public university in Malaysia. The previous empirical study conducted by Salleh (2014) had also proved that leadership, embedded system and empowerment with system connections are among the significant LO components for the integration concept of LO and the KMP of tacit knowledge for the future value of academic and research excellence in terms of knowledge performance and innovation the selected public university in Malaysia.

References

Bennet, D., & Bennet, A. (2003). *The Rise of the Knowledge Organization*. In C. W. Holsapple (Ed.), Handbook on Knowledge Management 1: Knowledge Matters (pp. 5-20). Berlin, Germany: Springer-Verlag.

Buckler, B. (1998). "Practical steps towards a Learning Organization: Applying Academic Knowledge to Improvement and Innovation in business Process". *The Learning Organization*, Vol 5, No 1, pp 15 - 23.

Davenport, T. H., DeLong, D. W., & Beers, M. C. (1998). "Successful Knowledge Management Projects". *Sloan Management Review*, Vol 39, No 2, pp 43 - 58.

Gupta, B., Iyer, L. S., & Aronson, J. E. (2000). "Knowledge Management: Practices and Challenges". *Industrial Management & Data Systems*, Vol 100, No 1, pp 17 - 21.

Hernandez, M. (2000). "*The impact of the dimensions of the learning organization on the transfer of tacit knowledge process and performance improvement within private manufacturing firms in Colombia*". Doctorate Dissertation. University of Georgia, Athens, Georgia.

Hernandez, M. (2003). "Asessing tacit knowledge transfer and dimensions of a learning environment in a Colombian business". *Advances in Developing Human Resources*, 5(2), 215 - 221.

Hussein, N., Omar, S., Noordin,F. & Amir Ishak,N. (2016). "Learning Organisation Culture, Organisational Performance and Organisational Innovativeness in a Public Institution of Higher Educaation in Malaysia: A Prelimanary Study" for *Fifth International Conference on Marketing and Retailing (5th INCOMaR 2015)*, Procedia Economics and Finance 37 (2016) 512 – 519, Elsevier, ScienceDirect

Rowley,J. (2000). "From learning organization to knowledge entrepreneur", *Journal of Knowledge Management*, Vol4, No. 1, pp 7 - 15

Meso, P., & Smith, R. (2000). "A resouce - based view of organizational knowledge management systems". *Journal of Knowledge Management*, Vol 4, No 3, pp 224 - 234.

Misha, B & Bhaskar, A.U. (2010), "Knowledge Management Process in two learning organizations", *Journal of Knowledge Management*, Vol.15, No.2, pp 344 – 359

Nonaka, I., & Takeuchi, H. (1995). *The Knowledge-Creating Company: How Japanese Company Create the Dynamics of Innovation*. Oxford, UK: Oxford University Press.

Quinn, J. B., Anderson, P., & Finkelstein, S. (1996). "Managing professional intellect: Making the most of the best". *Harvard Business Review*, Vol March - April, pp 71 - 80.

Salleh, K. (2014). "Learning Organization and Knowledge Management: Transfer Process of Tacit Knowledge in a Public university for Academic Excellence" for *11th International Conference on Intellectual Capital, Knowledge Management and Organizational Learning (ICICKM 2014)* in the University of Sydney, Australia, 6 – 7 November 2014 (ISI Indexed, E-Book ISBN: 978-1-910309-73-5 and E-Book ISSN: 2048 -9811)

Salleh, K., Chong, S.N., Syed Ahmad, S.N., & Syed-Ikhsan, S.O.S. (2012), "Learning and Knowledge Transfer Performance among Public Sector Accountants: An Empirical Survey", *Knowledge Management Research & Practice,* Vol 10, pp 164 - 174

Salleh, K., Syed Ahmad, S.N., Syed-Ikhsan, S.O.S. & Lin, B. (2011), "The Joint Effects of Organizational Leadership and Learning Factors of Professional Intellects in Sharing Knowledge and Innovation", *International Journal of Innovation and Learning*, Vol. 10, No. 2, pp 103 - 122

Salleh, K. (2013a), "Knowledge Sharing And Knowledge Management Modelling In Public Sector Accounting Organization: Case Evidence From Malaysia", *International Journal of Knowledge-Based Development*, Vol. 4, No. 4, pp 363 – 381.

Salleh, K., Chong, S.C., Syed Ahmad, S.N. & Syed-Ikhsan, S.O.S. (2013b), "The Extent of Influence of Learning Factors on Tacit Knowledge Sharing among Public Sector Accountants", *The Journal of Information and Knowledge Management Systems*, Vol 43 No 4, pp 424 - 441

Sekaran, U. (2000). *Research methods for business: A skill-building approach* : NJ: John Wiley and Sons.

Selden,G. & Watkins, K. (2001). "Learning organizations: what impact do they really make?". *Business and Economics Review*, Vol 25, No 2, pp 8-12. Troy State University.

Tabachnick, B.G. & Fidell, L.S. (2001), *Using Multivariate Statistics*, Allyn and Bacon Publishers, Boston, MA,2001

Watkins, K. E., & Marsick, V. J. (1993). *Sculpting the Learning Organization: Lesson in the Art and Science of Systematic change*. San Francisco: Jossey – Bass

Watkins, K. E., & Marsick, V. J. (1996). *In Action: Creating the Learning Organization*. Alexandria, VA: ASTD Press.

Oulu Edulab: University-Managed, Interdisciplinary Edtech Incubator Program from Finland

Blair Stevenson
Department of Media and Performing Arts, Oulu University of Applied Sciences, Finland
blair.stevenson@oamk.fi

Abstract: The Oulu EduLAB is a permanent and innovative EdTech (education technology industry) pre-incubator and incubator higher education training program based at the Oulu University of Applied Sciences in Finland. The curriculum of the Oulu EduLAB is based on the LAB studio model (Heikkinen and Stevenson, 2016) which can be characterized as a project-based and problem-based training program with entrepreneurship at its core. With its first full cohort enrolled in January 2016, this program has become a hub for digital prototyping in the education sector in Finland. Three key factors make the Oulu EduLAB unique. Firstly, it is a full-time program that allows students from any degree program to complete their studies in a project-based format and create startups at the same time. Secondly, it is interdisciplinary in nature which brings together participants from fields such as information systems/programming, graphic design, business and education. And thirdly, the program is offered in English which means that participants are drawn from around the world. The Oulu EduLAB is part of a larger series of incubator programs at the Oulu University of Applied Sciences called Oamk LABs (www.oamklabs.fi). This paper highlights the Oulu EduLAB as a case study and provides an overview of the structures and content of the program. Based on the on-going expansion of this program both in Finland and internationally, it represents an innovative model that is relevant both for practitioners interested in redesigning higher education programs, and for academics interested in interdisciplinary models of entrepreneurship education.

Keywords: interdisciplinary, studio learning, EdTech, pre-incubation, innovation

1. Introduction

Increasingly, technology is being seen as a disruptive force in the field of education at all levels. One can observe at the primary, secondary and tertiary education levels that technology is rapidly becoming an essential component of the formal classroom. Teachers are now expected to use both hardware and software to support their teaching activities and students are expected to be building their digital competencies. With this rise in the use of technology, a corresponding growth of interest has developed within the private sector to expand the product offerings available to schools. As a result, an education technology (EdTech) industry led by many of the largest global technology companies has begun to view education as a field of potential business growth. At the same time, entrepreneurship education is increasingly being offered at the higher education level with new models of higher education observable internationally that support studies and business development at the same time (Potter, 2008). In order to connect these two realities, this paper outlines the Oulu EduLAB program as a case study of a unique model for entrepreneurship education and business development focusing on the rapidly expanding global Edtech industry (http://www.oamklabs.fi/oulu edulab/).

The Oulu EduLAB program is located in the Finnish city of Oulu. This city of approximately 200,000 people has traditionally been a key centre for ICT research and development in Finland as seen by the long presence of the Finnish firm, Nokia. During the years 2012-2014, the ICT industry in the city experienced a significant downturn with thousands of unemployed ICT-professionals in the region. In part as a response to this economic situation, a unique model of higher education was established as a pilot in 2012 at the Oulu University of Applied Sciences (Oamk: Oulun ammattikorkeakoulu in Finnish) to support innovation. This model, referred to as the LAB studio model, has now become a permanent university-managed pre-incubator and incubator program called Oamk LABs.

As of 2016, Oamk LABs consists of three separately managed full-time LABs with the same structure which each focus on a different global industry: Game LAB (established in 2012 targeting the games industry); DevLAB (established in 2015 targeting the theme of sustainability including health and wellbeing, energy and the environment); and EduLAB (established in 2016 targeting the EdTech industry). As one of these three LABs, Oulu EduLAB develops interdisciplinary teams of university students and professionals to build prototypes, products and startups targeting the global education technology (EdTech) industry. This paper is structured into four sections. The first section is an introduction, while the second section outlines the theoretical foundations for the pedagogy behind Oulu EduLAB. The third section summarizes the key structures and content of the LAB. Lastly, a fourth section is added as a conclusion within which next steps and planned development of the LAB is discussed.

2. Theoretical Foundations

In the past decade, entrepreneurship education has become increasingly offered across higher education disciplines such that it is not just delivered in the field of business, but it is also increasingly finding its way into fields such as health and engineering. This development is connected with attempts within universities to support new models of education that target innovation and business creation. Along with these entrepreneurship programs, teaching methods are being re-evaluated at universities to support the outcome of innovation with specific regard to how creativity and innovation can be taught at the theoretical level (Sawyer 2012).

In the case of the Oulu EduLAB, the program is grounded in a project-based learning approach (Blumenfeld et al 1991). Additionally, the concept of self-regulated learning (Winne, 2010) is used to conceptualize how students are expected to develop as learners within their project work in teams. In this way, participants in Oulu EduLAB teams are encouraged to become effective self-regulated learners. Overall, Oulu EduLAB is grounded in a concept of education called the LAB studio model (Heikkinen and Stevenson, 2016). This model was established at the Oulu University of Applied Sciences as a way to bridge interdisciplinarity and entrepreneurship education and has been adapted from previous concepts of studio education (Bull, Whittle and Cruickshank 2013). The concept of studio education is not new and has traditionally been used in fields such as architecture and arts education to deliver education using authentic learning tasks (Schön 1985; Boyer and Mitgang 1996; Burroughs, Brocato and Franz 2009). Boyer and Mitgang (1996) define studio based learning as: "reflective; design project-centred; master craft-person supervised; with varying group sizes; discussion intensive; individual project driven; highly integrated across multiple knowledge elements of the profession being practiced; and fostering of the learning habits needed for the discovery, integration, application, and sharing of knowledge over a lifetime" (5).

Grounded in the tradition of studio based learning, the Oulu EduLAB uses an interdisciplinary education model with the pedagogical objective of developing skilled professionals, self-directive teams and start-ups targeting the global education technology industry. Specifically, the LAB studio model has two phases: the Lead phase, within which concepts are defined and articulated; and the Lab phase, within which a demo is built. Teams begin their work by undergoing a concept development phase structured using design thinking principles from an initial 'problem' provided by an existing company or organization. These problems represent a real challenge in need of innovation – for example, a school needing a particular digital tool that is not yet available on the market. As a result, an authentic learning scenario is created since, if the teams are successful, a real business opportunity and innovation can be possibly created as a result of participating in the program.

3. Summary of Oulu EduLAB

Oulu EduLAB is defined as a pre-incubator and incubator since participating in its interdisciplinary teams can lead to the development and testing of real prototype digital products and the creation of a startup at the conclusion of the incubator phase. All teaching is offered in English and therefore the program offers a strong international and intercultural experience. Additionally, the program supports career development since participants engage with local, national and international companies involved in the global Edtech industry. The Oulu EduLAB has two program goals: 1 to offer a high-quality interdisciplinary and project-based program of learning; and 2. to support an increase in employment and business development opportunities targeting the EdTech industry. While the development of new startups is considered as a key inductor of success, it is also recognized that not all students will become entrepreneurs. Therefore, teaching is principally offered in a personalized form such that the experience in the LAB can at least support each individual's professional growth. The following section details the Oulu EduLAB program as a case study with particular attention to the program structure, infrastructure, connections to the public and private sectors and challenges encountered.

3.1 Program Structure

Studies in Oulu EduLAB are full-time and are designed for 3rd and 4th year Bachelor students and Master's students studying for professional skills in fields such as graphic design, ICT, business and education. In this way, students apply to enter the Oulu EduLAB program while remaining in their respective degree program. Since the LAB program works as a form of work-life placement experience, students can additionally participate in the LAB as a work placement or as project work. Furthermore, students can complete their research theses during the experience as well. While the majority of LAB participants are Oulu University of Applied Sciences students involved in Bachelor or Master's degree programs, the program also accepts international exchange students and unemployed professionals undertaking retraining. Oulu EduLAB has also been integrated with an English language cohort of vocational teacher education students from the university's School of Vocational Teacher Education. In this case, these vocational teacher students can complete a component of their teaching qualification while participating in the Oulu EduLAB team development process.

After its first full year, 93 students had taken part in Oulu EduLAB from 30 different countries. Participants receive ECTS credits for their participation (30 credits per semester for full-time studies) and the LAB is structured as two parts, each one semester long (5 months). The first LAB (semester 1) is called the Demo Path and involves placing new participants into interdisciplinary and international teams to produce a working digital prototype (demo), draft a business plan and conduct initial user testing. The second LAB (semester 2) allows teams from the first phase to continue development from a prototype to a full product (typically a minimum viable product) and establish a startup. It is expected that once a startup has been formed then that group is encouraged to enter into either national or international accelerator programs and / or apply for public or private seed funding beyond the scope of the university program. It is also noteworthy that within the LAB studio model, student teams end up owning the products that they create with the university taking no equity stake.

The types of products created during Oulu EduLAB focus primarily on digital innovations such as mobile applications and educational games, however the program is also open to the building of prototypes such as components for learning management systems (LMSs), e-books and products that combine hardware and software such as Internet of Things (IOT) and sensor technology. Ultimately, it is expected that current and future products developed within the LAB will be globally focused and scalable beyond the Finnish market.

3.2 Program Infrastructure

The Oulu EduLAB is located at the Kotkantie campus of the Oulu University of Applied Sciences in Oulu, Finland. The current facility is made up of roughly 350 m^2 of teaching, meeting and coaching spaces as well as designated 'office' spaces for each team once they are fully formed. The LAB also has access, when requested, to relevant campus laboratories and workshops such as the university's virtual reality CAVE environment and printed technology workshops. Teams are offered unlimited access to the space and are encouraged to treat the physical space like a business office environment. As a result, teams take ownership over their designated spaces and are offered the technology (hardware and software) and furniture necessary to create a working space for all team members.

Since the LAB program is project-based, teaching is offered to support the effective development of the team products under development. As a result, LAB teams are supported by both coaches and tutors either from the university staff or from representatives from relevant industry companies. The LAB is managed by two staff from the university with a majority of their work time to oversee the administration, support networking and actively support the daily operations of the LAB. As well as the LAB managers, a wide range of internal university staff (between 8 and 12) are allocated with varying amounts of work hours to support the teaching in the LAB based on the skills and expertise necessary. For example, university staff from faculties such as education, information systems, communications and media, and business are often scheduled to provide keynotes and targeted coaching for the teams to support their project work and team development. Since the LAB has an open door policy, teams are exposed to frequent visitors and guest coaches (face-to-face and virtual) who can augment the support offered to teams. Ultimately, these external partners represent potential clients or investors, and act as new sources of knowledge and feedback to teams.

3.3 Connections to the Private and Public Sectors

There are a number of critical partnerships that Oulu EduLAB has been cultivating to support its effectiveness. Key partners include private companies and public institutions. In the private sector, Oulu EduLAB has been collaborating with existing local, national and international companies working in the EdTech sector. The principal manner in which the LAB has been collaborating with these companies has been by receiving 'problems' which the LAB teams can then build concepts and prototypes around. Partner companies are interested in participating since there are no financial costs associated with the collaboration and the possibility represents "free prototyping" around ideas that have not yet been developed. In this way, LAB teams are not creating products for the companies, but rather they are creating products with advice from the companies. LAB teams are also not seen as developing competitors since the products under development are viewed as being strategically advantageous to the partner company.

With respect to the public sector, the key partners for Oulu EduLAB have been the local education and social institutions within the region that act as environments for user testing as well offering their own problems. In this way, partner institutions are willing to collaborate since it is viewed as a development tool for their own personnel and to support innovative delivery of services. In the case of schools, this collaboration has involved Oulu EduLAB teams conducting user testing of digital prototypes such as educational games with teachers and students in local schools.

3.4 Challenges Encountered

One of the key challenges that has been addressed as part of the on-going expansion of the Oamk LABs and the establishment of the Oulu EduLAB at the Oulu University of Applied Sciences is the creation of an internal management and teaching structure that is interdisciplinary in nature. Key early challenges that were addressed included a traditional university structure that was discipline-centred, and a teaching model that made collaboration between faculties difficult. As a result, Oamk LABs has broken down boundaries between the traditional disciplines of engineering, education and media for example. This internal development has been completed to the point that the majority of degree programs at the university can now have their students enroll in the LAB seamlessly. Furthermore, the LAB team involved at the university is also interdisciplinary in practice and is made up of members from a wide range of fields and disciplines such as health and social care, education, business, media and engineering. Having undergone this internal transformation, the Oulu University of Applied Sciences has now begun a process of development support with other universities internationally to facilitate the expansion of interdisciplinary study programs at partner institutions.

4. Conclusion and Next Steps

This paper highlights a brief case study of an innovative model of university-managed business incubation from Finland. Over the last four years, the curriculum and structure at the Oulu University of Applied Sciences has been revised to establish a permanent set of programs (Oamk LABs) to support the development of interdisciplinary teams and startups. More specifically, one of these programs targets the creation and testing of education technology products – Oulu EduLAB – which was established in 2015. It is suggested that the Oulu EduLAB is a unique and innovative higher education program due to three key factors. The first factor is that it is a full-time program allowing students to complete their ongoing studies and create startups at the same time seamlessly within a range of degree programs. The second factor is that the program consists of an interdisciplinary structure which brings together participants from a wide range of disciplines such as information systems/programming, graphic design, business and education to work in teams. In this way, all content within the program is delivered within a project-based learning approach. The third factor is that Oulu EduLAB is delivered in English which facilitates applications from all over the world and encourages an intensive international and intercultural experience for participants.

As the Oulu EduLAB reaches the end of its first year, further development is planned to expand both content and infrastructure associated with the program. Specifically, national and international collaborations and networks are being rapidly expanded to include a larger number of partner companies and universities to support not only the increasing mobility of students into the program, but to support further opportunities to localize LAB team products into international markets. Additionally, partner LABs in other countries are already being negotiated and under development. With respect to building connections for graduating startups from the program, current and future teams will continue to be encouraged to apply to EdTech accelerator programs in Finland and other countries such as the UK and the United States. On the content side, collaborations with schools and public institutions in the Oulu region and nationally are expected to increase through the establishment of projects that can support interactions between Oulu EduLAB teams and users in education at all levels. The current listing of partner companies is also expected to increase as the LAB builds further collaborations with games companies, publishers and education service providers. As teams continue to solve real problems and create businesses and innovations, it is planned that the Oulu EduLAB will expand its capacity to act as an Edtech hub for both the public and private sectors in Oulu and Finland.

This case study is expected to be of interest for both researchers interested in models of interdisciplinary higher education and for practitioners exploring examples of how higher education programs can be constructed to support the development of education technology prototypes with university students from a wide range of disciplines. Overall, the development of increasingly stronger connections between the university, governments and businesses both in Finland and internationally will support the continued development of the Oulu EduLAB as a leading EdTech product design program.

References

Boyer, E. L., and Mitgang, L. D. (1996) *Building Community: A New Future for Architecture Education and Practice. A Special Report.* Princeton, NJ: The Carnegie Foundation for the Advancement of Teaching.

Blumenfeld, P.C., Soloway, E., Marx, R., Krajcik, J., Guzdial, M. and A. Palincsar. (1991) Motivating project-based learning: sustaining the doing, supporting the learning. *Educational Psychologist* No. 26, 369-398.

Bull, C. N., Whittle, J., and Cruickshank, L. (2013) Studios in software engineering education: Towards an evaluable model. In *2013 35th International Conference on Software Engineering* (ICSE) pp 1063–1072. Ieee. doi:10.1109/ICSE.2013.6606656

Burroughs, S., Brocato, K., and Franz, D. (2009) Problem based and studio based learning: Approaches to promoting reform thinking among Teacher candidates. *National Forum of Teacher Education Journal*, Vol 19, No.3, pp 1–15. Retrieved from http://nationalforum.com/Electronic Journal Volumes/Burroughs, Susie Problem Based and Studio Based Learning-NFTEJ-19-3-09.pdf

Heikkinen, K-P. and Stevenson, B. (2016) The LAB studio model: enhancing entrepreneurship skills in higher education, *Int. J. Innovation and Learning*, Vol 20, No. 2, pp 154–168.

Potter, J. (2008) Entrepreneurship and higher education: future policy directions, in Potter, J. (Ed.): *Entrepreneurship and Higher Education*, pp313–335, OECD Publishing, Paris.

Sawyer, K. (2012) *Explaining Creativity: The Science of Human Innovation*. Oxford: Oxford University Press.

Schön, D. (1985) *The design studio: An exploration of its traditions and potentials*. Intl Specialized Book Service Inc.

Winne, P.H. (2010) Bootstrapping learner's self-regulated learning, *Psychological Test and Assessment Modeling*, vol. 52, no.4, pp. 472-490.

The PIPE® Model and Tools for Teaching Innovation and Entrepreneurship in Chinese universities

Hongyi Sun
Department of Systems Engineering & Engineering Management, City University of Hong Kong, Hong Kong, China
mehsun@cityu.edu.hk

Abstract: There are quite a few questions related to entrepreneurship education (EE). For example, why do we teach entrepreneurship? What should we teach? How should we teach, and how should we assess the learning? Previous studies have addressed the question of why, but in this study the aim is to address the questions of what and how. This paper reports a Problem-Idea-Product-Enterprise (PIPE®) model that aims to motivate and inspire students to actively learn along the multi-disciplinary process from discovering problems and generating new ideas to proposing new products and planning new enterprises. Creativity, innovation and entrepreneurship are interrelated during the entrepreneurship process, but research and education of the three generally occur in parallel, with little interaction. The PIPE model provides a systematic vehicle for students to go through the multi-disciplinary process of creativity, innovation and entrepreneurship learning. The PIPE model is consistent with the outcome-based syllabus, as it covers learning objectives (problem, idea, product and enterprise plan), teaching and learning activities (use eyes to observe, use brain to think, use hands to make and move feet to search), capacities to nurture (discovery, creative thinking, innovation and planning) and assessment criteria (desirability, originality, feasibility and viability) at each step. The model supports problem-driven, team-based, project-based, student-centred and experiential learning (learning by doing). Culture has been identified by scholars as a major factor influencing innovation. The PIPE model has been enriched by considering Chinese culture along the process of teaching and learning entrepreneurship. The model has been implemented in regular courses over the past 10 years, and in a recently launched MOOC course. It has also been shared in over 100 seminars and workshops in Chinese and other Asian universities. The PIPE model and the MOOC course triggered many interesting discussions on cultures and innovation capabilities. The PIPE model can easily be adopted and implemented by any university.

Keywords: Creativity, innovation, entrepreneurship, the PIPE® model, cre8map, 9P canvas

1. Introduction

Entrepreneurship is a major driving force behind economic growth. Entrepreneurship education (EE) has developed very rapidly worldwide, for example in England (Levie, 1999), Iran (Arasti et al., 2012), China (Sun, 2011) and Malaysia (Hamzah et al., 2016), and is one of the fastest-growing subjects at colleges and universities, not only in schools of business but also in engineering, social science and the arts (Kuratko, 2005). Studies have reported that entrepreneurial education (EE) can influence students' entrepreneurial intention (Autio et al., 1997; Davidsson, 1995; Kolvereid, 1996; Tkachev and Kolvereid, 1999). Chen et al. (1998) found that entrepreneurship students have significantly higher self-efficacy than other students, which significantly determines entrepreneurial intention. This is also supported by Lüthje and Franke (2002), who found that students who studied entrepreneurship in undergraduate curricula were more likely to create their own businesses.

However, these studies only answer the question of whether EE is important and whether it influences students' entrepreneurial intention. They do not answer the question of how it should be taught. Entrepreneurship is extremely complicated and is related to creativity, discovery and technology. Almost all models for teaching entrepreneurship start with ideas, but experience and research have shown that a) it is still difficult for young students to generate new ideas and b) even when they do, their ideas rarely reach the market because the entire process from idea to market is rarely taught and practiced. Some creative thinking methods require students to generate ideas from nothing and for nothing. Our research and experience shows that creativity or innovation is not sufficient. Creativity, innovation and entrepreneurship must be integrated into one process from multi-disciplinary perspectives (Sun 2011).

This paper reports a Problem-Idea-Product-Enterprise (PIPE) model to motivate and inspire students to actively learn along the process from discovering problems and generating new ideas to proposing new products and planning new enterprises. The Chinese government recently recommended that an entrepreneurship courses should be offered to all university students, so they can gain a preliminary understanding of innovation and entrepreneurship. If they find it interesting, they can then go further and take more and advanced courses on entrepreneurship management and practices. The PIPE model introduced here is specifically for a general education course for junior university students.

Culture is identified by scholars as a key factor influencing innovation in China, as in other countries. According to Hofstede (1997), one of the foremost empirical researchers on culture, 'National Culture is about the value differences between groups of nations and/or regions'. China has a very long history, a rich culture and different religions and philosophies such as Confucianism, Taoism and Buddhism. It also had a glorious history of science and technology (Needham, 1954). However, research has found that contemporary Chinese culture does not support innovation as much as some other cultures (Sun 2009). While there are no 'good' or 'bad' cultures – they are just different – pertinent cultural issues must be considered while learning about innovation and entrepreneurship in China, and elsewhere, so cultural issues related to other places will also be addressed.

2. The PIPE® model

The PIPE acronym stands for Problem, Idea, Product and Enterprise. The **PIPE®** model is a summary of the four steps of teaching **P**roblem discovery, **I**dea generation, **P**roduct proposal and **E**nterprise plan, as illustrated in Table 1. It is an effective teaching model for motivating student-centred learning from multi-disciplinary perspectives. Students are motivated to actively look for what they need throughout the process, from the problem to the enterprise plan. The PIPE model aims to help students (from any field) to discover problems in daily life, generate new ideas aimed at solving these problems, design new products accordingly and develop a simple business plan for the enterprise. If sufficient support is available, the team can produce a prototype of the product and prepare an integrated yet simple business plan to present.

Determining how to measure and assess discovery and innovation is often a difficult task, not only in education but also in industry. Additionally, confusion can arise in innovation and entrepreneurship education over what is assessed. Some tools assess creativity while others assess innovation. Assessments may focus on personality, attitude, ability and/or accomplishment. The student outcomes under the PIPE model are mainly about accomplishments in terms of problems, ideas, products and the enterprise plan. The accomplishments are measurable and assessable. The assessment will cover the problems discovered, the number of ideas generated, ideas and idea screening, technical and market feasibility, financial feasibility and the whole business plan and course.

Entrepreneurship is related to innovation, creativity, invention and discovery, which may often overlap and be difficult and confusing to teach in one course. The PIPE model distinguishes and then integrates discovery, creative thinking and innovation into entrepreneurship, removing any confusion about the differences or similarities among creativity, innovation and entrepreneurship. The PIPE model supports multiple teaching and learning philosophies and/or methods. It is process-oriented from multidisciplinary perspectives. It supports problem-driven learning (PDL) where students identify problems themselves, unlike problem-based learning (PBL) where problems are given to students. The model suggests that a product or service must be proposed. It requires a simple business plan to integrate the problem, idea, product and basic market information. It supports team and project-based learning. Finally, it provides teaching tools along the PIPE process, which will be elaborated below.

Table 1: The **PIPE®** model for teaching innovation and entrepreneurship

PIPE® / Details:	**Problem discovery**	**Idea generation**	**Product development**	**Enterprise plan**
Pedagogical focus	Exploration and discovery	Creativity and creative thinking	Innovation and new product development	Entrepreneurship and business plan
Learning objectives	To discover problems in daily life or work	To generate new ideas to solve the problem identified.	To conduct a basic but comprehensive feasibility study of a new idea (for the product)	To incorporate all the above factors into a simple business plan (of the enterprise)
Teaching and learning activity (LTA)	Eye and mouth (Explore, observe and ask)	Brain (Creative thinking)	Hand (Design and make)	Feet (Go and do market search)
Warm-up games	2 groups of tourists	Purpose of a glass	Air plan	Toilet
Assessment criteria of the learning outcome	-Complexity, -Commonality -Number of problems discovered -Observation and curiosity	-Newness, -originality and attractiveness -Number of ideas generated	-Technical feasibility, -Technology availability, -Cost-effective feasibility	-Market feasibility -Financial feasibility - Team spirit and collaboration
Teaching and learning tools	7W4H	Cre8map	BAH	9P Canvas

3. Teaching tools along the PIPE® process

Entrepreneurship education is different to standard education. In addition to lecturing and case studies, special teaching and learning tools are needed to support participative and experiential learning in a project.

3.1 WH questioning and observation for problem discovery

Entrepreneurship starts with an entrepreneurial opportunity (Timmons et al., 2004). How do entrepreneurs find such opportunities? Research suggests that it is their own work experiences helps entrepreneurs to find opportunities (Lambing and Kuehl, 2006). In China, up to 90% of startup opportunities are derived from practical work experiences (Zhang et al., 2013), which is exactly what university students are missing! It is not feasible for students to identify an entrepreneurial opportunity. For students without practical working experience and relevant knowledge, observing daily life and finding problems is the best way to identify entrepreneurial opportunities.

What is a problem? A problem is a perceived gap between the existing state and the desired state. As long as this gap between the two states is observed, and it makes people feel uncomfortable and uneasy, causes them pain or makes their life difficult, then the gap is a problem. Even if you are not quite sure what the expected state will be, if you are not satisfied with the current state, it is a problem.

Observing and questioning are the main methods students can use to find problems. They can use WH questions to get started. What is it about? Whose lives can be made easier? How can it make their lives easier?

By observing and asking these questions about particular phenomena, many problems will be found. This works with students and real-life entrepreneurs alike.

Of course, not all questions lead to problems and not all problems lead to entrepreneurial opportunities, so the assessment and selection of problems from an entrepreneurial perspective are needed.

The key to finding the problem is not the tool but the attitude. Problems exist everywhere. Yet, some people may not see problems at all, while others may avoid them. Some may see the problems but ignore them. Entrepreneurs, however, not only see problems but they also turn them into opportunities. Some entrepreneurs even discover problems that are not visible to others and then imagine how the problems can be turned into great opportunities. Thus, attitude determines whether a person can find problems or not, and this attitude is influenced by the local culture. In Chinese culture, the idea that 'satisfaction is happiness' may have a heavy negative influence on finding problems.

3.2 The Cre8map for idea generation

After finding the problems, the next step to learn is to find solutions to solve the problems. This is related to creativity and idea generation. There is some confusion about the word 'creativity' in the Chinese language. Creativity has been translated into at least three different Chinese terms. One, 'creative idea', is different from 'creativity', which must be emphasised when teaching about creativity in a Chinese context or working with Chinese students or employees. In current Chinese creativity education, creativity is often misunderstood as a mere snap of the fingers and then ideas flow out. 'Creativity' is actually a process, whereas 'creative ideas' are the outcomes of the process. The renowned Graham Wallas model from the 1920s can help students understand that creativity is a process, and details this through Preparation, Incubation, Illumination to Verification (Wallas, 1926). This model is still influential today (Runco, 2014; Sadler-Smith, 2015). Idea generation at the illumination step has been over-emphasised in China, while the other steps are mostly ignored.

Hundreds of tools are available for idea generation. One website offers over 50 different methods (Creative Minds, 2015). The most popular include brainstorming, mind maps and SCAMPA. However, perhaps not everybody knows that the mind map is not really a tool for idea generation. It is a tool mostly for recording, organising or memorising ideas. Other tools like TRIZ or SCAMPA are either too complicated or difficult for non-English students in a general education course. Idea generation cannot result from a tool that people check like using a manual. It must be learnt by heart and inspired spontaneously.

The author has developed a Cre8map (i.e., creating an idea map) for students. The Cre8map is a tool based on the mind map and eight simple mathematical signs, standing for combining (+), deleting (-), similar principle (=), different principle (≠), increasing (↑), decreasing (↓), reserving backward (←) and moving forward (→), as illustrated in Figure 1.

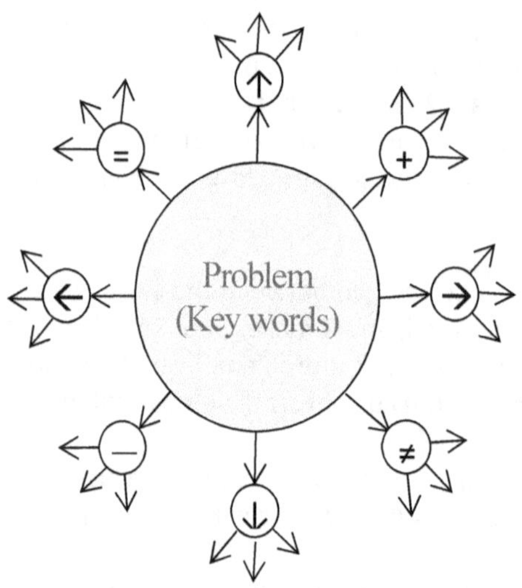

Figure 1: The Cre8map for generating ideas

These mathematical signs are used in most countries and can visually inspire the generation of new ideas. The map is visual and easy to remember and use. The Cre8map can be used to generate ideas and uses a table to organise and record these ideas. Table 2 lists examples of new ideas following the eight signs. In teaching, the students must select a problem first. Without a problem, creativity will be simply for its own sake, generating many ideas for no purpose. Cre8map is problem driven.

Table 2: Explanation and examples of the eight symbols in the Cre8map

Sign	Formula	Examples
+	Combine A + B?	Mobile phone + camera; clothes + heart monitor; earphone + radio; earphone + earring; necklace + wireless microphone
—	Eliminate A - B?	Radio - loud speaker ☞ portable music player; sales - middleman ☞ direct sales
↑	Increase, enlarge A ↑?	Low speed prop plane ↑ ☞ high speed jet plane; cassette tape audio player ↑ → digital music player with thousands of songs

↓	Decrease, shrink A ↓?	A sonar system for navies ↓ ☞ smaller one for fishermen ↓☞ even smaller for hobby fishing; House vacuum cleaner ↓ ☞ keyboard vacuum cleaner
→	Forward A1 → A2?	iPhone5 → 6; penicillin → amoxicillin
←	Backward, reverse ? A2 ← A1	Simple phone for senior citizens ← mobile (→smart phone)
=	Association, analogy A = f(B) ?	Inkjet printer = principle of capsule coffee maker; digital camera sensor = insect eyes; airplane = bird
≠	Alternative, substitute A ≠ f(B) ?	Mobile phone case made of: plastic ≠ leather ≠ metal ≠ nano-material

There can be many ideas on how to solve any particular problem. Not all ideas are suitable for entrepreneurship. Some ideas may be temporary solutions. Whether an idea is good and useful from the entrepreneurial perspective depends on whether it can be developed into an independent product or service. Culturally, Chinese are very flexible in their thinking and behaviour (Hall, 1976), but are in general shy! In a brainstorming session, either nobody talks or everybody talks at the same time, so the controlled version may be appropriate. The 635 brainstorming method has been found to be suitable for Chinese students. The 635 method recommends about six students per group. With each turn, every group member is supposed to generate three ideas so that each has an equal chance. The members then submit their three ideas to the moderator, and no-one then needs to feel shy or to worry about lacking confidence. Each round can take about five minutes, which can be adjusted according to the speed and productivity of the participants.

3.3 The BAH model for product development

A product or service is the core of a business and is essential for business success. New product development (NPD) is the process of turning an initial idea into a product or service, but currently this is not considered in EE in Chinese universities. Most EE teaching focuses on business model development even without a product, possibly because most EE courses are taught by business school teachers who are not familiar with NPD.

There are many models of NPD, and the generic model introduced here is based on the BAH model by Booz, Allen & Hamilton (1982). This model includes the following steps: the generation of a product idea, a patent search, market research, product design, product development and product testing, as illustrated in Figure 2.

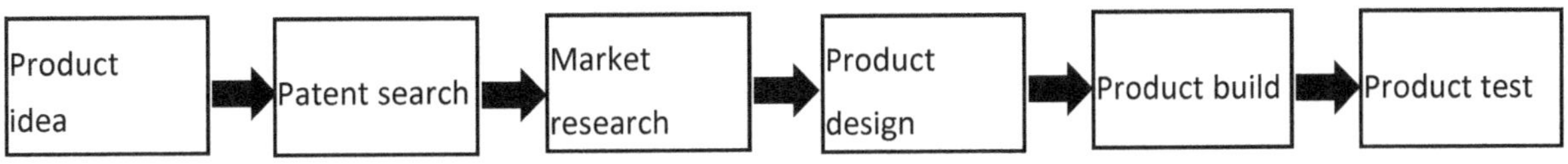

Figure 2: The NPD process of entrepreneurship

After identifying the problem and the idea for solving the problem, the team must turn the solution idea into a product idea. First, the startup must ensure that no other company or person owns the idea behind its product, so they must conduct a patent search. The students can do this, but hiring a professional patent attorney or agent is also possible in some universities. Patent search websites are effective and rapid methods of checking patents. Even if the product idea is similar to existing patents the idea does not necessarily have to be immediately dropped. Sometimes a new startup can be inspired by these patents and create new products, or improve the products and generate new product ideas. If a service is being developed, market research is also required, to ascertain whether similar services exist. Students are recommended to research a physical product so that they can learn the NPD steps. A patent search report can be required if patent search resources are available.

After the patent search is conducted, the next step is to carry out what is called 'market research' to understand the potential market and collect the necessary information to make good business decisions. Product designers should do their best to provide features in the new product which will benefit future customers. However, this does not mean a product should contain as many features as possible. The concept of the minimum viable product (MVP) advocates that a startup should first develop a product that has as few features as possible; just enough for a user test.

For students on a basic course the level of product development can range from high to low – from a verbal description of a 2D model drawing to a 3D printout or a digital prototype. A fully functional prototype, whether physical or non-physical, can be developed for user tests or to study user experiences. The level of new product development attained is determined by the level of support.

In a user test, the students ask potential customers to test the product and particularly to find problems or weaknesses with it. The comments on the product performance are then collected. Thus, to conduct a real user test, a functioning prototype is required.

3.4 The 9P canvas for developing business model and business plan

A business model describes how a business will make money. Business models can range from simple to very complex. In either case, the design of the model must specify the core elements of the business and identify the relationships and sequences among those elements.

Common canvases or tools for developing a business model include the canvas of Osterwalder (Osterwalder and Pigneur, 2010) and the lean canvas model by Maurya (2012). However, both these canvases have shortcomings in terms of teaching models for junior undergraduate students.

As Maurya (2012) pointed out, the Osterwalder canvas was based on cases that were successful and did not use the canvas at all, such as Apple and Skype. It does not clearly specify the problem to be solved. He believes that most startups fail not because they fail to build what they set out to build, but because they waste time, money and effort building the wrong product. A significant contributor to this failure could be a lack of proper 'problem understanding' from the outset. Ironically, both canvases miss this product block, and many of their examples are IT or website businesses. Additionally, the logic and flow are relatively complicated for students. The need for pre-requisite knowledge in developing business models based on these canvas tools is rarely mentioned. Crittenden et al. (2015) suggested that operations management and management accounting are required for developing business models, while Zhang et al. (2013) recommended that knowledge of management, managerial economics, strategy management, marketing and finances is needed to learn entrepreneurship and business models. According to Crittenden et al. (2015, p.119), before studying operations management and management accounting, the business model is a black box! However, students in general education courses on entrepreneurship do not possess the basic knowledge.

In this paper, the 9P canvas for business model development is introduced. The nine Ps are people, problem, proposal, product, process, price, profit, place and finally promotion, as illustrated in Figure 3. The 9P Canvas is a fundamental, people-centred tool. All of the elements revolve around people. A beginning learner in entrepreneurship should ask the following questions, guided by the 9P canvas, which correspond to each of the nine blocks.

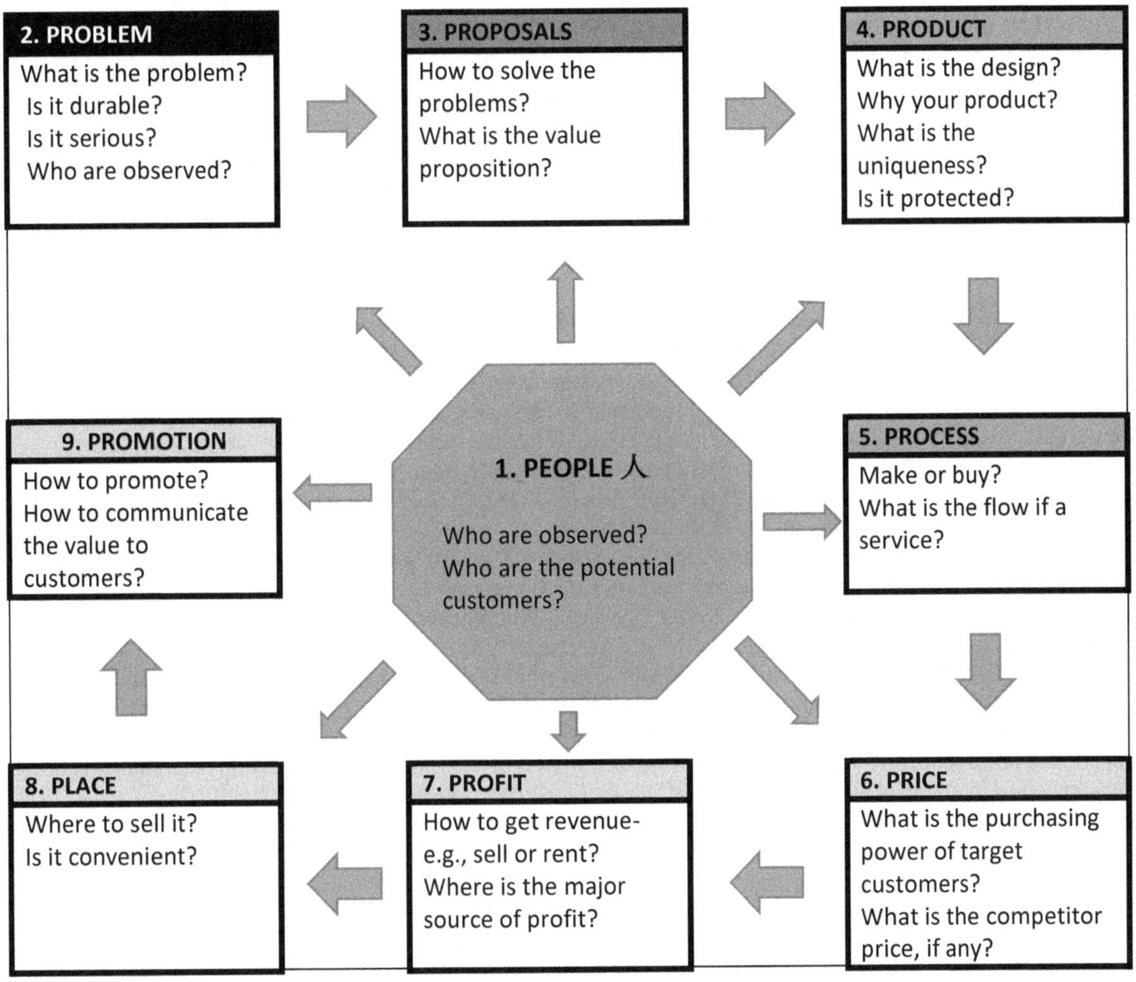

Figure 3: The 9P canvas for developing a simple business model

The 9P business model canvas is not only for documenting a business model step by step, but is also a tool to explore, analyse, revise and justify a business model. There will be much back and forth revision. There could be a Plan B or a Plan C, so it is useful to bear in mind that it takes time to develop a viable business model. The 9P canvas can be expanded to include other factors in advanced courses, such as partners, resources and performance, which can be considered in related blocks.

Very often students confuse business models and business plans. The business model explains the rationale while the business plan provides the details. The business plan builds upon a business model and explains the implementation steps to achieve the goals of the model.

4. Conclusions and future work

For GE students with little technical knowledge, embarking on the discovery of problems in daily life can be very useful. All students can join this course, and will have the chance to practice the discovery of problems and idea generation under the PIPE model. The mindset and methodology will influence students in the future when they join more technical or professional courses.

Innovation and entrepreneurship involve the basic strategies of market-pull versus technology-push. The PIPE model is a typical market-pull approach. In future, we will explore the TIME model, (i.e., from Technology, Idea, Market and finally to Enterprises). The TIME model is suitable for senior students with technical knowledge. If technical issues are involved, colleagues from relevant technical departments/units can be invited to be additional supervisors of the entrepreneurship teams.

A further development of the PIPE model would be to discover problems in industries and invite the relevant managers to be the assessors. The author plans to invite industrialists to be guest speakers and assessors of new ideas, new products and the new businesses. The preliminary version of the PIPE model was used for training in two Hong Kong companies. While preparing this proposal, another Hong Kong industry organisation is enquiring about whether we can provide training for their members.

Due to the time limitation warm-up games are not introduced in this paper . These games are not only for warming up participants but also explain the basic theories and concepts. They are available in other reference books and readers can develop their own versions.

References

Arasti, Z., Falavarjani, M. K. and Imanipour, N. (2012) "A study of teaching methods in entrepreneurship education for graduate students", Higher Education Studies, 2(1): 2-10.

Autio, E., Keeley, R. H., Klofsten, M. and Ulfstedt, T. (1997) "Entrepreneurial intent among students: testing an intent model in Asia, Scandinavia and USA", in Frontiers of Entrepreneurship Research, 1997: Proceedings of the Seventeenth annual Entrepreneurship Research Conference / [ed] Paul D. Reynolds, Wellesley, Mass.: Babson College, pp. 133-147.

Booz-Allen and Hamilton, (1982) New Products Management for the 1980s, Booz-Allen & Hamilton.

Chen, C. C., Greene, P. G. and Crick, A. (1998) "Does entrepreneurial self-efficacy distinguish entrepreneurs from managers?" Journal of Business Venturing, 13(4): 295-316.

Couger, J.D. (1995) Creative Problem Solving and Opportunity Finding, Danvers, MA: Boyd and Fraser Publishing Company.

Creating Minds (2015) Tools for Creating Ideas, http://creatingminds.org/tools/tools_ideation.htm.

Crittenden, V. L., Esper, K., Karst, N. and Slegers, R. (2015) Evolving Entrepreneurial Education, Innovation in the Babson Classroom, Emerald, Bingley.

Davidsson, P. (1995) "Determinants of entrepreneurial intentions", Working paper series 1995-1, Jonkoping International Business School, Sweden, http://eprints.qut.edu.au/2076/1/RENT_IX.pdf.

Hall, E. T. (1976) Beyond Culture, New York: Anchor Press.

Hamzah, H., Yahya, Z., Sarip, A. G. and Mohd Adnan, Y. (2016) "Impact of entrepreneurship education programme (EEP) on entrepreneurial intention of real estate graduates", Pacific Rim Property Research Journal, 22(1): 1-13.

Hofstede, G. (1997) Cultures and Organizations: Software of the Mind, London: McGraw-Hill.

Kolvereid, L. (1996) "Prediction of employment status choice intentions", Entrepreneurship: Theory and Practice, 21(1): 47-58.

Kuratko, D. F. (2005) "The emergence of entrepreneurship education: Development, trends, and challenges", Entrepreneurship: Theory and Practice, 29(5): 577-598.

Lambing P. A. and Kuehl C. R. (2006) Entrepreneurship, 4th ed, Prentice Hall, YN.

Levie, J. (1999) "Entrepreneurship education in higher education in England: A survey", UK, Department for Employment and Education.

Lüthje, C. and Franke, N. (2002) "Fostering entrepreneurship through university education and training: Lessons from Massachusetts Institute of Technology", in European Academy of Management 2nd Annual Conference on Innovative Research in Management, Stockholm, pp. 9-11.

Maurya, Ash. (2012) "Why lean canvas vs business model canvas." Available at: http://practicetrumpstheory. com/why-lean-canvas.

Needham, J. (1954) Science and Civilization in China: Introductory Orientations. Cambridge: Cambridge University Press.

Osterwalder, Alexander and Yves Pigneur. (2010) Business Model Generation: A Handbook for Visionaries, Game Changers, and Challengers. John Wiley & Sons, , NJ.

Runco, M. A. (2014) Creativity: Theories and Themes: Research, Development, and Practice, Burlington, MA: Elsevier.

Sadler-Smith, E. (2015) "Wallas' four-stage model of the creative process: More than meets the eye?" Creativity Research Journal, 27(4): 342-352.

Sun, H. (2009) "A meta-analysis on the influence of national culture on innovation capability." International Journal of Entrepreneurship and Innovation Management, 10 (3/4), 353-360.

Sun, H. (2011) "The 3-3-3 framework and 7P Model for teaching creativity, innovation and entrepreneurship" Journal of Chinese Entrepreneurship, 3(2): 159-166.

Timmons, J. A., Spinelli, S. and Zacharakis, A. (2004). Business Plans that Work: A Guide for Small Business, New York: McGraw-Hill.

Tkachev, A. and Kolvereid, L. (1999) "Self-employment intentions among Russian students", Entrepreneurship & Regional Development, 11(3): 269-280.

Wallas, G. (1926). The Art of Thought, New York: Harcourt Brace.

Zhang, Y. L., Xue, H. Z. and Chen, H. S. (2013) Entrepreneurship Management (in Chinese), Ed. 4., Mechanical Industry Publisher, Beijing.

Attitude Towards Eating "Green": Do Consumer Consciousness, Healthy Lifestyle, and Value Orientation Matter?

Booi Chen Tan[1], Lau Teck Chai[2] and Pang Suk Min[3]
[1]Faculty of Management, Multimedia University, Cyberjaya, Malaysia
[2]Faculty of Accountancy and Management, Universiti Tunku Abdul Rahman, Kajang, Malaysia
[3]Faculty of Management, Multimedia University, Cyberjaya, Malaysia
[1]bctan@mmu.edu.my
[2]lautc@utar.edu.my
[3]psmin90@hotmail.com

Abstract: Due to the increasing pressure on environmental deterioration, consumers have begun to be more concerned over sustaining green environment and living a healthy lifestyle. Consumers have started to worry about the negative effects of chemical residues on their health and on the environment in conventional production methods. As a result, organic food and products which produced without synthetic fertilizers, pesticides, genetically modified organisms, food additives, sewage sludge and others are perceived by consumers as safer and healthier, and expected to have greater nutritional value. Hence, the organic food market is growing because more people are willing to eat "green" as they lose confidence in the quality of food, resulting from the conventional method of production. Although the studies conducted to understand the organic food markets has certainly been on the increase, the information about consumer attitude towards eating "green" that helps firms to assess the feasibility of entering or expanding their operations in the green market is still not widely discovered. Therefore, this paper proposes a conceptual framework to examine the effect of consumer consciousness, healthy lifestyle, and value orientation on attitudes towards eating "green" simultaneously in a single study in Malaysia context. Green" is referred to the locally grown organic food and products in this research. Besides, the mediating role of healthy lifestyle in the relationship between consumer consciousness and attitudes towards eating "green" is examined in this study. An individual's healthy lifestyle that focuses on physical health-related activities may increase the effect of consumer health and environmental consciousness on their attitudes towards eating "green". The result of this study is expected to provide a better understanding for marketers to better design marketing promotion strategies for organically grown food and product consumption, given that the consumer lifestyle and value orientation are the psychographic variables that give a clearer orientation to identify green consumer segment.

Keywords: Attitudes, Eating Green, Lifestyle, Organic, Values

1. Introduction

Worldwide, the global organic food market had shown continuous positive growth with retail sales reaching $80 billion in 2014 (Lernoud & Willer, 2016). The United States is the largest organic food market, followed by Germany and France. In Asia, it was reported that the total organic agricultural area was 3.6 million hectares in 2014, which represented 8 percent of the world's organic agricultural land (Lernoud & Willer, 2016). This phenomenal growth in the global organic food market can be attributed to the increasing health concerns among consumers as well as growing awareness pertaining to health benefits of organic food. Other factors that drive organic food sales across the world include increasing disposable income, improving standard of living, changing lifestyle and easy accessibility.

Nevertheless, the food supply crises frequently highlighted have prompted consumers to lose confidence in the quality of food, resulting from the conventional method of production (Chen, 2009). Consumers have become more conscious about the nutrition, health, and quality of the food they consume. As a result, more and more organic food products are being marketed and the organic food market is growing because more people are willing to eat "green". Through green eating, this will not only benefit their health and save the environment, but will support small scale or local farmers who usually do not use pesticide in their farming method. Most conventional food are cultivated with the assistance of pesticides and other toxins and these are shown to poison one's body and weaken the immune system. The best defence for the body is to consume food that are natural (such as organic food), that are produced without the help of any harmful chemicals (Walker, 2009).

In Malaysia, the organic food market experienced rapid growth of about 20% per annum, valued at around RM150 million (Stanton et al., 2011). However, the definition of consumers who are interested in eating "green" are still vague. "Green" is referred to locally grown organic food and products in this research. Consumer lifestyle and value orientation are the psychographic variables that give clearer orientation on green consumer segment (Fraj & Martinez, 2006). Although there are numerous studies in the past that investigate the perception, attitudes, purchase intention and behaviour of consumers towards organic food and products, studies conducted in examining the effect of consumer consciousness, healthy lifestyle, and value orientations on attitudes towards eating "green" in Malaysia is still under-explored. This paper aims to address this gap by analysing several aspects of the organic food market and provides critical review from past studies in the similar setting. The paper will also propose a research framework to understand the influencing factors of consumer attitudes towards eating green. Lastly, sections on research methodology, implication, and conclusion will be addressed as well.

2. Literature Review

2.1 Organic farming in Malaysia

Organic farming in Malaysia was started in 1980s. The Centre of Environment, Technology and Development Malaysia (CETDEM) started its first experimental organic farm in Subang New Village, on one acre of land (CETDEM, 2010). The success of the experiment has motivated other farms to follow and grow organic agriculture. Besides, Malaysian government gives support to the small-scale producers to venture into organic farming with the objectives to raise income, overcome problems of chemical residues in food production, protecting the environment, reducing food import as well as enhancing the country's export of high quality safe food. Under the 9th Malaysia Plan (2006-2010), the government is aiming to grow the organic farming market to be worth RM800 million in 5 years time. Besides, Ministry of Agriculture plans to reach 20,000 hectares under organic farming method by year 2010, increasing local production by 4,000 hectares per year.

Nevertheless, organic agriculture in Malaysia is still in a development phase (Zhen, 2013). Number of farmers involved in organic agriculture industry increased from 900 in 2010 to 1500 in 2012 (Suhaimee et al., 2016). Furthermore, there was only 131 hectares of organic farms in Malaysia in 2001 (Omar et al., 2016). The number has increased to 963 hectares in 2007 (Omar et al., 2016) and 1700 hectares of organic farms in 2014 (Suhaimee et al., 2016). According to the Malaysian Department of Agriculture (2007), organic products are food that are produced, processed or handled in compliance with the organic standards. There are several organic certification logos used in Malaysia and shown in Figure 1 (Suhaimee et al., 2016). Consumers can differentiate certified organic products from the conventional products by looking for the Organic Malaysia mark. The Organic Malaysia mark is a label scheme operated by Organic Alliance Malaysia in association with Department of Agriculture Malaysia and it is used by registered operators on certified organic products (Department of Agriculture, 2007).

Figure 1: Organic certification logo in Malaysia

(Source: Suhaimee et al., 2016)

2.2 Consumer consciousness

According to Velmans (1996), the term "consciousness" is synonymous with "awareness" or "conscious awareness. Tassi & Muzet (2001) who states that someone is considered conscious when he is aware of things and the things may be objects outside himself or in his memories, thoughts and feelings. Consciousness is also refers to knowledge or experience itself (Velmans, 2009). In this paper, health consciousness, environmental consciousness, and price consciousness will be discussed.

2.2.1 Health consciousness

Health consciousness is a concept reflecting a person's readiness to do something to his or her own health (Kaynak & Ekşi,. 2014). Consumers nowadays are becoming more health conscious and concerned about the safety of the food they consume, which resulted in a change in their food preferences (Chen, 2009). Besides, Basha et al. (2015) found out that health conscious lifestyle is the primary motivating factor for purchase intention of organic products. Organic consumers are also aware of the benefits of organic products and considered themselves more responsible for their own health. According to Walker (2009), consuming organic food is beneficial for some reasons:

- Organic consumers will have a healthier body with more strength and energy as compared to conventional consumers, because conventional food contains more chemicals which linked to many types of diseases and cancer.
- Organic food contains at least 50% more nutrients, vitamins and minerals than conventional food.
- Hormones and antibiotics added in the conventional food may lead to early maturation in children. Therefore, it is advised to have a diet that rich in organic food in order to make sure that children will mature as nature intends.
- Organic food is normally lower in fat, therefore it helps to prevent obesity and diseases that cause by a diet high in fatty food, such as heart disease and stroke.
- Consumers should avoid taking conventional food if they have allergies. This is because allergies normally caused by the antibiotics found in the conventional food.
- Consumers will be able to taste the original flavour of the organic fruits and vegetables as these food are grown naturally without any added toxins that tend to ruin the true taste.
- Organic food protects consumers from toxic metals such as cadmium, lead and mercury which may damage nerve function, block haemoglobin production, and leads to anemia as well as other diseases.

In short, consumers choose organic food in order to avoid pesticides and other chemicals. For example, tomatoes are rich in flavonoids and other phytochemicals that have anticarcinogenic properties (Mercola, 2013). Researchers found out that the level of flavonoid in organic tomatoes was almost doubled the level of flavonoid in conventionally grown tomatoes (Nagourney, 2007). For this reason, organic tomatoes are said to be healthier for consumers as there is evidence that flavonoids may be protective against age-related diseases and prevent diseases such as cancer, cardiovascular disease or neurodegenerative diseases (Cassidy & Kay, 2012). However, Bravata and Spangler who conducted a meta-analysis to compare organic and conventional foods, found out that organic products are not necessarily 100% free of pesticides, but organic products had 30% lower health risk as well as risk of pesticide contamination than conventional products (Brandt, 2012).

2.2.2 Environmental consciousness

Schlegelmilch et al. (1996) describe environmental consciousness as a motive raising individuals' awareness of the negative environmental outcomes associated with humankind careless behaviors as well as companies, products or brands which are reshaping their attitudes and behaviors to decrease hazards of these agents' operations upon nature. According to Toth et al. (2008), consumer is said to be environmentally conscious if he purchase something that he believes to have positive or less negative impact on the environment. Past studies reported that environmental concern has a direct and positive influence on green purchase (Sinnappan & Abd Rahman, 2011; Wahid et al., 2011). Environmentally conscious consumers are more likely to purchase organic products (Kaufmann et al., 2012) as they will take into account the ecological impacts when they make a purchase decision. In addition, Meffert and Kirchgeorg (1993) suggest that environmental consciousness might occur in several ways: (i) reduce the consumption of traditional goods, (ii) adjust demand-purchase of green products instead of conventional products, (iii) consume environmentally efficient products, (iv) participate in recycling the products and separate waste collection, and (v) take part in environmentally conscious complaints or protests.

2.2.3 Price consciousness

Past studies found out that most of the consumers consider price as an important determinant of a purchase (Tan & Govindan, 2014: Alfred, 2013;) with the lowest price being the most preferred (Furnols & Guerrero, 2014). Price consciousness is that consumers use price as a decision criterion within a negative role (Lichtenstein et al., 1993), which means higher prices negatively affect purchase probabilities. Price conscious consumers will not willing to pay higher price for a product or they will only focus on searching for low price products (Lee, 2008). This is supported by Monroe (2008) who states that consumers with high price consciousness are less likely to pay higher price for products.

Consumers often perceive organic products as more expensive than conventional products (Somasundram et al., 2016; Azzurra & Paola, 2009). According to a survey conducted by RetailMeNot, an American multinational company in online coupons industry, more than 81% of respondents think green products are more expensive than non-green products and 61% of respondents would only consider to purchase green products if it cost the same or less than a non-green product (Skirboll & Nelson, 2015). One of the reasons why organically grown food and products are not the main selection among the consumers as compared to the conventional food in the market was due to its premium price (Pellegrini & Farinello, 2009; Lea & Worsley, 2005). However, some consumers are willing to pay more for organic products as they are attracted to the organic qualities of the product (Saleki & Seyedsaleki, 2012; Xia & Zeng, 2006).

2.3 Value orientations

Schwartz (1992, p.21) defined value as "a desirable transsituational goal varying in importance, which serve as a guiding principle in the life of a person or other social entity". Studying human values is important because values play a significant role in affecting attitudes and behaviour (Stern, 2000). Schwartz Value Theory (Schwartz, 1992) is the most commonly utilised method in recent environmental research (Harring & Jagers, 2013; Saris et al., 2013; de Groot & Steg, 2008). Schwartz presented 10 different types of values and grouped them into either four separate clusters (self-enhancement, self-transcendence, openness to change, and tradition values). Stern et al. (1998) suggested three types of value orientations to predict environmental attitude and behaviour. These three are (a) egoistic values, (b) altruistic values, and (c) biospheric values. An individual with an egoistic value focuses on his/her self and self-oriented goals, such as health, quality of life, prosperity, and convenience. Individuals with an altruistic value focus on other people or human elements, such as children, families, the community, and humanity. Last but not least, individuals with a biospheric value emphasise on the well-being of living things or non-human elements, which can include plants, animals, and trees.

Although numerous studies in the past reported a direct effect of value orientation on consumer attitudes in the context of environmental domain (Lopez-Mosquera & Sanchew 2012; de Groot & Steg, 2008), the results are still inconclusive and the similar study is still under-explored in Malaysia context towards eating "green". As in this study, value orientations from the environmental perspectives based on egoistic, altruistic, and biospheric values will be employed as the independent variables to understand their effects on the attitudes towards eating "green".

2.4 Healthy lifestyle

Suprapto & Wijaya (2012) defined healthy consumption lifestyle as the step taken to prevent health problem and maximize an individual prosperity through consumption pattern. Consumers with healthy lifestyle tend to do something which is good for their health, such as sports, consume natural or organic food, and have a balanced diet. A consumer is said to have positive attitude towards eating green (Suprapto & Wijaya, 2012; Chen, 2009;) and higher chance to purchase organic products when he possess a healthy lifestyle. It seems to be a growing trend for consumers to choose a lifestyle based upon an organic diet (Essen & Englander, 2013). Divine and Lepisto (2005) found out that people who maintain a healthy lifestyle tend to be more educated older female, place less importance on the value of excitement, have a greater tendency to plan ahead and more likely to experience less role overload. This is supported by Arganini et al. (2012) study that states women generally engage in more health-promoting behaviours than men and have healthier lifestyle patterns. Besides, Botchway et al. (2015) study suggests that healthy lifestyle is determined by a consumer's health consciousness. Basha et al. (2015) study found out that health conscious lifestyle is one of the motivating factors for purchasing organic products and Magistris and Gracia (2008) also reveal that consumers who tend to pursue a healthy diet and balanced lifestyle are more likely to have positive attitude towards organic products. Regardless of the premium price of organic products, the demand for organic products is still increasing because of the higher standard of living and healthier lifestyle of consumers (Hassan et al., 2015). Interestingly, Chen (2009) in Taiwan reported that healthy lifestyle mediates the relationships between health consciousness, environmental consciousness, and the consumer's attitude toward organic foods. Therefore, a healthy lifestyle should be advocated to render the consumer's attitude toward organic foods more positive. However, the similar group of study in Malaysia context is still lacking.

2.5 Attitudes towards eating "green"

According to Fishbein and Ajzen (1975, p.211), attitude can be defined as "a learned predisposition to respond in a consistently favourable or unfavourable manner with respect to a given object". It is an enduring set of beliefs about an object that predisposes people to behave in particular ways toward the object. In the environmental domain, Hines et al. (1987) proposed that attitudes can be divided into attitude towards the environment and attitude towards undertaking pro-environmental behaviour. In this research, attitude towards eating "green" referred to the consumer attitude towards eating locally grown organic food and products.

Some studies conducted on the relationship between attitude and intention to buy organic food consistently showed positive relations. For example, Thogersen (2007) indicate that positive attitude encourages the consumer's intention to purchase organic food. It occurs because positive attitude tends to be followed up with the intention to make it happens. Squires et al. (2001) study also found out that consumer who confessed himself to have green attitudes is more likely to purchase organic products than those without green attitudes. In addition, consumer's attitudes towards eating green and organic products attributes are important to explain consumers' purchase intention of organic products (Salleh et al., 2010). Therefore, it is vital to encourage positive attitudes among the consumers towards eating "green" as it leads to their future intention to purchase organic food and products.

2.6 Research Framework and Hypotheses

Based on the previously cited theoretical and empirical literatures, Figure 2 shows a proposed research framework by showing how consumer consciousness, healthy lifestyle, and value orientation affect the attitude towards eating "green". Therefore, the following hypotheses are proposed:

H1: The health consciousness of consumers has a significant effect on their attitudes towards eating *"green"*.

H2: The environmental consciousness of consumers has a significant effect on their attitudes towards eating *"green"*

H3: The price consciousness of consumers has a significant effect on their attitudes towards eating *"green"*.

H4: The value orientation of consumers has a significant effect on t their attitudes towards eating *"green"*

H5(a): The healthy lifestyle mediates the relationship between health consciousness and attitude of consumers towards eating *"green"*.

H5(b): The healthy lifestyle mediates the relationship between environmental consciousness and attitude of consumers towards eating *"green"*.

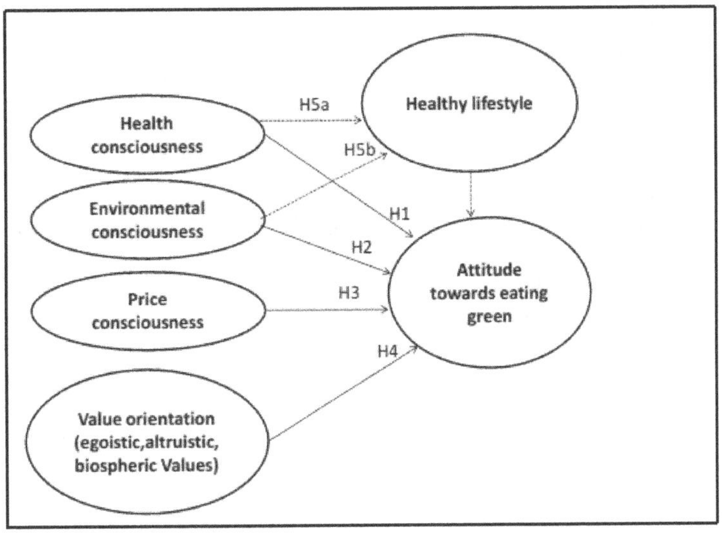

Figure 2: A Research Framework

3. Methods

This study is quantitative in nature. A survey questionnaire deemed appropriate to collect the primary data to answer the hypothesis and research question of this research study. In order to obtain reliable information from the respondents, established and validated scales were adopted/adapted from the past studies to suit the context of this study. The unit of analysis in this study is the individual consumers (aged 18 and above) who live in Klang Valley, Malaysia. A convenience sampling method is used to ensure largest possible sample with the least amount of administration. Prior to the field study, a pilot study on about 30 responses will be carried out. Next, the final refined questionnaires will be distributed randomly to a sample of 300 participants, via face-to face method. The survey form will be collected immediately after completed by the participants. Several statistical analysis techniques were used to test the data collected. These techniques included SEM and descriptive, correlation, factor, reliability, and validity analyses. SPSS and AMOS statistical software were used to analyse the descriptive and inferential study data.

4. Conclusion

The level of awareness among the public on the existence and usage of organic products and the many health benefits delivered by organic products seems to be on the rise (Basha et al, 2015; Wright, 2012). The growing interest in organic agriculture has led many to embark on the study to compare organic with conventional farming practices. According to McCarthy et al. (2015), fruit and vegetables are two of the most popular types of organic products favoured by consumers. Those who are aware of the many health benefits linked to the regular consumption of organic products are also willing to pay more for these products. For this reason, organic producers should expand their farm and output in order to meet the strong demand among consumers and also exploring the possibility of exporting these products to other countries. Wholesalers should be encouraged to enter the organic industry as there is high demand for organic products with many retail stores as well as hypermarkets that require large quantities of organic products to be supplied to these establishments on a regular basis.

As a conclusion, there is a high need to conduct a study to examine the influencing factors on attitudes towards eating "green" in the context of Malaysian organic food market. This paper proposes a research framework to address this research gap by including the variables of consumer consciousness, healthy lifestyle, and value orientation to explain such attitudes. By knowing the influencing factors, marketers can better design suitable campaigns and to target both new and existing consumers who have positive attitude towards eating "green". Doing such campaigns on a regular basis will help increase awareness and knowledge of existing and potential customers on the many benefits associated with organic products. Marketers should also focus on the supply chain management to ensure that their organic products are of the highest quality and to ensure the efficient delivery of these products to their customers.

References

Alfred, O. (2013). Influences of price and quality on consumer purchase of mobile phone in the Kumasi Metropolis in Ghana A comparative study. *European Journal of Business and Management*, *5* (1), 179-198.

Arganini, C., Saba, A., Comitato, R., Virgili, F., & Turrini, A. (2012). Gender differences in food choice and dietary intake in modern Western societies. In J. Maddock, *Public health -Social and behavioral health* (pp. 83-102). Rijeka: Intech.

Azzurra, A., & Paola, P. (2009). Consumers' behaviours and attitudes towards healthy food products: The case of organic and functional foods. *112th European Association of Agricultural Economists (EAAE) Seminar* (pp. 1-14). Chania: European Agricultural and Applied Economics Publications Foundation (EAAEP Foundation).

Basha, M. B., Mason, C., Shamsudin, M. F., Hussain, H. I., & Salem, M. A. (2015). Consumers attitude towards organic food. *Procedia Economics and Finance*, *31*, 444-452.

Botchway, I., Akenteng, B. W., & Atefoe, E. A. (2015). Health consciousness and eating habits among non-medical students in Ghana: A cross-sectional study. *Journal of Advocacy, Research and Education*, *2* (1), 31-35.

Brandt, M. (2012). *Little evidence of health benefits from organic foods, study finds*. Retrieved 14 November, 2016, from Stanford Medicine News Center: https://med.stanford.edu/news/all-news/2012/09/little-evidence-of-health-benefits-from-organic-foods-study-finds.html

Cassidy, A., & Kay, C. (2012). Phytochemicals: Classification and occurrence. In B. Caballero, *Encyclopedia of human nutrition* (3rd ed., pp. 39-46). Amsterdam: Academic Press.

CETDEM. (2010). *Organic farming*. Retrieved 12 November, 2016, from Centre for Environment, Technology and Development, Malaysia (CETDEM): http://cetdem.org.my/wordpress/?page_id=22

Chen, M. F. (2009). Attitude toward organic foods among Taiwanese as related to health consciousness, environmental attitudes, and the mediating effects of a healthy lifestyle. *British Food Journal*, *111* (2), 165-178.

Cho, Y. Y. (2012). *Consumers' value orientations and green advertising effectiveness: The moderating role of public self-awareness.* Retrieved 10 November, 2016, from University of Oregon: https://scholarsbank.uoregon.edu/xmlui/bitstream/handle/1794/12952/Cho_oregon_0171A_10573.pdf?sequence=1

De Groot, J. I., & Steg, L. (2008). Value orientations to explain beliefs related to environmental significant behaviour how to measure egoistic, altruistic, and biospheric value orientations. Environment and Behaviour, 40(3), 330–354.

Divine, R. L., & Lepisto, L. (2005). Analysis of the healthy lifestyle consumer. *Journal of Consumer Marketing , 22* (5), 275-283.

Essen, E. V., & Englander, M. (2013). Organic food as a healthy lifestyle: A phenomenological psychological analysis. *International Journal of Qualitative Studies on Health and Well-being , 8:20559*, 1-10.

Fishbein, M., & Ajzen, I. (1975). Belief, attitude, intention, and behaviour: an introduction to theory and research. Massachusetts.: Addison-Wesley Pub. Co.

Furnols, M. F.-i., & Guerrero, L. (2014). Consumer preference, behavior and perception about meat and meat products: An overview. *Meat Science , 98*, 361-371.

Gul, M. C. (2013). Long-term orientation, perceived consumer effectiveness, and environmentally conscious consumer behavior: The case of Turkey. *International Journey of Marketing Studies , 5* (5), 24-30.

Hai, H. V., & Mai, N. P. (2013). Environmental awareness and attitude of Vietnamese consumers towards green purchasing. *VNU Journal of Economics and Business , 29* (2), 129-141.

Harring, N., & Jagers, S. C. (2013). Should we trust in values? Explaining public support for pro-environmental taxes. Sustainability, 5(1), 210–227.

Hassan, S. H., Yee, L. W., & Ray, K. J. (2015). Purchasing intention towards organic food among Generation Y in Malaysia. *Journal of Agribusiness Marketing , 7*, 16-32.

Kaufmann, H. R., Panni, M. F., & Orphanidou, Y. (2012). Factors affecting consumers' green purchasing behavior: An integrated conceptual framework. *Amfiteatru Economic , 14* (31), 50-69.

Lee, C. H. (2008). The effects of price consciousness, brand consciousness and familiarity on store brand purchase intention. *Management Review , 27*, 113-117.

Lernoud, J., & Willer, H. (2016). *The world of organic agriculture: Statistics & emerging trends 2016.* Bonn: Research Institute of Organic Agriculture (FiBL) and IFOAM -Organics International.

Lichtenstein, D. R., Ridgway, N. M., & Netemeyer, R. G. (1993). Price perceptions and consumer shopping behavior: A field study. *Journal of Marketing Research , 30* (2), 234-245.

Magistris, T. d., & Gracia, A. (2008). The decision to buy organic food products in Southern Italy. *British Food Journal , 110* (9), 929-947.

McCarthy, B. L., Liu, H. B., & Chen, T. (2015). Trends in organic and green food consumption in China: Opportunities and challenges for regional Australian exporters. *Journal of Economic and Social Policy , 17* (1), 1-24.

Mercola, J. (2013). *Organic tomatoes, while smaller, are more nutritious than conventional counterpart, stude shows*. Retrieved 11 November, 2016, from Mercola: http://articles.mercola.com/sites/articles/archive/2013/03/25/organic-tomatoes.aspx

Nagourney, E. (2007). *Organic food may help against heart disease*. Retrieved 11 November, 2016, from The New York Times: http://www.nytimes.com/2007/07/17/health/17iht-snvital.1.6694779.html

Nordlund, A. M., & Garvill, J. (2002). Value structures behind proenvironmental behavior. *Environment and Behavior , 34* (6), 740-756.

Omar, N. A., Nazri, M. A., Osman, L. H., & Ahmad, M. S. (2016). The effect of demographic factors on consumer intention to purchase organic products in the Klang Valley: An empirical study. *Malaysian Journal of Society and Space , 12* (2), 68-82.

Saleki, Z. S., & Seyedsaleki, S. M. (2012). The main factors influencing purchase behaviour of organic products in Malaysia. *Interdisciplinary Journal of Contemporary Research in Business , 4* (1), 98-116.

Salleh, M. M., Ali, S. M., Harun, E. H., Jalil, M. A., & Shaharudin, M. R. (2010). Consumer's perception and purchase intentions towards organic food products: Exploring attitude among academician. *Canadian Social Science , 6* (6), 119-129.

Saris, W. E., Knoppen, D., & Schwartz, S. H. (2012). Operationalising the theory of human values: Balancing homogeneity of reflective items and theoretical coverage. Survey Research Methods, 7(1), 29–44.

Schlegelmilch, B.B., Bohlen,G.M., & Diamantopoulos,A. (1996). The link between green purchasing decisions and measures of environmental consciousness. European Journal of Marketing, 30(5), 35-55.

Schwartz, S. H. (1992). Universals in the content and structure of values: Theoretical advances and empirical tests in 20 countries. Advances in Experimental Social Psychology, 25(1), 1–65.

Schwarz, N., & Bohner, G. (2001). *The construction of attitudes.* Retrieved 15 November, 2016, from University of Southern California: https://dornsife.usc.edu/assets/sites/780/docs/schwarzz___bohner_attitude-construction-ms.pdf

Skirboll, S., & Nelson, K. (2015). *4 in 5 consumers think eco-friendly products cost more "green"*. Retrieved 10 November, 2016, from PR Newswire: http://www.prnewswire.com/news-releases/4-in-5-consumers-think-eco-friendly-products-cost-more-green-300061649.html

Somasundram, C., Razali, Z., & Santhirasegaram, V. (2016). A review on organic food production in Malaysia. *Horticulturae , 2* (12), 1-5.

Stern, P. C. (2000). New environmental theories: toward a coherent theory of environmentally significant behaviour. Journal of Social Issues, 56(3), 407–424.

Stern, P. C., Dietz, T., & Guagnano, G. A. (1998). A brief inventory of values. Educational and Psychological Measurement, 58(6), 984–1001.

Squires, L., Juric, B., & Cornwell, T. B. (2001). Level of market development and intensity of organic food consumption: cross-cultural study of Danish and New Zealand consumers. *Journal of Consumer Marketing , 18* (5), 392-409.

Suhaimee, S., Ibrahim, I. Z., & Wahab, M. A. (2016). *Organic agriculture in Malaysia*. Retrieved 15 November, 2016, from Food and Fertilizer Technology Center for the Asian and Pacific Region (FFTC-AP): http://ap.fftc.agnet.org/ap_db.php?id=579

Suprapto, B., & Wijaya, T. (2012). Intentions of Indonesian consumers on buying organic food. *International Journal of Trade, Economics and Finance , 3* (2), 114-119.

Tan, B. C., & Yeap, P. F. (2011). Relationships among the antecedents of behaviour intention towards environmentally friendly restaurants: A casual model. *International Conference on Environment and Industrial Innovation* (pp. 193-199). Singapore: IACSIT Press.

Tan, W. L., & Govindan, S. (2014). Emerging issues in car purchasing decision. *Academic Research International , 5* (5), 169-179.

Tassi, P., & Muzet, A. (2001). Defining the states of consciousness. *Neuroscience and Biobehavioral Reviews , 25*, 175-191.

Toth, A. H., Kelemen, K., Piskoti, M., & Simay, A. E. (2008). *Examining the differences between the environmentally conscious consumer behavior in China and Hungary.* Retrieved 11 November, 2016, from Corvinus University of Budapest: http://korny.uni-corvinus.hu/cneucoop_fullpapers/s1/agneshofm1.pdf

Velmans, M. (1996). An introduction to the science of consciousness. In M. Velmans, *The science of consciousness: Psychological, neuropsychological, and clinical reviews* (pp. 1-22). London: Routledge.

Velmans, M. (2009). How to define consciousness -and how not to define consciousness. *Journal of Consciousness Studies , 16* (5), 139-156.

Walker, D. (2009). *Seven reasons to eat organic foods*. Retrieved 10 November, 2016, from Article Base: http://www.articlesbase.com/wellness-articles/seven-reasons-to-eat-organic-foods-797275.html#ixzz0oenU3M6N

Wright, K. (2012). *Human Health Benefits of Eating Organic Foods*. Retrieved 14 November, 2016, from SF Gate: http://healthyeating.sfgate.com/human-health-benefits-eating-organic-foods-5174.html

Xia, W., & Zeng, Y. (2006). Consumer's attitudes and willingness-to-pay for green food in Beijing. *SSRN Electronic Journal* , 1-10.

Zhen, M. (2013). *Organic farming in Malaysia -what needs to be done*. Retrieved 12 November, 2016, from Business Circle: http://www.businesscircle.com.my/organic-farming-in-malaysia-what-needs-to-be-done/

Uncertainty Analysis and Success Prediction for Start-ups

Sarath Tomy and Eric Pardede
La Trobe University, Melbourne, Australia
ssarathtomy@students.latrobe.edu.au
E.pardede@latrobe.edu.au

Abstract: Uncertainties exist in business environment pose challenges for new start-ups. Knowledge of these uncertainties influences the success and growth of a firm, which is important in the pre-start-up phase of the entrepreneurial process. Entrepreneurs need support when making decisions and the decisions have to be made swiftly, with sufficient and reliable data. The purpose of the study is to examine how the analysis and evaluation of uncertainty factors with the help of data can predict the future of an organization success. The research adopts a mixed methods approach incorporating both qualitative and quantitative techniques, building a robust technique to investigate complex cognitive phenomena in entrepreneurial contexts. In the first phase the main uncertainty factors influence the success or failure of a firm are identified and categorized using existing literatures. In the second phase a success prediction model is implemented using machine learning techniques and trained it with survey information collected from the ICT companies operating in Victoria, Australia and data from GEM consortium. The approach here is to apply machine learning algorithm to train the model and to predict the success or failure depends on the input values. The model is trained in such a way that when new data comes in, the qualitative data is transformed into quantitative data and the probability of success or failure is calculated as the result output in the pre-start-up phase. This allows nascent entrepreneurs to make likelihood predictions on the basis of data. The model is implemented as a web interface and the accuracy of the prediction model is evaluated using Confusion Matrix. The model is used to uncover the frequency of the relations that links the input uncertainty factors with the success or failure of a firm. The particular strength of this method is to evaluate the opportunity based on unrelated factors and identify the patterns by the exploration of relations between them. The method and findings would be relevant for nascent entrepreneurs and researchers focusing on entrepreneurship.

Keywords: Entrepreneurship, Start-ups, Uncertainties, Opportunity Evaluation, Machine Learning, Predictive Analytics.

1. Introduction

Opportunity evaluation and success prediction in start-ups is a hot topic in entrepreneurship and a growing number of researchers define the domain of the entrepreneurship field as centering on opportunity recognition, evaluation, and exploitation. An ability to identify and select right opportunities for new businesses is one important characteristic for successful entrepreneur (Ardichvili et al., 2003, Wood and McKelvie, 2015). Often entrepreneurs are challenged by the external environment, not only by globalization but also by their liability of newness especially when they operate in environments that are subjected to change (Van Gelderen et al., 2006, Giardino et al., 2015).

Uncertainties are the lack of information or knowledge which can create confusion about the future. Uncertainties are also created by rapid change in technology that is more prevalent these days (Giardino et al., 2015). However, there is little research on success prediction by evaluating the uncertainties, even though it is widely-accepted that an entrepreneur cannot act on the opportunity successfully until he addresses uncertainties surrounding the opportunity. Majority of individuals who start new firms often have scientific or technical competency and may have prior experience in related industries. Therefore their education and experience may facilitate them to identify and act on an opportunity (Christensen et al., 2000). Having said that, the fundamental job of entrepreneurs is to create value by exploiting the identified opportunity.

Environmental indicators can be used to predict the success of opportunities for new start-ups. In some region or some industries at particular time, probability of success is more than in the other. Therefore, the market uncertainties affect the entrepreneur's perspective to act on an opportunity(Meijer, 2008, Butler et al., 2010). The fact is that many potential entrepreneurs are capable of identifying opportunities, but yet their ventures are failed because they do not have proper understanding of the risks surrounding these identified opportunities (Ireland et al., 2003). Therefore, in today's hostile and dynamic business environment, it is vital for nascent entrepreneurs to assess the market uncertainty factors which influences business success before making a decision (Giardino et al., 2015).

In this research we first review the literature to identify the market uncertainty factors that can affect the growth of a new venture. Our goal is to identify those factors which have heavy influence on the success or risk of a new business and use these factors as a scale to predict the business success. Once the factors are identified, we propose a method to use machine learning techniques to evaluate the chance of business success with the help of data. Then we employ three most widely used machine learning classification algorithms to evaluate the model and compare the result using confusion matrix. Based on the result of this experimental study, we identify the best technique that could predict the success of new business creation reliably.

2. Related Works

There are existing works that have modelled the opportunity evaluation process in the context of entrepreneurship. Many of the existing works evaluate the success of business opportunities by utilizing social, cultural and personal factors. The outcomes of the opportunity evaluation are then used by nascent entrepreneurs to decide whether or not to proceed. The objective of the elaboration is to understand the opportunity in a way to reduce the uncertainties by identifying the anticipated problems and to maximize the potential benefits (Van der Veen and Wakkee, 2006).

Despite the rich literature in opportunity evaluation in entrepreneurship, there are only few studies associated with the impact of uncertainty factors in entrepreneurship. De Koning and Muzyka (De Koning and Muzyka, 1999) identify a socio-cognitive framework of opportunity recognition by considering three cognitive activities such as information gathering, thinking through talking and resource assessing through the interacting with the extensive network of people. Baron and Ensley (Baron and Ensley, 2006) research explains the influence of cognition and behaviour in the evaluation of opportunities.

Erikson (Eriksson and Li, 2012) proposed a conceptual framework to relate the general company success factors and factors driving success for companies. There are also many other studies (Butler et al., 2010, Shane and Venkataraman, 2000, Wallace, 2000, Lin et al., 2012) which mainly concentrate on strategic planning of the opportunity evaluation process. Existing researches in the entrepreneurial process fail to provide a method to evaluate the market uncertainty to predict the success or failure in the pre-start-up phase.

3. Proposed Model

Entrepreneurship involves opportunity identification, evaluation and exploitation. The main barrier restricting an execution on an identified opportunity is the uncertainties or the risk. We utilize uncertainties as a method to evaluate opportunities, because these are factors which have heavy influence on the success and growth of a firm. The evaluation of opportunities based on these factors are important in making decisions not only for the entrepreneurs, but also for the government and other agencies promoting entrepreneurship.

On the normative level, the preliminary decisions on starting up a business is important and must be made according to the long-term goals of an enterprise (Luggen and Tschirky, 2003).The purpose of the study is practical and is conducted in order to examine how the analysis and evaluation of uncertainty factors with the help of data can predict the future of an organization success.

Entrepreneurs facing extreme uncertainty about how the different factors influence the existing businesses in their intended industry and how other businesses perform. For nascent entrepreneurs market analysis is considered as the best method to assess the attractiveness of a specific industry for the enterprise and to reduce uncertainties (Kraus and Kauranen, 2009). Based on the analysis, nascent entrepreneurs can identify which are the dominant factors influencing the success and growth and how these factors contribute to the profitability and success.
Our proposed model consists of two stages. (1) Uncertainty Analysis and (2) Success Prediction.

Uncertainty Analysis Stage: In this stage, we identify and analyze the main uncertainty factors influence the success or failure of a firm from the existing literatures. These factors are categorized into Political, Economic, Social and Technological as shown in Table 1.

Table 1: Uncertainty Factors of Business Opportunities

PEST	*Identified Uncertainty Factors*	*References*
Political	Political Environment	(Dollinger, 2005, Meijer, 2008, Eriksson and Li, 2012)
	Government Support	(Meijer, 2008, Alkemade et al., 2006, Skinner, 2008)
	Economy	(Meijer, 2008, Alkemade et al., 2006, Skinner, 2008)
	Potential market size	(Skinner, 2008, Eriksson and Li, 2012)
	Living conditions	(Shi et al., 2014, Ruokolainen and Igel, 2004)
	Employment laws	(Wallace, 2000)
	Taxation	(Eriksson and Li, 2012, Alkemade et al., 2006)
Economic	Capital	(Eriksson and Li, 2012, Ng et al., 2014)
	Social networks	(Dollinger, 2005, Ng et al., 2014)
	Revenue streams	(Rose, 2012, O'Brien et al., 2003)
	Availability of grants and funds	(Ng et al., 2014, O'Brien et al., 2003)
	Exchange rates	(Misra et al., 2012, Rose, 2012)
	Inflation	(Rose, 2012)
	Number and type of competition	(Meijer, 2008, Alkemade et al., 2006, Skinner, 2008)
	Existence of leading competitors	(Hoskisson and Busenitz, 2002, Wenzel, 2012)
	Market share	(Mehler-Bicher, 2002, Meijer, 2008, Skinner, 2008)
	Marketing strategy	(Wenzel, 2012, Skinner, 2008)
	Existing distribution channels	(Rose, 2012, Ruokolainen and Igel, 2004)
	Possible alliances	(Hoskisson and Busenitz, 2002)
Social	Skilled human resources	(Eriksson and Li, 2012, Dollinger, 2005)
	Customer needs	(Ng et al., 2014)
	Purchasing power of potential customers	(Rose, 2012, Wenzel, 2012)
	Segmentation	(Rose, 2012, Dollinger, 2005)
Technological	Physical and technological infrastructure availability	(Meijer, 2008, Alkemade et al., 2006, Skinner, 2008)
	Alternate technological solutions	(Meijer, 2008, Alkemade et al., 2006, Skinner, 2008)
	Technological Resources	(Ng et al., 2014, Dutot et al., 2014)
	Innovation speed	(Meijer, 2008, Skinner, 2008)
	Technological developments	(Meijer, 2008, Lin et al., 2012)
	In house and external R&D expenditures	(Ng et al., 2014, Dutot et al., 2014)

Our model is designed for nascent entrepreneurs to do a PEST analysis and input the values for each factor in relation to their business opportunity. PEST analysis is a strategic environmental analysis tool which identifies the political, economic, social and technological factors that influences an industry (Kraus and Kauranen, 2009, Hosseinzadeh et al., 2016). However, in this paper test data is used instead of manual PEST analysis by an entrepreneur as the input to the next stage, which is the success prediction model.

Success Prediction Stage: In this stage we employ data analytics and machine learning techniques to predict a firm's success. Data analysis is the process of inspecting data in order to extract useful information. Decision makers commonly use this information to drive their choices. [13]. Entrepreneurs can learn, analyze and evaluate the business success from the data of existing businesses in a particular region. Here we try to predict the success of an opportunity by analyzing the uncertainty factors as shown in the Figure 1.

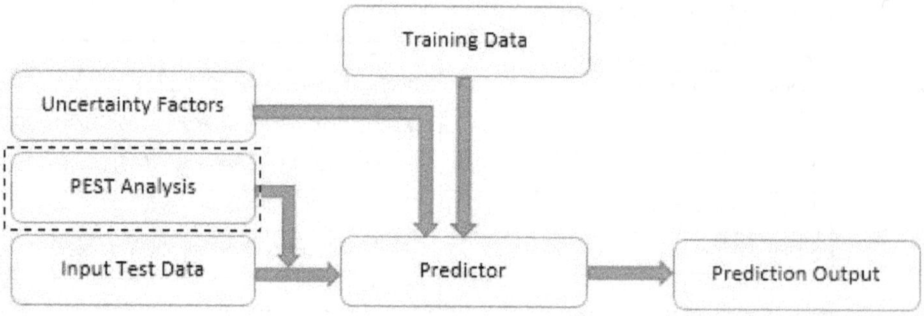

Figure 1: Prediction Model

The approach here is to apply machine learning algorithm to train the model and to predict the success or failure depends on the input values. The model is used to uncover the frequency of the relations that links the input uncertainty factors with the success or failure of a firm. Analyzing the data of other companies can help to make an experience-based decision making. This allows nascent entrepreneurs to make likelihood predictions on the basis of relevant dataset even though the dataset that we use do not represent the total population.

At the beginning, we filter the training set. We extract only the external factors and their economic performance and train the model with this dataset. As our explanatory factors are categorical and independent, the predictor in our model is built using supervised classification machine learning algorithm in order as statistical tool to manage uncertainty and predict the success. Once the 'Predictor' is constructed by using the training data, whenever a new data comes in, the qualitative data is transformed into quantitative data and the probability of success or failure is calculated as the result output. It computes the maximum likelihood of success or failure based on the training data distribution and predict the output accordingly.

The success prediction system is trained by giving input based on the classified uncertainties. It will then adjust the probabilities for each factor. After training, the system calculates the probabilities for each inputs and classify it as either success or failure with the corresponding percentage. The dataset is divided into training data set and test data set. The training dataset are used for train the model and test data is to evaluate the result. In order to choose the best machine learning algorithm, we evaluate the accuracy of three main widely used classification algorithms in the area of machine learning applications for probabilistic induction. They are Naïve Bayes, k-NN (k-Nearest Neighbours) and SVM (Support Vector Machine) which work well even with small amount of training data. Naïve Bayes classification algorithm is a classification algorithm based on Bayes rule with conditional independence assumptions (Xhemali et al., 2009, Patil and Sherekar, 2013). KNN is a simple algorithm, which stores all cases and classify new cases based on similarity measure. SVM is a robust and effective method which generates a model based on the training data that predicts the target values from the test data (Warriach and Claudel, 2013). The evaluation of the three algorithms are discussed in detail in the following sections.

The particular strength of this method is to evaluate the opportunity based on unrelated factors which are crucial for start-ups from experienced companies and identify the patterns by the exploration of relations between them. The quality of the information extracted by this process greatly benefits from the availability of extensive datasets. Through the data collection and analysis, we could identify and examine patterns of relationship of different external environmental factors to assess an opportunity. Thus we can get a sense of whether a factor is important or not in the success and growth of a firm.

4. Implementation and Evaluation

To implement and evaluate our prediction model, we used two different datasets which matches the requirements for our purposeful sampling method. One is industry specific datasets in a particular region while the other is a global dataset. The uncertainty factors from these datasets can incorporate the uncertainties that we identified from the literatures and they are categorised as Political, Economic, Social and Technological as shown in Table 2.

4.1 Dataset

The search for the datasets which can map the uncertainty factors with the firm performance lead us to the use the 2013 Victorian ICT Industry Statistics survey conducted by the Government of Victoria in Australia with 265 ICT companies as the participants as the primary dataset (Department of Economic Development, 2013). After cleaning and filtering, a final dataset consists of 248 records was used in this study and the success is measured in terms of firm's profitability. The survey contains of questions regarding the companies' products and services, export regions, total revenue and so on. However, for our purpose we are only interested in how the external market factors influence the company's success and failure with respect to these factors.

The second dataset is from GEM (Global Entrepreneurship Monitor) consortium and GEDI (The Global Entrepreneurship and Development Institute) which measures the level and nature of entrepreneurial activity around the world based on the survey data they collected in 2015 (Global, 2015). The factors from the dataset that match with the uncertainties identified from the literatures are used for the analysis. After filtering, a dataset consists of records of 61 economies which is ranked on the basis of Global Entrepreneurial Index are used for this study. The success is measured in terms of GEI (Global Entrepreneurship Index) and countries with GEI score of at least 40 are indicated as successful economies.

4.2 Implementation

The initial analysis and evaluation are done using Microsoft Excel and RStudio. The prediction model is implemented as a web interface using HTML, PHP, and JavaScript with MySQL database. As mentioned in the previous section, we use the Victorian ICT survey data as the primary dataset and the dataset from GEM AND GEDI is used as secondary dataset.

Table 2: Uncertainty Factors of Business Opportunities – From Data

Factors from ICT Survey Dataset	PEST	Factors from GEM Consortium Dataset
Domestic Economic Environment	Political	Governmental Support and Policies
Global Economic Environment		Governmental Programs
Government Regulation		Taxes and Bureaucracy
Access to Finance	Economic	Financing for Entrepreneurs
Exchange Rates		Internal Market Dynamics
Competitive Environment		
Access to Export Market		
Availability of Skilled Employees	Social	Cultural and Social Norms
Access to Target Market		Internal Market Openness
Availability of Infrastructure	Technological	Physical and Services Infrastructure
Innovative Environment		Commercial and Professional Infrastructure
Cost of R&D		R&D Transfer

In the first step of the uncertainty analysis stage, we extract the uncertainty factors such as Domestic Economic Environment, Global Economic Environment, Government Regulation, Access to Finance, Exchange Rates, Competitive Environment, Access to Export Market, Availability of Skilled Employees, Access to Target Market, Availability of Infrastructure, Innovative Environment and Cost of R&D from the ICT survey dataset. These are the twelve main factors influence the performance of the existing businesses operating in a region. In the second step, the uncertainty factors identified from the literatures were matched and grouped with respect to the factors identified from the data and then categorized it into Political, Economic, Social and Technological uncertainties as shown in the first column, labelled as "Factors from ICT Survey Dataset" of Table 2.

Likewise with the ICT Survey Dataset, we extract the uncertainty factors such as Governmental Support and Policies, Governmental Programs, Taxes and Bureaucracy, Financing for Entrepreneurs, Internal Market Dynamics, Cultural and Social Norms, Internal Market Openness, Physical and Services Infrastructure,

Commercial and Professional Infrastructure and R&D Transfer from the GEM consortium dataset. These ten main factors which influence the entrepreneurial performance and growth are matched with respect to the uncertainty factors identified from the literatures and then categorized it into Political, Economic, Social and Technological uncertainties as shown in the first column, labelled as "Factors from GEM Consortium Dataset" of Table 2. Even though all the uncertainty factors that we identified from literatures cannot be matched with the factors from data, we could match most of the factors with regards to the main PEST uncertainty category as shown in the Table 2.

4.3 Evaluation

As a way to validate the proposed method, we evaluate the accuracy of our model the dataset is split into training data (80%) and test data (20%). The task of the classifier is to determine the class (Success or Failure) depending upon the input factor values. The training data of the classifier was to label the test data output as either a positive or a negative. This task was performed on both the ICT survey data set, and the GEM consortium data set. The experiments in this research are evaluated using the standard method of accuracy, Precision/Recall method which is calculated using the predictive classification table, known as Confusion Matrix. In binary decision problem, the classifier labels as either positive (success) or negative (failure). The confusion matrix has four categories as shown in the Table 3.

Table 3: Confusion Matrix

		Predicted Condition	
		Negative	**Positive**
True Condition	**Negative**	**TN** (True Negative): *No. of correct predictions labelled as negative*	**FP** (False Positive): *No. of incorrect predictions labelled as positive*
	Positive	**FN** (False Negative): *No. of incorrect predictions labelled as negative*	**TP** (True Positive): *No. of correct predictions labelled as positive*

Precision is defined as the fraction of records predicted as positive that are actually positive. Recall reflects the probability of correctly predicting positive cases. Specificity is the probability of correctly predicting negative cases. The accuracy measures the probability of correctly predicting cases while the error rate represents the measure of incorrect predictions. The formulae for calculating these are shown in Table 4.

Table 4: Definition of Evaluation Matrices

Precision	Recall	Specificity	Accuracy	Error Rate
$\frac{TP}{TP+FP}$	$\frac{TP}{TP+FN}$	$\frac{TN}{TN+FP}$	$\frac{TP+TN}{TP+TN+FP+FN}$	$\frac{FP+FN}{FP+FN+TP+TN}$

4.4 Results and Discussion

The experiments are carried out to test the model in order to determine the accuracy. For this we execute the proposed prediction model with both the training data and test data of both the datasets using the three classification algorithms. All three algorithms were initially trained with 198 sampling units and tested with a further 49 records using the ICT Survey dataset and the results were compared to find out which algorithm performs better in predicting the pre-start-up success. Likewise, the three algorithms are validated using 49 training records and 12 test records with the GEM consortium dataset and the results were compared. The results are summarized in Table 5 and Table 6 which shows that all three classification algorithms achieved impressive results in the classification of attribute data. However, the Naïve Bayes classifier outperforms both k-NN and SVM in predicting the outcome by achieving the highest accuracy and lowest error rate with both the datasets.

Table 5: Comparison of Results – ICT survey Data

Classifier	Precision (%)	Recall (%)	Specificity (%)	Accuracy (%)	Error Rate (%)
Naive Bayes	87.87	80.56	69.23	77.55	22.45
k-NN	82.35	77.78	53.85	71.43	28.57
SVM	87.09	75	69.23	73.47	26.53

Table 6: Comparison of Results – GEM Consortium

Classifier	Precision (%)	Recall (%)	Specificity (%)	Accuracy (%)	Error Rate (%)
Naive Bayes	100	77.77	100	83.33	16.67
k-NN	100	55.56	100	66.67	33.33
SVM	66.67	85.71	40	66.67	33.33

The results shows that the probability of success can be predicted successfully using Naïve Bayes classifier as the predictor in our model with relevant data sets. The success of the start-ups can be efficiently predicted if the training data set maintained with accurate information. This is an easy, efficient and less expensive method to assess the pre-start-up success using uncertainty factors with data analysis. The result is further confirmed by changing the test data set by randomly choosing some records from the training data set.

Through this model, we have studied a range of approaches and external environmental factors in their relationships with start-up success. The results show that all the independent factors are significantly related to the success or failure of the firm. The factor input values may differ depending on the knowledge of nascent entrepreneurs, characteristics of the intended business and region where they are going to operate. Some of the factors having direct effects with the success of a firm such as global economic environment. In comparison with other factors, factors under economic situations are more having direct effect with the success and growth of a firm. The main focus of our research was to identify the uncertainties in entrepreneurship and analyse it to predict the probability of success in the pre-start-up phase based on the evaluation of uncertain external environmental factors from different datasets and thus foster the entrepreneurial opportunities by reducing the uncertainties.

5. Conclusion and Future Work

Our environment is too complex to be perfectly analyzed. But analyze the environment and assume the action using the current knowledge is better than planning without having any idea on the outcome (Rose, 2012). To summarize we have found a way for nascent entrepreneurs to assess and evaluate the success of the firm in the pre-start-up phase. Firstly the market uncertainty factors influence a firm's performance are identified from existing research works. The factors are then analyzed using machine learning techniques in order to predict firm's success using uncertainty factors. The performance of our proposed approach has been tested with Victorian ICT survey dataset and GEM consortium datasets using Naïve Bayes, k-NN and SVM algorithms and the results from all systems were compared to one-another. The accuracy of the predictor tested using Confusion Matrix and the results show that Naïve Bayes classifier achieved better results than other two classifiers in predicting the firm's success. We conclude that our success prediction model implemented with Naïve Bayes classification algorithm is an effective tool to understand the uncertainties and correctly predicts the outcome based on the available data set. The technique will also benefit the nascent entrepreneurs to predict the future and understand the most influential factors in order to gain a competitive advantage and finally become a champion as expected.

One of the most promising areas for future research is the pre-start-up planning stage. Knowledge of relevant factors and its importance in influencing the success of existing organizations are important for nascent entrepreneurs in order to create successful business venture. This research is aimed at addressing the importance of uncertainties in opportunity evaluation and attempted the practicality of employing machine learning approach in predicting the success of start-up ventures. This model is designed as a practical tool to analyze the available datasets to predict the business success in uncertain situations. In the future, all other factors including personal characteristics and resources can be included in order to enrich the prediction model. The method and findings discussed in this paper would benefit nascent entrepreneurs and researchers focusing on entrepreneurship.

References

Alkemade, F., Hekkert, M. & Suurs, R. (2006) "Strategic expectations management for emergent sustainable technologies" Paper presented at the DRUID summer conference on knowledge, innovation, and competitiveness: dynamics of firms, networks, regions and institutions, Copenhagen, June 18-20.

Ardichvili, A., Cardozo, R. & Ray, S. (2003) "A theory of entrepreneurial opportunity identification and development", *Journal of Business Venturing,* Vol 18, No.1,pp 105-123.

Association, G. E. R. (2015) *GEM 2007 - 2015 NES Global Key Indicators,* Global Entrepreneurship Research Association, London Business School, London.

Baron, R. A. & Ensley, M. D. (2006) "Opportunity recognition as the detection of meaningful patterns: Evidence from comparisons of novice and experienced entrepreneurs", *Management science,* Vol 52, pp 1331-1344.

Butler, J. E., Doktor, R. & Lins, F. A. (2010) "Linking international entrepreneurship to uncertainty, opportunity discovery, and cognition", *Journal of International Entrepreneurship,* Vol 8, No.2, pp 121-134.

Christensen, P. V., Ulhøi, J. P. & Madsen, H. (2000) "The Entrepreneurial Process in a Dynamic Network Perspective : a review and future directions for research", LOK working paper 6-2000, LOK Research Centre, Copenhagen.

De Koning, A. & Muzyka, D. (1999) "Conceptualizing opportunity recognition as a socio-cognitive process", Centre for Advanced Studies in Leadership, Stockholm.

Department of Economic Development, J., Transport and Resources, Victoria (2013) Victorian ICT Industry Statistics Survey, Victoria.

Dollinger, M. J. (2005) *Entrepreneurship: Strategies and Resources*, Singapore: Pearson's Educational.

Dutot, V., Bergeron, F. & Raymond, L. (2014) "Information management for the internationalization of SMEs: An exploratory study based on a strategic alignment perspective", *International Journal of Information Management,* Vol 34,No.5, pp 672-681.

Eriksson, J. & Li, M. (2012) "Success factors of entrepreneurial small and medium sized enterprises in the Gnosjö municipality", Master's Thesis, Mälardalen University.

Giardino, C., Bajwa, S. S., Wang, X. & Abrahamsson, P. (2015) "Key challenges in early-stage software startups" Paper presented at the International Conference on Agile Software Development, Helsinki, Finland, May, SpringerInternational Publishing, pp 52-63.

Hoskisson, R. E. & Busenitz, L. W. (2002) "Market uncertainty and learning distance in corporate entrepreneurship entry mode choice", *Strategic entrepreneurship: Creating a new mindset*.

Hosseinzadeh, S., Van Der Wee, M., Vlassenroot, S. & Verbrugge, S (2016) "Using PEST as a framework for analyzing open mobility dataz" Paper presented at the 11th Intelligent Transport Systems European Congress, Glasgow pp 1-10.

Ireland, R. D., Hitt, M. A. & Sirmon, D. G. (2003) "A model of strategic entrepreneurship: The construct and its dimensions", *Journal of management,* Vol 29, No.6, pp 963-989.

Kraus, S. & Kauranen, I. (2009) "Strategic management and entrepreneurship: Friends or foes", *International Journal of Business Science and Applied Management,* Vol 4, No.1, pp 37-50.

Lin, C., Tsai, H. L., Wu, Y. J. & Kiang, M. (2012) "A fuzzy quantitative VRIO-based framework for evaluating organizational activities", *Management Decision,*Vol 50, No.8, pp 1396-1411.

Luggen, M. & Tschirky, H. (2003) "A conceptual framework for technology and innovation management in new technology-based firms (NTBF)" Paper presented at the Portland International Conference on Management of Engineering and Technology, pp. 342-347, Portland, Oregon, July.

Mehler-Bicher, A. (2002), "Evaluating e-business investments by defining profiles", Paper presented at the 9th European conference on IT evaluation, Paris, July.

Meijer, I. (2008) *Uncertainty and entrepreneurial action. The role of uncertainty in the development of emerging energy technologies,* PhD diss., Utrecht University.

Misra, K., Memili, E., Welsh, D. H. B. & Sarkar, S. (2012) "The determinants of venture creation time: a cross-country perspective", *International Entrepreneurship and Management Journal,* Vol 10, No. 2, pp 253-276.

Ng, A. W., Macbeth, D. & Southern, G. (2014) "Entrepreneurial performance of early-stage ventures: dynamic resource management for development and growth", *International Entrepreneurship and Management Journal,* Vol 10, No.2, pp 503-521.

O'brien, J. P., Folta, T. B. & Johnson, D. R. (2003) "A real options perspective on entrepreneurial entry in the face of uncertainty", *Managerial and Decision Economics,*Vol 24, No.8, pp 515-533.

Patil, T. R. & Sherekar, S. (2013) "Performance analysis of Naive Bayes and J48 classification algorithm for data classification", *International Journal of Computer Science and Applications,* Vol 6, No.2, pp 256-261.

Rose, J. (2012), "Software Entrepreneurship: two paradigms for promoting new information technology ventures", *Software Innovation, Aalborg University.*

Ruokolainen, J. & Igel, B. (2004) "The factors of making the first successful customer reference to leverage the business of start-up software company—multiple case study in Thai software industry", *Technovation,* Vol 24, No.9, pp 673-681.

Shane, S. & Venkataraman, S. (2000) "The promise of entrepreneurship as a field of research", *Academy of management review,* Vol 25, No.1, pp 217-226.

Shi, Y., Xu, D. & Green, P. (2014) "Software Startup Growth: The Role of Dynamic Capabilities, IT, Innovation and Customer Involvement", Paper presented at the 19th Pacific Asia Conference on Information Systems, Chengdu, China, June.

Skinner, G. D. (2008) "A study into fostering entrepreneurship in information communication technology (ICT)" *International Journal of Computers and Communications,* Vol 4, No.2, pp 108-116.

Van Der Veen, M. & Wakkee, I. (2006) "Understanding the entrepreneurial process", In *New Firm Startups,* Cheltenham: Edward Elgar.

Van Gelderen, M., Thurik, R. & Bosma, N. (2006) "Success and risk factors in the pre-startup phase", *Small Business Economics,* Vol 26, No.4, pp 319-335.

Wallace, S. W. (2000) "Decision Making Under Uncertainty: Is Sensitivity Analysis of Any Use?", *Operations Research,* Vol 48, No.1, pp 20-25.

Warriach, E. U. & Claudel, C. (2013) "A machine learning approach for vehicle classification using passive infrared and ultrasonic sensors" Paper presented at the 12th international conference on Information processing in sensor networks, Philadelphia, April.

Wenzel, A. M. (2012) *The entrepreneur's guide to market research*, Santa Barbara, CA: Praeger.

Wood, M. S. & Mckelvie, A. (2015) "Opportunity evaluation as future focused cognition: Identifying conceptual themes and empirical trends", *International Journal of Management Reviews,* Vol 17, No.2, pp 256-277.

Xhemali, D., Hinde, C. J. & Stone, R. G. (2009) "Naive Bayes vs. decision trees vs. neural networks in the classification of training web pages", *International Journal of Computer Science,* Vol 4, No.1, pp 16-23.

A Case Study of Lean Data Driven Innovation in Government

Khimji Vaghjiani, Ian Oppermann, Jeremy Moon, Eleanor Rogers and Hannah Stacey
New South Wales Government Data Analytics Centre, Sydney, Australia
Khimji.Vaghjiani@finance.nsw.gov.au
Ian.Oppermann@finance.nsw.gov.au
Jeremy.Moon@finance.nsw.gov.au
Ellie.Rogers@finance.nsw.gov.au
Hannah.Stacey@finance.nsw.gov.au

Abstract: The New South Wales Data Analytics Centre (NSW DAC) was set up by the NSW Government to explore government-based data innovation projects addressing key opportunities within Australia's largest state by economic and Gross Domestic Product (GDP) size according to the Nicholls and Rosewell (2015) from the Reserve Bank of Australia (RBA). The specific charter of the DAC was to explore 'wicked problems' that cross interdepartmental boundaries using evidence or data-based decision making. Wicked challenges are ill-defined (Rittel and Webber, 1984), subtle and ultimately have people's behaviour at their core. They manifest across multiple agencies and are a challenge for all governments in all jurisdictions, complex, intractable, open-ended and very different in nature to routine problems (Head, 2008)

Core to this paper is exploring the challenge of providing better services to the citizens of NSW using data driven approaches. This is achieved through lean methodology: an approach that so far appears to be a unique combination of the use of data analytics and science to solve complex, citizen-centric service challenges. A world first, the DAC has so far been assigned twenty-five complex, multi-layered projects covering fields such as human services, transport, industry, health justice and community services to highlight the importance and the value of unlocking data assets. Further, the Lean Approach has been used to define, challenge, and scope projects to better understand, communicate and deliver outcomes – very likely another world first.

Providing unique insight into innovation within government structure in a space that has never been traversed before; our research is an ongoing exploration of work undertaken by the NSW DAC in high impact, high agility areas. Through exploring learning gained from a number of projects, following our adapted model for innovation, we will detail the process of engaging, ideating and executing high impact projects with big data at their core; looking at models for disruption and the impact of data science in informing public policy.

Insight will be gained into the process of identifying opportunities, scoping complex data projects, and exploring how best to extract outcomes and insights driven by data using an adapted version of the Lean Canvas approach, tailored to the emerging space of data analytics with its intrinsic challenges of data in government. The case studies are presented in consultation with the relevant product leads, and key insights into business structure and disruption will be shared.

The paper includes an outline and rationale for the process of converting ideas into successful project scoping: ensuring that project pitfalls are avoided, and efficient multi-stakeholder engagement and measurable outcomes are achieved through the process. The process of data governance, privacy, data management, and analytics will be covered as part of the case studies.

Attendees will experience the process used by one of the world's first government-funded data analytics centres through case studies across a range of projects with impact to the larger community. This is a unique opportunity for insight through the first academic release of the Data Analytics Centre, a privileged position in an emerging and exciting field.

Keywords: Case study of innovation in Government, Data analytics to solve every day wicked problems, lean framework to develop citizen centric solutions.

1. Introduction

The field of data analytics has undergone rapid expansion in recent years, and is awash with new possibilities for the mining and organisation of complex, refined data. Yet somehow, the abundance of this valuable resource is leading to its being overlooked and undervalued by those who have the most to gain. The acquisition of data is simply seen to highlight the superficial wealth of an organisation, so as in some countries ownership of cattle demonstrates wealth in the community. However, agencies are unprepared for the operational challenges of data analysis, having no idea how to effectively put this vast asset into use. Research done by Keystone Strategy (2006) has discovered that companies with more advanced data capabilities experience greater operating profits, as well as more sophisticated business processes. This is due to the way they store, process and use data for effective and timely decision-making. More and more evidence is emerging of the ability to earn significant revenue and gain understanding through data, and a current gap in the market exists, encouraging interest from non-traditional players who are beginning to enter this space (Plansky et al, 2013). One such player is the NSW Data Analytics Centre.

In this paper we explore how data modelling by an Australian state, New South Wales', (NSW) Government became the centre of data analytics to solve 'wicked problems' for the citizens of the state. The Data Analytics Centre, commonly known as the DAC, was set up in 2015 by the NSW Government to solve emerging challenges using data, or evidence-based problem solving. A complex myriad of data sets was to be collected across government to explore what they may unearth and in doing so understand what could be done to solve the original problem, or alternatively solve other otherwise unidentified problems. Under these circumstances, data can be used to create alternative business models to generate innovation and, ultimately, revenue opportunities from the commercialization of these projects. However, the initial purpose of data innovation should be to learn as much as we possibly can about the effective and efficient use of information (Corkindale, 2008). Opportunities for commercialisation and conversion are being explored, but are peripheral at this preliminary stage of the process.

The availability of information is changing the interactions between governments and citizens as the population becomes more connected, particularly in the digital space (Chun et al, 2010). It is essential that we optimise on these new abilities and opportunities in order to maximise the effectiveness and efficiency of government services.

1.1 NSW Data Analytics Centre

This paper is an empirical case study based on observations as well as work on various projects by the researchers at the NSW Data Analytics Centre.

The NSW Data Analytics Centre (DAC) is the first of its kind in Australia, set to become a world leader in using government data for analytics and insight to design solutions for NSW's complex community and policy challenges. The DAC aims to address 'wicked problems'; which are complex, unique, subtle, have many potential solutions and ultimately have people's behaviour at their heart (Rittel and Webber, 1973). Through advanced data analysis, the DAC connects data and people across government and develops insights, tools and models to improve the effectiveness and efficiency of government services. In some cases, this involves new ways of delivering services, or even the development of entirely new services. As of 15th of February 2017, the DAC has been assigned by the NSW Government to work on 25 different projects across different government departments, ranging from Community Services, Industry, Financial Services, Justice and Insurance bodies, looking to benefit communities around the state. All of these projects have been approved by the Cabinet of the State.

It is within this context that the researchers have identified data innovation and commercialisation opportunities. In other words: opportunities to explore using data developed algorithms, models and techniques for commercial use. This may occur in the business in which it was originally intended, or by another "data-reuse" strategy, which effectively enables the partially built algorithms to be commercially sold for other, similar, purposes.

We explore a Lean Approach for data commercialisation and the creation of innovative solutions, and discuss the value and benefits of these approaches. The canvas used by the DAC for the Lean Approach is shown in the figure below.

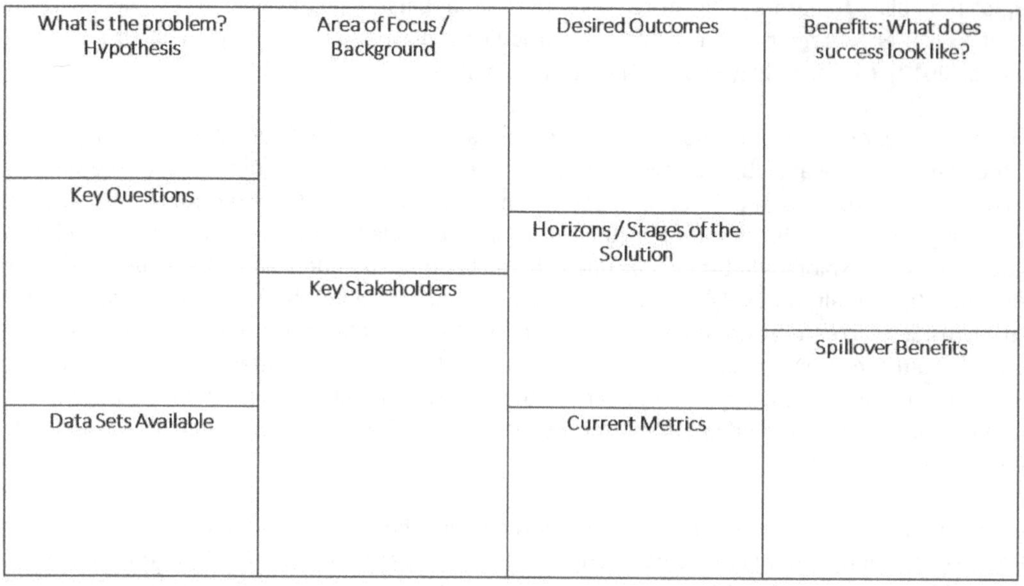

Figure 1: DAC Lean Data canvas

2. The Lean Approach to delivering data innovation projects: the flow of information from left to right

The DAC has developed an approach similar to that commonly used by start-ups to identify the value proposition, channels, cost structure, and revenue structure (Chesbrough and Rosenbloom, 2003). However, data-driven innovation in government has a different focus, therefore the Lean Approach is not to be confused with what is being used in the corporate world. The concern is more on ensuring that the problem is clearly captured and articulated by all the stakeholders, and to ensure an open mind to outcomes is preserved. A process of unravelling the complexity travels from building a Lean Approach to problem solving. The Lean Approach is effectively a business plan on a page that captures the entire project attributes: the hypothesis, the problem, the background, datasets, stages or horizons, the current metrics, the expected outcomes and, a new addition based on the case studies, spillover benefits. These involve benefits that may not be entirely attributed to the original scope, but that have resulted as an indirect effect of conducting the project. The various aspects and steps that have been undertaken at the DAC toward delivering data-driven innovative solutions in government using a Lean Approach will be unwrapped in the following sections.

2.1 What is the hypothesis you are concerned with?

The first aspect of the process is the hypothesis. In other words, is there a link between aspects of delivering service that could lead to further research? An example of a hypothesis could be: "the sky is blue", or, "the sky is also red at times", or the "sky is grey at some times and drops water during some periods". This, though a very simplistic example, is nevertheless a powerful way of assessing what the exact problem or challenge we are aiming to solve. From this point we may consider accompanying questions as we delve deeper into the issues that may each contribute to a refined and well-rounded response to the hypothesis.

2.2 Identification of valuable questions that data can answer

When embarking on a data-driven innovative solution, it is important to determine the right set of hypotheses and accompanying questions to ask of the sponsor organisation. If the right questions are not asked, an answer that effectively addresses the key issues will not emerge. The data will not simply give you information and insights on its own, and here data innovation is dependent on the correct start. In terms of the previous example, the accompanying questions may list as follows: "when is the sky blue, or grey?" "When are small droplets of water dispersed from the sky?"

The background and context of the study: i.e. the environment, location, longitudinal range and geographic setting, age group of the cohorts (if humans are part of the analysis), and overall context are at this point essential for consideration. It is important that these are clearly outlined and understood, otherwise the project endeavours to 'boil the ocean when only the kettle needs boiling'. The tendency to over-scope and under-deliver can consume the initial set of exercises, and hence it is very important to ensure the right questions are being asked to ensure the correct results, or as close as possible, are reached. Incorrect questions will lead to the wrong conclusion and lead to wasted resources, frustration and loss of credibility. The outcomes of the initial phase should ensure that a follow on future question or phase is developed, leading to a better, enhanced primary question.

Experience based on the projects so far suggests that an ideal set of questions to ask is between three and five, all linking to the hypothesis. More than five would make the project larger than practically possible to handle, and less would give the endeavour limited value.

2.3 Stakeholders: help or hinder?

Stakeholders can make or break the project. They can either provide useful insights and data that would optimise the capabilities of the model, or stall the progress through an additional set of expectations and potential adverse reactions to the project outcomes. As aptly noted by Corkindale (2008), there is no use in the enhanced ability of one stakeholder to perform certain tasks if they do not have the support of the network of other organizations with which they interact. Hence, it is essential to engage both the internal and external stakeholders of the project at an early stage. Service providers may also be consulted, depending on the situation. Stakeholders need to be identified in order to establish appropriate input that they may provide, data they may hold and the likely impact of their presence at the table. The early involvement of a variety of stakeholders also allows the impact of certain outcomes on the project as a whole to be identified in the first stages. However, when scoping the project amongst a number of stakeholders there is a tendency to reach too far, attempting to solve all the world's challenges. It is important to ensure this is resisted.

In many cases the concept of data-driven innovation, as a relatively new and unknown field, is encountered with scepticism. Under these circumstances, it is best to ensure that 'bite-sized' pieces of the project are undertaken, and stakeholder expectations managed adequately to ensure quick wins are possible rather than to over-promise and be embroiled in the larger complexity of the data. Once stakeholder confidence in the ability and power of the data has been received, additional or even disruptive options can be undertaken. Hence, the power in a manageable scope becomes even more important in data-driven innovation.

2.4 Scope

Once the elements above have been identified, the next step is to scope the overall project for outcomes that can be informed by data. At this point it is often very difficult to ensure stakeholder expectations are met, while at the same time ensuring the outcomes adequately represent value to the sponsoring executives as part of their annual achievements. The scope also has to be mindful of the possible deliverables and the measurable outcomes that can be achieved within the timeframe allocated. This approach then brings to the process the concept of identifying different horizons that break a project down into manageable pieces of work over a period of time. This not only creates value and builds intelligence; but encourages the confidence of the team and organisation, and ensures the stakeholder group are well-informed and buy into the vision. Focus on the overall outcomes hence becomes vital at this phase of the project.

2.5 Outcomes

In many cases, particularly at the start, it is not unusual for stakeholders to be unclear of the size or features of the problem that they are dealing with. Data analytics is a new space, a new sphere and a new approach to problem-solving. Despite the fact that most organisations have held some form of data for a long period of time, the domain of data analytics is one that may often feel daunting and threatening, as an untrodden path. Hence, the power of data analytics is one that has to be shared, promoted, and highlighted to business executives in a way that matters to them. The questions that need to be asked must relate to the overall problems that are envisaged by the organisation while serving their customer and the outcomes that they desire from the data.

Outcomes usually include solutions to issues such as hindering of service delivery, inefficiencies, or negative impacts on sales or compliance. In this instance, the outcomes may target the specific product or solution being offered. In some cases the question may be based on a potential future scenario such as "what will the infrastructure look like in ten years' time?" In this instance, various competing and complementary factors may collude in providing the outcomes. Stakeholders will likely develop questions that result in benefits at least twelve months out to ensure adequate lead time is available for potential implementation, and so as not to disturb regular business activities. It is hence important that a mechanism be developed to measure the outcomes. In a data analytics project, the newness of the overall project must not be an excuse for inability to measure its success and its potential benefits over a period of time. Stakeholders require a short, medium and long term ability to measure the benefits of their data analytics exercise before committing to the unknown. These different stages ensure small wins gather momentum for the project and build on every aspect of the project. At the DAC, these have been classified as "horizons of the project".

2.6 Horizons

Every successful organisation, despite its function, requires the establishment of a sound business model (Lambert, 2006). That of the DAC is based on three different horizons we have developed: the Proof of Concept (PoC), the Minimum Use Case (MuC), and the Minimum Viable Product (MvP). Each of these phases strengthens the project and adds greater value to the overall goal by increasing the insights that data can bring and asking additional questions of the stakeholders. Each phase may require additional data sets and new stakeholders, define new outcomes, and provide greater information of the depth of the challenge. The three horizons all allow for the achievement of quantifiable outcomes that address the original question.

The Proof of Concept phase focuses on determining what value data-driven capability may add to the issue at hand by gaining an understanding the data sets available and the quality of the data. Hence, it primarily involves the gathering and analysis of key data and the creation of a number of recommendations for the actions that may be taken. These are most often in the form of the development of a model or primitive dashboard that allows for greater collection, clarity and organisation of information. At this phase, it is important to ensure the expectations of the stakeholders are managed and not to attempt to solve too many problems. A set of basic outcomes that demonstrate the power of the data and allow for next steps, e.g. input into potential policy changes or further development of the project, is critical.

The second phase, once a project has progressed beyond policy recommendations, is the Minimum Use Case, and involves the creation of a model of limited scope and focus, to allow for a working tool that may be demonstrated to and evaluated by all stakeholders of the project to ensure that their needs are being met. Should this phase prove valuable to the stakeholders in terms of insights and outcomes, the project may move to the final stage.

During the final horizon, the Minimum Viable Product phase, the model created during the previous horizons is further refined, developed and placed into the client stakeholder system for testing under a production environment. The solution can now be road-tested against a set of data that may be able to, in real-time, provide valuable insights into a set of outcomes and be used to solve challenges to the stakeholders. This final MvP solution has the potential to result in a usable, deliverable product that not only can be utilised by the relevant agency/agencies, but also other stakeholders that may experience similar challenges within the same government jurisdiction or other, national, or even international jurisdictions.

2.7 What data do we need?

The million dollar question in data analytics is data. This is the oil in the well that needs to be extracted, cleaned and processed before it can be used. Data can exist in two different forms: open data, and organisation-specific data that has limited and restricted access. This may contain confidential information and can only be used by external entities when an appropriate governance and privacy framework is in place. The wide spectrum of data available on any subject can make the process of determining what is necessary for the current project a difficult one. This is why it is essential to determine the scope and focus of the issue at a very early stage of the process. It is vital that the data available and ultimately collected adds significant value to your ability to answer the questions at hand whilst remaining within the scope of your research. Otherwise, the project stalls under the weight of infinite data quantity, and is unable to progress in a timely manner past the data collection and analysis phases. On the other hand, if not all necessary data is collected, the project loses significance as an analytical tool, as it may not include all necessary variables, or have a broad enough scope to provide true commercial value to the stakeholders. Hence, the data collection phase is vital, as it provides the framework on which all future actions, and potential success or failure, are based. A balance between too much and not enough data must be found to ensure adequate value is developed at the PoC and MvU phases. Once the data collection has been conducted, the data scientists analyse and develop outcomes, and establish benefits that can be assumed, inferred, or partially developed further.

2.8 Benefits: what does success look like?

One of the more significant aspects of 'wicked problems', as discussed earlier, is the many stakeholders involved in the pursuit of success. Each individual or organisation has their own idea of what success looks like, and the optimum gain which the project may provide to them. The DAC must unite the varied and potentially conflicting priorities of the stakeholders in the planning stage of the project in order to find the true measure of success.

Success metrics in DAC projects are generally based on benefit to the NSW government and community, improving the social, economic, mental, and physical well-being of the state – either as a whole or focusing on a specific group. Specific attention is also paid to the Premier's Priorities and state priorities, as established by the NSW government in 2016. Success can depend on the stakeholders' needs, and understanding of the size of the problem and the value of the work needed to develop outcomes. In any case, when data is involved, a clear understanding that was not previously available is a valuable benefit. The ability to then convert that outcome to realised benefits becomes the key. Another measure of success is the movement from PoC to MuV to MvP, eventually making the solution available to other agencies.

Often in data projects while direct and observable benefits may be seen, projects may demonstrate what the DAC has observed as 'spillover' benefits. These are external benefits that have been observed from the insights of combining different data sets and visualising in different formats and outcomes, causing unforeseen contributions to the stakeholders. An open view on the project is essential for the optimisation of spillover benefit value.

2.9 Spillover benefits

As previously discussed, work on multiple DAC projects has led to the establishment of another category worth considering in the planning stage: the previously unforeseen benefits of the project to other government areas. These spillover benefits provide another indirect variable through which the necessity, validity and success of a project may be determined. Most often, the advantage is gained through a greater level, or superior organisation, of knowledge about a certain group, industry, geographical area, etc. This information may be translated into more informed decision-making in a number of other fields. In addition, a model, once created and refined, has the potential to be either delivered to other governments / agencies as is for the same purpose, or transformed into a similar tool for an alternative use. This allows for the provision of further commercial benefit whilst requiring limited expenditure of resources.

3. Case studies

The two case studies outlined below are examples of projects that are currently being worked on by the DAC. Note that both have a multi-disciplinary governmental background, and a focus on data collection and organisation.

3.1 'Non-Compliance Hot Spots'

This project was proposed by an organization of NSW government agencies, after their identification of a number of localised areas of general non-compliance. It is believed that a better understanding of non-compliant actions and activities may be gained through the identification and challenging of the relationships between drivers and behaviours of non-compliant individuals and businesses across a range of regulatory areas. In addition, the project aims to increase information-sharing and collaboration between NSW government regulators.

The key objective of the project is to bring together data from a number of agencies, exploring the relationship between drivers of non-compliance and identifying current and future indicators of non-compliance. This will allow the eventual building of a solution to this issue for all involved parties. The project is also intended to create a model to classify levels or types of non-compliance to draw relationships between various NSW government regulators with legislative compliance and enforcement responsibilities. This will help identify areas for regulatory improvement and undertake better regulation initiatives, including red tape reduction and regulatory reform.

3.2 'Ease of Doing Business in NSW'

This project was proposed by the department responsible for improving business conditions within the state, under the belief that increased ease of doing business in NSW will lead to a stronger economy. To make sure the government is creating the right environment to attract and support business to NSW, it is necessary to better understand the drivers of a successful business environment and compare these with other jurisdictions in Australia and the world. The project is intended to prioritise a set of specific metrics to compare NSW performance with other local and international jurisdictions. This will then allow the NSW Government to agree on robust, fact-based baselines and targets to improve on these measures. An analytics and predictive outcome of the project is to develop potential predictors of various variable inputs.

4. Conclusion

In this paper, the DAC process of developing a project, scoping, and delivering outcomes has been outlined. The process is innovative in nature, with an aim to deliver a scalable and measurable outcome, based on agile needs, to the stakeholders. The process has been developed in-house for the needs of the NSW Government, based on the learnings of a number of complex projects. The findings so far, in the nascent stages of an eighteen month-old start-up within Government, appear to demonstrate strong support from across agencies, have delivered measurable benefits, and enabled other agencies new to data science to explore their emerging challenges using data analytics. The lean methodology has enabled both the DAC and the sponsoring agencies to establish a valuable and efficient framework to identify the core issues, define the problem and ask key questions of the challenge, and understand the data that may be required. The process has further provided an approach that enables small, manageable functions of work to create small wins for the agencies, further demonstrating the power of data. The success to date has ensured a further eight to twelve projects are being considered by various agencies of the NSW Government for using the capabilities of the DAC to help with providing better and innovative service solutions to the citizens of NSW. A number of key learnings from the process of innovating in data are provided below.

4.1 Summary of 10 key learnings from the Lean Approach to solving data challenges in govenment

1. Ensure the lead agency needs the problem to be solved, and is looking at the right problem.
2. Ensure there is adequate data available to solve the problem.
3. Ask the right questions of the project. The wrong question will yield unexpected results and lead to frustration and loss of trust in the data and the entire data-driven innovation process.
4. Ensure expectations are managed in terms of outcomes and findings throughout the whole process.
5. Ensure timely and useful feedback is given to stakeholders during the different phases. Silence is *not* a virtue in this instance.
6. Ensure all discussions are based on outcomes and driven by value, tangible or intangible.
7. Ensure data from stakeholders is available and there is willingness to provide in a timely manner.
8. Deliver outcomes in clear, understandable language. Jargon may not mean anything to the business stakeholder. Stakeholders understand benefits and outcomes, hence it is important to speak their language.
9. Ensure there are adequate elements that demonstrate useful insights and knowledge.
10. Ensure that there are small and demonstrable wins along the journey
11. Always have a strategy for the next steps, and provide options to the stakeholders when moving forward.

References

Chesbrough, H.W. and Rosenbloom, R.S. (2002) "The role of the business model in capturing value from innovation: evidence from Xerox Corporation's technology spin-off companies", *Industrial Corporate Change*, Vol 11, No. 3, pp 529-555.

Chun, S.A., Shulman, S., Sandoval, R. and Hovy, E. (2010) "Government 2.0: Making Connections between Citizens, Data and Government", *Information Polity*, Vol 15, No. 1, pp 1-10.

Corkindale, D. (2008) "Towards a business model for commercializing innovative new technology", *Innovative Marketing,* Vol 4, No. 2, pp 7-15.

Head, B,. (2008) "Wicked Problems in Public Policy", Public Policy, Vol. 3, No. 2, 2008:1001-118

Keystone Strategy, (2016) *Data & Analytics Maturity Model & Business Impact,* Keystone Strategy, Boston.

Lambert, S. (2006) "A business model research schema", *BLED 2006 Proceedings*, pp 43-57.

Nicholls, S., Rosewall, R., (2015) "The Economic Performance of the States", Reserve Bank of Australia, Bulletin, March Quarter

Plansky, J., Solomon, J., Karp, R. and Drisko, C. (2013) "The data gold rush: Companies need the right models and capabilities to monetize data" in *Perspective*, Booz & Company, Boston, pp 1-8.
Rittel, H.W. J. and Webber, M.M., (1973) "Dilemmas in a General Theory of Planning", *Policy Sciences*, Vol 4, pp 155–169.
Rittel, H.W. J. and Webber, M.M., (1984) "Planning are wicked problems" John Wiley & Sons, edited by Nigel Cross, The Open University

The World's Best Practices of Entrepreneurship Education in the Universities

Maxim Vlasov[1] and Svetlana Panikarova[2]
[1]Assistant Professor, Ural Federal University named after the first President of Russia, Ekaterinburg, Russia
[2]Professor, Ural Federal University named after the first President of Russia, Ekaterinburg, Russia
Mvlassov@mail.ru
panikarova_s@mail.ru

Abstract: In the article results of the analysis of factors of efficiency of educational programs for business at universities of the different countries are presented. The authors use economic, statistic and sociological methods of data collection, processing and analysis including expert questionnaires and interviews. Peculiar feature of author's approach is in attempt at complex comparative analysis of entrepreneurship educational programs offered by the leaders in the field in different aspects: starting from educational program content to peculiar features of training infrastructure. As a result of the conducted researches, it is proved that a success major factor in formation of enterprise competencies is existence of the full closed cycle of training and support of business from transfer of basic knowledge before real support of the beginning businessman and often subsequently consulting maintenance of the operating business.

Keywords: entrepreneurship; entrepreneurship training; educational program; teaching infrastructure; entrepreneurial competencies

1. Introduction

The development of small enterprises is the top priority of modern policy for a long – term perspective in many countries of post – soviet space. Strategic documents of many countries – former members of USSR necessarily formulate the task on developing smaller enterprises and stimulus for its activation. However, despite the state interest, public attention and overall support development of smaller enterprises in the majority of post – Soviet countries lags behind the levels demonstrated by countries with developed market economy and official prognostication figures. This situation calls for research on instruments, methods and approaches to stimulating smaller enterprises.

Entrepreneurship is an integral part of modern market economy without which economics of the country cannot properly function and develop. In the countries with developed economy from the point of view of economic position and level of life, entrepreneurs form the basis of middle class, which serves as the foundation of social and political stability of society. That is why development of small enterprises is the top priority of modern policy for a long – term perspective in many countries of post – soviet space. Strategic documents of many countries – former members of USSR necessarily formulate the task on developing smaller enterprises and stimulus for its activation. However, despite the state interest, public attention and overall support development of smaller enterprises in the majority of post – Soviet countries lags behind the levels demonstrated by countries with developed market economy and official prognostication figures. This situation calls for research on instruments, methods and approaches to stimulating smaller enterprises. One aspect of this research is an attempt to answer the following question: what should entrepreneurship education in post – soviet countries look like?

One of the reasons behind difficulties in defining approaches to entrepreneurial education is the ambiguity of the entrepreneurship phenomenon itself. Let's give several examples of the way scientists define the meaning of entrepreneurship:

- new way in (Lumpkin & Dess, 1996);
- creation of a new company (Low & MacMillan, 1988);
- creation of new organizations (Gartner, 1988);
- obtaining advantages from new combination of different resources capable of influencing the market (Wiklund, 1998);

- process by means of which individuals by themselves or within some organization jump to opportunities and it does not matter if they have relevant resources at hand at the moment (Stevenson & Jarillo, 1990);
- the process of creating something different in terms of value, related to time and efforts put into it; considering accompanying financial, psychological and social risks; obtaining reward in the form of financial or moral benefit (Hisrisch & Peters, 1989).

Most of entrepreneurship researchers do not introduce their formal terms and generally accept the definition given by J. Schumpeter (Schumpeter, 1934). For example, P. Drucker associates entrepreneurship with innovative and change - oriented behavior (Drucker, 1985), whereas I. Bull and G. Willard include also aim - oriented motivation, competencies and expectations of getting profit for oneself (Bull & Willard, 1993).

When forming entrepreneurial competencies one must consider which roles are set for entrepreneur by the society depending on the economic situation. E. Kirzner (Kirzner, 1982) suggests the following set of roles for an entrepreneur in different economic theories: engaged in a specific type of labor, ready to take risk, innovator, middleman in bank and trade operations, coordinator, organizer or actor filling the gaps, providing leadership, possessing true will, acting as a clean dealer, acting as an employer, acting as an executive officer in manager, acting as a source of information, attentive to opportunities ignored by the market earlier.

Using empiric approach to the question of nature and meaning of entrepreneurship B. Gartner defined the following eight topics arising during the conversation about the meaning of entrepreneurship with those people using entrepreneurship concept on a professional basis (not only to researchers) (Gartner, 1990): entrepreneur, innovation, organization creation, value generation, profit or loss, growth, unique, proprietor or manager.

Content analysis of articles and books conducted by a research team (Morris at all, 1994), demonstrated the following most wide - spread key definitions: start, creation; new business; innovation, new product, new market; aspiration to use the opportunity; risk acceptance, risk management, uncertainty; desire to get profit, personal advantages; new production methods; management; resource coordination; value generation.

Authors conclude that all possible entrepreneurship definitions are related to the fact that development and renewal of any society, economy or organization requires subjects acting at micro-level that possess necessary initiative and persistence to make such changes happen. Institutions, as well as market and organizational structures, can facilitate or hinder changes and development. One of these important institutions is the institutions of entrepreneurship education development.

Works of the following authors present examples of innovative approach to entrepreneurship training: E.A. Scherbakova (2012), S.V. Khachin (2012), L. Pittaway, C.Missing (2009), J. Zang, E. Hamilton (2010). Experience of training in innovative entrepreneurship in the context of a construction educational cluster in the system of technical and technological education is given in the work by R.S. Safin (2012). Certain problems faced by entrepreneurship education in Russia are highlighted in publications by N.S. Zaripova (2014), G.N. Franovskaya (2013) et al. Research on student entrepreneurship is made by G.V. Shirokova, A.V. Kulikova (2011). Works by J. Copp, G. Watts (2000), L. Bisk (2002) reveal the role of mentoring in entrepreneurship training. Development of pedagogical practices of entrepreneurship training is described by D.Kirby (2009). Peculiar features of entrepreneurship education in the online format are given in the research by B. Mashaw (2012), J. Mills and S. Barakat (2010).

At the same time analysis of main trends in academic research devoted to entrepreneurship training demonstrates insufficient amount of complex comparative research concentrating on efficacy factors in entrepreneurship training based on best practices of universities from different countries.

The aim of the research is to identify efficacy factors for entrepreneurship training programs on the basis of analysis of existing approaches to forming entrepreneurial competencies at the leading universities.

Two main research questions were placed:

1. What features of key competencies of entrepreneurship education are usual for leading universities?
2. What elements of system entrepreneurial competencies can be useful for typical university practice?

The structure of the paper is as follows: The first section presents the methods of research. The second section characterizes the entrepreneurial knowledge and skills during the process of teaching. The third section presents the special infrastructure elements for entrepreneurship education. The forth section presents the role of academic research and networking in the entrepreneurship education and the last section is the conclusion.

2. Methods

The article takes an eclectic methodological approach to piece together extant literature and to discover new empirical knowledge about the factors of efficiency of educational programs for business. Peculiar feature of author's approach is in attempt at complex comparative analysis of entrepreneurship educational programs offered by the leaders in the field in different aspects: starting from educational program content to peculiar features of training infrastructure.

The research uses economic, statistic and sociological methods of data collection, processing and analysis including expert questionnaires and interviews.

Research project consisted of three stages.

On the basis of information presented at official websites of regional and international communities and network organizations engaged in entrepreneurship education we created an initial list of educational institutions offering entrepreneurship training that included 92 organizations from different countries (including the USA – 24; Canada – 18; the United Kingdom – 13; France – 9; Germany – 4; the Netherlands – 4; Singapore – 5; Russia – 10; others – 14). At the first stage with the help of experts from different universities, authors formed the list of educational organizations with best practices and approaches to entrepreneurship. Selection criteria included 1) positive academic reputation; 2) long successful experience of training entrepreneurs; 3) successful research activities; 4) possibility to disseminate successful experience of forming entrepreneurial competencies among educational institutions with developing educational environment; 5) top rankings in national and international ratings; 6) membership in regional and international associations of educational organizations. According to criteria 1-4, comparative evaluation of educational organizations form the initial list was conducted by means of expert poll. The choice of experts was made on the basis of three characteristics: employment sphere, work experience, qualification level.

Experts were asked to evaluate the degree of this or that characteristic manifestation according to 5 score scale. If expert had no information about educational institution activities in the field of entrepreneurship training, organization got 0 points. Analysis of expert poll was conducted by means of average score.

Data on criteria 5-6 was received by means of comparative analysis of information from rating agencies and educational institutions official websites listed in the description of Stage 1. According to the first criterion 5 scores were given to educational institutions with high positions in 4 or more ratings, 4 scores to 2 and more ratings, 3 scores to those with midlevel positions in 2 and more ratings, 2 scores to one and more ratings and 1 to not present in ratings. According to the second criterion: 5 scores to organizations with membership in 5 an more educational associations, 4 scores to those with 3 or 4 memberships, 3 scores to those with 2 memberships, 2 scores for one membership and 1 score to organizations with no membership in any of the listed educational associations.

With the use of expert poll method each of the chosen criterion was given a certain weight coefficient.

The final educational environment evaluation for an educational institution (Q) is defined by a sum of derivates of the sums of all indicators (criteria) (I) at the relevant weight to a relative indicator importance (W) according to the following formula (1):

$$Q = \sum_{i=1}^{n} I_i \times W_i \qquad (1)$$

where:

Q - evaluation of educational structure quality;

Ii- evaluation according to indicator i;

Wi- weight of i-indicator.

Therefore considering expert opinion concerning criteria importance we suggested the following formula for evaluating educational environment quality (2):

$$Q = 0{,}11R+0{,}19P+0{,}07M+0{,}13S+0{,}24C+0{,}26E \qquad (2)$$

Where *R* – is an academic reputation of educational organization;
P – position in national and international ratings;
M – membership in educational associations;
S – academic activities results in the field of entrepreneurship problems;
C – ability to disseminate successful experience in forming entrepreneurial competencies;
E – presence of a significant successful experience of entrepreneurship training;

Each of the reviewed organizations got scores for educational environment quality as a sum of all individual indicators results

The list of universities whose programs were chosen for further analysis consisted of 24 higher educational institutions from 9 countries (including the USA, Great Britain, the Netherlands, Singapore, France, Canada, etc.). The list of universities chosen for such analysis features both those universities that are considered entrepreneurship education leaders (University of Cambridge - Judge Business School, Manchester Business School, London Business School, Babson College, Baylor University, Nanyang technological university, etc.), and less well known universities whose experience in forming entrepreneurial competencies (according to expert opinion) can be most useful for the post-Soviet countries (Moscow State Technical University named after N.E. Bauman, Higher School of Economics, Moscow State University named after M.V. Lomonosov, Riga International School of Economics and Business Administration, University of Huddersfield, , Erasmus University Rotterdam, Maastricht University, Aalto University, University of Alberta, University of Maryland, Texas Christian University, Syracuse university, etc.).

The second stage included distant analysis of chosen educational programs according to the following parameters: educational program structure; teaching infrastructure; teaching personnel characteristics; academic and practical teaching environment characteristics. Informational sources for the second stage included web-sites of analyzed educational institutions; marketing materials received at Russian and international conferences; information from closed databases (ICSB и USASBE); materials provided for open access by regional and international unions and networks engaged in entrepreneurship training; printed and electronic Mass Media; portals in the relevant field.

The third stage included a series of structured interviews with representatives of leading organizations in the field of entrepreneurship education. This work was aimed at obtaining more detailed information on peculiar features of entrepreneurship education and clarification of certain results of previous analysis.

3. Results

Entrepreneurship training at leading universities usually has a complex character. The system of forming entrepreneurial competencies consists of several elements:

1. forming entrepreneurial knowledge and skills during the process of teaching;
2. supporting entrepreneurial activities with the help of developed infrastructure;
3. developing communicational space for entrepreneurial networking;

4. conducting academic research in the field of entrepreneurship.

Let's look at each of these elements in more detail.

Forming entrepreneurial knowledge and skills during the process of teaching

One of the main tasks of the research was to find out which competencies play the most important role in the training of future entrepreneurs from the point of view of heads of teaching programs under analysis. Interviews provided a relatively long list of different competencies which are considered as important by universities. In general these key competencies can be subdivided into three groups: competencies forming entrepreneurial thinking; entrepreneurial communication and entrepreneurial skills (Figure 1.).

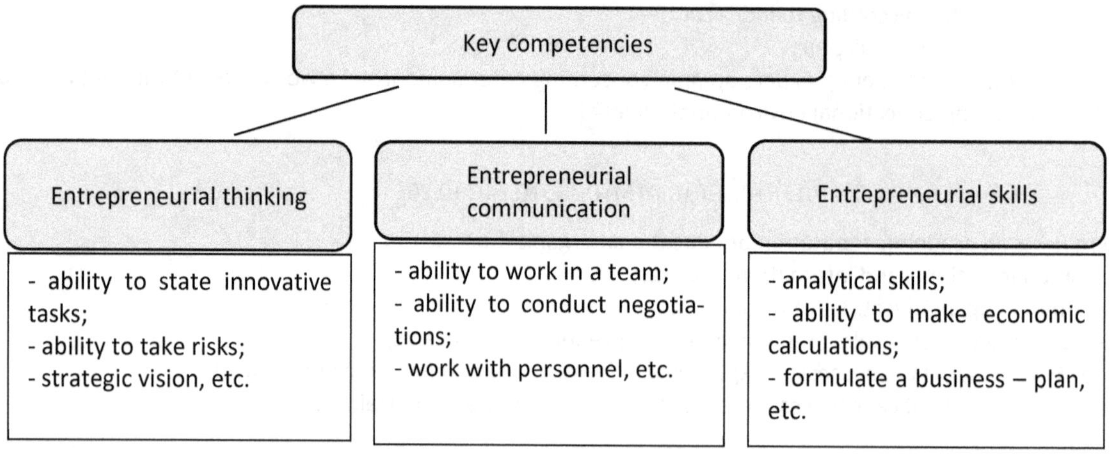

Figure 1: Key competencies of entrepreneurship education, developed by the author.

Educational programs in entrepreneurship offered by the leading universities have the same following characteristics:

1. *Wide di.versification of educational programs on entrepreneurship*. Most of higher educational institutions have created institutional chain of forming entrepreneurial competencies: starting from short-terms courses/programs developing basic skills in the field of entrepreneurship to maser and PhD research programs. Each of analyzed institutions offers several entrepreneurship programs that differ in terms of effort (short and long-term programs) level of specialization (branch, functional, process); profile (basic, supplementary, etc.). Besides bachelor and master programs all educational institutions under research offer short-term entrepreneurship courses. Forms of these courses can be different depending on the type of educational organization, type of main educational programs, qualitative characteristics of innovative infrastructure and external business – environment. It can be a series of open lectures and experience exchange; series of elective courses and master – classes on entrepreneurship; intensive short – term entrepreneurial activity stimulation courses; idea commercialization programs; summer entrepreneurial schools; trainings, etc.
2. *A large proportion of disciplines forming (developing) entrepreneurial thinking and oriented towards "building an entrepreneur"*, such as: creativity and innovation; discover your inner entrepreneur; creative thinking; presentation training; creativity development; etc.
3. *Practice oriented form of knowledge check (usually real business – project).* Knowledge check format combines successful mastering all disciplines and modules and a particular business – project, which is defended in front of practical experts, potential investors and venture funds representatives.
4. A large proportion of lecturers – entrepreneurs. Lecturers giving entrepreneurship training programs can be subdivided into 4 groups: lecturers – entrepreneurs; lecturers - practical experts; lecturers – academics; lecturers – administrators.

   Lecturers – entrepreneurs and lecturers – practical experts are the key figures in forming entrepreneurial competencies of leading universities in terms of entrepreneurship education. Quite often the main criterion in choosing lecturers for entrepreneurship course is their experience of working in entrepreneurial sphere.
5. *Use of active educational technologies.* In order to form competencies mentioned above the following technologies can be used: online training, design thinking, team facilitation, business game, cases instead of lectures and research articles instead of textbooks.

Supporting entrepreneurial activities with the help of developed infrastructure
Formation of entrepreneurial competencies is supported by a chance to implement them in the framework of special infrastructure elements (business – incubators, accelerators, techno-parks, etc.) (Figure 2).

Leadership training infrastructure in entrepreneurship education has many similarities. One of the main elements of the infrastructure is specialized institute or entrepreneurship center in charge of forming teaching courses and programs in entrepreneurship. Entrepreneurship centers frequently fulfil key task of forming entrepreneurial competencies. Besides educational functions entrepreneurship centers can support start-up programs, organize conferences, competitions and business ideas festivals, etc., issue copyright license for inventions, etc.

Entrepreneurship centers are usually integrated with other elements of innovational infrastructure: network communities, technology transfer departments; business – incubators and sometimes techno-parks.

Technological licensing center/department is an important element of the infrastructure. It supports technology transfer process and communication between research (science) and business.

Techno-parks are not the main element of entrepreneurship training infrastructure though for some major universities (particularly technically oriented) they play an important role in the infrastructure.

Entrepreneurship training infrastructure often includes business excavators and business – accelerators. The main task of business – incubator is to facilitate successful development of businesses created by young entrepreneurs. Accelerators are short-term programs aimed at supporting start-ups which are initiated on the basis of business – incubators and techno-parks. For a short period of time project team finds itself in an environment that allows for speedy creation of a project or project prototype strong enough to enter the market and attract investments.

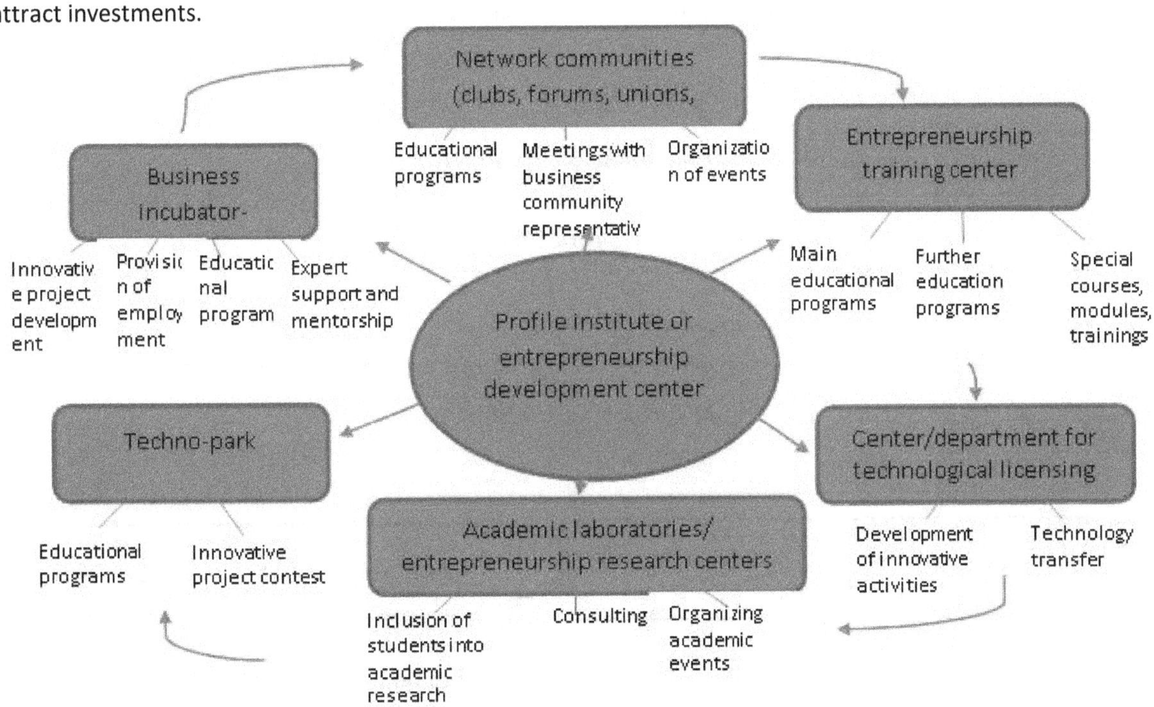

Figure 2: Entrepreneurship education infrastructure at the leading universities, designed by the author.

Conducting academic research in the field of entrepreneurship.
All educational institutions support projects on academic research in the field of entrepreneurship, formulate research topics in the field of entrepreneurship development and actively involve students into the research process. We can identify several research trends supported by leading entrepreneurship education structures: entrepreneurial instruments; markets and competitiveness factors; entrepreneurial behavior; innovative processes; fundamental economic problems.

Leading universities in the field of entrepreneurial behavior usually exist in an environment stimulating research and project activities of the students. All of the educational programs we have analyzed offer competitions, conferences, business games, etc. on the regular basis. The most wide – spread event is student project/start-up competition (business – ideas, innovative projects, business – plans, business models, etc.). Competition winners get an opportunity to implement their project (grants, money, etc.).

Some universities conduct annual Olympiads and nosiness games for student teams. It is obligatory to conduct conferences on entrepreneurial topics. More than half of the universities conduct Annual entrepreneurship weeks. In general leading universities organize up to 20 entrepreneurship events per year.

Developing communicational space for entrepreneurial networking.
The next important element of entrepreneurship training system is network community: entrepreneurship clubs, forums, young entrepreneurs' unions, etc. Such associations functions at almost all universities and facilitate close communication of entrepreneurial community of the universities, organize meetings and events. An important role in the functioning of such communities is played by alumni. In most of the analyzed organizations entrepreneurship training infrastructure includes different events aimed at improving networking skills and developing contacts, meeting-places with investors and coaching programs are organized.

Discussion and Conclusions
Therefore the research on the leading entrepreneurship training universities has demonstrated several key *educational program efficacy factors*:

- broad diversification of educational programs on forming entrepreneurial competencies;
- presence of institutions providing inclusion of entrepreneurial community representatives into the teaching process;
- opportunity to start business simultaneously with mastering educational program;
- systematic inclusion of students into the interaction with real-life economy and science.

The main features of forming entrepreneurial competencies within the best educational programs are given in the Figure 3.

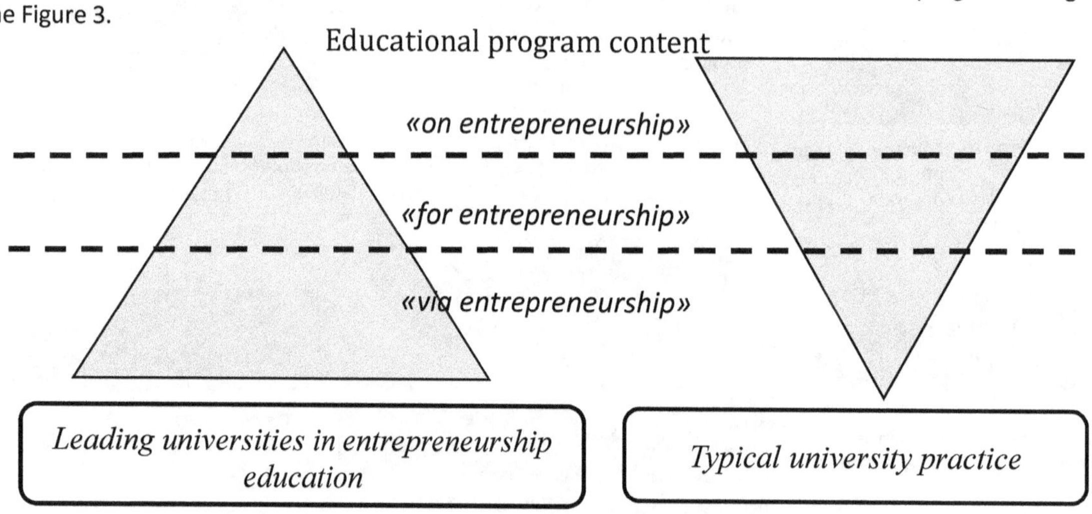

Figure 3: Comparison of approaches to forming entrepreneurial competencies at the universities.

Therefore the key factor of successful formation of entrepreneurial competence is the presence of a full educational cycle an entrepreneurship support starting from basic knowledge transfer to real support of aspiring entrepreneurs and frequently further consulting services to a real business.

According to the results of conducted research on the leading entrepreneurship training programs the following conclusions have been made:

1. In terms of forming entrepreneurial competencies leading universities offer complex training. Entrepreneurship education includes: training, provision of necessary knowledge and ability to apply tit in practice; support of entrepreneurial activities with the help of developed infrastructure; studying aca-

demic aspect of entrepreneurship development; construction and support of student, research and entrepreneurial networks.

2. Most universities design institutional chain of forming entrepreneurial competencies: from short-terms courses/programs forming initial entrepreneurial skills to master and doctoral research programs. Each of analyzed universities offers several different entrepreneurship programs different in terms of effort (long-term, short-term, etc.), specialization (branch, functional, processual) and profile (basic, supplementary, etc.), etc.
3. Formation of entrepreneurial competencies is supported by opportunity to implement them in the framework of special infrastructure elements (business – incubators, accelerators, techno-parks, etc.).
4. One of the main elements of entrepreneurship education infrastructure is a special institution or entrepreneurship center in charge of developing teaching courses and programs on entrepreneurship. These branches usually solve key tasks on forming entrepreneurial competencies, accumulate new supplementary teaching programs, projects and initiatives.
5. Leading educational organizations in the field of entrepreneurship education can render financial support to entrepreneurs – students by means of picking the best project and ideas. Most of analyzed universities have structures supporting innovative entrepreneurial aspirations of their students by means of financial or other resources or incorporating business – incubators, techno-parks, foundations, grants and other opportunities.
6. Majority of analyzed organizations organize different events on networking and establishment of new contacts, offer opportunities for meeting investors and coaching programs.
7. An important factor is systematic conducting of different events related to entrepreneurship and its development: business – project competitions, trainings and seminars, business games, meetings with entrepreneurs, conferences, forums, youth schools, etc.
8. All educational institutions support research projects in the field of entrepreneurship, formulate research topics on entrepreneurship development and actively involve students onto the research process.

Acknowledgements

The study was financially supported by the grant of President of Russian Federation, Project MD-5743.2016.6 "Influence of sociocultural factors on institutional development of regional innovative system"

References

Bull, I. & Willard, G. E. (1993). Towards a Theory of Entrepreneurship. *Journal of Business Venturing*, 8, 183-195.

Bisk, L. (2002). Formal entrepreneurial mentoring: the efficacy of third party managed programs. *Career Development International*, 7 (5), 262-270

Cope, J., & Watts, G. (2000). Learning by doing – An exploration of experience, critical incidents and reflection in entrepreneurial learning. *International Journal of Entrepreneurial Behaviour and Research*, 6 (3), 104-124

Drucker, P. F. (1985). *Innovation and Entrepreneurship: Practice and Principles.* New York: Harper and Row.

Franovskaya, G. N. (2013). Entrepreneurship education: peculiarities and objectives. *Voronezh State University Herald. Series: Economics and management*, 1, 190-194.

Gartner, W. B. (1988). "Who is an entrepreneur?" is the wrong question. *American Journal of Small Business,* 12(4): 11-32.

Gartner, W. B. (1990). What are we talking about when we talk about entrepreneurship? *Journal of Business Venturing*, 5(1), 15-28.

Hisrisch, R.D. & Peters, M.P. (1989). *Entrepreneurship. Starting, Developing and Managing a New Enterprise.* Homewood, IL: Irwin.

Khachin, S. V., Kizeev, V. M., & Ivanchenko, M.A. (2012). Experience of Tomsk Polytechnic University in the field of engineering entrepreneurship training. World of education – education in the world, 4, 13-143.

Kirby, D. A. (2007). Changing the Entrepreneurship Education Paradigm. In Handbook of Research in Entrepreneurship Education, Vol. 1, A. Fayolle, A. (Ed.), 21-45. Cheltenham, UK: Edward Elgar

Kirzner, I. M. (1982) Uncertainty, Discovery and Human Action: A Study of the Entrepreneurial Profile in the Misesian System. In: Kirzner, I. M. (ed.) Method, Process and Austrian Economics. pp. 139–160. Canada: D.C. Heath

Low, M. B., & MacMillan, I. C. (1988). Entrepreneurship: Past research and future challenges. Journal of Management, 14(2): 139-161.

Lumpkin, G. T., & Dess, G. G. (1996). Clarifying the entrepreneurial orientation construct and linking it to performance. *Academy of Management Review*, 21(1), 135–172.

Mashaw, B. (2012). A model for measuring effectiveness of an online course. *Decision Sciences Journal of Innovative Education*, 10 (2), 189-221

Mills, J., Barakat, S., & Vyakarnam, S. (2010). The impact of e-learning strategies for entrepreneurship education. The Institute of Small Business and Enterprise (ISBE) Annual Conference, London

Pittaway, L., Missing, C., Hudson, N., & Maragh, D. (2009). Entrepreneurial Learning through action: a case study of the Six-Squared programme. *Action Learning: Research and Practice*, 6 (3), 265-288

Morris, M.H., Lewis, P.S., & Sexton, D.L. (1994). Reconceptualizing entrepreneurship: an input/output perspective. *SAM Advanced Management Journal*, 59 (1), 21-31

Safin, R. S., Matukhin, E. L., Shaydulina, A. R., & Zyalaeva, R. G. (2012). Innovational entrepreneurship education in the system of continuous professional education. *Kazan pedagogical journal*, 5-6(95), 79-96.

Scherbakova, E. A. (2012). Innovative approach to entrepreneurship training. Sothern Russia State Technical University (Novocherkassk Polytechnic Institute) Herald. Series: Social and economic sciences, 3, 83-86.

Schumpeter, J. A. (1934). *A theory of economic development*. Cambridge, MA: Harvard University Press.

Shirokova, G. V., & Kulikova, A. V. (2011). Global research on students' entrepreneurial spirit: national report, Moscow: NRU HSE

Stevenson, H. H. and J. C. Jarillo (1990). A paradigm of entrepreneurship: Entrepreneurial management, *Strategic Management Journal*, 11, 17-27.

Vlasov, M.V. (2015). Knowledge Generation Managing at Universities. Mediterranean Journal of Social Sciences, 6(1), 453-458.

Wiklund, J. (1998). Small firm growth and performance: entrepreneurship and beyond, Jönköping: Jönköping International Business School.

Zaripova, N.S. (2014). Entrepreneurship training in the modern socio-cultural environment. *Information and education: communications limits,* 6 (14), 220-222.

Zhang, J., & Hamilton, E. (2010). Entrepreneurship Education for Owner-Managers: The Process of Trust Building for an Effective Learning Community. *Journal of Small Business and Entrepreneurship*, 23 (2), 249-270

Formation of Organization Development Strategy on the Basis of New Knowledge

Maxim Vlasov
Assistant Professor, Ural Federal University, Ekaterinburg, Russia
Institute of Economics, Ural Branch of the Russian Academy of Sciences, Ekaterinburg, Russia
mvlasov@mail.ru

Abstract: American and European researchers started emphasizing the role and meaning not only of information but knowledge which gave rise to a whole set of new definitions for modern society, including «knowledge society», «knowledgeable society», etc. Modern market conditions require businesses to find new approaches to corporate management, planning and control. The right choice of direction in introducing new knowledge largely predetermines efficacy of achieving stated objectives. We often see how insufficient evaluation of initial economic opportunities leads to a halt of many perspective innovation and investment projects and programs because of the lack of financial and economic resources for their completion. It is possible to avoid such situations if at the stage of practical implementation strategy formulation, we exclude "unreachable" projects based on low initial innovative activity of the company. The aim of this research is to formulate methodological approaches to selecting innovative projects based on widespread investment design methods considering peculiarities of investment development strategy. The author offers methodological approaches to selection of results of new knowledge generation based on widespread methods of investment design and considering features of innovative development strategy. New methodological approach includes the following stages: company economic opportunities analysis; innovative ideas generation; preliminary innovation selection; presentation of innovation idea in the form of innovation project; innovation project efficacy evaluation from the point of view of investment perspectives; evaluation of innovation project efficacy from company economics point of view; multidimensional analysis of obtained quantitative evaluation with the aim of choosing the most perspective innovation projects. Theoretical importance of obtained results is in the development of methodological approaches to innovation project selection based on widespread methods of investment design considering peculiar features of innovation development strategy. These methodological approaches can be the basis for designing company activities on new knowledge generation. Practical importance of obtained results is in increased transparency of activities on new knowledge generation results application in the work of a company by means of improving managerial decisions on developing innovation activities and implementation of innovations.

Keywords: knowledge generation, innovative development, investment design.

1. Introduction

Joseph Schumpeter was the first who separeted inventions and innovations. In his 1912 study entitled "The Theory of Economic Development" he noted that "new discoveries and inventions are constantly replenishing the existing stock of knowledge... The function of the inventor and the general technician does not coincide with the function of the entrepreneur. As such, the entrepreneur is not the spiritual creator of new combinations" (Schumpeter, 1912). According to Schumpeter, entrepreneurs implemente new combinations through the following stages: "1) the production of new goods or the creation of a new quality of goods, 2) the introduction of a new mode of production, 3) the development of a new market, 4) providing a new source of raw materials, 5) carrying out an appropriate reorganisation" (Eggertsson, 2001). Thus, for Schumpeter, inventions precede innovations.

Modern market conditions require businesses to find new approaches to corporate management, planning and control. The right choice of direction in introducing new knowledge largely predetermines efficacy of achieving stated objectives (Soldatov A.A, Tanchuk R. S., 2013). We often see how insufficient evaluation of initial economic opportunities leads to a halt of many perspective innovation and investment projects and programs because of the lack of financial and economic resources for their completion. It is possible to avoid such situations if at the stage of practical implementation strategy formulation, we exclude "unreachable" projects based on low initial innovative activity of the company.

The aim of this research is to formulate methodological approaches to selecting innovative projects based on widespread investment design methods considering peculiarities of investment development strategy.

As is well known, the process of the knowledge transformation into the primary productive factor was predicted by Peter Drucker and Daniel Bell in the 1960-70s (Bell, 1973). Now the competitive advantages of the firm is interpreted as the ability to benefit from the electronic resources of the Internet, e-commerce, and preservation of "knowledge workers", to create a "learning organisation" and, more rapidly than their competitors, to identify and commercialise global opportunities of technological and organisational innovations. So one of the most effective efforts of strategic management in recent years, formed in the framework of the resource approach, has been the concept of "knowledge creation company" (Nonaka, & Takeuchi, 1994), that develop the concept of intellectual capital of the firm (Teece, 2001).

Since the 1990 economic science and practice have been actively using two notions: "knowledge based economics" and "information based economics". These terms were coined to cover the new sector of economics: together they form the notion of post-industrial society which has been actively researches since the second half of XX century.

American and European researchers started emphasizing the role and meaning not only of information but knowledge which gave rise to a whole set of new definitions for modern society, including «knowledge society», «knowledgeable society», etc.

Unlike traditional economics, the key role in such economics belongs not to financial capital and material assets but to knowledge, intangible assets and particularly intellectual capital.

According to the opinion of several researchers, many economic subjects find themselves in a situation when research organization potential is underused and research products are not always competitive because of discordance between science and manufacture and almost universal gap in communication between them (Goncharenko L.P. Arutyunov Yu.A., 2011).

It would be reasonable to start the process of forming strategy for introducing new knowledge into the activity of economic units from the analysis of economic opportunities of the organization. The choice of this or that strategy predetermines formation of a relevant patent, licensing, marketing, manufacturing, staff and other types of functional policy in innovational an economic activities.

In this research author looks into formalized knowledge. As knowledge is the basis of innovation process it should be new.

2. Methods

Preliminary selection of the most effective innovations can be conducted on the basis of innovation behavior evaluation (Trifilova A.A., 2003). Such approach allows for evaluating the scope of perspective reserves appearing as a result of mastering innovations. There are many features according to which we can classify reserves as the source of economic growth. For example depending on the mobilization period we can point out current and perspective reserves and on the basis of their source – external and internal. Current reserves can be mobilized in the nearest planned period and they usually do not require substantial costs. On the contrary perspective reserves need considerable financial support as they are related to reconstruction and broadening of production processes. External reserves sources can be macroeconomic (features of state financial, tax and customs systems functioning) and microeconomic (regional monetary, climate relations with customers, investment and other terms of economic functioning).

Areas in which internal reserves can be found largely depend on the practice of economic activities organization at the company and are derived from the analysis of principles and results of managing costs, finance, purchases, price, assortment, retail net, personnel, investments and innovations. In modern economics development reserves of the company can be activated by the following internal and external sources of generating new knowledge:

- intensification of information exchange between organization and external environment, internal units and staff, including those in research sphere;
- more complete knowledge and diverse use of research and development products;

- experience and latent knowledge of staff members in the field of research, technology, organization, management, production, sales, academic and other spheres;
- review of labor division principles, including introduction of innovative production technologies, latest technical developments and computer infrastructure;
- selection of effective innovative projects, offer of unique or new services and improved products, etc. (Korobeinikov I.O., 2000).

Evaluation of implementing new knowledge generation results at the stage of forming economic activities strategic policy defines potential reserves appearing due to the introduction of new and improved technologies and answers the question concerning possible changes of external cooperation terms with competitors, consumers, strategic partners, suppliers, shareholders and creditors as the result of innovation commercialization (Makarova I.A., 2012).

Innovation ideas are presented in a form of innovation projects and are evaluated based on the ratio between investment costs and further economic results. Evaluation of innovation projects efficacy is a central point in the process of forming innovation strategy management (Popov V.M., Lyapunov S. I., 2007).

A starting point for defining investment efficacy for development and implementation of new technologies can be project evaluation in general or evaluation of its social significance (Popov V.M., Lyapunov S. I., 2007). Such sequence of new knowledge evaluation is usually used for the analysis of large scale innovation projects of federal significance. Depending on aims and scope of investments evaluation covers ecological, social, budget and regional efficacy.

For innovation projects of local importance evaluation usually covers efficacy analysis for individual investors and expected financial flows are evaluated according to commercial profit. In that case according to existing practice such indicators as pure discount profit and profit index, internal profit rate and discount term are calculated. Net present value (NPV), profitability index (PI), internal rate of return (IRR), discounted return index (T_{OK}).

These indicators are well known and their calculation is widely presented in literature (Popov V.M., Lyapunov S. I., 2007) (see Table 1).

Table 1: Overall scheme of evaluating project participation efficacy

Efficacy indicator	Calculation formula
NPV is a difference between the sum of current effects for calculation period led to basis period and discounted investment sum	$NPV = \sum_{t=0}^{T} (P_t - C_t) \times a_t$ IRR > 0
PI is a balance of presented effects sum to the sum of discounted capital investments for the same moment.	$PI = \sum_{t=0}^{T} (P_t - C_t) \times a_t / C_u$ PI > 1
IRR is the discount norm (EDD), at which the sums of effects led to a basic time moment equals capital investment amount for the same time period	$\sum_{t=0}^{T} \frac{P_t - C_t^+}{(1+E)^t} = \sum_{t=0}^{T} \frac{K_t}{(1+E)^t}$
Тoк defines the period during which cumulative sum of financial inflows equals discounted investment sum C.	$T_{ок} = \frac{C_u}{P_s}$

Where:
i – the number of step in the calculation horizon T, years;
E – discount norm (capital efficacy coefficient) equaling income per capital % acceptable for the investor;
R_t – results achieved at t-step of calculation in rubles:
$З_t$ - costs;
$К_t$ – capital investment.

If new investment meets requirements of commercial evaluation of investment efficacy processes of new technology design and implementation should be analyzed from the point of view of internal economic opportunities of the company. One must make quantitative evaluation of costs and understand if it is possible to implement innovation objectives using resources of separate functional units at a certain company considering or its individual development characteristics. In order to do so we can use innovation perceptiveness and implementation probability indicators for real economic conditions. The final stage of innovation project efficacy can include multi-dimension analysis of obtained qualitative characteristics in order to choose the most perspective options of new technologies or products for financing.

3. Results

Let us look at the stages of innovation project selection on the example of telecommunication company growth project.

At the stage of preliminary selection four projects were chosen.

1. Project: broadening the range of internet services using individual channels (the first project).
   Individual channel Internet connection is a priority for clients as it provides Internet access with high quality and minimal time lag. Individual Internet access allows for solving such tasks as information host network access, connecting local workstations to the Internet the use of World Wide Web (WWW) servers, email exchange and creation of own post server in the Internet. Permanent access allows for unlimited work of all corporate network stations in the Internet. Besides permanent access to the Internet you can order other services, such as provision and registration of IP addresses set, domain registration, database, e-mail. Project implementation allows for larger number of potential users.
2. Project: broadening telephone connection network (the second project).
   Telephone connection in its different forms is a technological basis for all modern business communication. Quality and costs of telephone connection is significant for success of any progressive company. Most of the companies with more than 5 staff members and more than one external phone number must manage telephone connections in the office. Such tasks as call transfer, additional numbers, intellectual answering machine (autosecretary) and others are successfully solved by installing office telephone stations. Implementation of the project would allow for broadening the client base and obtaining more profit.
3. Project: broadening the range of Wi-Fi services (third project).
   Wireless technology Wi-Fi has stable demand among customers. Virtually all modern equipment used by businessmen has necessary options for working with the Internet via Wi-Fi access. Project implementation would allow for broadening the area of Wi-Fi coverage, attract new clients and improve company competitiveness.
4. Project on broadening the range of hosting services (the fourth project).
   Hosting is a service of providing calculating capacity for physical placement of information at the server with permanent access to the Internet. The term hosting is also used to name the service of placing client's equipment at provider's premises, providing access to high speed channels.

Complex efficacy evaluation for business development with the use of new technologies should start from defining innovation project costs.

In order to calculate these costs one must define the sum of innovation costs and group them according to relevant expenses.

Investment costs and basic financial results on innovation project should be structured according to legislative basics of company activities.

All costs related to company growth can be subdivided into:

- financial costs;
- salary;
- amortization;
- other costs.

Financial costs usually include costs for purchasing raw materials and spare parts. They also cover purchase of water, fuel, power and all other technology – related costs, as well as costs for production services rendered by external organizations.

Costs related to salary include all payments to all employees involved in the project.

The next important element in the project cost structure is amortization of laboratory and production equipment and intangible assets.

Initial cost of amortization intangible assets is defined by the sum of purchase price and cost of maintenance necessary for its exploitation. The price of intangible assets created by organization itself is defined by the sum of factual costs of their generation and production, including financial costs on labor payment; external organization services; patent and license costs.

When forming innovation project costs the sum of amortization on main funds and intangible objects should include the size of costs in the reported period.

The forth and the last innovation project cost type is "other costs" category. It covers taxes and other similar payments.

The sum of all four cost categories allows for calculating company costs of an innovation project, that is evaluate the price of broadening innovation activities.
Project costs are grouped according to cost categories (see Table 2).

Table 2: Costs of projects on broadening the range of activities

Cost category	Project costs (thousand rubles)			
	First project	Second project	Third project	Fourth project
1	2	3	4	5
1. material costs	91,2	573,6	60,8	3275,69
2. labor costs	476,4	216	476,4	736,8
3. amortization	18,243	114,73	12,16	655,14
4. other costs	152,45	69,12	150,8	235,78
total	733,08	973,45	700,16	4 466,64

NPV, PI, IRR, cost return period serve as project efficacy criteria.
NPV reflects suggested evaluation of company economic potrntial change as a result of a project. This criteria has additivity criteria thst is NPV of diferent projectscan besummed up in order to define the overall effect. PI criterion shows return per cost unit: this is a go to criteria when it comes to structuring independent projects for creating an optimal portfolio in case of limited overall investment amount. This criterion shows maximum level of costs which can be associated with this project. That is if the price of capital attracted for project financing is larger that IRR, the project shoukd be turned down. Criterion $T_{ок}$ demonstrates the number of basic periods in which investments will be compensated by financial returns from the project.
On the basis of commercial efficacy evaluation one cn make conclusions concerning eceonomic attractiveness of project under consideration (see Table 3).

Table 3: Overall project efficacy evaluation

Economic analysis indicators	Calculations for each project			
	First project	Second project	Fourth project	Third project
1	2	3	4	5
Pure discounted profit	-80,89	12 461,91	1 441,28	1 584,9
Profitability index	0,113	4,459	3,513	27,07
Internal profitability norm	profit	76,86	10,77	318,5
Investment return period	No profit	1,4	1,6	1
Preliminary project rating position according to NPV	4	1	3	2

From Table 3 we can see rating evaluation of project efficacy for each project.

The first project is the least effective, will not reach break - even point and will incur losses. According to efficacy indicators second and third projects are the most attractive in terms of NPV, PI, IRR and time to breakeven point.

Implementation of these projects at the given company considering its resources and economic growth perspectives seems the most feasible.

Therefore company development strategy should be based on the basis of the third project.

On the basis of broadening these activities profit will increase significantly, allowing the company work on its further development strategy.

4. Discussion and Conclusions

Therefore we suggest new methodological approach to selection of new knowledge generation results for further implementation. It includes the following stages: company economic opportunities analysis; innovative ideas generation; preliminary innovation selection; presentation of innovation idea in the form of innovation project; innovation project efficacy evaluation from the point of view of investment perspectives; evaluation of innovation project efficacy from company economics point of view; multidimensional analysis of obtained quantitative evaluation with the aim of choosing the most perspective innovation projects.

Theoretical importance of obtained results is in the development of methodological approaches to innovation project selection based on widespread methods of investment design considering peculiar features of innovation development strategy. These methodological approaches can be the basis for designing company activities on new knowledge generation.

Practical importance of obtained results is in increased transparency of activities on new knowledge generation results application in the work of a company by means of improving managerial decisions on developing innovation activities and implementation of innovations.

Acknowledgment

The study was financially supported by the Russian Science Foundation at Udmurt State University (Izhevsk, Russia) project №15-18-00049.

The work was supported by Act 211 Government of the Russian Federation, contract № 02.A03.21.0006.

References

Bell, D. (1973). The Coming of Post-Industrial Society: A Venture of Social Forecasting. N.Y.: Basic Books.
Eggertsson, T. (2001). Economic Behavior and Institutions. M: Business.
Goncharenko L.P. Arutyunov Yu.A. (2011). Innovative policy. Moscow: KNORUS. 350p.
Korobeinikov I.O. (2000). Reserves of development of the enterprises. N. Novgorod: NSU publishing house of N. I. Lobachevsky. 22 p.
Krylov E.I., Vlasov V. M., Zhuravkov I.V. (2003). Analysis of efficiency of investment and innovative activity of the enterprises. M.: Finance and statistics. 419 p.
Makarova I.A. (2012). Mekhanizm of optimization of innovative policy at the enterprise. Modern problems of science and education. No. 3.
Nonaka, I., & Takeuchi, H. (1994). The Knowledge-Creating Company: How Japanese Companies Create the Dynamics of Innovation. Oxford: Oxford University Press.
Popov V.M., Lyapunov S. I. (2007). The analysis of financial decisions in business. Moscow: Knorus, 2007. 240 p.
Schumpeter, J.A. (1952). The Theory of Economics Development. London: George Allen & Unwin.
Soldatov A.A, Tanchuk R. S. (2013). Strategic management and innovative development of the enterprises and firms. Management of economic systems. 2013 . No. 3. Pp. 2-3.
Teece, D.J. (1996). Firm organization, Industrial Structure and Technological Innovation. Journal of Economic Behavior and Organization. 31 (2). 193-224
Trifilova A.A. (2003). Management of innovative development of the enterprise. Moscow: Finance and statistics. 73p.

Innovation Management: A Study of Woman Entrepreneurs in Klang Valley

Lim Ooi Wei[1] and Lee Kean Yew[2]
[1]Assistant Professor, Herriot-Watt University Malaysia Branch
[2]PhD, Asia Europe Institute, University of Malaya
ms.erinlim@gmail.com

Abstract: This paper explores the implementation of innovation management among women entrepreneurs in Klang Valley. The study highlights the issues and challenges faced by women sole proprietors and copreneurs in operating their businesses. The research also describes the differences in how female sole proprietors and copreneurs implement innovation management based on factors such as their business nature and demographic profile. The research adopts a qualitative approach to data analysis due to the small number of respondents. It is an exploratory study based on the analysis from the in-depth interview of eleven respondents who are involved in retail and service industries. The in-depth interviews were carried out in the business premises or homes of the respondents. Some of the respondents also preferred to be interviewed in a more relaxed environment. The interview was conducted face-face for at least an hour based on the semi-structured, open-ended questionnaire. From the analysis of the interview transcripts, prevalent themes that have been identified include entrepreneurial intention, issues and challenges, as well as types of innovation. On top of that, this study explained the difference in the implementation of innovation management among woman entrepreneurs involved in sole proprietorship and copreneurship respectively in Klang Valley.

Keywords: women entrepreneurs, copreneurs, innovation, innovation management, challenges

1. Introduction

Entrepreneurship has been playing a very important role in the economic growth of a country contributing to gross domestic product. Entrepreneurship encourages the economic growth in a region because it is a driving force and decisive factor which provides job creation and contributes to personal development as agreed by Hisrich (1996). Entrepreneurship has been a discussion topic since the eighteenth century. Kuratko & Hodgetts (2007, p.33) mentioned that the analysis of entrepreneurship has been introduced by economists such as Richard Cantillan (1680 – 1734) and Jean Baptiste Say (1803). Entrepreneurship consists of three major key elements which include innovation, proactivity, and risk taking (Miller, 1983).

Innovation was actually derived from a Latin word : "innovate" which means to take something new" (Tidd et al, 2001, p.24). There were many researches done in innovation. Therefore, innovation is an important element in entrepreneurship to maintain worldwide competitiveness for profitable performance in enterprise. However, a system-wide dedication to track exceptional opportunities is required. There are various definitions of innovation. Therefore, innovation is a major field to study in the areas of economics, business, technology, sociology, and engineering. Entrepreneurs consist of male entrepreneurs, copreneurs (husband and wife) and woman entrepreneurs. However, research has been done in foreign countries like United Kingdom, Sri Lanka, Australia and United States of America which showed the importance of women involved in entrepreneurship.

Undoubtedly, women penetrated in many industries such as retail businesses, service industries, science and technology field consisting of prospects which enable women entrepreneurs to excel in the entrepreneurial world and contribute towards employment opportunities in the country. Women entrepreneurs are getting more proactive in the participation of entrepreneurial activity being in a small or large scale industry. It shows the capabilities and ambition of women entrepreneurs for achieving excellent performance in entrepreneurship. From the study conducted by Soyeon Shim abd Eastlick (1998) on Hispanis female entrepreneurs, Ayadurai Selvamalar (2004, p.6) noted that there were ten business problems faced by the female entrepreneurs which include sales and profit forecasting; obtaining lines of credit; capital management; working capital management and gender problems.

Research done on women entrepreneurs on the other hand is limited and is not extensively done in Malaysia. However, judging by the growing number of Malaysian women involving in entrepreneurship, one cannot help but to be drawn into an in-depth study on the challenges and issues faced by Malaysian women entrepreneurs and how they solve these problems by implementing innovation management. There were some examples of successful women entrepreneurs who have inspired and motivated generations of Malaysian women generation, for example, Melinda Looi, Bridget Lai, and Dr. Zaha Rina Zahari. Having said that, women entrepreneur in Malaysia face different challenges and the arguments presented above have created an interesting study.

2. Malaysia Woman Entrepreneurs

In Malaysia, an increasing number of female labour force in various industry displays the important role of women in the economic growth of the country. It has been identified from the summary of statistics of the World Bank that starting form 1991 to 2014, the female labour force increases from 43% to 44.5%. The occupation involved by female employees varied from clerical workers, professionals, legislators, elementary occupations, plant and machine-operators, craft and related trade workers. Besides, it is noticed that the female unemployment rate drops from 3.1% in 1991 to 2.2% in 2014. This scenario also relates to the increased female literacy rate in Malaysia in 2014 compared to 1991. From the Malaysia's gender Gap Index indicates that the female literacy rate has moved from 95.22% to 98.46%.

In line with the realization of vision 2020 that encourages Malaysia to reach a self-sufficient industrial and emphasizes on industrialization, privatization and business-oriented employment among the nation, Normah (2006) noted that 36% of the total employment in small and medium enterprise (SMEs) in 2003 was women. In addition, it is found that Malaysian women have involved the former male-dominated enterprises (Maimunah, 1996a; 1996b). Therefore, women entrepreneurship has become a significant resource in the economic growth of our country.

In view of the above, there has been establishment of organization and policy to develop and assist the growth of women entrepreneurship in Malaysia. For example, Ministry of Entrepreneurial and Cooperative Development (MECD) in 1995, the Ministry of Women Family and Community Development (MWFCD) in 2001, the formulation of National Policy for Women (NPW), Bumiputera Commercial and Industrial Community (BCIC), Federation of Women Entrepreneurs Association Malaysia (FEM), National Association of Women Entrepreneurs of Malaysia (NAWEM), Persatuan Usahawan Wanita Bumiputera (USAHANITA), the Women's Wing of the Malay Chamber of Commerce Malaysia of the State of Selangor and National Council of Women's Organisation (NCWO). It is indicated our government has been supporting the sustainability and development of women entrepreneurship in different ways.

In other studies (Ariffin, 1994; Ong and Sieh, 2003), it is established that Malaysian women entrepreneurs are most likely to be in the service industries, have prior working experience and are small operators that is, with fewer than 20 full-time employees and earning lesser than RM100,000 per annum. Their businesses are mainly funded by personal savings and most are either sole proprietorships or partnerships. More recently, Ndubisi and Kahraman (2005) found that the majority (62%) of Malaysian women entrepreneurs have received tertiary education but only a fraction have explored traditionally male-dominated areas such as transportation and communication.

The data indicates a high survival rate (78.4% have been operational for more than 5 years), however, only 48% display innovative characteristics such as adopting advanced technology in their business operations. The lack of innovativeness appears to be related to typical characteristics of women-owned enterprises, namely their small size and high service-orientation. Ndubisi and Kahraman (2005) suggested that further studies on innovation among Malaysian women entrepreneurs are timely. In particular, it should be determined whether there are additional contributing factors to the women's innovativeness or lack of besides firm's characteristics.

3. Copreneur and Innovation

Entrepreneur is someone who has allocated resources and bore the risks in entrepreneurship but an entrepreneur is not necessarily the innovator and the first creator of the product. Bolton and Thompson (2004) explained that *entreprendre* means 'to undertake', for instance, undertaking a venture or start a new venture. Further, Bolton and Thompson (2004, p.15) mentioned that entrepreneurs means contractors in French language. Apart from the various definition for entrepreneurs, it is agreeable to mention that entrepreneurs could be viewed as risk takers because of their bravery to face challenges and unforeseen circumstances may happen in businesses.

In 1988, Barnett and Barnett (1988) coined the term "copreneurs" are couples who are both romantically and professionally involved, they are responsible and committed couples who own a business together. In fact, research on copreneurship or couple entrepreneurs (Barnett & Barnett, 1998) has been looked into on how family relationship can benefit business. However, according to Neubauer & Lank (1998) :

> *"Family firms who consciously manage the balance between family and business needs are most likely to create and utilize the 'family' advantage."*

There were benefits offered by copreneurship (Thompson, 1990). For instance, copreneurs have a high degree of controls and enhanced work and family's fulfillment. Besides, Marshack (1998) highlighted the advantages of copreneurship. He mentioned that the common goal of copreneurs enables them to improve their professional and marital relationships. This will bring profitability in the copreneurial business. In addition, this will build entrepreneurial strength and courage to their family members, such as their children (Smith, 2000). In addition, in Marshack's (1994) previous examination of dual-career couples and copreneurs, this author concluded that copreneurs had more specific, traditional, and clearly defined roles. Marshack lamented the apparent rigidity of roles although the author observed that this may have been an adaptive response to the reality of such a relationship.

In addition, Peter Drucker (1985) mentioned that innovation is an additional core competency which is required by every organization. However, the innovation aspect applies to all sizes of industries which may be either large companies or small and medium-sized enterprises (SMEs) (Vrakking and Cozijinsen, 1997).

Finally, Johannessen *et al* (2001) identified innovation as newness implication because innovative activity may relate to new products, new services, new organizing methods, new markets venture, new production methods and new sources of supply.
Researcher also relates the conceptual relationship between entrepreneurship and innovation. The researcher, Sundbo (1998) has identified the basic theories of the economics innovation and three competing paradigms for current theoretical discussion of innovation: the entrepreneur paradigm, the technology-economics paradigm and strategic paradigm.

However, the entrepreneur paradigm was attempted by Schumpeter (1934) to create linkage between entrepreneurs and innovation in theory. Schumpeter (1934) viewed entrepreneurs as innovators who contribute to the economic growth of the nation. This is because the researcher views entrepreneurship as a creative act and as an innovation. Moreover, Zhao (2005) addressed innovation as a tool to identify market needs in order to achieve commercial achievement.

4. Challenges Faced and Innovation Barriers

From the literature review researchers have mentioned that there were challenges faced by copreneurs in business. The challenges consist of administrative restrictions in business as mentioned by Marshack (1998). The allocation of roles and decision making (Rosenberg, 1991) is also an issue because the duties among copreneurs overlapped. Constant monitoring of labors is also required in order to ensure the task was being carried out smoothly.

The constraint of work balance between family and business (Garrett, 1993), and discriminary feelings (Goffee & Scase, 1985) have shown that gender and equality issues arise in copreneurship because the husband is always the leader and decision maker compared to his wife who is a follower in a copreneurial enterprise.
On top of that, copreneurs may neglect personal requirements or desires in the process of copreneurship (Garrett, 1993). All these pressures created from copreneurship form a barrier in couple business venture. Therefore, innovative management process is a way to solve and minimize the tension in copreneurial business.

On the other hand, it is argumentative to confirm whether couple similarity in personal characteristics determines the professional relationship quality of copreneurs in business even if researchers (Nemecheck & Olson, 1999) mentioned that the function of personality similarity in marital excellence as a consequence of associate mate was well known.

Freel (2000) highlighted four major resource constraints which resulted as innovation barriers : Finance; Management and Marketing; Skilled Labour; and Information. From the literature of small firms, the most popular innovation barriers are the difficulties in assessing financial support. However, in recent literature, high technology small firms also suffered from this problem, Oakey (1997, pp.20-21) concludes that '... all... concerns are directly or indirectly influenced by shortages of capital.' Moreover, according to Oakey (1997) has also pointed out that small firms have difficulty to recruit, train and retain qualified and experienced staff such as managers.

Besides, because of the problems in management and marketing, small firms will have difficulty in recruiting skilled labour to implement existing technology in the organization. (Freel, 2000). Therefore, Freel (2000) feels that small firms are unable to obtain information due to the high costs involved. The above mentioned constraints will highly affect the effectiveness in the implementation of innovation in enterprise.

5. Study Framework and Methodology

Owing to the constraints in getting respondents, exploratory approach is more preferable in this study. According to Blumer (1969), he explained clearly the purpose of an exploratory investigation. : -

> *The purpose of an exploratory investigation is to move toward a clearer understanding of how one's problem is to be posed, to learn what are the appropriate data, to develop ideas of what are significant lines of relation and to evolve one's conceptual tools in the light of what one is about the area of life. (Blumer, 1969, p. 40)*

Therefore, qualitative research is recommended to carry out in this study by using in-depth interview approach to find out the inner experience from the respondents. The rationale of this approach is for the researcher to understand the personal experience of the respondents in innovation management regarding the research objectives of this study. Mason (2002, p.1) mentioned qualitative research is important, inspiring and exciting because researcher will be engaged with things that matter, in ways that matter. Qualitative research is capable to produce "the general picture" of how things actually work. The author explained one can explore the experiences and opinions of research participants/respondents. In addition, Mason (2002, p.3) further identified qualitative research as a method of data generation from the collected data which is flexible and sensitive to the social context.

Moreover, Eileen and Mary (2001, p.257) have highlighted that qualitative research has to be used properly in giving us rich and in-depth information than any other methods. In this chapter, researcher will describe in detail about the research design, data gathering methods, descriptions of the interviewees, themes of the interviews obtained and analysis techniques of the qualitative data in this study.
One of the most commonly recognized forms of qualitative research method according to Mason is interview (Mason, 2002, p.63). It helps the researcher to approach the inner questions in different angle in order to obtain sufficient information from the respondents. (Jennifer, 2002, p.66). However qualitative interview requires a lot of planning. A set of semi-structured interview questions has been prepared in order to carry out a purposeful interview.

The purpose of the interviews is to understand the issues or challenges faced by the woman entrepreneurs among the sole proprietors and copreneurs. From the interview, the researcher is required to identify the difference of how woman entrepreneurs to solve the problems/challenges which they faced in the enterprise when they involve either in sole proprietorship or copreneurship in relation to innovation management.

The 'open-ended questionaire' was designed according to the women entrepreneurs' involvement in sole proprietorship and copreneurship respectively. The interview questions is only a guideline for the researcher to follow in order to relate to the research objectives because the questions was changed according to respondents' business nature and background. However, the interview questions have been set according to the research questions of this study. The category of the questions are based on the tables as shown below: duration of business, reason of choosing the business category, challenges that they face and how do they solve the challenges. Finally, we also asked the preference of the woman entrepreneurs involvement in sole proprietorship and in copreneurship respectively.
Research questions in this study:-

1. What is the different issues faced by woman sole proprietors and copreneurs ?
2. How do woman sole proprietors solve the issues faced by them as compared to being copreneurs ?
3. What are the differences in innovation management process between woman sole proprietors and copreneurs?

Table 1

Question Category	Sample Questions	
	Sole Proprietor	**Copreneurs**
Entrepreneurial Intention	*Why do you want be a sole proprietor ?/ Why do you first become self-employed ?*	*What is your main aim/objective that you want to start your business as a couple business ?*
Duration of business	*How long your business started ?*	
Reason of choosing the business category	*Why do you choose this business nature ? Because of interest or is your expertise ?*	
How to solve challenges	*How do you solve issues/problems that you face in your business ?*	
Innovation management in business	*Do you forsee any problems if you start innovation in your business ?*	
	How do you differentiate your business with other competitor in the same field ?	
	What are the new ideas/innovation you have carried out in your business ?	

6. Results Discussion

6.1 Summary of the profiles

The summary of the demographic profile of respondents are shown in Table 2 which presents the age, educational background, ethnic group, marital status, tenure in business and industry involved of the respondents. The in-depth interviews were conducted in Klang Valley. There were fifteen (15) prospective respondents targeted, coming from various industry backgrounds. However, emphasis was given to the service and retail industry because of easy accessibility. Three (3) of the prospective respondents had declined the invitation for personal interview due to confidentiality. They did not want to reveal relevant business information to the researcher. Therefore, a total of twelve (12) respondents are involved in the in-depth interview. However, one respondent of the interview had to be removed because she was sleeping partner in the copreneurship. Therefore only remaining eleven (11) respondents are participated in the in-depth interviews for this study.

The respondents were interviewed face to face either in their business premises or at restaurants. Their ages range from late twenties to early sixties. All of the respondents had been employed before they started their own business. Additionally, the age range of the respondents indicated they might have some financial means to start a business on their own. Moreover, the age criteria also ensured that the respondents were mature and independent in dealing with challenges in their business. Most of the respondents were aged between 30 to 33 years old. However, 4 out of the 11 respondents were aged between 50 to 60 years old. There was only one respondent at the retirement age of 60 years old. Apart from that, when we looked into the educational background of the eleven (11) respondents, we found that the number of degree holders and secondary school leavers were equivalent. There was only one primary level respondent (respondent G). Therefore, it could be concluded that women entrepreneurs were more educated now compared to the previous research whereby they were only involved in home-based industry.

The majority of the respondents were Chinese women entrepreneurs who made up seven (7) respondents. This was followed by three (3) Malay women entrepreneurs and one Indian woman entrepreneur who participated in the personal interview.

In terms of marital status, four out of eleven respondents were single while the other seven (7) were married. There was only a couple who involved in service industry.

For the tenure in business, there were five out of eleven respondents (41.8%) who are involved in their businesses for less than 5 years. There was one couple who were in their business for the past ten months.

There were four (4) women entrepreneurs who had been in business for more than 5 years, ranging from 7 years to 20 years.

The respondents were involved in retail and service industry. The ratio of the industry involved by women entrepreneurs in retail and service industry were almost equivalent. 5 out of 11 respondents were involved in service industry whereas 6 out of 11 respondents were involved in retail industry respectively. The retail industry consists mainly of accessories, car accessories, food and beverage, bakery and fruits. As for the service industry, these respondents were involved in services such as dental, hair saloon, traveling, dancing and clinic.

Table 2: Demographic Profile of Respondents

Case	Age/ Sex	Education back ground	Marital Status	Business Nature/ activity	Duration of business	Number of employees	Location	Category	Date
A	29/ F	Secondary	Married with 2 daughters	Accessories (copreneur)	4 years	6	Kuala Lumpur	Retail	27-1-2009
B	22/ F	Degree	Single	Travel agent (sole proprietor)	2 years	N/A	Klang Valley	Service	1-2-2009
C	33/F 33/M	Degree	Married with a son	Clinic (copreneur)	10 months	2	Petaling Jaya	Service	11-2-2009
D	30/M3 1/F	Degree	Married (no children)	Dental Clinic (copreneur)	2 years	2	Cheras	Service	10-2-2009
E	32/F	Secondary	Single	Hair Saloon (sole proprietor)	4 years	1	Cheras	Service	6-2-2009
F	50/F	Degree	Single	Dance Academy (sole proprietor)	7 years	3	Cheras	Service	9-2-2009
G	60/F	Primary	Married with 2 children	Food stall (sole proprietor)	12 years	None	Kepong	Retail	20-6-2009
H	32/F	Degree	Single	Bakery (sole proprietor)	2 years	2	Pantai Hill Park	Retail	8-3-2009
I	Early 30's	Secondary	Married with 4 children	Coffee shop (copreneur)	1.5 years	None	Kepong	Retail	20-6-2009
J	53/F	Secondary	Married with 5 children	Fruit seller (shop) (sole proprietor)	20 years	None	Cheras	Retail	10-7-2009
K	53/F	Secondary	Married with a daughter	Spare Part Shop (copreneur)	20 years	8	Ampang	Retail	22-7-2009

7. Entrepreneurial Intention

From the interview conducted on the eleven respondents, it was identified that women entrepreneurs have various intention to be involved in entrepreneurship. By comparing women entrepreneurs who involved in sole proprietorship and copreneurship, the intentions varied. Generating income/finances was still the major factor for women to be involved in entrepreneurship. There were 9 out of the 11 respondents who considered this factor as the major reason because they want to provide financial support to the family. The respondents mentioned their entrepreneurial intention as follows:-

Respondent A: "To get more income basically."

Respondent B: "I want something I am satisfied. I am aiming RM10k per month. I can earn more than I was working for people".

Respondent C: "To have better income and can contribute knowledge we have learned. I can look after my son who is 1 year plus only. I also can take care of my family."

Respondent E: "Better time management and more free time. Do not need to report to superior and also can earn more income."

Respondent G: "To earn income for my family. It's more flexible working hours. More freedom."

Respondent H: "I want to make decision and I want to earn money."

Respondent I: "To earn a living. Before this, my husband was a driver. The salary is not enough to cover the expenses for the family. I was a housewife and we have four children. That's why my husband decided to start the business."

Respondent J: "To earn income and as a source of financial support to my family. I started because my application for shop (government) was successful. At that time, I already have two children and I was working as a clerk. So, I thought it's time for me to start my own business and at the same time, I can look after my children. Moreover, my husband failed in his partnership business."

Respondent K: "To be independent and earn money."

On the other hand, respondent D explained: "Because we are in the same field and we can work together." Respondent F stated, "Initially, it was my retirement plan. I would like to do something which is not so stressful and I love dancing."

In view of the above, we conclude that the entrepreneurial intentions of the women entrepreneurs was different and it was affected by demographic factors. For example, if the women entrepreneurs were degree holders, they tend to have similar careers and expertise as their spouses. Therefore, most of them would tend to involve in decision making such as case C and D who were degree holders. However, if women entrepreneurs have moderate education level and they were married, majority of them will be the follower in decision making when dealing with entrepreneurial intention. They are playing a role as support for their spouse. So, they tend to be agreeable to their business partner or spouse for example, women entrepreneur in case A and she will normally follow what has been decided by her husband.

From the entrepreneurial intention which the women entrepreneurs have mentioned during the in-depth interview, we may highlight that it reveals personal characteristics/personality among women entrepreneurs involve in sole proprietorship and copreneurship. For sole proprietors, it is noticed that most of the respondents are very individualistic. They have their own thinking and are independent and firm decision makers. It is also found that women entrepreneurs are creative because they want to try something new and they want to be decision makers. Moreover, from their conversation, it reveals that they are risk takers. According to Respondent B : "It's for me to work for myself. I am so confident that I don't need someone to work together with me. I have just resigned from my current job." Respondent J also mentioned : " I'll settle problems on my own." "I do not need to report to any superior," as stated by respondent E. Besides, respondent F and G also revealed that by venturing into entrepreneurship, it provides working opportunity after their retirement age.

8. Types of Innovations Involved

Based on the interview of respondents, it is discovered that most of the respondents were mainly involved in product innovation compared to other types of innovation. From the 11 respondents who have been interviewed, there was only one case involved in market innovation (case A) who started new branches for their business.

Respondent A: *"To venture into new market. For example, to start a new branch in Mid Valley. We also participated in Genting Highland's sales carnival. Lack of staff. Need to stay in Genting Highlands for a few days."*

On the other hand, product and/or service innovation was more popular among the respondents involved in either sole proprietorship or copreneurship. There were 10 of 11 respondents who applied product/service innovation in their business.

Respondent B : *"I plan to expand network besides Klang valley like Terengganu and Johor Bahru. I will make trips to Indonesia as well. My mother who used to travel to Indonesia, may be I can ask her to work for the hotels. I will also get information from exhibition. I will build network first. In addition, I would like to develop website for other company."*

Respondent C: *"Offer comprehensive package medical checkup package for the patients. We will tailor the package according to customers' request."*

Respondent D: *"Providing music by giving earphone to them when they are having dental treatment. So, patient will be more relax."*

Respondent E: *"To have some promotion package during festive season. Design hair style according to customers' taste."*

Respondent F: *"To conduct more exam-oriented dancing lessons for children. Two UK examinatiosn in a year."*

Respondent G: *"To cook at different way to provide good quality of food. To buy better equipment to cook. To save time. Provide more variety of food because all my customers are regular customers."*

Respondent H: *"The price is cheaper and the size of the buns are bigger. Then, the ingredient of the buns are also different from others. For example, I put vegetables on the mini pizzas."*

Respondent I: *"To prepare variety of food for customers' choice. My wife cook different menu everyday."*

Respondent J: *"To sell more products besides fruits. For example, provide coconut milk and selling sweet potatoes. I also fried banana crackles for selling."*

Respondent K: *"Our salesmen will implement sales or promotion for the regular customers."*

On top of that, some of the woman entrepreneurs are also involved in administrative innovation of which most of them are not aware. Based on the in-depth interview conducted, it is found that respondents in case D, E and I, respectively also implemented administrative innovation in their enterprise. The following responses are indicated by the respondents:-

Respondent E: *"Since there are only two workers in my saloon. My business is based on appointment. This will ease the crowd waiting for their turn in my saloon." I do not dare to take off in the beginning of the business. After 1 year plus, business become stable, I will be off on Thursdays."*

Respondent D: *"We did not have off day in the beginning of the business for a year. Now, we are off on every Wednesdays."*
Respondent I: *"I sell fruits in bulks. So, my fruits can be sold out faster."*

Finally, it is concluded that innovation management has been implemented by woman entrepreneurs in order to carry out their enterprise smoothly. However, from the interview conducted, the respondents revealed that they are not aware they have applied innovation in their enterprise. Majority of the respondents indicated that the resources determine whether they have to implement innovation in their business. Therefore, it is suggested that awareness has to be created for better knowledge regarding innovation management for their success.

From the various innovation management that have been implemented by woman entrepreneurs as indicated above, it is concluded that the type of innovation management applied depends on various factors such as business nature and demographic profile among women entrepreneurs.

9. Issues and challenges faced by Woman Entrepreneurs

Based on the content analysis from the personal interview, it is obvious that women entrepreneurs face issues and challenges in their enterprise which are quite similar to the previous researches mentioned such as financial, balance between work and family, gender issues, delegation of responsibilities among copreneurs and cultural issues. Most of the woman entrepreneurs in sole proprietorship faced staff problems because they need to depend on staff for assistance. However, they always face difficulty in recruiting suitable workers in their enterprise. For instance, the following are responses from the in-depth interview from sole proprietors:-

Respondent E shared her problem, *"First, will be staff recruitment problem. Because applicants will tend to prefer work in shopping complexes. The location here is housing area. So, a lot of applicants refuse to work here. The applicants also ask for salary and benefits through telephone interview. Some of them even tried the first time working but missing on the next day."*

Respondent G mentioned, *"If the business is not good, still have to pay staff's salary. So, I decide not to hire staff."*

In case F, respondent F stated that, *"Instructor problems. Very difficult to get fulltime instructors. I will have to relief the class once the instructor is absent."*

Respondent H replied, *"Problems from staff starting from the beginning because I have to handle everything, baking and delivery when my staff are new and not competent in baking."*

Besides, women entrepreneurs from copreneurship also faced staff problems in their enterprise which affects innovation management processes implemented in the business, for example, in case I, the main staff who handled cooking and menu left because of failure in salary negotiation. Ultimately, respondent I needs to become cook to in-charge of the menu for the coffee shop. She mentioned, " *Staff problems. It's difficult to get loyal and committed staff. That is why I join my husband in this business. The staff requested higher pay and refused to continue when we could not raise his pay."*

In addition, respondent K also mentioned that, *"We were disappointed that the staff who worked very long for us, end up cheating the company." Even if he is our relative who worked for us. They also betrayed us."*

From the feedback we gather from the respondents, it is found that more than 50%, 6 out of 11 respondents faced challenges dealing with staff. There was only one exceptional case because respondent C's husband informed that, *"The staff report to my wife directly. Of course, they will listen to my instruction too when dealing with official tasks. I served staff as friend and family. I gave them a treat when my wife and I invited them for Hari Raya Buka Puasa dinner in hotel. I believe if we treat the employees well, they will be motivated and dedicated in their work."*

On top of that, respondents also faced challenges other than staff problems.

There were 2 out of 11 respondents facing financial problems in the business. Respondent J faced financial problems in her starting phase of the business. She shared her experience , *"I faced financial problem at the beginning. However, my father gave me a helping hand. Then, my business can cover the cost and become profitable."* Additionally, the following are the responses from the interviewees who face financial problem :-
Respondent H : *"I need to expand my business. So, I need more capital. The major issue is looking for strategic location for my bakery which I need to consider time and petrol consumption for delivery purpose. I have applied for capital from PNB. Still waiting for approval."*

Moreover, women entrepreneurship involved in copreneurship also consider financial as an important factor to be concerned before they venture into copreneurship. This is because they require to ensure the daily expenses can be covered in their business. From the interview, we observed that some of the couples did not participate in the business as they need to make sure at least one of them has a permanent job. Normally, either, husband or wife will venture and start the business. After the business was stable and income had been generated then only both of them involve into the enterprise totally. We will observe the following responses from the women entrepreneurs in case A, C, D and K.

Respondent A: *"To ensure income cover expenses."*
Respondent C: *"Our business is still new. My husband is still working in a private hospital. I am the one who is fully in-charged of the clinic."*
Respondent D: *"To start business gradually. First, by my husband. He resigned from his job. Then only I join in. We need to consider the expenses and our income situation."*
Respondent K: *"We have to make sure that the all cost is sufficient to cover whatever expenses incurred."*

On the other hand, woman entrepreneurs also face gender issues in their enterprise. From the interview conducted among the respondents, it is concluded that women involved in sole proprietorship will face these issues very often. Below are feedback from the respondents in case B, E, H and J :-

Respondent B: *"I face with people who said I am young. Not trust me that I am able to do the task."*.
Respondent E: *"I will also face some difficult customers whereby they like to talk nonsense but I just ignore and do the service requested by them such as doing hair-cut, hair wash etc."*

Respondent H: "One more thing is chasing payment from the buyer. Normally, there will be verbal consent between us to collect payment after two months. There is no agreement to be set because we are still small business."
Respondent J: *"It may happen, difficult collection from the new buyers. Just talk to them, if they couldn't pay, I could not do much as well."*

In some certain circumstances, women entrepreneurs also faced different customers. Case E can be related to cultural issue. For instance, respondent E shared her experience when she needs to deal with different ethnic groups of customers. *"As for Malay lady customers, due to the culture, they will only cut their hair when no male customers are around."*

As for respondent F, she mentioned that: *"People copy or imitate what I am doing."* In addition, she also highlighted that as a sole proprietor, she is highly committed and dedicated to the company. However, she faced difficulty when she needs to attend conference or seminar in overseas to upgrade herself in dancing. She added: " *Facing problem to find relief for my classes once I need to attend conference in overseas."*

Respondent G faced varied problem. She mentioned:

> *"The price for ingredients of the food keep on increasing. However, I can't simply raise the food price. Customers are not willing to pay. So, I have little profit margin."*

On the other hand, for copreneurs in case C, they did not face much problems at the moment because they have just started their business lees than a year. Respondent C: *"We are glad we don't face much problem for the time being because we directly bought over the clinic. Everything is ready." But she* confided that to cure a patient is the biggest challenge to her at the moment. She stated: "*"Basically, the biggest challenge is to cure patients and win their hearts."*

However, it is noticed that respondent A who is involved in copreneurship revealed that different work styles and opinion will cause conflict between couples and will indirectly affect their marital relationship. She mentioned *"If it is not for profit, couple working together is not a good idea because most of the time argument will be created because of different opinions. It will affect our emotion and family relationship."*

Allocation of duty and responsibilities among women entrepreneurs in sole proprietorship and copreneurship also indicates different aspects. As for copreneurs in case D, respondent D's husband highlighted that he felt burdened when most of the responsibilities cross boundries and he needs to do it for his wife as he mentioned, : *"Sometimes, I feel very tired because if too many customers, my wife will pass her customers to me, so that the customers do not need to wait ."*

As a result, women entrepreneurs faced various challenges and issues in sole proprietorship and copreneurship respectively. It is noted that there were different issues faced by them in their enterprise depend on various business nature. However, women entrepreneurs managed to handle all issues by using innovation management creatively in their enterprise based on their experience.

10. Solutions Implemented by Women Entrepreneurs in Innovation Management

Based on the responses from the interviewed women entrepreneurs, it was noticed that women entrepreneurs face different problems and issues in their business depending on diverse business nature. However, they have implemented their own solutions to solve problems they faced. For instance, when the sole proprietor in case E faced staff problems in the salon industry, she would have to find other alternative to recruit staff and she revealed: *"For recruitment, I have to recruit other races such as Sabahan in order to get help in my business. By recruiting other races of staff, it can solve communication problem for multi-racial customers."* However, respondent G decided not to recruit staff to avoid additional expenses to her business because she explained: *"If the business is not good, still have to pay the staff's salary."* She needs to be multitasking in her business.

Respondent F found another way to solve instructor's issues in her dancing studio as she mentioned : *" Recruiting students according to the number of instructors. Train the students become instructor as well."* Besides, respondent H solved the staff problems in bakery by training the staff to be competent in bakery and she concentrate in marketing as she raised: *"I will be in-charge of marketing and delivery. I have trained my two staff to do bakery,"*

However, for respondents in case I and K, the copreneurs experienced staff problems when they had to depend on the major staff in their businesses. It revealed that copreneurs would ask their couple take over the responsibilities. Respondent I decided to assist her husband in their coffee shop : *"That's why I join my husband in this business."* Respondent K mentioned that : *" My wife will in-charge all clients' accounts and company's financial matters and the staff will handle marketing only."* As for respondents K who has dishonest staff, they solved the problem by delegating the important and major responsibilities to their spouses.
On the other hand, for women entrepreneurs who faced financial problems in their business such as respondent J, she obtained financial aid from her father : *" My father gave me a helping hand."* It is noticed that there is only one respondent in case H was aware of seeking financial aid from the government such as PNB.

From four out of eleven respondents, it is found that copreneurs would participate in copreneurship gradually to ensure financial stability in the family. For instance, respondent D revealed: *"First, my husband. He resigned from his job. Then only I join in. We need to consider the expenses and our income situation."*

From the feedback of respondents who faced gender issues especially women entrepreneurs among sole proprietors are required to face the challenge positively. Respondent B mentioned; *" Sometimes, it's good to have problems. At least I can learn to solve the problems. I faced with people who said I am young. Not trust me that I am able to do the task. After a while, I will show them I can do it."* Therefore, respondent B would show results to prove her ability in the business.

In addition, respondent E choose to tolerate when she faced difficult customers by not replying the irrelevant questions stated by the customers. However, respondent H and J who faced problems in payment collection have tried very hard to build a good relationship by informing the buyers in order to collect the payment on time. But respondent J sometimes choose to ignore and she mentioned: *"If they couldn't pay, I could not do much as well."* On the other hand, copreneurs were not facing the stated issues compared to sole proprietors. Sole proprietor in case F was responded that she had difficulties attend international conferences because of high commitment to the business. Therefore, she reduced her classes: *"I can only recruit less students and less class will be cancelled once I am in overseas."* Even if respondent F commented that: *"People copy or imitate what I am doing,"* she still keep up and ahead with the change of trend in order for her business to sustain.

For cultural issues faced by respondent E, she revealed that: *"As for Malays customers, they will only cut their hair when no male customers are around."* She will accommodate the customers' needs when she deal with customers form different culture background. Besides, respondent G mentioned that she had little profit margin in her business because the increase of ingredients' price. However, she needs to keep the customers by not raising the price of the food she sold : *"I can't simply raise the food price. Customers are not willing to pay."*

As for copreneurs in case A, the wife commented that : *"Have to give and take. After all, we have the same objectives : to earn a living and support the family,"* even though they have arguments in their business. Copreneurs would solve their conflicts by mutual understanding because they have the same mission and vision in the enterprise. To solve the allocation of duties and responsibilities issues among copreneurs, husband in case D tried to balance the task allocation with his wife. Respondent D added : *" I will be in-charged of hardware matters. Whereas my wife will handle software matters."*

Last but not least, based on the interviews, it is also revealed that the advantages that experienced by the copreneurs which was not enjoyed by women sole proprietors as stated by the following copreneurs:-

Respondent A: *"We trust each other. To work with my wife, I feel more reliable."*
Respondent C: *"Better income. I enjoyed myself. I can take care of my family."*
Respondent D: *"We were more understanding because we know about our work schedule each other. We will discuss and solve the problems together. Most importantly, the mental support that we have in couple business. Financially, we are stronger."*

11. Conclusion

This study demonstrates the differences among women entrepreneurs involved in sole proprietorship and copreneurship based on their implementation on innovation management in enterprise. The implementation of the different types of innovation is based on the issues and challenges arising from sole proprietorship and copreneurship respectively in enterprise. The innovation management process was implemented differently among women entrepreneurs based on the nature of business involved, business structure, demographic profile, family situation and personal characteristics. By comparing the distinction of innovation management carried out by sole proprietors and copreneurs, some family conflicts and relationship issues were revealed. Further, the findings also indicated that product innovation, service innovation and administrative innovation were popular and practised by women entrepreneurs.

12. Contribution of the study

This study is aimed at developing awareness among women entrepreneurs in entrepreneurship which reinforces the importance of innovation management in entrepreneurship. In the meantime, the findings also provide some suggestions which deal with preventive action for practitioners in entrepreneurship. It is therefore a beneficial guideline for women entrepreneurs who intend to be involved in entrepreneurship.

From the challenges faced by the respondents, it is hoped to create awareness among women entrepreneurs in Malaysia in order to encourage them to go through the proper channels to obtain various forms of assistance such as resources, raw material, microfinance, skills and training, technology assistance involved in entrepreneurship. In addition, more training and workshops should be conducted to train woman entrepreneurs in the areas of technological skills and equip themselves with the implementation of innovation management.

It is believed that this study contributed to the innovation theory : entrepreneur paradigm as attempted by Schumpeter (1934) which explained that entrepreneurs are recognized as innovators who contribute to the economic growth of the nation. This element was shown from the feedback of respondents who are innovative in enterprise.

References

Ariffin J (1994). *Readings on Women and Development in Malaysia.* Kuala Lumpur: University of Malaya.

Ayudurai, Selvamalar (2004), *"Profile of Women entrepreneurs in a War-Torn Area : Case Study of North East Sri Lanka, 2005,"* Paper presented at the 50th World Conference of the International Council for Small Business (ICSB), Washington.

Barnett, F. and Barnett, S. (1988), *Working together: entrepreneurial couples.* Berkelry, CA: Ten Speed Press.

Bolton, B. and Thompson, J. (2004). *Entrepreneurs: Talent, temperament, technique (*2nd edn.). Oxford: Elsevier

Bulmer, M. (1969), *"Concepts in the analysis of qualitative data,"* Sociological Review, 27(April), 651 – 677.

Drucker, P.F. (1994), *Innovation and Entrepreneurship: Practice and Principles.* London: Heinemann.

Eileen Kane and Mary O'Reilly-de Brun (2001), *Doing your own research.* London: Marion Boyars Publishers, 256 -276.

Frederick, H., Donald F. Kuratko and Richard Hodgetts (2007). *Entrepreneurship Theory Process Practice* (Asia-Pacific edition). Melbourne: Thomson Learning Australia.

Freel, M. (2000), *"Barriers to Product Innovation in Small Manufacturing Firms,"* International Small Business Journal, 18(60).

Garrett, E.M. (1993), *"And business makes three,"* Small Business Reports, 18(September), 27 – 33.

Goffee, R. & Scase, R. (1985), *Women in charge.* London: George Allen and Unwin.

Hisrich, R.D. and Brush, C.G.(1996), *Entrepreneurship: Starting, Develiopng and Managing a New Enterprise.* Illinois: Irwin.

Johannessen JA, Olsen B, Lumpkin GT (2001). *Innovation as newness: what is new, how new and new to whom?* Euro. J. Innovation Manage. 4(1): 20-31.

Maimunah, I. (1996a). *Gender needs analysis of women entrepreneurs*. Pertanika Journal of Social Science and Humanities, 4(1), 1-9.

Maimunah, I. (1996b). *Usahawan wanita: Satu analisis keperluan dari perspektif gender. Dalam Mazanah Muhamad dan Ezhar Tamam* (eds.). Rakan Kongsi, Komunikasi dan Media dalam Pembangunan. Serdang: Penerbit Universiti Pertanian Malaysia, 55-76.

Marshack, K. (1998), *Entreprenerial couples: Making it work at work and at home.* Palo Alto, CA: Davies-Black Publishing.

Mason, Jennifer (2002), (2nd edition), *Qualitative researching*. London, United Kingdom: SAGE Publications Ltd.

Miller, D. (1983), *"The correlates of entrepreneurship in three types of firms,"* Management Science, 29(July), 770 – 791.

Ndubisi NO, Kahraman C (2005). *Malaysian women entrepreneurs: Understanding the ICT usage behaviours and drivers*. J. Ent. Info. Manage. 18(6): 721-739.

Nemecheck, S. & Olson, K.R. (1999), *"Five-factor personality similarity and marital adjustment,"* Social Behaviour and Personality, 27(March), 309 – 318.

Neubauer, F. & Lank, A.G. (1998). *The family business – Its governance for sustainability.* London: MacMillan Press.

Normah, M. A. (2006). SMEs: *Building blocks for economic growth*. Paper presented at the National Statistical Conference, Kuala Lumpur.

Oakey, R. (1997), *A Review of Policy and Practice Relating to High-technology Small Firms in the United Kingdom,* WP 359, University of Manchester, 20 – 21.

Ong FS, Sieh LML (2003). Women Managers in the New Millenium: Growth Strategies. In Roziah Omar, Azizah Hamzah. *Women in Malaysia Breaking Boundaries*. Kuala Lumpur: Utusan.

Schumpeter, J. A. (1934). *The Theory of Economic Development.* Cambridge, MA: Harvard University Press.

Shim, Soyeon (1998), *"Characteristics of Hispanic female business owners. An exploratory study,"* Journal of Small Business Management, 36(March).

Smith, C.R. (2000), *"Managing work and family in small 'copreneurial' business: an Australian study,* Women in Management Review, 15(May), 283 – 289.

Sundbo J (1998). *The Theory of Innovation: Entrepreneurs, Technology and Strategy.* Northampton, MA: Edward Elgar.

Thompson, K.D. (1990), *"Married... with business,"* Black enterprise, 20(September), 46 – 52.

Tidd, J. (2001) *Innovation management in context: environment, organization and performance.* International Journal of Management Review, 3(3), 169–83.

Vrakking, W.J., and Cozijnsen, A.J. (1997), "Monitoring the quality of innovation processes and innovation successes," in Hassey, D.E. (ed.), *The Innovation Challenge,* Chichester: John Wiley & Sons, 25 – 49.

Zhao F (2005). *Exploring synergy between entrepreneurship and innovation.* Int. J. Ent. Behav. Res. 11(1): 25-41.

A Longitudinal Study Measuring Agropreneurship Behaviours Using Entrepreneurial Ladder Concept

Asliza Yusoff, Noor Hazlina Ahmad and Hasliza Abdul Halim
Universiti Sains Malaysia, Penang, Malaysia
asliza.uz@gmail.com
hazlina@usm.my
haslizahalim@usm.my

Abstract: Drawing on a well-established intention model, the present study focuses on the six-month longitudinal effect of factors in the Theory of Planned Behaviour on agropreneurial intentions and actual agropreneurship behaviours among 239 Gen Y agricultural students from six Malaysian public higher education institutions. This study conceptualised agropreneurship behaviour as a ladder to establish a firm that consists of five important steps which are gathering marketing information, estimating potential profits, finishing the groundwork for product or services, developing the company structure, and setting up business operations. The data gathered were analysed using partial-least squares-based structural equation modelling (PLS-SEM). The results showed that the model substantially explained agropreneurship behaviours among Gen Y students and thus confirmed the applicability of TPB in explaining individuals' intentions and behaviours in a developing country and across cultural context. The results also indicate that the Malaysian Gen Y's intention to become self-employed in the agriculture sector were successfully realized into subsequent behavioural actions within a six-month period. This study contributes methodologically via the application of a longitudinal research design to fill the gap in the existing local cross-sectional agropreneurship studies. It also contributes to the practice by showing that the Malaysian Government's indication to ensure graduate employability which is six months after graduation is practical. Hence, the Government, policy makers, and also university administrators could enhance the Gen Y's intention for agropreneurship by offering appropriate agropreneurial support to enhance their intentions in becoming successful players in the agropreneurship market.

Keywords: Entrepreneurial intentions, Entrepreneurial behaviours, Entrepreneurial ladder, Agropreneurship, Malaysia, Gen Y

1. Introduction

Entrepreneurship, the utmost source for economic growth and competitiveness, has captured the eyes of both scholars and policy makers in past decades. One of the entrepreneurship areas that has developed the interests of many parties is entrepreneurship in the agriculture sector or agropreneurship. Based on previous agropreneurship definition, agropreneurship involves activities of producing, distributing, and marketing of agricultural products to generate income and contribute to a sustainable community (Azer et al., 2014, Nagalakshmi and Sudhakar, 2013).

In Malaysia, agriculture is known as the third pillar of the country's economy after the service and manufacturing sectors (Selamat and Nasir, 2013). The agriculture sector plays a significant role in contributing to the country's economic development by contributing to the supplies of food, job opportunities for the people, earnings from export, and has also become major suppliers for agro-based industries (Siwar et al., 2013). Because of this reason and together with the concept "agriculture is business", the Malaysian Government endeavours to develop agropreneurial skills among the Gen Y segment, which are those born between 1979 and 2000 (Sox et al., 2014). Given the many optimistic characteristics of Gen Ys including high entrepreneurial spirit and their large population (Sox et al., 2014, Broadbridge et al., 2007, Lim, 2014), the local government has placed great emphasis on encouraging and motivating them to become agropreneurs with the objectives of ensuring increasing and continuous supplies of food for the nation and to decrease the youth unemployment rate (Abdullah et al., 2012, D'Silva et al., 2010).

Realizing the importance of the Gen Ys' involvement in agriculture, and based on previous findings that entrepreneurial intentions are the best predictor of entrepreneurship behaviours, scholars have devoted their time and interests to investigate agropreneurial intentions among youths particularly among graduates (D'Silva et al., 2010, Abdullah and Naem Sulaiman, 2013, Abdullah and Abu Samah, 2014, Soumiya Devi, 2015, Mohammad Nor et al., 2015). However, there has been little evidence that shows whether the intentions have been realized into subsequent agropreneurship behaviours. Although intention has been acknowledged as the single best predictor of entrepreneurship, intentions do not always end up in behaviour formation (Rauch and

Hulsink, 2015, Saeed et al., 2014, Solesvik et al., 2013). These arguments highlight the need for a longitudinal investigation when investigating agropreneurship activities in order to examine if intention is realized into actual agropreneurship behaviour. Thus, this study was conducted based on longitudinal design to heed a call for the study of such design that was found in literature (Chang et al., 2014, Saeed et al., 2014).

2. Literature Review

2.1 Agropreneurial Intention

The TPB was formulated by Ajzen (1991) to predict and explain human behaviour in specific contexts. The TPB variables have been shown to have a significant impact in explaining human behavioural intentions and behaviours. According to the TPB, human behaviour is influenced by their intention to perform the behaviour in question and that intention is influenced by attitude towards behaviour, subjective norm, and perceived behavioural control (PBC).

Attitude towards behaviour refers to how individuals evaluate a certain behaviour to be attractive and pleasant or not, and to acknowledge and respond to that behaviour consistently. Generally, attitude is a feeling one holds about a certain concept. People's behaviours are argued to be aligned with their attitude (Ajzen and Fishbein, 2005), where the behavioural action is more likely to be realised if one perceives that an engagement in a certain behaviour will produce positive outcomes. According to Chen and Lai (2010), "attitudes about and knowledge of entrepreneurship are likely to shape students' inclination to start their own business in the future" (pp. 2).

Scholars from numerous fields such as health behaviour, tourism, and marketing have examined the effects of attitude on intention and behaviour, and revealed that behavioural attitude had significantly predicted behavioural intention (Fen and Sabaruddin, 2009, Hsu and Huang, 2012, Taylor, 2012). Similar results were also found in the entrepreneurship field (Engle et al., 2010, Kautonen et al., 2013, Krueger et al., 2000, Küttim et al., 2014, Schlaegel and Koenig, 2014, Marques et al., 2012, Yousaf et al., 2015, Chang et al., 2014, Liñán and Rodríguez-Cohard, 2015, Solesvik et al., 2012, Liñán and Chen, 2009). Compared to other TPB predictors, attitude was found to be the strongest in explaining individual entrepreneurial intentions (Pouratashi, 2014, Liñán and Rodríguez-Cohard, 2015, Solesvik et al., 2012, Solesvik, 2013). In the case of agropreneurship, empirical data also showed similar findings. Attitude toward self-employment was found to correlate positively and significantly with interest to do agricultural activities (Movahedi et al., 2013). In the Malaysian context, Abdullah and Naem Sulaiman (2013) also found that attitude has significantly affected the interest among youth to be involved in agricultural entrepreneurship. Therefore, based on this, it was hypothesized:

H1: Attitude towards agropreneurship is significantly related to agropreneurial intention.

The second variable in TPB is subjective norms, which is defined as perceived pressures from people who are very important to oneself such as family, friends, and teachers. The influence of subjective norms on individuals' intention to become entrepreneurs have been the subject to many discussions and speculations since the 20th century. However, the results of these studies are still unclear. For example, while a few studies found that subjective norms significantly correlate with individuals' entrepreneurial intentions (Carr and Sequeira, 2007, Engle et al., 2010, Iakovleva et al., 2011, Kautonen et al., 2013, Kautonen et al., 2015, Kolvereid and Isaksen, 2006, Mueller, 2011, Pouratashi, 2014, Yousaf et al., 2015, Murugesan and Jayavelu, 2015, Joensuu-Salo et al., 2015), other studies revealed contradictory results (Krueger et al., 2000, Liñán and Chen, 2009, Solesvik et al., 2012, Autio et al., 2001, Shook and Bratianu, 2010, Shiri et al., 2012, Almobaireek and Manolova, 2012, Fini et al., 2009, Chang et al., 2014, García-Rodríguez et al., 2015). In these studies, no significant association between subjective norms and students' entrepreneurial intentions was found.

Despite the contradictory findings on the strength and power of subjective norm as a predictor of individual entrepreneurial intention, the involvement of social pressure in shaping agropreneurial intention and behaviour cannot be denied. The reason behind it is because entrepreneurship is surrounded by its social environment and individuals tend to follow and repeat the behaviour that is accepted and approved by their social group (Stephan and Uhlaner, 2010, Fischer, 2006, Shteynberg et al., 2009). Performing agropreneurial business activities involve many risks such as natural disaster, business, and also financial risks. In this case, approval, opinion, and judgement from people who are important to oneself are very salient. Based on the justification by Shook and Bratianu (2010), as long as an individual is governed by a strong motivation to comply with their subjective norm, intention to perform agropreneurship behaviour is more likely to be shaped as long as the behaviour is approved by these people. Therefore, the present study holds to believe that a higher subjective norm perceived by an individual will result in enhanced entrepreneurial drive and greater formation of an individual's intention to perform agropreneurship behaviour.

H2: Subjective norms is significantly related to agropreneurial intention.

The last predictor, PBC or the perception one holds that the act is in one's control. The concept of PBC refers to individuals' perceived relative ease or difficulty in performing a certain task. According to Engle et al. (2010), the behaviour in question is more likely to be executed when a person holds a stronger belief that the behaviour is within his/her control.

Research in the entrepreneurship area showed a different predictive power of PBC in explaining individuals' intention to become entrepreneurs. For example, research conducted by Liñán and Chen (2009) found that PBC influence entrepreneurial intention at different strength between students from two countries (Spain and Taiwan). Even that is the case, their study still revealed that PBC and the other TPB antecedents (attitude toward behaviour) contribute to more than half of the variance in students' intention to get involved in self-employment. Indeed, a positive association between PBC and entrepreneurial intention was empirically proven in many studies (Engle et al., 2010, Fini et al., 2012, Kautonen et al., 2013, Schlaegel and Koenig, 2014, Solesvik, 2013, Solesvik et al., 2012). Empirical evidence also showed that PBC has a statistically significant ability and power in explaining students' intention to become entrepreneurs meta-analytically (Schlaegel and Koenig, 2014), in a single country (Joensuu-Salo et al., 2015, Murugesan and Jayavelu, 2015, Pouratashi, 2014, Chang et al., 2014) and also across multiple countries (Mueller, 2011, García-Rodríguez et al., 2015, Kautonen et al., 2015, Liñán et al., 2013, Engle et al., 2010). Furthermore, Iakovleva et al. (2011) compared and contrasted the impact of TPB antecedents on entrepreneurial intention among respondents from developing and developed countries. They found that PBC impacts intention regardless of the types of countries. Thus, the above studies demonstrated the importance of PBC in enhancing intention to become self-employed.

H3: Perceived behavioural control is significantly related to agropreneurial intention.

2.2 Entrepreneurial Ladder and Agropreneurship Behaviours

van der Zwan et al. (2010) introduced the entrepreneurial ladder concept where entrepreneurship behaviour is modelled as a process and not as a binary choice of achieving the outcome of having started a business enterprise. In this concept, the implementation of an entrepreneurship behaviour is an obvious metaphor if a person is successful when these stages are successive. Under this concept, an entrepreneurship behaviour is described as a process that involves five stages beginning with 'never thought about an entrepreneurship', 'thinking', 'taking steps', 'running young business', and 'running mature business'. Interestingly, the 'taking step' and the 'running young business' are very similar to the concept of entrepreneurship behaviour used by Gatewood et al. (1995); where the authors categorised entrepreneurship behaviour into five major categories, namely gathering marketing information, estimating potential profits, finishing the groundwork for product or services, developing the company structure, and setting up business operations.

For an agropreneurial intention to be realized into actual agropreneurship behaviours, it requires time. Agropreneurship deals with perishable and fragile agriculture products in a risk-prone sector which can result in negative outcomes caused by imperfectly predictable biological, climatic, and price variables. Hence, different people require different time frames in creating an agropreneurship enterprise. Because of that, in investigating entrepreneurship behaviour, it is suggested that the behaviour is measured using various gestation activities to understand and to show whether different intention–action links hold for different start-up activities (Kautonen et al., 2015). Regarding the time taken to realise one's intention for agropreneurship, this study assumed that six-month of entrepreneurial preparation would suffice based on the Malaysian Government's indicator for graduate employability, which is six months after graduation. Therefore, based on Gatewood et al. (1995) and van der Zwan (2010), agropreneurship behaviour in this study is conceptualized as a 'taking steps' ladder to establish a firm which consist of five important steps which are gathering marketing information, estimating potential profits, finishing the groundwork for products or services, developing the company structure, and setting up business operations.

The literature showed that most of the longitudinal studies that investigated human actual behaviours in non-entrepreneurship areas such as retail, services, and community service had used intention as a single determinant of actual displayed behaviour (MacGillivray and Lynd-Stevenson, 2013, Taylor, 2012, De Cannière et al., 2010, Liao et al., 2014). In these studies, intention was showed to have a significant impact on actual behavioural actions (Liao et al., 2014, MacGillivray and Lynd-Stevenson, 2013, Taylor, 2012). Similar findings were also found in the entrepreneurship area (Kautonen et al., 2013, Kibler et al., 2014). Entrepreneurial intention was, indeed, acknowledged as the best and an important predictor of one's actual effort to form an enterprise (Iakovleva et al., 2011, Liñán and Rodríguez-Cohard, 2015, Sequeira et al., 2007, Kautonen et al., 2013). For instance, a study by Sequeira et al. (2007) found that entrepreneurial intention correlates highly with entrepreneurship nascent behaviour. The study indicated that students who have high intentions of becoming entrepreneurs have also engaged in at least two nascent entrepreneurship behaviours. A more recent study by Kautonen et al. (2015) also concluded similar findings in which intention is not only a significant predictor of entrepreneurship behaviour but it also predicted behaviour stronger than PBC. Another study by Hopp and Sonderegger (2015) also provided support for entrepreneurial intention-behaviour relationship by revealing that intention affects the progress entrepreneurs make when organising a new venture. Thus, the results from these empirical studies provided support that entrepreneurship behaviour is an outcome of one's behavioural intentions. Hence, the following hypotheses were developed:

H4: After six months, agropreneurial intention is positively related to the behaviour of gathering marketing information.

H5: After six months, agropreneurial intention is positively related to the behaviour of estimating potential profits.

H6: After six months, agropreneurial intention is positively related to the behaviour of finishing the groundwork for products or services.

H7: After six months, agropreneurial intention is positively related to the behaviour developing the company structure.

H8: After six months, agropreneurial intention is positively related to the behaviour of setting up business operations.

Figure 1 illustrates the research model in this study.

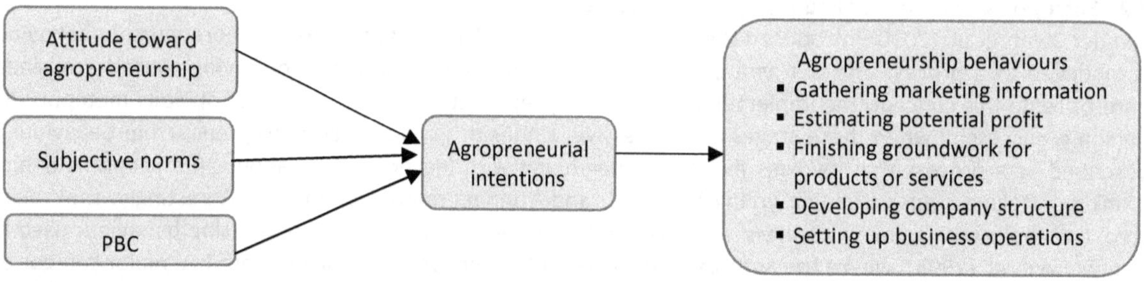

Figure 1: Research model of agropreneurial behaviours

3. Methodology

3.1 Samples

The respondents of the current study were 753 final semester Gen Y agricultural students from public higher educational institutions (HEIs) in Malaysia. The students were contacted via an email containing a cover letter and also a link to an online web-survey. At this time we asked the students if they would voluntarily participate in the second wave data collection. Only those who answered 'yes' to this question were contacted again for Time 2 (T2) data collection. During Time 1 (T1), 333 students responded to our web-survey, which yield 44.22% response rate. During T2, 243 of 333 T1 respondents answered the second online survey and yield a response rate of 72.54%. However, for final data analysis, 4 respondents from T2 data collection were eliminated as the students extended their studies. Thus, only 239 responses were used for further analysis. The sample size in the current study is considered sufficient based on G-Power analysis, in order to run structural equation modelling (SEM) analysis with $\alpha = 0.05$, anticipated effect size of 0.15 and desired statistical power of 0.95, the minimum required sample size is 119.

An independent t-test at significance level of 0.05 was conducted to detect if there is a difference in early and late responses. A 30-day cut-off point was applied to differentiate between early and late respondents. This 30-day cut-off point was similar to the cut-off point applied by Chen et al. (2003) and Vink and Boomsma (2008). The independent t-test results yield no significant difference in between the two groups. Hence, no response bias was detected.

The 239 graduates in the sample consist of 36.4% male and 63.6% female. Most of the students are pursuing a bachelor's degree in agriculture (73.2%) and the rest are studying at the diploma level. In regards to the age of respondents, the following distribution was reported: 21-22 years, 24.3%; 23-24 years, 66.1%; 25-26 years, 8.8%; 27-28 years, 0.4% (0.4% of the respondents did not specify their age category).

3.2 Measures

There were 49 items in our online web survey form, which were divided into two questionnaire sets. The first questionnaire was sent during T1 to gather information on the respondents' demographic information such as gender, age, level of education, and name of institutions and also information on TPB factors including attitude (ATT), subjective norm (SN), PBC, and agropreneurial intention (INT). On the other hand, the second set of questionnaire was emailed to the respondents during T2 and aimed to investigate the different dimensions of their agropreneurship behaviours.

The dependent variable in this study is the students' agropreneurial behaviours. In this study, agropreneurship behaviours consist of five dimensions which are gathering marketing information (MI); estimating my potential profits (PP); finishing the groundwork for my product or service (GW); developing the structure of my company (ST); and setting up business operations (BO). The items measuring agropreneurship behaviours were adapted from Gatewood et al. (1995). There were six items measuring MI; four items measuring PP; three items measuring GW; seven items measuring ST; and seven items measuring BO.

The independent variables in the model are the factors in TPB. There are six items measuring ATT which were adapted from Liñán and Chen (2009): six items with regards to their PBC were adapted from Tkachev and Kolvereid (1999) and four items developed by Autio et al. (2001) were adapted to measure SN. INT was measured using six items adapted from Thompson (2009). The items were assessed based on a five- and six-point Likert scale ranging from "Strongly Disagree" to "Strongly Agree".

4. Findings

Before we proceeded to data analysis, the common method variance (CMV) was first analysed by applying Harman's single factor analysis. Unrotated exploratory factor analysis (EFA) was performed. The analysis returned nine factors, explaining 76.36% of the variance with the first factor contributing 38.78% to the variance explained. Since the first factor did not account for the majority of the variance explained, the CMV was therefore not detected.

4.1 Assessment of the Measurement Model

The pattern of relationship between variables in our model was tested using partial least squares-structural equation modelling (PLS-SEM). Firstly, the assessment of the measurement model was performed by assessing the constructs' convergent and discriminant validity.

Convergent validity was performed to determine if all of the items measuring a certain construct are all in agreement. This can be done by referring to factor loadings, composite reliability (CR), and average variance extracted (AVE) (Hair et al., 2011). As suggested by Hair et al. (2014), the cut-off significant value of 0.5 for loadings was used. As such, eight items, namely GW3, BO4, BO6, BO7, ST1, ST2, ST7, and MI6 were removed from further analysis due to low loadings. The PLS algorithm was then rerun. The final loadings for all items ranged from 0.665 to 0.947, which is higher than the minimum loading recommended by Hair et al. (2014). The CR of all constructs ranged from 0.904 to 0.944 and meet the minimum value of 0.7. This depicts that construct indicators indicate a latent construct (Hair et al., 2014). Finally, the AVE values of all constructs are higher than 0.5 (Hair et al., 2014, Hair et al., 2011). The results show that all nine constructs are valid measures of their respective constructs based on their parameter estimates and statistical significance. As such, convergent validity for this study was confirmed.

Following that, the discriminant validity test was performed by employing the Henseler et al. (2015) heterotrait-monotrait ratio of correlations (HTMT) criterion to assess discriminant validity. The results showed that the highest HTMT value is 0.892 and did not violate the 0.90 threshold. $HTMT_{inference}$, which indicate a value of less than 1 in all of the constructs, also did not indicate discriminate validity problem in this analysis. In addition, the standardized root mean square residual (SRMR) composite model also showed a value of 0.053, indicating that the data fit the model very well. Therefore, we can conclude that the measures' discriminant validity has been established. In conclusion, the measurement model in the current study is satisfactory in terms of convergent validity and discriminant validity.

4.2 Assessment of the Structural Model

The results of the measurement model discussed in the previous section are within the recommended values, therefore providing support to proceed with hypotheses testing.

Table 1: Hypotheses Testing

Hypothesis	Relationship	Std. Beta	Std. Error	t-value	Decision	R^2	f^2	Q^2
H1	ATT -> INT	0.463	0.066	7.046**	Supported	0.381	0.267	0.258
H2	SN -> INT	0.135	0.062	2.161*	Supported		0.022	
H3	PBC -> INT	0.150	0.060	2.507**	Supported		0.026	
H4	INT -> MI	0.349	0.058	6.019**	Supported	0.122	0.139	0.087
H5	INT -> PP	0.300	0.062	4.798**	Supported	0.090	0.099	0.068
H6	INT -> GW	0.317	0.060	5.260**	Supported	0.100	0.111	0.072
H7	INT -> ST	0.243	0.064	3.800**	Supported	0.059	0.063	0.04
H8	INT -> BO	0.323	0.059	5.514**	Supported	0.104	0.117	0.078

**p<0.01, *p<0.05

Table 1 represents the results for hypothesis testing. H1 to H3 examined the relationships between TPB factors and INT. It was found that all TPB factors were significantly related to INT ($0.135 \leq \beta \leq 0.246$, $p < 0.05$). Next, H4 to H8 examined the relationship between INT and five dimensions of agropreneurship behaviours. INT was found to significantly explain MI ($\beta = 349$, $p < 0.01$), PP ($\beta = 0.300$, $p < 0.01$), GW ($\beta = 0.317$, $p < 0.01$), ST ($\beta = 0.243$, $p < 0.01$), and BO ($\beta = 0.323$, $p < 0.01$). Hence, H1 to H8 were all supported.

In our study, TPB factors were found to explain 38.1% of the variance in INT. Subsequently, INT was found to explain 12.2%, 9.0%, 10.0%, 5.9%, and 10.4% percent of the variance in MI, PP, GW, ST, and BO respectively. In terms of the effect sizes (**f^2**), the results showed that one relationship showed medium effect size, and the rest seven relationships showed small effect sizes (Cohen, 1988). In terms of predictive relevance (**Q^2**), the results showed that the predictive relevance of TPB factors on INT was medium. On the other hand, the predictive relevance of INT on MI, PP, GW, ST, and BO were all small.

5. Discussion and Conclusion

In the current situation with the issue of sustainable agriculture and government emphasis on food security for the people, the country needs to make the most of its young and educated talents by injecting new image and hopes to the agriculture sector in Malaysia. As agropreneurship has become a very useful tool in uplifting the economy and also in redefining new and modern agriculture, the involvement of the young in agropreneurship business activities is seen as crucial. It has been argued that intention is the proximal determinant of individual actual behaviour (Ajzen, 1991, Kautonen et al., 2013) where intentions consistently and robustly predict planned behaviours (Murugesan and Jayavelu, 2015). Consequently, this research started with the intention to find out how the factors in a well-established TPB model can be tested as predictors of agropreneurial intention on actual agropreneurship behaviours among Malaysian graduates.

In examining the relationship between TPB factors and agropreneurial intention, this study found that with a positive mindset and attitude, the Gen Ys' ability to control possible outcomes (positive or negative) in becoming an agropreneur as well as their flexible ways of responding to the challenging and demanding environment together with the opinion and approvals from people who are important to them increases efforts toward future entrepreneurial goals. The positive attitudes of the Gen Ys such as being passionate and ambitious (Sox et al., 2014) enable them to have an optimistic perception regarding agropreneurship, thus developing their desire for agropreneurship.

The effects of PBC on agropreneurial intention is also very true for Gen Y individuals, as their flexible ways in responding to the challenging and demanding environment in the agriculture sector seem to give them the ability to have control over possible outcomes of venturing into agropreneurship. This observation was done by Sox et al. (2014), who characterized the Gen Ys as individuals who are very confident in what they are doing and will get great results from their venturing, thus allowing them to perform behaviours that they are able to control and master.

Furthermore, the significant impact of subjective norm on agropreneurial intention could be explained by specific characteristics of the local samples. The Malaysian Gen Y themselves prefer collective action (Lim, 2014). As the Gen Y is known for their politeness and respect for the elderly especially parents and grandparents (Broadbridge et al., 2007), the opinion, encouragement, motivations, and support from these important individuals in their lives help them to see that agropreneurship is a good and prosperous career to embark on.

This study also found that agropreneurial intention is related to the development of actual agropreneurship behaviours of agricultural Gen Y graduates six months after their graduation. In other words, agropreneurial readiness among agricultural Gen Y graduates could assist them in strategizing their actions along their agropreneurial ladder six month later. The finding accords with research done by Rauch and Hulsink (2015), who found similar findings among students in Netherland. Hence, the current findings proved that the impact of intention on entrepreneurship behaviour is similar in developing and developed countries. In addition, the current findings vindicate the decision to opt for a six-month longitudinal period. While longer longitudinal time is recommended to generate a stronger effect size of intention on actual behaviours, this study proved that six months is sufficient for the Gen Ys to make appropriate preparation for agropreneurship set ups.

The results of this study provide some directions for the Malaysian Government and policy makers in formulating strategies to develop more young agropreneurs to become active players in the agropreneurship market. Since attitude is a collection of personal traits that can be developed from learning, which encompasses general knowledge including cognitive, emotions, and actions (Chen and Lai, 2010), the Government and policy makers should specifically aim to supply the Gen Ys with meaningful knowledge related to the attractiveness of agropreneurship. Furthermore, education and training programmes, which focus on preparing the Gen Ys to have a positive mindset regarding their ability to control and uncover their hidden ability to deal with possible challenges in the agropreneurship business, should also be designed. It is also important for family and friends to allow the Gen Ys to voice out their agropreneurship intentions especially when it involves communicating ideas on unique and creative agropreneurship products and services. According to Chang et al. (2014), motivation serves as one of the key determinant of an entrepreneurial intention. Therefore, family and friends should act as motivators by providing support, both tangible and intangible, to increase the Gen Ys agropreneurial spirit. Also, the Government and policy makers should be aware that Gen Ys with higher agropreneurial intention are more likely to engage in performing agropreneurship behaviour than those with lower or no intention. Therefore, it is imperative for the Government, policy makers, and also university administrator to offer meaningful agropreneurship curriculum and content, thus ensuring the information regarding various types of government support to successfully reach the Gen Ys.

6. Limitations and Directions for Future Research

This study focused on the empirical examination of the agropreneurial intention and agropreneurship actual behaviours among the Malaysian Gen Y from the lens of TPB only. As there is no single concept or model that best describes entrepreneurship intention and behaviour, integrating a few competing intention models could increase the predictive ability of the model. Furthermore, the longitudinal effect of intention on actual agropreneurship behaviours was limited to six months only. Thus, the intention-behaviour relationship could not be strongly demonstrated. Hence, a future study on agropreneurship behaviour can replicate this study by extending the longitudinal time frame beyond six months. Finally, this study investigate agropreneurship behaviours from the entrepreneurial ladder concept. However, Reynolds (2000) disputes that entrepreneurship with a birth of infant firm is a successful culmination of an entire and long entrepreneurial process. Therefore, it is suggested that a future study should be carried out to investigate agropreneurship behaviours from this angle.

References

Abdullah, A. A. and Naem Sulaiman, N. (2013) "Factors That Influence the Interest of Youths in Agricultural Entrepreneurship", *International Journal of Business and Social Science,* Vol 4, No. 2, pp 228-302.

Abdullah, F. A. and Abu Samah, B. (2014) "Factors Influencing Inclination toward Agriculture Entrepreneurship among Students in Agriculture Learning Institute", *Asian Social Science*, Vol 10, No. 2, pp 273-278.

Abdullah, F. A. Abu Samah, B., and Othman, J. (2012) "Inclination towards Agriculture among Rural Youth in Malaysia", *Journal of Basic and Applied Scientific Research*, Vol 2, No. 11, pp 10892-10894.

Ajzen, I. (1991) "The Theory of Planned Behavior", *Organizational Behavior and Human Decision Processes*, Vol 50, No 2, pp 179-211.

Ajzen, I. and Fishbein, M. (2005) The influence of attitudes on behaviour. In: D. Albarracín, B.T. Johnson, & M.P. Zanna, (eds.), *The handbook of attitudes*, Erlbaum, Mahwah, NJ.

Autio, E., Keeley, R. H., Klofsten, M., Parker, G. G. C. and Hay, M. (2001) "Entrepreneurial Intent among Students in Scandinavia and in the USA", *Enterprise and Innovation Management Studies*, Vol 2, No. 2, pp 145-160.

Azer, I., Mohamad, S. A., Abdullah, N. S. and Mustapha, M. (2014) "Agro-preneurial Obstacles among Students in the Faculty of Plantation and Agrotechnology, UiTM Pahang", *Social and Management Research Journal*, Vol 11, No. 1, pp 1-8.

Broadbridge, A. M., Maxwell, G. A. and Ogden, S. M. (2007) "13_2_30: Experiences, Perceptions and Expectations of Retail Employment for Generation Y", *Career Development International,* Vol 12, No 6, pp 523-544.

Carr, J. C. and Sequeira, J. M. (2007) "Prior Family Business Exposure as Intergenerational Influence and Entrepreneurial Intent: A Theory of Planned Behavior Approach", *Journal of Business Research*, Vol 60, No 1, pp 1090-1098.

Chang, H. C., Tsai, K. H. and Peng, C. Y., (2014) "The Entrepreneurial Process: An Integrated Model", *International Entrepreneurship and Management Journal,* Vol 10, No. 4, pp 727-745.

Chen, R., Wei, L. and Syme, P. D. (2003) "Comparison of Early and Delayed Respondents to a Postal Health Survey: A Questionnaire Study of Personality Traits and Neuropsychological Symptoms", *European Journal of Epidemiology*, Vol 18, No. 3, pp 195-202.

Chen, Y. F. and Lai, M. C. (2010) "Factors Influencing the Entrepreneurial Attitude of Taiwanese Tertiary-Level Business Students", *Social Behavior and Personality*, Vol 38, No. 1, pp 1-12.

Cohen, J. (1988) *Statistical Power Analysis for the Behavioural Sciences, Second Edition*, Lawrence Erlbaum Associates, Hillsdale, NJ.

D'Silva, J. L., Mohamad Shaffril, H. A., Uli, J. and Abu Samah, B. (2010) "Socio-demography Factors that Influence Youth Attitude towards Contract Farming", *American Journal of Applied Sciences*, Vol 7, No 4, pp 603-608.

De Cannière, M. H., De Pelsmacker, P. and Geuens, M. (2010) "Relationship Quality and Purchase Intention and Behavior: The Moderating Impact of Relationship Strength", *Journal of Business and Psychology*, Vol 25, No 1, pp 87-98.

Engle, R. L., Dimitriadi, N., Gavidia, J. V., Schlaegel, C., Delanoe, S., Alvarado, I., He, X., Buame, S. and Wolff, B. (2010) "Entrepreneurial Intent: A Twelve-Country Evaluation of Ajzen's Model of Planned Behavior", *International Journal of Entrepreneurial Behaviour & Research,* Vol 16, No 1, pp 35-57.

Fen, Y. S. and Sabaruddin, N. A. (2009) "An Extended Model of Theory of Planned Behaviour in Predicting Exercise Intention", *International Business Research*, Vol 1, No 4, pp 108-122.

Fini, R., Grimaldi, R., Marzocchi, G. L. and Sobrero, M. (2009) "The Foundation of Entrepreneurial Intention", *DRUID Society Summer Conference,* Copenhagen, Denmark, pp 17-19.

Fini, R., Grimaldi, R., Marzocchi, G. L. and Sobrero, M. (2012) "The Determinants of Corporate Entrepreneurial Intention within Small and Newly Established Firms", *Entrepreneurship Theory & Practice*, Vol 36, No 2, pp 387-414.

Fischer, R. (2006) "Congruence and Functions of Personal and Cultural Values: Do My Values Reflect My Culture's Values?", *Personality and Social Psychology Bulletin,* Vol 32, No 11, pp 1419-1431.

García-Rodríguez, F. J., Gil-Soto, E., Ruiz-Rosa, I. and Sene, P. M. (2015) "Entrepreneurial Intentions in Diverse Development Contexts: A Cross-Cultural Comparison between Senegal and Spain", *International Entrepreneurship and Management Journal*, Vol 11, No 3, pp 511-527.

Gatewood, E. J., Shaver, K. G. and Gartner, W. B. (1995) "A Longitudinal Study of Cognitive Factors Influencing Start-Up Behaviors and Success at Venture Creation", *Journal of Business Venturing*, Vol 10, No. 5, pp 371-391.

Hair, J. F., Hult, G. T. M., Ringle, C. and Sarstedt, M. (2014) *A Primer on Partial Least Squares Structural Equation Modeling (PLS-SEM).* SAGE Publications, Incorporated,Thousand Oaks, CA.

Hair, J. F., Ringle, C. M. and Sarstedt, M. (2011) "PLS-SEM: Indeed a Silver Bullet", *The Journal of Marketing Theory & Practice*, Vol 19, No. 2, pp 139-152.

Henseler, J., Ringle, C. M. and Sarstedt, M. (2015) "A New Criterion for Assessing Discriminant Validity in Variance-Based Structural Equation Modelling", *Journal of the Academy of Marketing Science*, Vol 43, No. 1, pp 115-135.

Hopp, C. and Sonderegger, R. (2015) "Understanding the Dynamics of Nascent Entrepreneurship—Prestart-Up Experience, Intentions, and Entrepreneurial Success", *Journal of Small Business Management*, Vol 53, No 4, pp 1076-1096.

Hsu, C. H. and Huang, S. S. (2012) "An Extension of the Theory of Planned Behavior Model for Tourists", *Journal of Hospitality & Tourism Research*, Vol 36, No 3, pp 390-417.

Iakovleva, T., Kolvereid, L. and Stephan, U. (2011) "Entrepreneurial Intentions in Developing and Developed Countries", *Education+ Training*, Vol 53, No 5, pp 353-370.

Joensuu-Salo, S., Varamäki, E. and Viljamaa, A. (2015) "Beyond Intentions–What Makes a Student Start a Firm?", *Education+ Training,* Vol 57, No 8/9, pp 853-873.

Kautonen, T., Gelderen, M. and Fink, M. (2015) "Robustness of the Theory of Planned Behavior in Predicting Entrepreneurial Intentions and Actions", *Entrepreneurship Theory and Practice*, Vol 9, No. 3, pp 655-674.

Kautonen, T., Van Gelderen, M. and Tornikoski, E. T. (2013) "Predicting Entrepreneurial Behaviour: A Test of the Theory of Planned Behaviour", *Applied Economics,* Vol 45, No 6, pp 697-707.

Kibler, E., Kautonen, T. and Fink, M. (2014) "Regional Social Legitimacy of Entrepreneurship: Implications for Entrepreneurial Intention and Start-Up Behaviour", *Regional Studies*, Vol 48, No 6, pp 995-1015.

Kolvereid, L. and Isaksen, E. (2006) "New Business Start-Up and Subsequent Entry into Self-Employment", *Journal of Business Venturing*, Vol 21, No 6, pp 866-885.

Krueger, N. F., Reilly, M. D. and Carsrud, A. L. (2000) "Competing Models of Entrepreneurial Intentions", *Journal of Business Venturing*, Vol 15, No 5, pp 411-432.

Küttim, M., Kallaste, M., Venesaar, U. and Kiis, A. (2014) "Entrepreneurship Education at University Level and Students' Entrepreneurial Intentions", *Procedia-Social and Behavioral Sciences*, Vol 110, pp 658-668.

Liao, Y. W., Wang, Y. S., Yeh, C. H. and Jansen, J. (2014) "Exploring the Relationship between Intentional and Behavioral Loyalty in the Context of E-Tailing", *Internet Research*, Vol 24, No 5 pp 668-686.

Lim, K. C. (2014) *"How to achieve alignment of the Malaysian Gen Y workforce with the systems and structures of organisations in Malaysia".* DBA Thesis, Southern Cross University, Australia.

Liñán, F. and Chen, Y. W. (2009) "Development and Cross-Cultural Application of a Specific Instrument to Measure Entrepreneurial Intentions", *Entrepreneurship Theory & Practice*, Vol 33, No. 3, pp 593-617.

Liñán, F., Nabi, G. and Krueger, N. (2013) "British and Spanish Entrepreneurial Intentions: A Comparative Study", *Revista de Economía Mundial,* Vol 33, pp 73-103.

Liñán, F. and Rodríguez-Cohard, J. C. (2015) "Assessing the Stability of Graduates' Entrepreneurial Intention and Exploring Its Predictive Capacity", *Academia Revista Latinoamericana de Administración*, Vol 28, No 1, pp 77-98.

Macgillivray, G. S. and Lynd-Stevenson, R. M. (2013) "The Revised Theory of Planned Behavior and Volunteer Behavior in Australia", *Community Development*, Vol 44, No 1, pp 23-37.

Marques, C. S., Ferreira, J. J., Gomes, D. N. and Rodrigues, R. G. (2012) "Entrepreneurship Education: How Psychological, Demographic and Behavioural Factors Predict the Entrepreneurial Intention", *Education + Training,* Vol 54, No 8/9, pp 657-672.

Mohammad Nor, N. A. A., Nik Mohd Masdek, N. R. and Maidin, M. K. H. (2015) "Youth Inclination Towards Agricultural Entrepreneurship", Economic *and Technology Management Review,* Vol 10a, pp 47-55.

Movahedi, R., Latifi, S. and Sayyar, L. Z. (2013) "The Factors Affecting Agricultural Students' Attitude Towards Self-Employment and Entrepreneurship", *International Journal of Agriculture and Crop Sciences,* Vol 5, No 16, pp 1813-1819.

Mueller, S. (2011) "Increasing Entrepreneurial Intention: Effective Entrepreneurship Course Characteristics", *International Journal of Entrepreneurship and Small Business*, Vol 13, No 1, pp 55-74.

Murugesan, R., and Jayavelu, R. (2015) "Testing the Impact of Entrepreneurship Education on Business, Engineering and Arts and Science Students Using the Theory of Planned Behaviour: A Comparative Study", *Journal of Entrepreneurship in Emerging Economies,* Vol 7, No 3, pp 256-275.

Nagalakshmi, T. and Sudhakar, A. (2013) "Agri-preneurs: A Case Study Of Dharmapuri Farmers", *International Journal of Science and Research*, Vol 2, No. 8, pp 208-214.

Pouratashi, M. (2014) "Entrepreneurial Intentions of Agricultural Students: Levels and Determinants", *The Journal of Agricultural Education and Extension*, Vol 21, No 5, pp 467-477.

Rauch, A. and Hulsink, W. (2015) "Putting Entrepreneurship Education Where the Intention to Act Lies: An Investigation into the Impact of Entrepreneurship Education on Entrepreneurial Behavior", *Academy of Management Learning & Education*, Vol 14, No. 2, pp 187-204.

Reynolds, P. D. (2000) National panel study of US business startups: Background and methodology. In: J. A. Katz & A. C. Corbett (eds.), *Databases for the study of entrepreneurship*, JAI, New York, Vol 4, pp 153-227.

Saeed, S., Muffatto, M. and Yousafzai, S. Y. (2014) "Exploring Intergenerational Influence on Entrepreneurial Intention: The Mediating Role of Perceived Desirability and Perceived Feasibility", *International Journal of Entrepreneurship and Innovation Management*, Vol 18, No. 2/3, pp 134-153.

Schlaegel, C. and Koenig, M. (2014) "Determinants of Entrepreneurial Intent: A Meta-Analytic Test and Integration of Competing Models", *Entrepreneurship Theory & Practice,* Vol 38, No 2, pp 291-332.

Selamat, Z. and Nasir, A. M. (2013) "Efficiency Measurement of Malaysian Agriculture Firms", *International Journal of Trade, Economics & Finance*, Vol 4, No. 2, pp 79-85.

Sequeira, J., Mueller, S. L. and Mcgee, J. E. (2007) "The Influence of Social Ties and Self-Efficacy in Forming Entrepreneurial Intentions and Motivating Nascent Behavior", *Journal of Developmental Entrepreneurship*, Vol 12, No 3, pp 275-293.

Shiri, N., Mohammadi, D. and Hosseini, S. M. (2012) "Entrepreneurial Intention of Agricultural Students: Effects of Role Model, Social Support, Social Norms and Perceived Desirability", *Archives of Applied Science Research*, Vol 4, No 2, pp 892-897.

Shook, C. L. and Bratianu, C. (2010) "Entrepreneurial Intent in a Transitional Economy: An Application of the Theory of Planned Behavior to Romanian Students", *International Entrepreneurship and Management Journal*, Vol 6, No 3, pp 231-247.

Shteynberg, G., Gelfand, M. J. and Kim, K. (2009) "Peering Into the "Magnum Mysterium" of Culture: The Explanatory Power of Descriptive Norms", *Journal of Cross-Cultural Psychology,* Vol 40, No 1, pp 46-69.

Siwar, C., Yasar, M., Ghazali, Z. and Mohd Idris, N. D. (2013) "Vulnerability and Sustainable Livelihood of Paddy Farmers in the North Terengganu Integrated Agriculture Development Area (IADA KETARA), Malaysia", *Prosiding PERKEM*, Vol 8, No 2, pp 778-789.

Solesvik, M. Z. (2013) "Entrepreneurial Motivations and Intentions: Investigating the Role of Education Major", *Education + Training*, Vol 55, No 3, pp 253-271.

Solesvik, M. Z., Westhead, P., Kolvereid, L. and Matlay, H. (2012) "Student Intentions to Become Self-Employed: The Ukrainian Context", *Journal of Small Business and Enterprise Development*, Vol 19, No 3, pp 441-460.

Solesvik, M. Z., Westhead, P., Matlay, H. and Parsyak, V. N. (2013) "Entrepreneurial Assets and Mindsets: Benefit from University Entrepreneurship Education Investment", *Education+ Training*, Vol 55, No. 8/9, pp 748-762.

Soumiya Devi, M. K. (2015) "A Study on the Influencing Factors for a Literate Youth to Take Up Agricultural Entrepreneurship", *International Journal of Management and Commerce Innovations*, Vol 3, No. 1, pp 692-700.

Sox, C. B., Kline, S. F., and Crews, T. B. (2014) "Identifying Best Practices, Opportunities and Barriers in Meeting Planning for Generation Y", *International Journal of Hospitality Management,* Vol 36, pp 244-254.

Stephan, U. and Uhlaner, L. M. (2010) "Performance-based vs Socially Supportive Culture: A Cross-National Study of Descriptive Norms and Entrepreneurship", *Journal of International Business Studies,* Vol 41, No 8, pp 1347-1364.

Taylor, S. A. (2012) "Evaluating Digital Piracy Intentions on Behaviors", *Journal of Services Marketing*, Vol 26, No 7, pp 427-483.

Thompson, E. R. (2009) "Individual Entrepreneurial Intent: Construct Clarification and Development of an Internationally Reliable Metric", *Entrepreneurship Theory & Practice*, Vol 33, No. 3, pp 669-694.

Tkachev, A. and Kolvereid, L. (1999) "Self-employment Intentions among Russian Students", *Entrepreneurship & Regional Development*, Vol 11, No.3, pp 269-280.

van der Zwan, P., Thurik, R. and Grilo, I. (2010) "The Entrepreneurial Ladder and Its Determinants", *Applied Economics*, Vol 42, No. 17, pp 2183-2191.

Vink, J. M. and Boomsma, D. I. (2008) "A Comparison of Early and Late Respondents in a Twin–Family Survey Study", *Twin Research and Human Genetics*, Vol 11, No. 02, pp 165-173.

Yousaf, U., Shamim, A., Siddiqui, H. and Raina, M. (2015) "Studying the Influence of Entrepreneurial Attributes, Subjective Norms and Perceived Desirability on Entrepreneurial Intentions", *Journal of Entrepreneurship in Emerging Economies*, Vol 7, No 1, pp 23-34.

PhD Research papers

Driving Green Practice Adoption in Restaurant Sector: Restaurant Operator's Perspectives

Surendev Singh, Booi Chen Tan and Nasreen Khan
Faculty of Management, Multimedia University, Cyberjaya, Malaysia.
dev_joel85@yahoo.com
bctan@mmu.edu.my
nasreen.khan@mmu.edu.my

Abstract: The deteriorating condition of environment globally has caused both profit and socially oriented companies to adopt green practices in operating their businesses. The environment faces degradation triggered by global warming, depletion of ozone layer, water, air, noise and light pollution and acid rain. These negative impacts initiate green movement among businesses to resolve environmental issues. The green movement minimizes the environmental problems and helps to build a better company image, thus gaining the competitive advantages in the competitive business world today. Hence, there is a high need for companies to take more proactive role in protecting the environment while marketing their products and services. In addition, some groups of consumers are getting more concerned about the environment and willing to pay premium price for environmental friendly products, thus increasing the market demand for products and services that consist of eco-friendly characteristics. In spite of that, the pressure to adopt green practices in food service sector is insignificant compared to other business sectors in Malaysia. With the evidence of fast growing number of restaurants and the widespread habit of eating out in Malaysia which bring with it an increasingly detrimental environmental impact, little research attention is paid towards environment initiatives from the perspectives of restaurant operators. The past research focusing on the factors that affect the intention of restaurant operator to adopt green practices in operating the restaurant is still under-explored. Therefore, this paper aims to propose a theoretical framework which derives from the Technology-organization-environment (TOE) framework and Value-attitude-behaviour (VAB) concept to better explain the green practice adoption within the restaurant context in Malaysia. The framework will be able to cover internal, external and individual aspect of environmental that contributes towards intention to adopt green practices. The result is expected to enhance the environmental literatures and provide a better understanding to the policy maker about the important factors that lead to such intention. This will spur the demand for green products and services business opportunities and create a healthy business environment in the context of restaurant sector.

Keywords: Adoption, Green practices, Restaurants, TOE, VAB

1. Introduction

One of the biggest and fastest growing industries in the world is related to the hospitality and tourism industry (Sulaiman and Haron, 2011). The hospitality industry especially restaurant sector is growing from time to time which is causing environmental issues. In the restaurant industry natural resources and physical environment is their most valuable asset (Kasim, 2009). The components of the hospitality industry consist of food services, airlines, hospitals and hotels (Line and Runyan, 2011). In relative to that, the food service in Malaysia is considered the fastest growing sector in hospitality recently (Lee et al., 2012). The food service industry generates pollution and produces huge amount of waste in their daily operations. Therefore, if appropriate action is not taken, the food sector could be one of the reasons that destroying the natural resource and physical environment as Malaysia are rich ecological geographical location (Siti-Nabiha et al., 2011).

In Malaysia lack of attention is paid towards environment issues caused by restaurant sector. On other hand restaurant operators are unaware of the requirements that need to be met in order to implement green practices. This study aims to investigate how the innovation, organizational, external, and individual environmental characteristics affect restaurant operators' intention to adopt such a system. This paper will explore and identify the possible internal, external and individual factors that need to be considered for the adoption of green practices in food service sector. Technology-Organizational-Environment (TOE) and Value-Attitude-Behaviour (VAB) model will both be used to develop the study framework. The results are anticipated to motivate organizations to incorporate green practices by food service operators in the daily operations.

2. Literature Review

2.1 An Overview of Food Service Sector in Malaysia

According to the National Restaurant Sodality, the restaurant industry is still one of the economy's top employers. Forecasters expect the industry to increment its job count to 14.1 million positions by 2020.

Learning the major segments of the restaurant industry can avail a minuscule business owner position his locations efficaciously. Malaysia has enjoyed remarkable growth over the last decades with industrialization, agriculture and tourism playing leading roles in its achievements. The industry is expected to perpetuate its excellent performance due to the magnification of urbanization and transmuting in the lifestyles. Malaysia's population has a significant pool of active consumers, with evolving eating habits, and growing consumption of imported food and beverages. Over 60 percent of the population is in the middle to high-income group with growing purchasing power, and increasingly sophisticated and modern lifestyles. In addition, unemployment remains very low. This is leading to greater consumption of imported food and beverages from western countries. Solid waste spawned yearly with roughly 7.34 million tonnes and spends between RM110 and RM130 to collect and dispose one tonne of garbage by the local authority. Years after that environmental issue in Malaysia continues to rise such as deforestation, climate change and global warming and in 2007 Intergovernmental Panel on Climate Change (IPCC) forecasted that by the year 2060 temperatures in Malaysia will increase by 0.6 to 4.5 Celsius.

Malaysia has a wide variety of dining establishments, including full accommodation restaurants, expeditious pabulum restaurants, cafes, aliment stalls, pabulum courts, victual-in bakeries, and pubs and bars. A majority of the restaurants provide Asian cuisine, with Chinese dominating the mid and high end restaurants. These trends will boost demand in the foodservice sector. The majority of the customers that frequent restaurants emanate from the middle to upper income families, business persons and the affluent people working adults. Most of the customers are well-travelled, well-apprised, sophisticated, prefer to dine in comfort and appreciate the highest culinary standards in Malaysia. A casual dining restaurant serves moderately-priced food in a relaxed atmosphere where table service is provided. That is, casual dining restaurants are a less expensive version of fine dining restaurants and are frequently used as a place to celebrate an event (Morgan, 1993).

2.2 Green Initiatives in Malaysia

Distinct from US as till today there is no association which grants green certification to restaurants establishment that meets the criteria in Malaysia. However, in Malaysia going green and practicing green is highly encouraged but just there is no association to name as certified green restaurants. In Malaysia, there are initiatives by government and agencies to promote green practices related to the restaurant sector. For example Ministry of Energy, green technology and water known as KeTTHA in 2011 introduce National green technology policy (NGTP) for hotel industry on Malaysia. Another initiative from the government is by launching eco labelling plot beneath Standard and Industrial Research Institute of Malaysia (SIRIM). The initiative was create for any businesses in Malaysia that could apply if they wish to park their product under SIRIM eco labelling scheme. According to SIRIM (2016), their current product range categories under the scheme includes construction, building, home appliances, cleaning substance, lights, office supplies, food and plant, packaging containers and other product categories. Therefore restaurant operators are able to register themselves with SIRIM if the green practices stated is been practiced. The programme encourages much of businesses in Malaysia to produce green product and services and registered under the SIRIM scheme in order to be certified as green product. Malaysian government also stressed their green ascendency in the 10th Malaysia Plan by looking for alternative source of energy which will cause less damage to the environment as the demand of energy, water, gas and others has increased.

2.3 Areas of Green practices in the Restaurant

Restaurants are the food establishments that by nature uses large amounts of products for food, energy consumptions, water and detergents agents, disposable solid and liquid waste from food and also packaging of products. According to Green Restaurant Association (GRA, 2016) there are seven (7) categories of green practices which the restaurant establishments should follow to be certified as a green restaurant. The seven practices consist of (1) water efficiency, (2) waste reduction and recycling, (3) sustainable durable goods and building materials, (4) sustainable food, (5) energy, (6) reusable and environmentally preferable disposables and (7) chemical and pollution reduction are used to deliver transparency on the guidelines followed to measure restaurant's environmental accomplishments. Based on Wang (2012) research resulted on finding that green practices divided into two dimensions. Mohindra (2008) research on greening public health in India found and used 3R model; Reduce, reuse and recycle as the factors to encourage health industry to move into greener future. Manaktola and Jauhari (2007) discovers that minimizing negative environmental impacts require green practices such as saving energy, saving water and reducing solid waste in terms of lodging industry. According to Chan et al., (2009), hotels consumption of water, energy, and non-durable goods is high as functions that contribute the effects to the environment. Research also discovered that hotels affect the environment in terms of air and water pollution, waste generation and energy emission (Park, 2009 and Kasim, 2009).

2.4 Underpinning theory - Technology-Organizational-Environment (TOE)

Technological, organizational and environment that forms TOE model is known as an integrative schema which incorporates all the three factor characteristics and the elements from macro environment (Tornatzky and Fleischer, 2008). The TOE framework suggests that a firms capabilities to adopt and implement innovations is intensely influenced by the three characteristics of technology context (Kauffman and Walden, 2001), organizational context (Chatterjee et al., 2002) and environment context (Kowath and Choon, 2001). In terms of technology context, it is defined as the adoption of technology innovation by the firm relies on the application on relative advantage, compatibility, and complexity. Meanwhile, organizational context describes the firm's available resources in terms of quality of human resources and organizational support as part of intention to adopt green practices (Jeyaraj et al., 2006). Environment context completes the external characteristic which depends on government support, regulatory pressure, customer pressure and environmental uncertainty (Al-Qirim, 2007 and Jeyaraj et al., 2006).

2.4.1 Technological Factors

Technology is common factors that are found in literatures that research on improving technology innovation in businesses. Technology innovation is also considered and accepted environmental management system as one of the practices (Lin et al., 2011). Diffusion of innovation framework by Roger (2003), been used in variety of disciplines as Dooley (1999) and Stuart (2000) stated that broad industries relating to economics, technology, politic science, education. Moreover Rogers (2003) said that the decision to adopt or reject adoption of innovation will reflect each other as adoption will make full use of innovation and rejection will ignore the importance of innovation in business operations. Technology plays a role in restaurants to adopt green innovation in business operations. Rogers (2003) suggested attributes of innovation which is relate to innovation diffusion process to help reduce innovation uncertainty levels. The attributes consists of five characteristics which are; (1) relative advantage, (2) compatibility, (3) complexity, and (4) observability. These attributes are widely used by researchers in various industries in terms of environment management system adoption. The technology factor will look into the technological factor that contributes towards restaurant operators to adopt technology practices that are able to conserve environment impacts.

2.4.2 Organizational Factors

Organizational is another factor that commonly used by research related to technology innovation and environment management. in order to define organizational some of the constructs that been used such as size of the organization, quality of human resources, management skills, organization culture, strategy implementation and organizational support, are used to discuss influences on technology innovation (Tornatzky et al., 2008 and González-Benito and González-Benito, 2010). Organization is the internal variables that are able to influence restaurants to practice green management practices. Organizations with superior capabilities to innovate and willing respond to environmental friendly practices call from the society are more successful to develop and lead to competitive superiority (Hurley and Hult, 1998). Organizational is a factor that contributes restaurant operators to adopt green management practices in restaurant operations to reduce environmental effects. Study also found that positive relationship between attitudes at the organizational level towards environmental management practice is the most significant (Le et al., 2006). Therefore attitude of the organization towards environmental practices are significant to determine level of risk taking towards environmental friendly practices.

2.4.3 Environmental Factors

Environmental factors are the external environment characteristics that indicate the organization relationships with others. In other terms, it is also described as the stakeholder of the organization. According to Friedman (2006) stated that a clear bond between stakeholders and the organization is what defines who are the real stakeholders. Stakeholders are usually having rights and certain benefits gain from the organization relationship. Based on Friedman (2006) they are (1) the media, (2) general public, (3) business partners, (4) future generations, (5) past generations, (6) academics, (7) competitors, (8) NGOs or activist, (9) trade unions, (10) financiers, (11) competitors, (12) government and others. In restaurant sector, stakeholders are the individual or firms that directly have contact with the restaurant daily operations. The common major variables that are used in TOE constructs are governmental support, customer pressure, regulatory pressure and environmental uncertainty (Etzion, 2007). These variables are able to define the external factor that influences restaurant operators to adopt green practices in their operations. As restaurant operation are customized based on the demands and availability of resources that determines the restaurant products and services. Therefore if the stakeholders demands for greener restaurant practices, restaurant operators will customised products and services based on that demands.

2.5 Underpinning theory - Value-Attitude-Behaviour (VAB)

Value, attitudes, and behaviours are three variables part of VAB model framework. This model explain the structure process from value to attitude to behaviour model whereby it recommends that perception of value will influence individual attitudes, which than ultimately impact the individuals behaviour towards an action taken (Homer and Kahle, 1988). The process is related to each other form value affects attitude and then will triggers individual's behaviour. The behaviour on an individual is than determined by the individual's attitude Ajzen, (2005). Rajani, (2010) stated that social awareness is the bases of understanding values which is resulting of attitudes and behaviour of an individual. Therefore, value is a concept that is vital to guide actions or decision making process of an individual in any situation. Values concerning nature are personal and subjective to slowly grow in individual psychological and social development stage. Therefore it showed the hierarchical order of value-attitudes-behaviour model. This is also confirmed by Vaske and Donnelly (1999) as stated that individual environment perceptive is dependent on the hierarchy of cognitive consisting of values, value orientation, attitudes, behavioural intentions and behaviour itself which than builds on one another to form actions.

2.5.1 Value orientation

Schwarts, (1992, 1994) discussed the general value orientation scale which consist of ten distinctive types of value denoting core motivation structures. Value is defined as desirable transituational goals which plays important role in serving as guidance in people's lives (Schwartz, 1992). The ten values stated by Schwarts are (1) power, (2) achievement, (3) hedonism, (4) stimulation, (5) self-direction, (6) universalism, (7) benevolence, (8) tradition, (9) conformity, and (10) security. The types of value are separated in two dimensions which are self-transcendence versus self-enhancement and openness to change versus conservation. The self enhancement value dimension combines the value types of power and achievement and the self-transcendence combines universalism and benevolence value types. Studies have shown that differentiating self-transcendence values into two groups applies: as biospheric values attend to quality if nature and the environments concerns and meanwhile altruistic values attends to well-being of other human being interest (de Groot and Steg, 2010, Schultz, 2001, Steg et al. 2005, Stern, 2000). Therefore based on the assumptions scholars suggested in order to understand beliefs and actions towards the environment behaviour, value to be grouped into three different types: (1) egoistic, (2) altruistic, (3) biospheric values (de Groot and Steg, 2010, Steg et al., 2005, Stern, 2000).

2.5.2 Attitude towards green practices

A classic definition of attitude define by Allport (1935) expresses that attitude is a mental and neural state of readiness, which results a directing, influence upon the individual response to an objects and situations. According to Fishbein and Ajzen (1975) attitude is defined as individual various overt behaviours evaluated base on mediating response. Attitude towards green practices are said to be rooted in ones perception to the degree the person perceives as personal integrity integrated in her or herself natural behaviour (Schultz and Zelezny, 2000). Moreover in regards of environmental knowledge, behaviour and social economic variables are examined towards environmental studies in general in order to address the individual attitudes towards green practices by researchers (Hens et al., 2010). Some researchers looked into how to improve environmental awareness among younger generation in a situation (Chapman and Sharma, 2001), by looking at personal environmental responsibility behaviour in relation with environmental attitudes (Scott and Gough, 2003). Furthermore researchers look at the emotions point of view as the encouraging role played in positive environmental attitudes (Keles, 2011) and looking into the change of structure as the reason for environmental friendly behaviour (Kollmuss and Agyeman, 2002).

2.6 Intention to adopt green practices

According to Warshaw and Davis (1985), defines intention as "the degree to which a person has formulated conscious plans to perform or not perform some specified future behaviour". The decision to perform a specific behaviour by a person is determined by the degree of the person consciousness to perform or not to perform the behaviour. Several empirical literatures have shown that accuracy of measuring attitude towards certain behaviour could predict intention of a person (Ajzen, 1985). Meanwhile, in the hotel industry consumers green purchase intention is likely to influence consumer to visit a green hotel (Han et al., 2009). Additionally Han et al., (2009) has created a framework that investigates the relationship between attitude towards green behaviour whereby studies hotel consumers overall image and green behavioural in a hotel. On the other hand, Schubert et al., (2010) studies have shown restaurant customer attitudes and behavioural intentions in casual dining restaurant in Columbus, Ohio towards environmentally friendly restaurants.

2.7 Proposed Framework

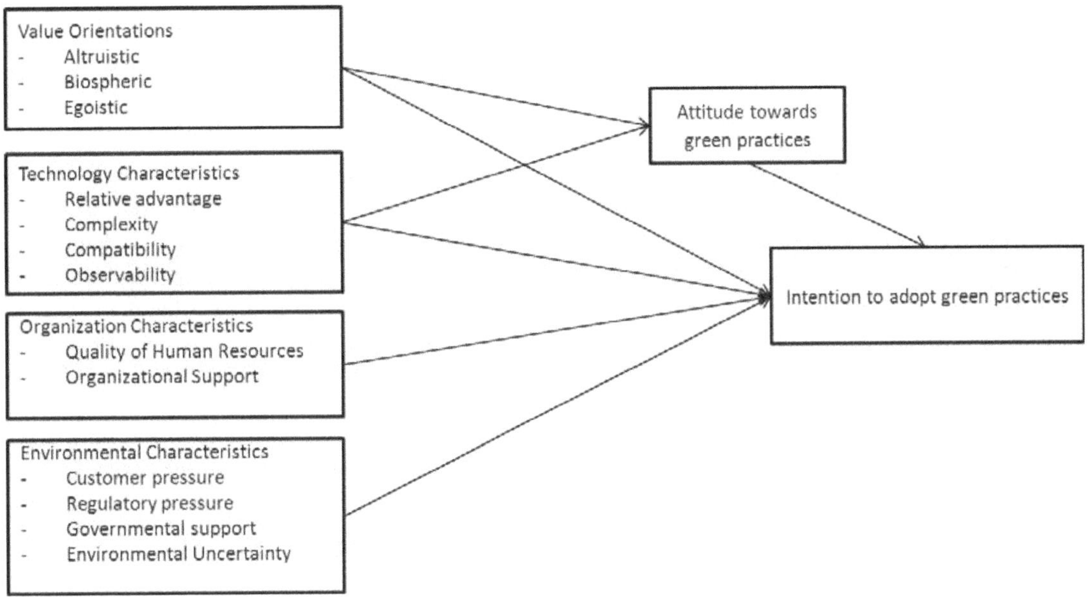

Figure 1: A Conceptual Framework of restaurant operator's intention to adopt green practices.

Hence, the research hypotheses are develop and presented as follows:

- **H1:** Value orientations have a positive effect on restaurant operator's intention to adopt green practices in restaurants.
- **H2:** Technology characteristics have a positive effect on restaurant operator's intention to adopt green practices in restaurants.
- **H3:** Organization characteristics have a positive effect on restaurant operator's intention to adopt green practices in restaurants.
- **H4:** Environmental characteristics have a positive effect on restaurant operator's intention to adopt green practices in restaurants.
- **H5:** Attitude towards green practices mediates the relationship between value orientations and restaurant operator's intention to adopt green practices in restaurants.
- **H6:** Attitude towards green practices mediates the relationship between technology characteristics and restaurant operator's intention to adopt green practices in restaurants.

3. Research Methodology

This study takes the perspective of organization/restaurant as unit of analysis. Quantitative approaches will be used in this study. The survey instrument will be covering four independent variables (innovation, organization, external and individual) with one mediating variable (attitude towards green practices) and dependent variable (intention towards EMS adoption) will be discussed during the preliminary study. Specifically, the subject measures for each variable will be assessed using Likert Five-point interval scales. Prior to the field study, a pilot study on about 30 responses will be carried out. This helps to ensure the reliability and validity of the survey questionnaire. The final refined questionnaires will be distributed randomly to a sample of 300 participants, via face-to face method. The questionnaires will be distributors and collected from sample population of full service casual upscale restaurants in Malaysia which refers to restaurants that have one or more. The characteristics of these full service casual upscale restaurants are normally offers fine dining with full table services and focuses on quality compared to pricing. Other characteristics of casual dining restaurants are to be more relaxed type of services, friendly staff, and informality of staff treating guests and professional efficiency and table service offerings (Walker, 2008). The restaurants chosen are from the categories whereby the interior design is pleasant with concepts, linen setting tables, cutleries above average qualities, air conditioned and prices are slightly higher than normal restaurants. Survey data will be analysed using the Statistical Package for the Social Sciences (SPSS) and structural equation modelling SEM. The data analyses performed range from univariate analysis, reliability analysis, correlation analysis, factor analysis, and multiple regression analysis. Lastly, a research framework of EMS adoption in the context of restaurants in Malaysia can be confirmed via the Exploratory and Confirmatory Factor Analysis (EFA and CFA).

4. Implications

4.1 Theoretical Implications

By using the TOE framework researcher is able to understand the factor levels that will influence the firm's decision to make environmental decisions. However, the problem raised from T-O-E framework is the lack of behavioural, attitude and awareness construct influences towards green practice adoption decision (Awa et al., 2012). Therefore, by integrating Value-Attitude-Behaviour (VAB) model with T-O-E framework will provide and offer finer theoretical explanation towards understanding intention to adopt green practices behaviour. The combination will cover internal, external, technological, and individual behaviour factors determining intention to adopt green practices in restaurant operation. T-O-E framework will cover aspects of the organizational point of view of adopting technology innovation in business operation (Tornatzky and Fleischer, 1990) and meanwhile VAB will cover the individual aspect of value orientations, environmental attitude and environment behaviour intention (Ajzen, 1985) to adopt green practices. This study integrates both TOE and VAB models, therefore it will investigates technological, organizational, environmental and value orientation factors with attitude mediating technology and value orientation towards intention to adopt green practices in Malaysia restaurant industry.

4.2 Practical Implications

The research will result in a win-win situation among policy makers, business players and customers in terms of encouraging environment friendly practices. Policy makers are able to develop green restaurant certification which could be awarded to restaurants that meets the environmental guidelines in restaurant operations. Moreover, restaurants are able to create competitive advantage compared to other restaurant operators by meeting the green practice guidelines. As customers are more concern about the environment impacts and willing to pay more for green product and services. Therefore customers who are concern on environmental issues will have restaurant to go to while creating a unique attraction to the restaurant. The surrounding society will benefit the environmental friendly behaviour as the level of pollution around will be lower.

5. Conclusion

The restaurant industry in Malaysia is growing rapidly which brings detrimental environmental impact. Although the deteriorating environment faces degradation and pressure to adopt green practices in the food service sector increasing, yet little research attention is paid towards this area. Therefore this study proposes a theoretical framework which derives from the Technology-organization-environment (TOE) framework and Value-Attitude-Behaviour (VAB) model to better explain the factors that affect operator's intention to adopt green practices in restaurants. The framework focuses on aspects of internal, external, and individual factors towards intention to adopt green practices.

References

Ajzen, I. (1985) From intentions to actions: a theory of planned behaviour, in Kuhl, J. and Beckmann, J. (Eds), Action-control: From Cognition to Behaviour, Springer, Heidelberg, 11-39.

Ajzen, I. (2005) Attitudes, Personality and Behavior, 2nd ed. Open University Press: Maidenhead, UK.

Ajzen, I., and Fishbein, M. (1980) Understanding Attitudes and Predicting Social Behaviour, Prentice-Hall, Englewood Cliffs, NJ.

Allport, G.W. (1935) Attitudes. In C. Murchison (Ed.), Handbook of social psychology. Worcester, Mass: Clark University Press

Al-Qirim, N. (2007) The adoption of ecommerce communications and applications technologies in small businesses in New Zealand. Electronic Commerce Research and Applications, 6(4), 462-473.

Awa, H. O., Emecheta, B. C., and Ojiabo, U. (2012) Integrating TAM and TOE Frameworks and Expanding their Characteristic Constructs for E-Commerce Adoption by SMEs Electronic Commerce. In Informing Science and IT Education Conference.

Chan, W., Wong, K., and Lo, J. (2009) Hong Kong Hotels' Sewage: Environmental Cost and Saving Technique, Journal of Hospitality and Tourism Research, 33(2), 329 – 346.

Chapman, D. and K. Sharma, (2001) Environmental attitudes and behavior of primary and secondary students in Asian cities: An overview strategy for implementing an eco-schools programme.

Chatterjee, D., Grewal, R., and Sambamurthy, V. (2002) Shaping up for e-commerce: Institutional enablers of the organizational assimilation of web technologies. MIS Quarterly, 26, 65–89.

de Groot, J. I. M., and Steg, L. (2010) Relationships Between Value Orientations, Self-determined Motivational Types and Pro-Environmental Behavioural Intentions. Journal of Environmental Psychology 30, 368–378.

Dooley, K.E. (1999) Towards a holistic model for the diffusion of educational technologies: An integrative review of educational innovation studies. Educational Technology and Society 2(4), 35-45.

Etzion, D. (2007) Research on Organizations and the Natural Environment, 1992-Present: A Review. Journal of Management, 33, 637-664.

Friedman, A.L. and Miles, S. (2006) Stakeholders: Theory and Practice. Oxford University Press. .58.

González-Benito, J., and González-Benito, Ó. (2010). A study of determinant factors of stakeholder environmental pressure perceived by industrial companies. Business Strategy and the Environment, 19(3), 164-181.

Green Restaurant Association (GRA). (2016) Environmental guidelines, from: https://dinegreen.com/restaurants/standards.asp, accessed on 16 January 2016.

Han, H., Hsu, L.T., and Sheu, C. (2010) Application of the Theory of Planned Behavior to green hotel choice: Testing the effect of environmental friendly activities. Tourism Management, 31(3), 325-334.

Homer, P.M., and Kahle, L.R. (1988) A structural equation test of the value-attitude- behavior hierarchy. J. Pers. Soc. Psychol, 54, 638–646.

Hurley, R. and Hult, T. (1998) ``Innovation, market orientation and organizational learning: an integration and empirical examination'', Journal of Marketing, Vol. 62, July, pp. 42-54.

Jeyaraj, A., Rottman, J. W., and Lacity, M. C. (2006) A review of the predictors, linkages, and biases in IT innovation adoption research. Journal of Information Technology, 21, 1-23.

Kasim, A. (2009) Managerial attitudes towards environmental management among small and medium hotels in Kuala Lumpur. Journal of Sustainable Tourism, 17(6), 709–725.

Kauffman, R. J., and Walden, E. A. (2001) Economics and electronic commerce: Survey and directions for research. International Journal of Electronic Commerce, 5(4), 5-116.

Kollmuss, A.; Agyeman, J. (2002) Mind the gap: Why do people act environmentally and what are the barriers to proenvironmental behavior? Environ. Educ. Res., 8, 239–260.

Kowath, N., and Choon, T. (2001) Determinants of website development: A study of electronic commerce in Singapore. Information and Management, 39, 227–242.

Le, Y., Hollenhorst, S., Harris, Ch., McLaughlin, W. and Shook, S. (2006) Environmental management: A Study of Vietnamese hotels. Annals of Tourism Research, 33(2), 545-567.

Lee, C. H., Wahid, N. A. and Goh, Y. N. (2012) Assessing determinants of green practices adoption: a conceptual framework, Elixir Journal, 45, 7760-7766.

Lin, C., and Ho, Y. H. (2011) Determinants of Green Practice Adoption for Logistics Companies in China. Journal of Business Ethics, 98(1), 67-83.

Line, N. D. and Runyan, R. C. (2011) Hospitality marketing research: recent trends and future directions, International Journal of Hospitality Management, 31(2), 477-488.

Manaktola, K. and Jauhari, V. (2007) Exploring consumer attitude and behaviour towards green practices in the lodging industry in India. International Journal of Contemporary Hospitality Management, 19 (5), 364-377.

Mohindra, K. S. (2008) Greening Public Health Conferences: Educating Ourselves. Health Education, 108 (4): 269-71.

Morgan, M. (1993) Benefit dimensions of mid-scale restaurant chains. The Cornell Hotel and Restaurant Administration Quarterly 34(2), 40-45.

Park, J. (2009) The Relationship between Top Managers' Environmental Attitudes and Environmental Management in Hotel Companies. Virginia Polytechnic institute and State University, Virginia.

Rajani, N. (2010) Values, attitudes and intention to consume wild fish versus farmed fish in Nha Trang. Master's Thesis, Nha Trang University, Nha Trang, Vietnam.

Rogers, E.M. (2003) Diffusion of innovations (5th Ed.). New York: Free Press.

Schubert, F., Kandampully, J., Solnet, D. and Kralj, A. (2010) Exploring consumer perceptions of green restaurants in the US. Tourism and Hospitality Research, Vol. 10 No. 4, 286-300.

Schultz, P. W. (2001) The Structure of Environmental Concern: Concern for Self, Other People, and the Biosphere. Journal of Environmental Psychology 21, 327–339.

Schultz, P.W. and Zeleny, L.C. (2000) Promoting environmentalism. The Journal of Social Issues, 56, 443-457.

Schwartz, S. H. (1994) Are there universal aspects in the structure and content of human values? Journal of Social Issues, 50, 19 – 45.

Schwartz, S.H. (1992) Universals in the content and structure of values: Theory and empirical tests in 20 countries. In Advances in Experimental Social Psychology; Academic Press: New York, NY, USA.

Scott, W.A.H. and S.R. Gough. (2003) Sustainable Development and Learning: Framing the issues. London: Routledge Falmer.

SIRIM. (2016) Eco-Labeling scheme, from: http://www.sirim-qas.com.my/index.php/our-services/sustainability/eco-labelling, accessed on 16 January 2016.

Siti-Nabiha, A. K., George, R. A., Wahid, N. A., Amran, A., Abustan, I. and Mahadi, R. (2011) A field survey of environmental initiatives at selected resorts in Malaysia. World Applied Sciences Journal, 12, 56-63.

Steg, L., Dreijerink, L., and Abrahamse, W., (2005) Factors Influencing the Acceptability of Energy Policies: Testing VBN Theory. Journal of Environmental Psychology 25, 415–425.

Stern, P. C. (2000) Toward a Coherent Theory of Environmentally Significant Behavior. Journal of Social Issues 56 (3), 407–424.

Stuart, W.D. (2000) Influence of sources of communication, user characteristics and innovation characteristics on adoption of a communication technology.

Sulaiman, S. and Haron, M. S. (2011) Foodscapes: The effects towards future behavioral intentions in casual dining restaurant. Proceedings of the 9th Asian Academy of Management International Conference, October14-16, 2011, Penang, Malaysia.

Tornatzky, L. G., and Fleischer, T. (1990) The Process of Technological Innovation. Lexington: Lexington Books.

Tornatzky, L. G., Fleischer, M., and Chakrabarti, A. K. (2008) The processes of technological innovation Issues in organization and management series. Lexington Books.

Vaske, J.J. and Donnelly, M.P. (1999) A value-attitude-behavior model predicting Wild land preservation voting intentions. Soc. Nat. Resour. 12, 523–537.

Walker, J.R. (2008) Introduction to Hospitality (5th Edition). New Jersey: Pearson International Edition.

Wang, R. (2012) Investigations of important and effective effects of green practices in restaurants. Procedia – Social and behavioral Sciences, 40. 94-98.

Warshaw, P., and Davis, F. (1985) The accuracy of behavioral intention versus behavioral expectation for predicting behavioral goals. The Journal of Psychology, 119(6), 599-602.

Enterprise Culture: Impact on Malay Entrepreneurs

Kamaruzaman Ujang, Rugayah Hashim and Norziana Lokman
Faculty of Administrative Science and Policy Studies, Universiti Teknologi MARA, Shah Alam, Selangor, Malaysia
kamaruzamanujang@hotmail.com
guy73106@yahoo.com
norziana2001@yahoo.com

Abstract: The entrepreneurship phenomenon has attracted enormous attention all over the world from almost all sectors; economic, politics, social, psychology, finance, management and even religious institutions. Many initiatives are taken at all levels to accommodate and ultimately generate successful entrepreneurs but at the same time, problems in entrepreneurship remain. To policy makers, understanding issues and problems of entrepreneurship are to help their quest to influence entrepreneurial behaviours to facilitate national policies. The findings revealed that 66.2% of the Malay entrepreneurs ventured into business with no entrepreneurial culture. Currently, however, there is a significant change with 78.4% have acquired and practised entrepreneurial culture. The analysis of the findings has also succeeded in establishing the correlation between entrepreneurial culture and entrepreneur and business performance and addressed the two key issues. The first key finding infers that the Malay entrepreneur who has a successful business has acquired the entrepreneurial culture. The entrepreneurs generally acknowledged that entrepreneurial culture is an important factor that impacted their performance. The second finding has no definitive conclusion about the impact of entrepreneurial culture on business performance. The hypothesis tests indicate that there is no correlation between entrepreneurial culture and change in business income. This implies that change in business income is not influenced by an entrepreneurial culture. On the other hand, there is a positive relationship between entrepreneurial culture and change in business capital, suggesting that as the entrepreneur's entrepreneurial culture strengthened, they tend to increase their business capital. As for the result of business turnover, considering the analysis of the case study and in-depth interview, the study suggests concluding that there is a positive correlation; implying that entrepreneurial culture does influence the performance of business turnover.

Keywords: Malay Entrepreneurship, entrepreneurial culture, business performance, successful entrepreneurs attributes

1. Introduction

The entrepreneurship phenomenon has attracted enormous attention all over the world from almost all sectors; economic, politics, social, psychology, finance, management and even religious institutions. Many initiatives are taken at all levels to accommodate and ultimately generate successful entrepreneurs but at the same time, problems in entrepreneurship remain. To policy makers, understanding issues and problems of entrepreneurship are to help their efforts to influence entrepreneurial behaviours to facilitate national policies. The entrepreneurs, on the other hand, may not realise that entrepreneurial culture plays a significant role in determining business success. This paper provides the answer to the unending issue facing the Malay entrepreneurs; that they are lacking entrepreneurial culture (Lim, 2000). For the first time, this study proved that the successful Malay entrepreneurs do possess and practice entrepreneurial culture and tested the impact of the entrepreneurial culture on their business performance. The study thus established the need for the Malay entrepreneurs to nurture and develop an entrepreneurial culture to become successful.

2. Background

The importance of entrepreneurship has attracted many Governments worldwide to establish policies and programs to support entrepreneurship (Gangyi & Timan, 2013) In most countries the Governments have invested much resources and efforts to the development and enhancement of entrepreneurship (Obaji & Olugu, 2014). Most governments develop policies that favour the development of entrepreneurship. Some provide limited assistance whilst others extended almost all instruments available (Oni & Daniya, 2012); including financial, training and education, access to opportunities, consultancies and contracts. Some countries even instituted entrepreneurship education to nurture their young population with the entrepreneurial culture and prepare them to become entrepreneurs once the complete their studies (Akuegwu & Nwi-ue, 2016). However, the Malaysian government effort on the development of entrepreneurial culture is the least. Many studies have indicated the significance of culture on economic activities, businesses and entrepreneurship (Armington & Acs 2002; Goetz & Freshwater 2001; Johannisson, 1984) and the impact of culture on entrepreneurs and entrepreneur success (Beugelsdijk, 2007; Bergman,

2009; Wong 2014). However, the study on the impact of entrepreneurial culture on business performance is recent.

3. Problem Statements

Despite what the Government has done to uplift the Malay community's participation in entrepreneurship and businesses, findings by Zainol & Daud (2011) indicate that government-aided policies and other initiatives to promote Malay entrepreneurship have been less successful. Taking into cognition the government efforts and initiatives and a large number of implementing agencies involved, there is one important aspect that has not been given much emphasis; entrepreneurial culture. This aspect has been extensively studied and the results have indicated entrepreneurial culture as among the factors contributing to entrepreneurs and business success (Wong, 2014, Yusof 2011). In the context of Malaysia and Malay businesses and entrepreneurs, studies related to the impact of entrepreneurial culture on Malay entrepreneurs and their businesses are negative. Since entrepreneurial culture is significant to business performance it is of interest to investigate and examine the impact of entrepreneurial culture on the performance of the Malay entrepreneurs and their business.

4. Research Objectives

The research aims to address the question related to the practice of entrepreneurial culture by the Malay entrepreneurs and the impact on their business performance. To enable the study finds the answers to this question, the research analyses how the entrepreneurial culture affected the Malay entrepreneurs and their business performance.

5. Literature Review

The concept of entrepreneurial culture is not new and has existed for decades (Wong, 2014). The concept, however, is interpreted or defined in many ways; some relate it to organisational culture, some to business culture or enterprise culture (Hull, 2003; Belak & Milfilner, 2012) whilst others describe entrepreneurial culture as values practice by entrepreneurs (Sexton & Bowman, 1986). From entrepreneur perspective, an entrepreneurial culture is where one creates a project to develop a product either goods or services, that have a clear market value, and through them creates a sustained and sufficient source of revenue to meet its future needs.From an organisational perspective, the entrepreneurial culture is described "as an organisational culture embodying and championing entrepreneurial characteristics and attributes" and is related to positive organisational outcomes such as generating new business and improving firms' performance" (Wong, 2014, p ii). Entrepreneurial culture affects individual attitude towards entrepreneurship and the likelihood the individual choosing entrepreneurship as a career or plan to set up a business or new venture (OECD, 2012). The effect also influences the individual's ambitions to success and if he (or she) fails, there is the urge to start again.

No empirical attempt to measure the impact of entrepreneurial culture on entrepreneur performance has been studied. Suddle et.al.,(2007) investigating the relationship between entrepreneurial culture and the rate of nascent entrepreneurship, develops a composite measure of entrepreneurial culture using data from the World Values Survey. However, this exercise on entrepreneurial culture only interprets the role of entrepreneurial culture in explaining international differences in entrepreneurship rates. Earlier studies on culture indicate that culture was measured by individual perceptions (Calori & Sarnin, 1991). According to Wong (2014), in general, there are inconsistencies with the approaches in measuring entrepreneurial culture. Among the noteworthy observations relate to the respondents: Minguzzi & Passaro (2000) study covers individual entrepreneurs and Bradley et.al (2011) covers the chief executives. Another approach is the Corporate Entrepreneurship Assessment Instrument (CEAI) model developed by Hornsby, Kuratko & Montagno in (2002) and Wyk and Adonisi (2011). This model, however, assesses organisational entrepreneurial culture. This study measures the impact of the entrepreneurial culture on the attributes associated with it and business performance. Business performance is measured through the change in capital and business turnover. Thus to measure the impact of entrepreneurial culture on entrepreneurial performance, entrepreneur performance is assumed to equate business performance.

There is no single theory that can explain adequately business growth and success (Gibb & Davies, 1990; Bustamam, 2010). Traditional measures of success (and failure) have used statistical models based on financial characteristics (Keasey & Watson, 1991). On most cases, success is measured by business turnover and profit. Other tangible measures include income, assets, return on investments, growth in firm's size (Kalleberg and

Leicht,1991; Hall, 1992) and the increase in the number of employees (Alpander et.al, 1990). Intangible measures include competitiveness (Man et.al, 2002), achieving the desired objectives and target (Reijonen and Komppula, 2007) and customers' satisfaction. Yusof (2011) uses both financial and non-financial factors to measure entrepreneurial success; sales growth, income and satisfaction. Acknowledging the various scholarly attempts to measure success, this research focuses on business turnover, profits and capital to measure enterprise growth and success.

6. Methodology

This study applies the mixed method model. The research is designed to be both exploratory and explanatory. Currently, the issues of entrepreneurial culture among the Malay entrepreneurs are not clearly defined. Through case studies and interviews, the study attempts to gain familiarity with the phenomenon facing Malay entrepreneurs related to entrepreneurial culture. The entrepreneurs' survey provides the study with an avenue to make statistical inferences on the subject matters in relation to the entrepreneurs. This methodology integrates both quantitative and qualitative research methods of data collection and analysing. The reason for taking a mixed method is to enhance the capabilities of this research and provide additional validity to assertions made by the researcher, the participants in the case studies and the respondents for the survey. In combining both quantitative and qualitative research techniques, the approach provides a better understanding of a research problem or issue than either research approach alone. The methodology applies both the content analysis approach and statistical data analysis approach.

The case study covers 8 entrepreneurs and the in-depth interview 10. A total of 231 respondents was received from the sample survey. Data collection was conducted between August 2015 and February 2016. The respondents are Malay entrepreneurs who initiated, owned and managed the business and have been in operation for not less than five years, within the state of Selangor. The study uses the stratified random sampling approach on two strata; urban and rural. Since a large number of Malay entrepreneurs are located in the urban area, the ratio of urban to rural is fixed at 7.5:2.5 to determine the sample size. The types of businesses are categorised into two; formal and informal. A ratio of 3:7 on informal to formal businesses is used to determine the sample. The entrepreneurs in the case study and in-depth interview were also randomly selected from the list of 76 entrepreneurs randomly identified to have fulfilled the selection criteria; Malay, have been in the same business for more than 5 years, operating in Selangor, and most importantly the business is considered a successful venture.

Among the important elements of the study are the attributes that encapsulate entrepreneurial culture and business performance. The questions raised are to determine the entrepreneur's acquisition and practice of the key attributes related to the entrepreneurial culture to relate them to change in business capital, turnover and income. The respondents were also asked to assess the level of importance and contribution of entrepreneurial culture to business performance.

7. Findings

7.1 Entrepreneurs and Entrepreneurial Culture

Measuring entrepreneurial culture by the entrepreneurial attributes, all the entrepreneurs in the case study and in-depth interview, with an exception of one, have acquired an entrepreneurial culture. They have maintained at least six out of the nine entrepreneurial attributes as indicated in the following Table7.1

Table 7.1: Entrepreneurial Attributes among the entrepreneur

Variable\Test Analyses	YES	NO
Understand the business	18	-
Planning the business	17	1
Business Mission & Vision	16	2
Business Research	6	12
Sales & Marketing skill	14	4
Self-manage business finance/account	15	3
Management skill	16	2
Attended business related training	14	4
Willingness to take a risk	17	1

Table 7.2 shows the result of the correlation test between the respective entrepreneurial attributes and the entrepreneurs. Except for the sale and marketing attribute, the results show that there is a statistically significant relationship between the attributes and the entrepreneurs. Since the majority of the entrepreneurs indicate they do acquire and practice entrepreneurial culture, the finding is consistent with the case study and in-depth interview. It implies that most successful Malay entrepreneurs acquired and practices entrepreneurial culture.

Table 7.2: Entrepreneurial Attributes among the entrepreneur

Variable\Test Analyses	Test Result
Planning the business	$r_s = .422, p < .01$
Business Mission & Vision	$r_s = .356, p < .01$
Business Research	$r_s = .312, p < .01$
Sales & Marketing skill	$r_s = .011, p > .05$
Self-manage business finance/account	$r_s = -.158, p < .05$
Management skill	$r_s = .511, p < .01$
Attended business related training	$r_s = .256, p < .01$
Willingness to take a risk	$r_s = .236, p < .01$

7.2 Importance of EC to an entrepreneur in managing the business

The findings from the case study and in-depth interview reveal that the entrepreneurial culture is an important aspect that influences the performance of an entrepreneur in managing the business. Only two of the entrepreneurs indicate that entrepreneurial culture is not an important factor the influence business performance. Seven out of eighteen indicate that it is a slight important whilst the other nine indicate a moderately important. The result from the survey is shown in Table 7.3. It indicates 60.6% of the entrepreneurs believe that entrepreneurial culture is an important contributor to their business performance. On the other hand, 36.4% claims otherwise whilst a small group (3.0%) is unsure of its contribution.

Table 7.3: The importance of Entrepreneurial Culture Among Entrepreneurs

	Frequency	Percent	Cumulative Percent
Agree/Important	140	60.6	60.6
Not Agree/Not Important	84	36.4	97.0
Not Sure	7	3.0	100.0
Total	231	100.0	

The statistics in the following Table 7.4 indicate that it is the entrepreneurs with the entrepreneurial culture who claimed that entrepreneurial culture is important. The finding implies that entrepreneurs without entrepreneurial culture believe that entrepreneurial culture is not an important element that affects their performance in managing the business. The statistics also depict that not all entrepreneurs with an entrepreneurial culture agree to such notion of entrepreneurial culture. The table indicates only 77.3% of the entrepreneur with an entrepreneurial culture agree that entrepreneurial culture is important to their business performance; the other 22.7% thinks otherwise.

Table 7.4: The importance of Entrepreneurial Culture Among Entrepreneurs - with and without entrepreneurial culture

	With EC		Without EC		Total	
	Frequency	Percent	Frequency	Percent	Frequency	Percent
Agree/Important	140	77.3	0	0.0	140	60.6
Not Agree/Not Important	39	21.5	45	90.0	84	36.4
Not Sure	2	1.2	5	10.0	7	3.0
Total	181	100.0	50	100.0	231	100.0

7.3 Level of the contribution of EC to business success

The findings from the case study and in-depth interview indicate the different level of contribution of entrepreneurial culture to business success. Using a 5-point Likert Scale measure, the outcome is displayed in the following Table 7.5. Out of the 64.9% who indicate positive contribution, more than thirty-six percent indicate a moderate contribution while about a quarter claims a small contribution. Less than five percent of the entrepreneurs indicate above average contribution. Not only the entrepreneurs without entrepreneurial culture (21.6%) indicate no contribution of entrepreneurial culture to business performance, the finding also reveals that the respondents include those with entrepreneurial culture (about 13.5%). Table 7.6 indicates this group accounts for 17.7% of the entrepreneurs with an entrepreneurial culture.

Table 7.5: Level of EC contribution to business success

	Frequency	Percent	Valid Percent	Cumulative Percent
No contribution	81	35.1	35.1	35.1
Small contribution	56	24.2	24.2	59.3
Moderate contribution	84	36.4	36.4	95.7
High Contribution	9	3.9	3.9	99.6
Very High Contribution	1	0.4	0.4	100.0
Total	231	100.0	100.0	

The two main contribution levels are a small contribution and moderate contribution. More than thirty percent of the entrepreneurs describe the contribution of entrepreneurial culture to business performance as small compared to more than thirty-six percent describes as a moderate contribution. Only a small group of the entrepreneurs, slightly more than five percent, thinks that entrepreneur culture has a high contribution to the performance of a business.

Table 7.6: Level of Entrepreneurial Culture Contribution to business performance

	With Entrepreneurial Culture		Without Entrepreneurial Culture	
	Frequency	Percent	Frequency	Percent
No contribution	32	17.7	49	98.0
Small contribution	55	30.4	1	2.0
Moderate contribution	84	46.4	0	0.0
High Contribution	9	5.0	0	0.0
Very High Contribution	1	0.5	0	0.0
Total	181	100.0	50	100.0

7.4 Entrepreneurial Culture & Performance

The business performance of the entrepreneurs in the case study and in-depth interview indicate a positive correlation between entrepreneurial culture and business performance. Only four of the entrepreneurs record a sustaining business, including the entrepreneur without entrepreneurial culture. It indicates the business performance of the fourteen entrepreneurs grows in tandem with the entrepreneur's possession and practice of entrepreneurial culture. From the survey, a high percentage of the entrepreneurs indicate a positive performance with an entrepreneurial culture, Comparing business turnover and entrepreneurial culture, the result of the survey indicates the majority of the entrepreneurs indicate at least an increase. The same applies to both business income and capital. To test the significance of the result, the study conducted the Spearman rho test, Pearson test and the Mann-Whitney test on the three indicators and.the entrepreneurs own assessment on their performance.

Table 7.7: Spearman rho correlation test on Entrepreneurial Culture and Business Performance

Variables	Correlation Coefficient	Significant Level
Change in Business Turnover	-.178	.007 = 0.01<
Change in Business Income	.023	.728 = >0.05
Change in Capital	-.159	.016 = 0.05<
Performance based on entrepreneurs' own assessment	.105	.112 = >0.05

Table 7.8: Pearson chi-square correlation test on Entrepreneurial Culture and Business Performance

Variable	Critical Value	Degree of freedom	Asymp. Sig. (2-sided)
Change in business turnover	13.343[a]	3	.004 = 0.01<
Change in business income	.846	2	.655 = >0.05
Change in capital	5.846	1	.016 = 0.05<
Performance based on entrepreneurs' own assessment	8.934	2	.011 = 0.05<

Table 7.8: Mann-Whitney correlation test on Entrepreneurial Culture and Business Performance

Variable	Critical Value	Z	Asymp. Sig. (2-sided)
Change in business turnover	219.000	-1.644	.100 = > 0.05
Change in business income	192.000	-.894	.372 = > 0.05
Change in capital	2271.500	-2.413	.016 = 0.05<
Performance based on entrepreneurs' own assessment	798.000	-2.983	.003 = 0.01<

- Entrepreneurial Culture and Business Turnover
  The result of the correlation analysis in Table 7.7, technically, suggests that there is a correlation between entrepreneurial culture and change in business turnover. Similarly, the Pearson chi-square indicates a positive correlation between both variables. The Mann-Whitney test, however, shows that the is no correlation between the two.

- Entrepreneurial Culture and Business Income
  All three tests indicate that there is no correlation between entrepreneurial culture and business income. The outcome implies that entrepreneurial culture has no impact on business income. Technically, business income is determined by the trade profit margin, cost and pricing.

- Entrepreneurial Culture and Change in Capital
  The results of the three tests suggest that there is a correlation between entrepreneurial culture and change in capital. It shows that once the entrepreneurs have acquired and practice the entrepreneurial culture, the positive correlation on business turnover will result in the entrepreneur investing more capital into the business.

- Entrepreneurial Culture against the entrepreneur's assessment of performance
  The Spearman rho test for these two variables suggests that there is no correlation between the two. However, the Pearson chi-square and Mann-Whitney indicates that there is a correlation. This analysis is consistent with the earlier finding.

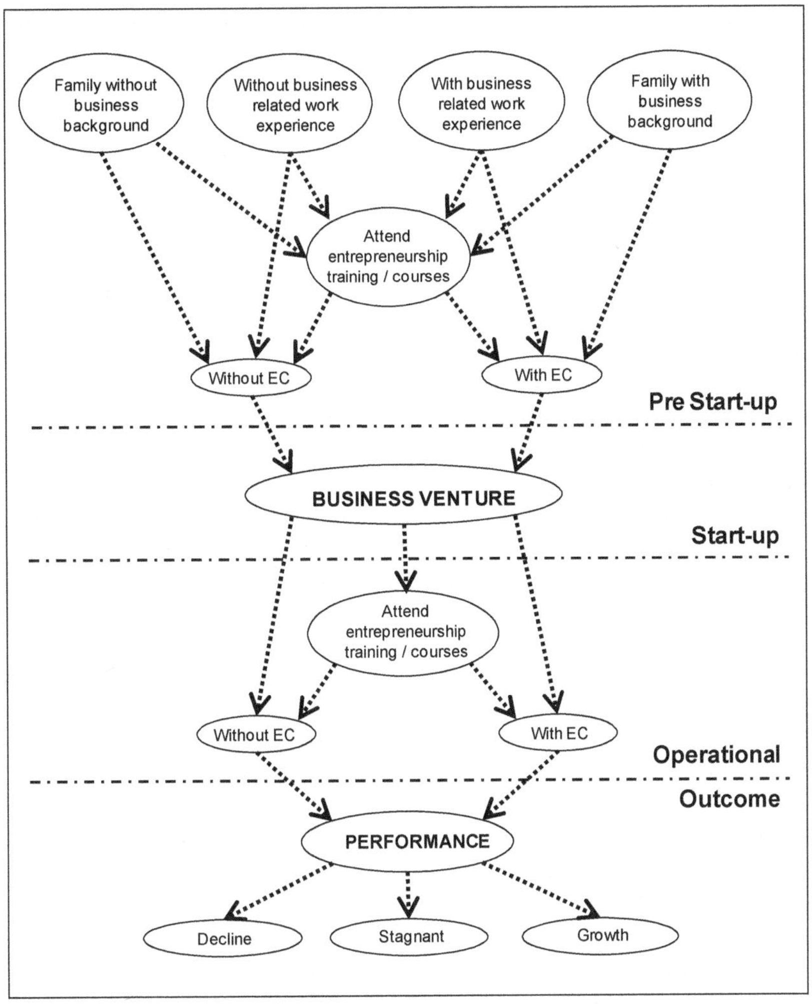

Figure 7.1: Entrepreneurial Culture and Performance Model

Figure 7.1 establishes the entrepreneurial culture environments that relate to the performance of the enterprise. The model is derived from the inputs received from the entrepreneurs in the case study and in-depth interview and the findings. With or without entrepreneurial culture, an individual may venture into a business. Once they started operating, those with entrepreneurial culture may want to improve and enhance their knowledge on entrepreneurship. As indicated in the result of the tests conducted, the outcome of their business performance is growth in business turnover. This has been made possible for those with entrepreneurial culture will be able to overcome issues and problems that affected their performances. Some, nevertheless, may experience business stagnation or decline not due to entrepreneurial culture, but other factors beyond the entrepreneur's control.

The entrepreneurs who started the business without entrepreneurial culture often take the same path once they realised the need to apply the culture of an entrepreneur to run their business either attending formal training programs to acquire and practise entrepreneurial culture. The enterprising may attend an informal training or self-learning approach while others may remain as entrepreneurs without practising entrepreneurial culture. The energetic may experience growth business, whilst the lethargic will experience a slow growth or stagnation. On the other hand, the passive entrepreneurs will see a decline in business and finally leave, since those without entrepreneurial culture will not be able to overcome business issues and problems. Among the entrepreneurs, there will be a group who may observe the opportunities to grow and decide to learn further about the culture of an entrepreneur to be successful and expand. Entrepreneurs who are willing to accept risky ventures, will decide to increase their business capital to meet increasing demand, and expect an increase in business turnover, although that may not lead to increase in business income.

One most distinguished difference between the two groups of entrepreneurs is that an entrepreneur with entrepreneurial culture will continue to venture into the business even after a failed business until becoming successful, whilst an entrepreneur without entrepreneurial culture will exit without attempting to venture into new business or other business opportunities.

8. Implication and Conclusion

This study further develops existing theories and explores the relationship between entrepreneurial culture and business performance. The theories established in this paper are relevant to the legitimacy of the relationship between entrepreneurial culture and business performance. The key findings corroborate with past research and consistent with the theory constructed by Wong (2014) that inferred entrepreneurial culture as desirable because it has a positive relationship to growth, performance, and success. The study important contribution is the relationships established between entrepreneurial culture and business performance. For once, the findings empirically proved wrong the general belief, as indicated by Lim (2000), that Malay entrepreneurs do not have an entrepreneurial culture. The significance of the relationship implies that on the normal business environment as the entrepreneurial culture enhance, the business performance will further improve. Another important contribution of this study, the entrepreneurial culture and performance model, explains the relationship between the entrepreneurial culture and the impact on performance. The model projects the process undergone by the entrepreneurs from start-up to growth and to some, no growth or a decline. Further research is recommended for this model. Since it is derived from input provided by the entrepreneurs in the case study and in-depth interview, the model needs further empirical evidence representing a broader business community.

Following the findings, similar studies involving the nascent entrepreneurs and failed entrepreneurs and other economic sectors, especially manufacturing, is recommended. The limitation of the study is it covers only entrepreneurs within the distributive trade and services sector who have been successful. A study of nascent entrepreneurship, and especially the failed entrepreneurs, will provide an in-depth view of the business environment faced by these groups and hopefully, the findings will enable the new entrepreneurs a better chance to survive and finally succeed and the failed entrepreneurs the second chance.

The result of this study should enlighten the policy makers and implementing agencies on the real need to be sensitive to the culture and value need of the Malay entrepreneurs in particular and the Malay community in general. The entrepreneurial culture is not a one-off training program and nurturing entrepreneurial culture is an ongoing life experience process. It is thus timely for the policy makers and implementing agencies to consider better and more effective measures and support programs that will enhance entrepreneurial culture not only among the entrepreneurs but the Malay community at large. One of the measures is entrepreneurship education in school by introducing a subject in entrepreneurship as one of the elective subjects.

References

Akuegwu, B.A., & Nwi-ue, F.D. (2016). Developing Entrepreneurship Culture among University Students in South-South Nigeria, *Mediterranean Journal of Social Sciences, 7(2),* 315-324

Alpander G.C., Carter, K.D., and Forsgren, R.A. (1990). Managerial issues and problem solving in the formative years. *Journal of Small Business Management,* 28(2), 9-19.

Armington, Catherine.,& Acs,Zoltan J.(2002). The Determinants of Regional Variation in New Firm Formation, *Regional Studies,* 36;33-45

Belak, Jernej., & Milfilner, Borut., (2012). Enterprise Culture as One of the Enterprise's Key Success Factors (Integral Management Approach): Does the Internal and External Cultural Orientation Matter? *Acta Polytechnica Hungarica,* 9 (3); 27-44

Beugelsdijk, S. 2007. Entrepreneurial Culture, Regional Innovativeness and Economic Growth, *Journal of Evolutionary Economics* 17 187–210

Bergmann, H (2009). Cultural Aspects of Entrepreneurship: In strengthening entrepreneurship and economic development in East Germany: Lessons from local approaches. (pp 59-71). Paris, France Trento/Italy: *Organization for Economic Cooperation and Development (OECD) Centre for entrepreneurship, SME and Local development (CFE).*

Bustamam, Ummi Salwa Ahmad (2010). Entrepreneurial Growth Process of Malay Entrepreneurs- A Malaysian. *International Journal of Business and Social Science* Vol. 1 No. 3; December 2010, 206-218

Calori, Roland & Sarnin, Philippe (1991). Corporate culture and economic performance: A French study. *Organizational studies* 12(1); 49-74

Gangi, Y.A. and Timan, E., (2013). An empirical investigation of entrepreneurial environment in Sudan. *World Journal of Entrepreneurship, Management and Sustainable Development*. 9(2/3): p. 168-177.

Goetz,SJ & Freshwater, D (2001). State-level determinants of entrepreneurship and a preliminary measure of entrepreneurial climate *Economic Development Quarterly,* 15 (1), 58-70

Hull, Louise (2003). A promotion of enterprise culture: Theory and practice

Hornsby, J.S., Kuratko, D.F. & Zahra, S.A. 2002. Middle managers' perception of the internal environment for corporate entrepreneurship: Assessing a measurement scale. *Journal of Business Venturing*, 17: 49–63.

Johannisson, B. (1986). Network strategies. Management technology for entrepreneurship and change. *International Small Business Journal*, 5 (1), 19-30

Kalleberg, Arne L., and Leicht Kevin T. (1991). Gender and organizational performance: determinants of small business survival and success. *The Academy of Management Journal,* 34(1),136-161

Keasey, K. and Watson, R. (1991), Financial distress prediction models: a review of their usefulness[1]. *British Journal of Management*, 2, 89–102.

Lim, L. (2000). A Dynamic Bumiputera Commercial and Industrial Class? A mismatch with market rationality. *Southeast Asian Studies, 37(4),* 443-457.

Man, T. W. Y., Lau, T. and Chan, K. F. (2002). The competitiveness of small and medium enterprises - A conceptualization with focus on entrepreneurial competences. *Journal of Business Venturing,* 17, 123-142.

Minguzzi, A. & Passaro, R. (2000). The network of relationships between the economic environment and the entrepreneurial culture in small firms, *Journal of Business Venturing*, 16;181–207.

Obaji, Nkem Okpa., and Olugu, Mercy Uche (2014). The role of government policy in entrepreneurship development. *Science Journal of Business and Management*. 2(4); 109-115

Oni, Emmanuel., & Daniya A.A (2012). Development of Small and Medium Scale Enterprises: The role of Government and other Financial Institutions *Arabian Journal of Business and Management Review* 1(7);16-29

Reijonen, H., & Komppula, R. (2007) Perception of success and its effect on small firm performance. *Journal of Small Business and Enterprise Development*, 14 (4), 689-701

Sexton, D. L,. & Bowman, N. (1986). Validation of a personality index: Comparative psychological characteristics analysis of female entrepreneurs, managers, entrepreneurship students, and business students. *Frontiers of entrepreneurship research*, Wellesley. MA: Babson College.

Suddle, Kashifa., Beugelsdijk, Sjoerd., and Wennekers, Sander. (2007). Entrepreneurial Culture and its Effect on the Rate of Nascent Entrepreneurship, SCALES, *Netherlands Ministry of Economic Affairs,* Zoetermeer

Wong, Matthew A (2014). *Entrepreneurial Culture: Developing a Theoretical Construct and its Measurement*. PhD Thesis, The University of Western Ontario, Ontario, Canada

van Wyk, Rene., & Adonis Mandla (2011). An eight-factor solution for the Corporate Entrepreneurship Assessment Instrument. *African Journal of Business Management.* 5 (8); 3047-3055

Yusof, Siti Nor Wardatulaina Mohd (2011), Success factors in Enterpreneurship: The Case Study of Malaysia, *Pilot Research Work (Phd Thesis), Department D'Economia De L'Empresa*, Universitat Autonoma de Barcelona

Zainol, Fakhrul Anwar & Wan Daud, Wan Norhayate (2011). Indigenous ("Bumiputera") Malay Entrepreneurs in Malaysia: Government Supports, Entrepreneurial Orientation and Firms Performances. *International Business and Management,* 2(1); 86-99

Work in Progress Papers

Toward Entrepreneurial Bricolage: a Longitudinal Perspective on Organizational Learning and Dynamic Capability in Emerging Market

Shao-Ning Chang[1] and Kai-Tang Fan[2]
[1]Warwick Business School, University of Warwick, UK
[2]the Graduate Institute of Technology Innovation & Intellectual Property Management (TIIPM), National Chengchi University, Taiwan
Jackmiaoli@gmail.com

Abstract: This study reports on a longitudinal study of how iStaging Corp (iStaging), a successful start-up company in the global augmented reality and virtual reality industry, has evolved a set of entrepreneurial bricolage across a combination of resources and collaborators in a turbulent ecosystem. Our analysis builds on existing approaches to firm-level entrepreneurial bricolage process in two ways. First, by explicitly connecting internal change with external drivers; we identify some of micro-foundations of entrepreneurial bricolage (Baker & Nelson, 2005) and link these with the adaptive demands of the start-up' competitive environment (Nelson & Winter, 1982; Teece, 2007; Zollo and Winter, 2002). Second, we take a longitudinal approach to better-understand the micro-macro connection over time and to analyse the underlining learning mechanisms by which an innovative start-up firm continually upgrades its capabilities and knowledge (and those of its co-specialists). Both elements of this approach enable a more detailed understanding of how a born global firm can deploy its entrepreneurial bricolage evolving its innovation capabilities in turbulent ecosystems

Keywords: Entrepreneurial Bricolage; Dynamic Capability; Organizational Learning; Strategic Change.

1. Background/ Objectives and Goals

The research goal of this study explains the evolution process of Entrepreneurial Bricolage with learning mechanism and dynamic capability. This study is based on the bricolage theory of Baker & Nelson (2005), dynamic capability (Teece, 2007), and organizational learning (Nelson & Winter, 1982; Zollo and Winter, 2002). Through this study, the theory gap among entrepreneurial bricolage process, organizational learning, and dynamic capability can be integrated toward a novel model of entrepreneurial bricolage. In addition, this comprehensive model can get more understanding on the innovation process of new ventures and reveal their organizational capability and strategic change through the entrepreneurial bricolage model. This study reports on a longitudinal study of how iStaging Corp (iStaging), a successful start-up company in the global augmented reality and virtual reality industry, has evolved a set of entrepreneurial bricolage across a combination of resources and collaborators in a turbulent ecosystem.

2. Facing the challenges of strategic change: entrepreneurial bricolage, dynamic capability and organizational learning

2.1 Entrepreneurial bricolage and Dynamic capability

Baker & Nelson proposed the theory of bricolage in 2005. According to Baker and Nelson (2005), the behavioral theory of "entrepreneurial bricolage" attempts to understand what entrepreneurs do when faced with resource constraints. Recently, the researches about bricolage, defined it as "making do by applying combinations of the resources at hand to new problems and opportunities". (Baker & Nelson 2005: 333, Senyard, Baker & Davidsson, 2009) This definition is kind of creating the conjunction with the theory of dynamic capability. Facing the turbulent external ecosystem, entrepreneurs merely can rely on exploring and exploiting the limited recourses and also store the organizational slack to facing the next strategic change and seizing the business and technology opportunity. In the other word, "entrepreneurial bricolage" is sort of a social interactive process underpinning the embeddedness and resource dependence. (Wu et al., 2015)

Dynamic capabilities have been viewed as higher-level competences in leveraging internal and external resources/knowledge to deal with the rapidly changing environment (Teece, 2010, 2012) through the capacities to (1) sense and shape opportunities and threats, (2) seize opportunities, and (3) maintain competitiveness through enhancing, combining, protecting, and reconfiguring business enterprises' tangible and intangible assets (Teece, 2007).

2.2 Organizational learning, routine, and strategic change

As defined by Feldman (2000) routines are seen as "a capability for repeated performance that has been learned by an organization in a context of selective pressures". This builds on earlier concepts of routines associated with Nelson and Winter's (1982) evolutionary theory of economic change (Zollo and Winter, 2002; Winter, 2003). They can be described as inherited procedures or decision rules that promote the survival of their 'carrier' in a changing environment.

The 'variation stage' in this cycle is emphasised as a key junction at which new combinations of external and internal knowledge may be used to solve existing problems in new ways, or cope with new challenges. In the context of this study, variations in routines and capabilities stem from the exploration activities of the focal firm as it searches for new ways of developing new products independently of outside firms. "Retention occurs when selected variations are preserved, duplicated, or otherwise reproduced so that the selected activities are repeated on future occasions or the selected structures appear again in future generations" (Aldrich 1999: 30).

3. Methods

The design of this study not only allows within-case analysis over time (Eisenhardt, 1989; Yin, 1994), but also enables a dual method which combines longitudinal study (Pettigrew, 1990) and multiple retrospective cases at the micro level (Leonard-Barton, 1990). Our central case, iStaging, comes from a larger empirical study of Global AR/VR industry, which provides an excellent example of a turbulent ecosystem. We investigate how the focal firm evolved its "entrepreneurial bricolage routines" to achieve and maintain its leading competitive position in Global AR/VR industry.

The study began in 2013, encompassing interviews in Taiwan, Beijing, Silicon Valley, Shanghai, and Hangzhou, including industry experts and stakeholders. Semi-structured interviews in iStaging Corp. were mainly conducted between 2013 and 2016. Cross-level informants were interviewed, including the top management team, middle managers, and frontline engineers. In addition, several kinds of internal archive data were analyzed, including technical reviews, daily reports, meeting records, and enterprise journals. To ensure the accuracy of the case, the research team continued to feedback and validate findings via emails, phone calls, and repeat interviews.

A certain degree of triangulation and validation was achieved by interviewing iStaging Corp. top management team, managers and employees at different levels and external industry experts and policymakers. The total interviews during 2013-1016 from iStaging Corp. related informants is 76 interviews. The interviews distribution is as below.

Table 1: Status of Interviews

Interviewee	2013	2014	2015	2016	Total
CEO (founder)	1	3	4	4	12
CTO (co-founder)	1	1	3	3	8
Board Members	0	0	1	2	3
Vice President	0	0	3	4	7
Directors	1	1	3	6	15
PM	1	1	4	5	12
others	1	2	8	8	19
Total	5	8	26	32	76

Note: Interview frequency, including face to face interview, conference call, and questionnaires.

- CEO (founder); CTO (co-founder); Board of directors/ Board Members
- Vice President of Operations; Vice President of R&D (co-founder)
- Directors of Strategic planning; Directors of Global Marketing
- Product and Platform managers

External interviews of stakeholders included informants from suppliers, rival firms, major customers, and industry experts.

4. Industry Overview, case company, and ecosystem

iStaging aims to vertically integrate real estate industry from real estate developers, real estate agents, interior designers, and furniture makers through Virtual Reality and Augmented Reality technology. iStaging believes that VR/AR technology can disrupt the rigid real estate industry. They provide faster, cheaper, and more efficient options to enhance their sales kit and marketing approaches and also create a self-sustaining ecosystem for players in the industry to flourish and the network effect in the marketplace to increase the consumer switching costs. With strong partners, including CE makers, internet giants, telecom carriers and etc., around the world.

4.1 The overview of the turbulent industry changes and ecosystem: Virtual Reality and Augmented Reality Industry

VR/AR technology has the potential to change business models and the ways in which noe people transact. While virtual reality concept has been discussed back in the 1990s, the technology back then failed to catch up with people's imagination. However, the report indicated that virtual reality era is coming with powerful personal computers and significant performance of displays and sensors. Key technology companies, such as Google, Facebook, Microsoft, HTC, Samsung and Apple have been participating the development of the virtual reality world that human beings have been envisioning. The application of VR/AR is still very experimental; however, according to Goldman Sachs research, there are some industries are identified to be disrupted by the advancement of the technology. Real estate industry is one of the verticals that VR/AR technology is expected to overturn the user experience. (Bellini et al., 2016)

4.2 The evolution process of iStaging's entrepreneurial bricolage

Stage 1: Creation with real estate agent for AR technology

In 2013, iStaging starts to provide project based technology services to real estate agent which their client is the largest agent company in Taiwan. While they provide a special augmented reality technology (AR) for agent to enhance the user experience for customers of real estate agents. This project conducted a novel technology usage of AR which conducted the 3 times transaction speed of real estate agent who using it.

Stage 2: Co-Creation with target accounts for novel business model

In 2014, iStaging transformed to lift their services to product based which target the market of vertical industries that includes members who already interact among one another. This enables our platform to provide the effective matchmaking characteristic of a large market even in the earliest stage of growth. iStaging provides VR/AR APP as service portals that benefit a single group of users; later, converts the business into a platform business by attracting a second set of users who want to engage in interactions with the first group.

iStaging will reform the Real Estate and Furniture industries because their platform unlocks new resources of value creation and supply. iStaging plays an indispensable partner to the players who pursuit a more efficient and enriched experience for their customers. iStaging focuses on VR/AR content and partners with key players in order to build a marketplace for real estate players, including constructors, real estate agents, interior designers and furniture makers/channels. The enterprise-to-enterprise solution have been convinced the best approach under this environment with limited consumer installed base.

iStaging's platform ecosystem constructed by free 3D-content-making for furniture brands, 3D-VR-content generation for interior designers, Matchmaking for Real Estate developers, agents and end-users, agent refers the leads for interior designers, and interior refers the leads for furniture brands.

Stage 3: Co-Specialization with ecosystem partners for platform economy

During 2015 to 2016, iStaging develops specifications for AV/VR technology with leading technology players, CE vendor, Internet giants, E-commerce, Logistic vendor, and Banker & Escrow provider. They join specification development and industry standard processes; therefore, their technology development is way ahead of competitors.

They exhibit strong "network effects". It quoted by their CEO and TMT members: "a growing group of one sort of customer attracts more of the other, which again draws in more of the first and so on. And they are controlled by one company, which can dictate the terms of trade, such as what type of businesses are allowed on its digital property and what they have to pay for the privilege".

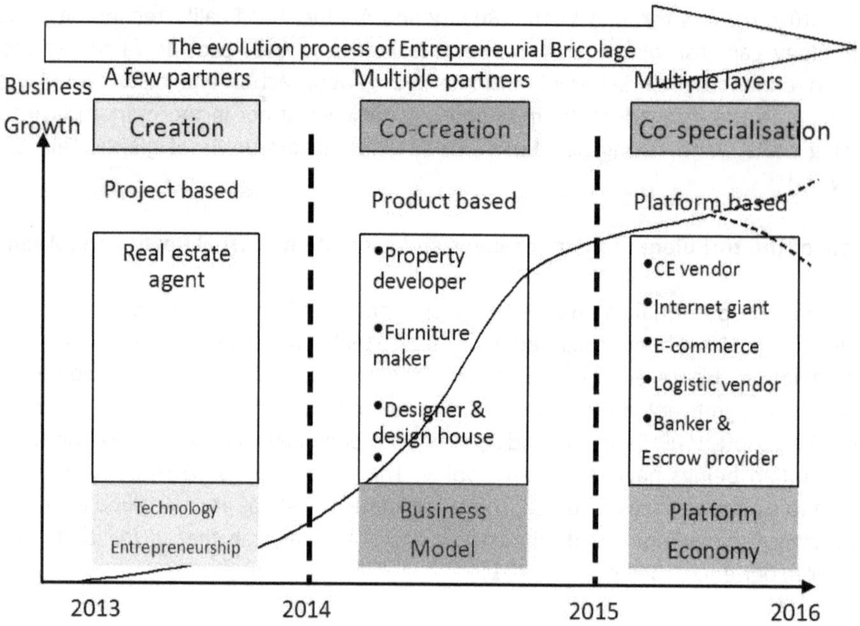

Figure 1: The evolution process of iStaging's Entrepreneurial Bricolage

5. Conclusion and Future study

As discussed cases and theory, we conducted the "evolution process of Entrepreneurial Bricolage" which combined the learning mechanism and dynamic capability. The learning mechanism includes experience accumulation, knowledge articulation, and knowledge codification. In this study, we can take the exploratory case and direction of how star-up companies modified and restructured internal to fit the changes from turbulent ecosystem. Further, we investigated how new ventures sensing, seizing, and reconfiguring to achieve the "fitness". Finally, underlying the Learning mechanism and dynamic capability, new ventures can lead the evolution process of "Entrepreneurial Bricolage".

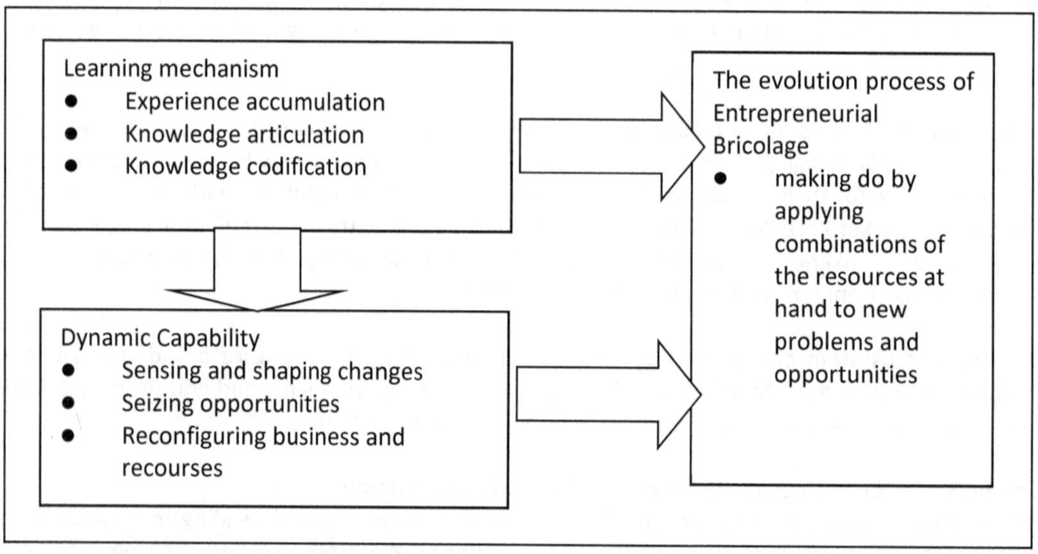

Figure 2: The evolution process of Entrepreneurial Bricolage

Our analysis builds on existing approaches to firm-level entrepreneurial bricolage process in two ways. First, by explicitly connecting internal change with external drivers; we identify some of micro-foundations of entrepreneurial bricolage (Baker & Nelson, 2005) and link these with the adaptive demands of the start-up' competitive environment (Nelson & Winter, 1982; Teece, 2007; Zollo and Winter, 2002). Second, we take a longitudinal approach to better-understand the micro-macro connection over time and to analyze the underlining learning mechanisms by which an innovative new ventures continually upgrades its capabilities and knowledge (and those of its co-specialists). Both elements of this approach enable a more detailed understanding of how a born global firm can deploy its entrepreneurial bricolage evolving its innovation capabilities in turbulent ecosystems.

References

Aldrich, H. (1999). *Organizations Evolving*. London: Sage Publications.

Baker, T & Nelson, R. (2005). Creating Something from Nothing: Resource Construction through Entrepreneurial Bricolage. *Administrative Science Quarterly*, 50:329-366

Bellini, H., Chen, W., Sugiyama, M., Shin, M., Alam, S., and Takayama, D. (2016). *Virtual and Agemented Reality: Understanding the race for the next computing platform*. Goldman Sachs: 2016

Eisenhardt, K. M. (1989). Building theories from case study research, *Academy of Management Review*, 14: 532–550.

Feldman, M.S. (2000). Organizational Routines as a Source of Continuous Change, *Organization Science*, 11(6): 611-629.

March, J.G. (1991). Exploration and exploitation in organizational learning, *Organizational Science* 2(1): 71–87.

Nelson, R. & Sidney Winter, S. (1982). *An Evolutionary Theory of Economic Change*. Harvard, Cambridge, 1982.

Prieto, I. & Easterby-Smith M. 2006. Dynamic capabilities and the role of organizational knowledge: an exploration, *European Journal of Information Systems*, 15(5): 500-510

Senyard, J., Baker, T. & Davidsson, P. (2009). Entrepreneurial Bricolage and Firm Performance: Some Preliminary Tests, in Frontiers of Entrepreneurship Research, Babson College, Wellesley, MA.

Teece, D. J. (2007). Explicating dynamic capabilities: The nature and microfundations of (sustainable) enterprise performance. *Strategic Management Journal*, 28: 1319-1350.

Teece, D. J. (2012). Dynamic capabilities: Routines versus entrepreneurial action. *Journal of Management Studies*, 49: 1395-1401.

Teece, D. J., Pisano, G., & Shuen, A. (1997). Dynamic capabilities and strategic management. *Strategic Management Journal*, 18: 509-533.

Zollo, M. & Winter, S.G. 2002. Deliberate learning and the evolution of dynamic capabilities. *Organization Science*, 13(3): 339-351.

www.ingramcontent.com/pod-product-compliance
Lightning Source LLC
LaVergne TN
LVHW060211210926
848481LV00008B/2696